JENNIE GEORGE

PALANI MOHA

BRAD NORINGTON is the Industrial Editor at the *Sydney Morning Herald* where he has covered industrial relations through the Hawke, Keating and Howard years—from the Accord to the turbulent implementation of Peter Reith's Workplace Relations Act.

Jennie George is the product of many years writing about the labour movement, and of having followed Jennie George's career for all that time. It draws on countless interviews with trade union officials and employer representatives; political activists; politicians and their staffers; Jennie, her opponents, and her supporters.

JENNIE GEORGE

BRAD NORINGTON

ALLEN & UNWIN

First published in hardcover in 1998
This paperback edition published in 1999
Allen & Unwin
9 Atchison Street
St Leonards NSW 1590
Australia
Phone: (61 2) 8425 0100
Fax: (61 2) 9906 2218
E-mail: frontdesk@allen-unwin.com.au
Web: http://www.allen-unwin.com.au

National Library of Australia
Cataloguing-in-Publication entry:

Norington, Brad, 1959– .
  Jennie George.

  Bibliography.
  Includes index.
  ISBN 1 86508 050 0.

  1. George, Jennie. 2. Australian Council of Trade Unions—
  Presidents—Biography. 3. Trade-unions—Australia—Officials
  and employees—Biography. I. Title.

331.87330994

Set in Bembo by DOCUPRO, Sydney
Printed and bound by Australian Print Group, Maryborough

10 9 8 7 6 5 4 3 2 1

CONTENTS

For my mother, Jacqueline
You gave so much of yourself

ACKNOWLEDGEMENTS

It is understandably daunting to have one's entire life laid bare to public examination in a biography. As I found researching and writing this biography of Jennie George, the exercise was necessarily intrusive and, knowing her as I do, she would have been more than a little nervous about how the words might land on the page. She is still mid-career—so there is the risk, as other biographers have noted, that revelations may be used or misused afterwards against the subject.

Although far from open about key aspects of her political background, Jennie George co-operated without any pre-conditions whatsoever or requests to see the manuscript in advance. I express my gratitude to her—and admiration. She was the model subject for a biography that is not authorised. She provided her time for a series of lengthy initial interviews, follow-up interviews, and dozens of telephone calls to check and recheck details, particularly related to sensitive passages. She also allowed me access to her papers, speeches, letters and photographs.

I also wish to especially thank her mother, Natasha Feodosiu, who provided photographs and much helpful information and whose journey, as related in chapter 1, was the all-important foundation of Jennie's own.

While Jennie George was my primary source, this biography is the result of material provided by many others. I express thanks to Brian Aarons, Les Ayres, Glenn A. Baker, Barry Blears, Cathy Bloch, Roger Boland, David Bunn, Meredith Burgmann, Maureen Burns, Sharan Burrow, Bronwen Campbell, Senator George Campbell, Senator Kim Carr, Rodney Cavalier, Ray Cavenagh, Joyce Clarke, Ray Clarke, Greg Combet, Senator Peter Cook, Phil Cross, Michael Danby, Martina Darnley, Russell Darnley, Van Davy, Joan Dawson, Cliff Dolan, Jenny Doran, Bruce Elder, Di Foggo, Gwen George, Bob Gould, Janet Hase, John Hennessy, Helen Hewett, Rex Hewett, Tim Hornibrook, John Hughes, Suzanne Jamieson, Bill Kelty, Cheryl Kernot, Martin Kingham, Ivor Lancaster, Tom McDonald, David McKnight, Bill Mansfield, Simon Marginson, Terry Metherell, Anne Milson, Matthew Moore, Jack Mundey, Max Ogden, Charles Ovadia, Doris Owens (Jobling), Tim Pallas, Peter Reith, Brian Rix, Mavis Robertson, Mark Robinson, Peter Robson, Iain Ross, Bob Sharkey, Stan Sharkey, Vera Shihoff, Greg Smith, Neal Swancott, Malcolm Turnbull, Richard Walsham, Vivienne White, Peter Wilson and Peter Woods.

I have been able to draw upon many conversations with Martin Ferguson in the past, but he declined to be interviewed for this biography, perhaps because of a falling out with Jennie George in the early 1990s. Martin Ferguson asked it be stated that he 'refused' to speak about her for this book—on the public record or off it. He said he had no comment to make, critical or otherwise, and did not want to respond to any criticism Jennie George made of him. He wished me well with the biography.

Andrew Casey, who was the ACTU's media officer during Martin Ferguson's term as ACTU president and is now Ferguson's press secretary in the Federal Parliament, adopted the same position.

A number of people provided background. Among them,

Terry Metherell, Education Minister in the NSW Government led by Nick Greiner, was reluctant to talk publicly about his feelings towards Jennie George but was prepared to recall the facts of the only time he met her while he was a minister.

For assistance in research, transcripts, work on early drafts and photographs, my appreciation goes to Jennifer Cooke, Amanda Wilson, Kate Southam, Sonia Modellino, Richard Coleman, Braham Dabscheck, Mark Davis, Palani Mohan, staff of the John Fairfax editorial library, staff of the NSW Teachers' Federation library, staff of Australian Archives, Voula Paschalis of the ACTU's Labour Information Network, Nina Blackwell of the Australian Republican Movement, Gordon and Jeanene Hodgkinson of Office Affairs, Charles Elias, Editor of the *Bankstown-Canterbury Torch*, and, last but not least, Jennie George's faithful assistant, Denise Power. For additional information I thank Shaun Carney, Shane Green, Ewin Hannan, Sid Marris and Michael Millett.

I am grateful to senior executives at the *Sydney Morning Herald* for their support. At Allen & Unwin, I thank John Iremonger and Rebecca Kaiser for their encouragement, and Annette Barlow for her editing.

ABBREVIATIONS

ABS   Australian Bureau of Statistics
ACOSS   Australian Council of Social Service
ACSPA   Australian Council of Salaried and Professional Associations
ACT   Australian Capital Territory
ACTU   Australian Council of Trade Unions
AEU   Australian Education Union (formerly ATF)
ALP   Australian Labor Party
AMWU   Amalgamated Metal Workers Union (later Australian Manufacturing Workers Union)
APEC   Asia Pacific Economic Co-operation group
ARCO   Atlantic Ritchfield Company
ARM   Australian Republican Movement
ASIO   Australian Security Intelligence Organisation
AWU   Australian Workers Union
BLF   Builders Labourers' Federation
BWIU   Building Workers Industrial Union (later CFMEU)
CEPU   Communications, Electrical and Plumbing Union
CFMEU   Construction Forestry Mining and Energy Union

CPA	Communist Party of Australia
DOGS	Defence of Government Schools
DP	Displaced Person
EYL	Eureka Youth League
FECCA	Federation of Ethnic Community Councils of Australia
GST	Goods and services tax
ILO	International Labour Organisation
IRC	Industrial Relations Commission (formerly Conciliation and Arbitration Commission)
IRO	International Refugee Organisation
ITF	International Transport Workers Federation
MHR	Member of the House of Representatives
MP	Member of Parliament
MTIA	Metal Trades Industry Association
MUA	Maritime Union of Australia (formerly WWF)
POW	Prisoner-of-War
SPA	Socialist Party of Australia
TAFE	Technical and Further Education college
TUTA	Trade Union Training Authority
UNO	United Nations Organisation
USA	United States of America
USSR	Union of Soviet Socialist Republics
WWF	Waterside Workers Federation (later MUA)

INTRODUCTION

MELBOURNE, 27 September 1995: It was the scene of many university graduations over the years but the stage, this day, was hers. Cheers and joyful applause swept through the crowded auditorium as Jennie George celebrated her triumph. Hers was a graduation of sorts too. This was the emotional moment Jennie would cherish long after she was installed as the highest-ranking trade unionist in the country and, most significantly, the first woman to lead Australia's trade union movement.

Jennie George had arrived, crashing through the doors of the boys' club. Her appointment symbolised an end to more than a century of overt male domination dating from the beginning of union history in the 1850s. It was no longer acceptable for women to have their rights in the workplace considered secondary to men, or for them to be denied a voice in organised labour.

Friends and supporters, mainly women as befitting the occasion, joined Jennie on stage, competing for space with streamers, balloons and bouquets of flowers. Among the guests were well-known figures such as Cheryl Kernot, Joan Kirner and Anne Summers. Others were close personal friends of Jennie's. After a resolution endorsing her as president-elect of the Australian Council of Trade Unions (ACTU) was carried by acclamation, Jennie led singing and dancing while Helen Reddy's feminist anthem, 'I am Woman', played over the loudspeaker: *'I am strong, I am invincible, I am woman . . .'*

Even Bill Kelty, on her immediate left, an ardent supporter of Jennie's but not noted for his advocacy of women's issues in earlier years, joined in, mouthing the words: *'I am woman, hear me roar . . .'*

Once the revelry had settled down, Jennie gave her inaugural speech as president-elect to the 700 union delegates in the audience, congregated for the 1995 ACTU Congress, at Melbourne University's Wilson Hall. Her new role, she declared, was a victory for all women. She told the sympathetic audience that her political life was shaped by her commitment to the union movement, defending workers' entitlements, first for teachers and then generally. The influences that set her on that path she attributed to her late husband, Paddy, and her involvement in anti-Vietnam War protests and the women's movement:

> It's not me, just me, Jennie George, that's achieved this very important position in the union movement. I see myself symbolising the aspirations of women and I know that they'll be rejoicing in a collective sense, knowing that whatever achievements I've made, I've made it for all of us.

As president-elect of the ACTU, Jennie had attained a position of considerable prestige and authority in the nation's affairs. She would be the union movement's most identifiable figure—the public voice of the ACTU—regarded widely as responsible for the effectiveness of unions in representing workers, the perception of unions in the community and whether or not unions made a credible contribution to public debate.

Since its establishment in 1927 as Australia's national trade union organisation, the ACTU had produced a strong line of leaders. Jennie George was its ninth president, keenly aware of the historic burden on her shoulders.[1]

In recent times, the ACTU's most spectacular individual was undoubtedly Bob Hawke, whose decade as president in the 1970s proved to be the career foundation, assisted by an extraordinary tide of publicity, for him to become prime minister. All those who followed Hawke, for better or worse, would be compared with him. Already one successor, Simon Crean, had repeated Hawke's transition to Federal Parliament. He was a possible future Labor Party leader and perhaps prime minister. Martin Ferguson, still officially ACTU president on the day Jennie was declared president-elect, was guaranteed a senior frontbench portfolio at the very least when he quit the ACTU and took up a safe Labor seat in Federal Parliament at the next election. Already expectations were raised in union circles about whether or not Jennie might follow the recent tradition and move to parliamentary politics after the ACTU.

Such talk now was premature, considering Jennie had not even started her new job. She faced immense challenges. She was assuming the presidency at a time of crisis. Unions were in serious decline because of a major fall in membership as a proportion of the total workforce, which showed no sign of rebounding. They faced further pressure only months away with the likely election of a Coalition government with a union-hostile agenda.

At 48 years of age, Jennie had the professional union experience and maturity for her new responsibility, having spent 20 years rising to the top of the NSW Teachers' Federation and the past four years as an assistant secretary of the ACTU. But the ACTU presidency was a long way from her humble beginnings as a migrant child from a poor refugee family who arrived in Australia speaking no English. She made a point of it to her audience in Wilson Hall:

> When I was growing up in the high-rise Housing Commission flats in Surry Hills in Sydney, of course I never dreamt that I'd be a

union officer, let alone one day reach the pinnacle and be standing before you as the president-elect of the ACTU.

One woman standing on Jennie's immediate right on the stage was the proudest of all to hear these words. She clapped enthusiastically and the emotion on her face was obvious. The white-haired woman knew more intimately than anyone present the trials of the journey taken to reach that pinnacle and the significance of what Jennie had just said. It confirmed to her that all the hard years had been worth the effort. The woman was the closest person in the world to Jennie George, her mother, Natasha.

1

REFUGEES

In the dry heat of the Mediterranean summer the heavily pregnant woman craved grapes. A forlorn hope, she thought. She had no money to buy them at the local markets. But the bountiful plantations on the outskirts of Barletta, a town on Italy's Adriatic south-east coast that was her temporary home, proved too much temptation. 'Come with us, Natasha,' her friends implored her. And so she joined them, leaving the camp gates behind, strolling far enough until all believed it was safe to leave the roadside and cross into one of the vineyards to steal grapes.

Natasha ate grapes as she picked and had bagged some for later when the vineyard owners arrived without warning. Her friends ran off but Natasha, in her condition, was caught quickly. 'I have a child! I have a child!' she shouted in Italian. The protests did not dissuade her captors. They took her to the police station where she was questioned about why she was stealing and the grapes were confiscated. Oleg, Natasha's husband, was summoned to take her back to the camp at Barletta. He cursed her. 'Why did you go with those stupid women? Couldn't you understand it was a crime?' Oleg was forced to pay for two kilograms of grapes. He scrounged what money he could from others in the camp.

A few weeks later, the labour pains began. The Hungarian doctor who had been treating Natasha recommended that she leave the camp immediately. He ordered an ambulance to take her the short distance to Trani, a Romanesque coastal town further south where British authorities in charge of post-war reconstruction in Italy had established a makeshift hospital at one of the ousted Mussolini regime's headquarters. Medical supplies were scarce but the 'hospital' was better equipped than the Barletta township to cater for a possibly difficult birth, and undoubtedly better than the displaced persons' camp in which Natasha Sinicky lived.

For five days Natasha waited in Trani until labour began in earnest, a twelve-hour ordeal that ran through the hot night. The birth was witnessed by one of the daughters of the conquering Allied commander in Italy, Field Marshal Earl Alexander. Outside the hospital room stood Oleg, who had been called from the camp and now heard his wife crying and screaming in pain. 'Will you shut up!' he kept yelling, when he could not bear the noise. The baby was born at around 11 a.m. on 20 August 1947. Natasha had wanted a son because that was Oleg's wish, and she wanted to please him. 'Tell me is it a son! Don't tell me I have a daughter?' she pleaded. 'No, you have a beautiful daughter.' There was a brief silence. 'God forgive me,' said Natasha. 'As long as she is healthy.' Healthy she was but Oleg was upset when he entered the room. 'Why didn't you bear me a son?'

The spartan hospital had no trolley, so the delivering doctor himself carried Natasha back to the general ward. Natasha's mother, Xenia, who lived in the nearby camp with them, came to see the new baby. The child was said to have her father's nose and mouth but have her grandmother Xenia's distinctive eyes. Later she would also demonstrate her grandmother's strength of character and survival instinct. Natasha had considered calling her daughter Victoria or Veronica but settled on Eugenie with Oleg's blessing. The name was popular before World War I because of the beautiful French empress who fired public imagination in the late nineteenth century. In its Greek form, Eugenia, the name meant 'noble excellence' and it was also the name of a third century Roman martyr, St Eugenia. Natasha's personal inspiration for naming her daughter was a childhood friend from her native Russia whom she remembered as being especially bright at school.

Back at the camp, Natasha had nothing for her baby. The Red Cross gave her a roll of gauze material, layers of which she stitched together as make-do nappies. Oleg managed to scavenge some baby clothes but most came from parcel donations sent by Russian communities in the United States and Australia to help many of the several million compatriots like Natasha and Oleg who were refugees after World War II. The family—as it was now—lived on meagre rations. They were housed in former army amenities, all supplied by the Refugee Rehabilitation Agency of the newly formed United Nations Organisation, which had taken over from the Western Allied Forces the role of caretaker of post-war displaced persons. When the Agency collapsed, the responsibility for relief and later for repatriation or resettlement was assumed by the International Refugee Organisation (IRO).[1]

Life in Barletta and other camps around Italy to which the family was shunted during this time was a waiting game. Natasha and Oleg, with their baby daughter, Eugenie, and Natasha's mother, Xenia, watched the months and then years roll past before the IRO processed their applications for migration to a new country. They were a stateless people, ethnically Russians loyal to their nationality and culture but disowning the post-war Communist Soviet Union of Joseph Stalin after strenuously resisting forced repatriation.

Eugenie spent the first three years of her life in Italian displaced persons' camps. She spoke her first words in Italian and did not use her parents' language at that stage. In the camps she mixed with children of many nationalities—Russian, Ukrainian, Polish, Czechoslovakian, Hungarian and Yugoslavian—whose parents were desperate to escape Soviet-occupied Eastern Europe. They would sing songs in Italian and play outside the huts. The deprivation of camp life was palpable and the future uncertain, but Eugenie's family had endured the worst already. They had survived the war by sheer determination and luck and by the time Eugenie was born there was optimism in the air. The authorities were assuring resettlement, not repatriation. For Natasha and her mother, Xenia, there was an end in sight at last to a long, hazardous journey.

Natasha and Xenia hailed from a powerful matriarchy—a pattern that was to repeat itself with Eugenie and have a profound influence on her. It began with Olga, Eugenie's great-grandmother on her mother's side, a White Russian aristocrat. Before the Russian Revolution in 1917, Olga had lived comfortably in the Volga region, married to a senior officer in the Tsar's army. All changed dramatically when her husband was killed fighting the communist Bolsheviks. Olga was left impoverished under the Soviet regime. But her daughter, Xenia, made her way in life by marrying a local, Frederich Lutz, a government printer and communist sympathiser who was paid well by Soviet standards. After a government posting to Warsaw, Xenia and Frederich returned to the Soviet Union in the late 1920s with their daughter, Natasha, and settled in Rostov, a city on the river Don almost 1000 kilometres south of Moscow and the place where world-famous writer Alexander Solzhenitsyn spent his youth.

In the midst of the Great Depression, with hunger, squalor and poverty everywhere around them in Rostov, the family survived well on Frederich's wage in a well-appointed apartment. In 1933, however, Frederich died suddenly. Xenia was forced to look for work in order to provide for herself and Natasha, now eight years old. By all accounts Xenia was a determined, resourceful and feisty woman. Although she despised the Soviets, she kept her thoughts to herself and persuaded authorities to give her a good government job. Colloquially called 'trade with foreigners', Xenia's job entailed supervising Russians bartering their family gold and silver for coupons that permitted them to buy flour or cheese or other basic rations. The Soviet government melted the gold and silver to trade it on the international market.

When her mother started work, Natasha became very much a 1930s version of the latch-key child, arriving to an empty home after school while her mother worked. The situation changed quickly though when Xenia asked Olga to join them and live in the apartment to look after Natasha. The arrival of Olga established a household of equally strong-willed women who were at once close but at times struggling under the dominance of the eldest.

Olga, in effect, reared Natasha while Xenia worked. She packed Natasha off to school each day and was always home to greet her granddaughter. The emotional support Olga offered to Natasha included pacifying her when she became upset at the lovers Xenia brought home. 'She was very much sexual,' Natasha recalled of her mother. 'Her lovers used to come, I remember, and I used to hate them all.'

When the bombs of Nazi Germany's advance into the Soviet Union started exploding on the outskirts of Rostov in July 1942, Natasha was seventeen and had just completed her school certificate. Olga had recently died and so was spared the traumas to come. Xenia and Natasha fled immediately, heading 500 kilometres south to the Caucasian town of Kislovodsk, not far from Chechnya. Xenia had friends there and gambled that it would be a haven, free of Nazi bombs and guns. They took with them just a suitcase each. The only personal items were some diaries. Behind them they abandoned the furnished flat, clothes and possessions, Xenia's job and Natasha's hopes of going to university to study geology. It was a harrowing twelve-day journey to Kislovodsk, made on foot and occasionally on the back of tractors. When they arrived, Natasha and Xenia were forced to live outside the town in the open with thousands of refugees. The weather was warm, fortunately, but they had no money and no food. Natasha became ill with diarrhoea and her body was riddled with lice. After a four-week search, Xenia found her friends living in a small village just outside Kislovodsk and they moved in with them. German occupation had already begun. Unlike Rostov, not a single shot was fired as soldiers roared into the town on motorbikes. Jews were rounded up. Statues of Lenin and Stalin were smashed.

Xenia found work almost immediately as a nurse for the Nazis, even though she spoke no German. Her German married surname, Lutz, was helpful. Her late husband was descended from one of many German families who had emigrated the previous century to the Volga River region of Russia. The Nazis in Kislovodsk looked kindly upon his widow. Xenia soon used her charm to lobby for her and Natasha's return to Rostov. The Nazis had overrun Rostov soon after their escape. There was no choice about German occupation now, so mother and daughter wanted to go home. Permission was granted and the return journey five months after walking into Kislovodsk was more comfortable—by train. The sight awaiting Xenia and Natasha at home, however, was shattering: their flat in the three-storey block was empty, ransacked by neighbours and others even before the Germans had arrived. 'We thought you weren't coming back,' some said. 'We thought you were dead,' said others. Xenia retrieved one portrait from neighbours and started inquiring about their other possessions, including a statue of Venus, which some fleeing Jewish neighbours had asked her to mind early on. That was when trouble with the Nazis began. Xenia and Natasha were summoned to the German headquarters on the other side of Rostov, strip-searched and put in a cell together. Xenia was suspected of harbouring Jews and helping them to escape. She presumed that Russian informants had told the Nazis about her Jewish connection with the statue, which apparently was in the hands of a German officer.

Xenia's instructions to Natasha during their detention were either to speak the smattering of German they had picked up or to shut up unless spoken to. For the next five days, they received just one meal a day of soup containing a few fish pieces. Then, separately, they were taken to a cellar and interrogated about whether or not Natasha's father was a communist or Jewish. Natasha followed her mother's advice, speaking with a nervous stutter said to have developed a decade earlier at the shock of her father's death. Afterwards, both were reminded that they were under the authority of the Third Reich and released.

The experience hardened the belief of mother and daughter that they had to leave Rostov—and the Soviet Union—for good. Despite her late husband's sympathies, Xenia had always disliked the Soviet system. The only certain escape and sure meal ticket during occupation was recruitment by the Nazis as cheap labour. Xenia and Natasha joined the ranks of the three million recruited or forced labourers, called *Ostarbeiter*, employed by the Reich. The two women helped fill the need for domestic servants in Germany and Austria.[2] The first stage of their escape was a long train journey west to Poland in 1943, where they spent almost a year in a camp waiting for their records, which eventually followed them from Rostov, to be checked by the Nazis. In early 1944 they were sent to Vienna to work as maids in non-military households—Xenia for an elderly well-to-do couple and Natasha for the couple's daughter and her husband, a businessman in the city's commercial district. Mother and daughter were able to keep in contact on Natasha's two half-days off a week. While Natasha stayed with her employers until virtually the end of the war with enough food to eat and the privacy of a small bedroom to herself, Xenia fell out with hers. She was moved to one of the war industry factories in Vienna, which meant basic rations and dormitory accommodation.

The Russian army advance was close to Vienna by April 1945 and the explosions of battle could be heard from the city. Austrians were not the only ones afraid. Russian labourers in the Reich were fearful about a future condemned to Soviet concentration camps, or worse, if they returned home. Natasha had heard horror stories about likely treatment by the Soviets, including having her head shaven and being called a German prostitute. She and Xenia agreed to meet at the closest main railway station in a bid to escape to the West. As she was leaving, Natasha's boss asked her to write a note for him in Russian, explaining to soon-to-arrive Soviets that he was anti-Nazi. She obliged but proudly refused the money he offered to her as payment for the favour.

The railway station was crowded and, amid the turmoil of an approaching enemy, foreigners like Xenia and Natasha were low priority for passage out of Vienna. Xenia persuaded a guard at the station gate to let them through by bribing him with a bottle of wine she had stashed in her luggage. She then talked her way onto a women and children-only carriage by telling Natasha to pretend she was younger and huddle in her mother's arms like a vulnerable child. The train barely travelled 60 kilometres before it stopped—the track ahead destroyed by Allied bombs—and all its occupants were forced to continue on foot. Xenia's preference was to head towards American troop lines, rather than British or French, but she had no idea where the Americans would be. In a remarkable journey in which they would traverse almost the entire breadth of war-ravaged Austria, Xenia and Natasha walked, rode on the back of trucks or, where the lines were sufficiently clear from bombardment to permit thoroughfare, clambered aboard trains. Their journey took them from Vienna in the east to Salzburg in the west, and then further south-west to Innsbruck near the Alps. 'There were craters everywhere around us from the bombs,' recalled Natasha. 'And soldiers fleeing on foot—some of them helped carry our bags.'

From Innsbruck it was a relatively short hop south to the Brenner Pass near the north Italian border, which held the prospect of freedom if they could cross into Allied-controlled Italy. They were fortunate that the remaining German military commanders at the Brenner Pass were benevolent and directed them to a train down the slope, standing on Austrian-annexed Italian territory. Xenia and Natasha scrambled down the mountainside and boarded the train. Overhead, Allied warplanes flew north while their train headed south, away from the conflict, to Bolzano, the major town in Italy's most northerly region. Arriving starved and exhausted, Bolzano offered a brief sanctuary but they were told that their safety could be assured only if they retraced their steps, almost halfway back to the Brenner Pass to the Red Cross town of Bressanone. They thanked God when their train pulled into Bressanone in May 1945, the end of the war, and they were accepted at a camp there. Throughout their ordeal, starting at Rostov, mother and daughter had managed to remain together always, unlike so many other families who were split up and never saw one another again.

It was on the streets of Bressanone two months after war's end that Natasha Lutz met Oleg Sinicky. Recognising each other as Russian and speaking the same language in this strange place, Oleg and Natasha struck up a conversation. Originally from Stalingrad, Oleg told Natasha how he had been captured on the eastern front while fighting in the Soviet infantry and sent to a prisoner-of-war camp in Nazi Germany. He was thin and wore part of an American uniform—trousers and boots—given to him by American soldiers who he claimed had liberated him from the POW camp. Somehow Oleg had parted company with fellow Russian ex-POWs bound for the Soviet Union and had made his way to the northern Italian town. Like Natasha, he was desperate to escape forcible repatriation. He had heard stories of the fate awaiting Russian army refugees—starvation and probable death in Siberian concentration camps. Stalin, it was said, did not want his people hearing what life was like in the West and treated returned POWs like traitors.

Natasha was smitten with the good looks and wit of this man, four years her senior. As they became more friendly, their relationship blossomed quickly into romance. It was cut short within weeks, however, when they were separated. Natasha and her mother were sent far south to a displaced persons' camp at Aversa, on Italy's west coast near Naples. Oleg remained in the north, claiming renewed interest in returning to the Soviet Union for reasons that are unclear.

Natasha heard nothing more from Oleg until Easter 1946. He sent her a postcard inviting her to join him at Bagnoli, one of the numerous displaced persons' camps dotted around Naples that happened to be a few kilometres away from her in Aversa. Reunited, Oleg told Natasha that after they had parted he was put on a train to the Soviet zone near the Austrian–Italian border so he could be sent back to Russia but had escaped after talking to compatriots about the dire prospect of Siberian camps. He now sought refugee status in Italy instead. The romance between them was rekindled, prompting Natasha to win permission for herself and her mother to be transferred to Bagnoli so she could be with Oleg.

The couple's attachment grew against a grim background. By August, Natasha and Oleg, along with Xenia, were moved yet again, far north to a camp on the eastern coast in the small town of Riccione, near Rimini, where they spent the next nine months. On the way at least one male refugee among the many nationalities on board their transport—a packed cattle train—tried to escape but was caught by British soldiers armed with batons. On arrival these soldiers corralled the refugees, effectively prisoners, to make sure there were no further escape attempts. The fear among Russians, especially the single men, that they were about to be sent back to the Soviet Union had reached fever pitch. It was a legitimate fear. On the insistence of the Soviet government, the IRO was not permitted to assist its citizens displaced during the war to gain new homes.[3]

Riccione was a former POW camp of corrugated-iron huts, surrounded by a barbed-wire fence, but its purpose now was to screen refugees. They were to be divided into three groups: 'A' was for refugees born outside the Soviet Union, 'B' was for Soviet-born single men and 'C' was for families. Group B was to be deported straight back to the Soviet Union while the others scored a chance at migration to new lands. Oleg, born in Stalingrad and unmarried, was at obvious risk of being forced home, a prospect he now flatly rejected. However, he got around the problem by registering himself as Bulgarian-born and so manipulated his place into Group A. Oleg then tried to convince a British officer to switch Natasha from Group C to Group A as well by claiming she was his fiancée. He almost succeeded but failed when the officer found that Natasha—who would not be parted from her mother—was not alone. The officer, annoyed by now, would not accept Xenia in the same category and reacted to Oleg's try-on by putting them all in the family category, Group C, which still carried some risk of deportation.

Oleg had to make a hasty choice. He could not maintain to the authorities the facade of being part of a family without being married to Natasha. She was in love with him and wanted to marry. His emotions were less clear, although his attempt to switch her to his non-Russian refugee category suggested a strong attachment. He could have declared himself solo once more but decided to stay. It is also possible he may have believed his prospects of immigration were higher if he was with Natasha.

Oleg and Natasha Sinicky, both non-practising Russian Orthodox, were married by a Catholic priest in the barbed-wire camp in October 1946. Oleg was safe for now. But the mood remained bleak at Riccione. A number of the young, single Russian men classed for return to the Soviet Union attempted suicide and some succeeded. They preferred to crush their own heads with rocks than return home to a miserable fate. Riccione inmates including Oleg and Natasha wore black armbands of protest and went on a hunger strike. For Natasha, the experience was filled with horror: 'I was in tears when I heard one of our friends had killed himself—it was such a waste of young life.'

There was also an uprising shortly before they left the camp, around the time the Russian men were to be deported, in which several British soldiers were killed. Partly in response to this uprising in May 1947, British authorities divided the refugees once more. Oleg, Natasha and Xenia were among those told they were 'free' and sent south to a new camp at Barletta on the Adriatic east coast. The strict internment of Riccione did not exist at Barletta. Although there were guards on the gates they could move freely about the local town. The change could not come at a better time for Natasha. She was pregnant and due to give birth in August.

Still Natasha went hungry. Her disastrous episode stealing grapes in late pregnancy only made her dwell on their poverty and the notion that they were 'unwanted people'. Oleg cadged extra food where he could, but his priorities were already different from his wife's. He preferred alcohol to food. Even during their time in Riccione, despite the fences and guards on the gates, Oleg always found *some* money, usually lira from local Italians willing to buy anything from pilfered tent cloth to firewood that he hid under his coat. He would return with cognac or grappa, not food. If he could not get alcohol, he would persuade Natasha, who did not drink, to buy some during sanctioned visits to the town doctor during her pregnancy. If conventional alcohol was not available, a desperate Oleg resorted to dentists' spirit used in the camp. Natasha recalled: 'The Italians, they would buy anything whatever. Then he would come back with drink. I would say, "I'm starving, I want to eat" and all he would say is, "Look, I bought for you polenta".' Xenia's assessment of her son-in-law to Natasha was typically strong: 'You don't need a child from that drunk.'

When Eugenie was eight months old, the family was moved from the Barletta camp on the south-east coast, their home for twelve months, to a series of camps in towns that surrounded the picturesque ancient city of Naples on Italy's south-west coast. A camp at Bagnoli was once again the family's temporary home.

Although a worldly 23-year-old when Eugenie was born, Natasha was new to motherhood. Disease or mishap could prove fatal to her baby in the tough conditions of the camps. Soon after arriving in Bagnoli, Eugenie developed severe gastroenteritis and was so sick that Natasha thought she would die. Distressed, she appealed to the local doctor for help. 'You stupid mother,' he told her. 'Don't you know how to cherish your child?' He instructed her to find a ripe apple, shred it, leave it until it went brown, then feed it to her baby. There were no apples in the camp so Oleg fetched one from a restaurant. Within 24 hours, their daughter began to recover.

The stay at Bagnoli was short because Oleg found work as a cook in the kitchen of the displaced persons' camp on the southern side of Naples, at Cava Dei Tirreni, a town set between Pompeii and Salerno. The family spent almost a year at the Cava Dei Tirreni camp. Oleg had no qualifications or training as a cook but took to the job quickly. It was to become his nominated profession from then on.

Tensions had surfaced by now not only between Oleg and Natasha but also between Oleg and Natasha's mother. While Xenia resented Oleg's drinking, Oleg resented Xenia interfering in his married life, in particular the strong pressure she exerted for them all to seek emigration to the United States. Xenia had been corresponding with friends there as the prelude to a formal application for the family to migrate. Oleg rejected the idea, refusing to let his future be dictated by his mother-in-law. He applied for them to migrate instead to Argentina, only to be rejected. Then he came up with a new notion. 'What about we go to Australia?' he said to Natasha. Initially she was sceptical, wondering what they would do in Australia. But he persisted. 'I want to go. If you love me, you will go with me. Forget about America.'

Forced repatriation of Russians had slowed down and later

stopped, reducing the need for Oleg to continue his pretence about Bulgarian nationality. But the word in the camps was that Australia was not welcoming Russians. In fact, official estimates of former Soviet citizens who came to Australia between 1947 and 1954 via assisted migration and were registered as Russians at some stage of their journey were as high as 7000.[4] It was common, however, for Russians to declare themselves as 'stateless' or to register under a convenient birthplace, as Oleg had. Russians who registered under another nationality did so either with no proof or with some form of documentation. Nansen passports were one form of documents accepted by authorities. They identified holders as refugees of World War I with Polish or Baltic ethnicity—from well before Soviet control of their lands—who were put under the IRO's care for resettlement in new countries. Oleg acquired false papers to change his origin to Bulgarian and applied for assisted migration to Australia using this nationality and putting Natasha, Eugenie and Xenia under his responsibility. They were elated when finally accepted to Australia, a signatory of the IRO constitution that adhered to its policy even though the country's Chifley Government was not bound legally to admit refugees. Prime Minister Ben Chifley had stressed when he signed the agreement that the IRO's primary role would be to send displaced persons home and Australia's immigration system remained skewed heavily in favour of a British intake. But the country's first Minister for Immigration, Arthur Calwell, subsequently changed the Australian Government's tune—with Chifley's approval. Calwell was encouraged to admit people under the IRO's care following the news that, if Australia acted quickly, many of the displaced persons available for resettlement were of a high standard and the IRO would provide their passage by ship.[5] Of the one million displaced people resettled after the war, Australia took almost 180 000 between 1947 and 1954, the second-largest intake after the United States.[6]

The lives of the Sinicky family had become a crisscross pattern of train trips from one camp to another. Their last year in Europe, from mid-1949 until final immigration clearance was granted to move to Australia as their permanent new home, was spent once more at a camp on the north-west side of Naples, at Aversa. Eugenie was now three years old and healthy apart from a serious bout of whooping cough. She seemed more Italian than Russian, thanks to her mixing with Neapolitan children. Natasha had befriended a woman who ran a local kindergarten and regularly minded Eugenie. Italian became Eugenie's first language. She did not speak Russian then, although she understood her parents' native tongue.

Passage to Australia meant a train trip, longer than any they'd taken before, from the south of Italy, north through Austria and all of what was then West Germany to the port of Bremerhaven, not far from Hamburg. They left Aversa in August 1950 and on arrival at Bremerhaven boarded a former American warship, the *General Muir*, a vessel hardly built for comfort and which had been used recently to transport Dutch troops from Indonesia.

If not for Oleg's stubbornness, the family probably would have migrated to America and young Eugenie would have grown up in another part of the world entirely. Were it not for the way the war changed their fates so dramatically in the first place, all would have remained under the rule of Stalinism. Natasha, her mother in tow, had agreed to Oleg's choice of Australia but was scared. She knew almost nothing about the country and none of them spoke English. She was worried for Eugenie's future.

The atmosphere when the ship berthed in Melbourne, on 25 October 1950, did not ease Natasha's concerns. Their immediate introduction to life in Australia was a strike. Waterfront workers under the new Coalition government of Robert Menzies had withdrawn their labour, so when the *General Muir* docked, the refugees' suitcases were thrown from the ship onto the wharf, smashing open as they landed and spilling possessions. Standing for the first time on Australian soil, the refugee family, carrying young Eugenie, looked on, helpless and appalled.

2

CHILDHOOD YEARS

Like most Russians arriving in Australia after World War II, the Sinicky family detested Stalin's communist dictatorship and had desperately wanted to escape it. But they were entering a country whose people were gripped by fears of a Cold War communist conspiracy—fuelled by the McCarthy-era witch-hunt for spies and sympathisers—and deeply suspicious of anything Russian. Just four months before the family's ship berthed in Melbourne in October 1950, North Korean communist troops had launched a full-scale invasion across the 38th parallel boundary into the South, sparking the Korean War. As tensions worsened between East and West, a thermonuclear war seemed a very real possibility.[1]

Eugenie Sinicky grew up in this politically paranoid, hostile environment, where the antipathy towards Russians reinforced the disadvantages they suffered in their new home. Most had a poor grasp of English and were employed in low-paying menial jobs. The Australia of the 1950s, with its dominant British heritage, was no multicultural society. The anti-Russian sentiment of the Cold War scare was to bring the tight-knit Russian community even closer, rather than fostering integration or opening the doors of the Russian culture in any meaningful way to the wider population.

The local manifestation of the Cold War when the Sinicky family arrived in Australia was a convulsive debate over efforts by the Menzies Government to pass draconian legislation banning the Communist Party of Australia. The legislation also gave the Government the power to outlaw organisations affiliated with the party and to remove people declared as members of the party from their jobs in the Commonwealth public service and unions. It appeared that this land, portrayed to new Russian settlers as a country of pioneer spirit and bold democracy, was attempting to smother the rights of people with views divergent from the political orthodoxy. Yet the fears that Russian settlers felt about the communist bogey from their own experience meant that they could only agree with the determination of Menzies to crush the local Communist Party. Communists were the enemy of the majority of the Russian community in Australia, hated because of the repressive Stalinist regime under which community members had suffered. Menzies ultimately failed in his endeavour to ban the Communist Party when he lost a High Court challenge to his legislation and the national referendum in 1951. But many Russians including Oleg, Natasha and Xenia came to admire him and became firm supporters at the ballot box when they were eligible to vote.

The strike that had greeted Oleg Sinicky and his family at the dock in Melbourne was part of a national protest campaign by militant left-wing leaders of the wharf labourers' union, the Waterside Workers' Federation, against Menzies's Communist Party Dissolution Bill. Other unions joined in a wave of strikes across the country. The protest was not just against Menzies's legislation but also to stiffen the arm of the Federal Opposition, the parliamentary Labor Party, which had been ordered by its central executive to drop its opposition to the legislation.[2]

The Sinicky family was not very politically minded and knew

little about Australia, but they knew about survival. The waterfront strike, their first taste of life in this supposed paradise after having escaped the cauldron of Europe, made it appear as though the Cold War was a day-to-day reality of this far away continent as well. It added to their trepidation about being penniless, unskilled, speaking no English, having no local relatives or friends and no choice about where they would be sent to live.

Convincing the Department of Immigration in Australia to accept his entire family had proved a tricky problem for Oleg. Under contract agreements introduced by Arthur Calwell, refugees entering Australia were obliged to accept a job designated to them soon after arrival. They would head straight from the wharf to a reception camp, where they would live for up to a month. It was the task of the Commonwealth Employment Service, acting as the department's agent, to find jobs and arrange transfer from the reception camp to the place of employment.[3]

Oleg's conundrum was Xenia. When he applied for immigration to Australia in Italy, he and Natasha were accepted but Xenia, being over 40 years of age, had been deemed by the department as too old under its guidelines to qualify under the system of bonded labour contracts. Thus she was at real risk of being left behind in Italy. It was ironic for Oleg that he had to go to extra lengths to ensure that the mother-in-law he disliked joined them on the journey. He would have preferred Xenia to have gone her own way to America—but Natasha would not be separated from her mother. A compromise satisfied the Australian authorities. Both Oleg and Natasha were placed on two-year work contracts. Natasha received the contract that was to have gone to Xenia had her age not made her ineligible. Xenia was allowed into the country on the basis that she was needed to rear Eugenie and could not work, the role originally intended for Natasha. So it was that when they arrived in Australia the pattern of the grandmother assuming a primary maternal role, established in Rostov for Natasha, was to be repeated for young

Eugenie. She was to live with her grandmother for long periods until her late teens. The arrangement would have an indelible effect on Eugenie and later prove explosive when the two strong-willed women, similar in character, were thrown together in confined circumstances.

The Sinicky family was given no opportunity to see Melbourne or to consider settling there. In line with official policy, the newcomers were sent immediately away from the city and had minimal contact with the locals at that stage. They were whisked from the wharf by bus and taken directly to the largest reception camp in the country at Bonegilla, a Victorian town near Wodonga on the NSW state border. The Bonegilla Immigration Centre was a former military barracks in which thousands of Calwell's 'New Australians' were housed in dormitory-style huts made of corrugated iron that had been partitioned into rooms. The huts had no ceilings and the partitioned walls were bare—and thin. There was the Italian block, the Ukrainian block, the Polish block, and the Russian block, among an array of nationalities. The Sinicky family was put with the Russians— Oleg, Natasha and Eugenie in one room and Xenia next door.

Jobs were easy to find in the early 1950s and, although labour market needs were not often matched with a person's background, Oleg was lucky. He left the family behind in Bonegilla almost immediately—placed within days as a cook in a British migrant hostel at Burwood, in Sydney's inner-west. It was a sweltering start to summer. When Oleg sent ten shillings by mail to Natasha in Bonegilla, she spoilt Eugenie buying her plenty of ice-cream and bananas.

Shortly before Christmas, Natasha and Xenia were summoned, with Eugenie, to attend the camp office. They were to be sent to Sydney too. But they were to be split up and scattered widely across the city. Natasha was placed as a nursing aide at King George V Hospital in the inner-city suburb of Camperdown. She was to live at the hospital's adjoining nurses' quarters. Xenia and Eugenie were sent to the Walgrove migrant hostel, another former military barracks at Rooty Hill, in Sydney's outer-western suburbs, a substantial distance away. Oleg remained at Burwood, working and living at Broughton Hostel for British migrants. Eugenie saw her mother once a week and almost nothing of her father for the next year or so. A shiftworker in the maternity ward, Natasha received one day off each week. Her arduous weekly routine on those days was to catch an electric train from Central Station to Burwood, visit Oleg and do his washing. Then she would catch a steam train in the afternoon to Rooty Hill, take a bus from the station to the camp and spend the night with Xenia and Eugenie. Often she would leave at four o'clock the next morning to make the early shift at the hospital.

Eugenie and her grandmother were fed in the community dining room at Walgrove but had no means of financial support, so Natasha contributed part of her wage to their needs. Oleg very rarely went to Walgrove to see his daughter during the year and a half she lived there with her grandmother. It was from this early time in his daughter's life that he started to become a remote figure for her. However, he doted on Eugenie when he did see her.

Oleg had easy access to alcohol now. His drinking increased and affected his behaviour more and more. He became jealous and possessive about Natasha, questioning her repeatedly about what she did and whom she saw when they were apart. A beneficial aspect of Oleg's anxiety was that it contributed to bringing the family together once again. Natasha had spent almost a year living and working at King George V Hospital when Oleg persuaded the manager of the Burwood hostel, Stan Benson, to arrange a job and living quarters for her at the hostel with Oleg. She was to clean the kitchen and dining room and prepare school lunches for the hostel's children. Benson, a kindly fellow who had a Russian wife, was sympathetic to the family's plight and was to bend the rules on a number of occasions over the years to do them favours. Natasha's next step was to be reunited with Eugenie. She was missing her daughter desperately and the travel to Rooty Hill, considering time and connections, was proving too much. Xenia had found a lover and intended moving to Queensland with him anyway, so it was convenient timing for Natasha as she pleaded with the hostel manager to allow Eugenie to shift to Burwood to be with her parents. He agreed.

Eugenie, now aged four, spoke good Russian, after living with her grandmother who refused to speak anything other than Russian for the rest of her life. Eugenie's second language was Italian, which she spoke when playing with Italian children around the Walgrove camp. She had also picked up some Polish the same way. Still she had no English, which was about to become an issue when she moved to Burwood and started school.

When Natasha tried to enrol her daughter at Burwood Primary School in February 1952, Eugenie was underage at four-and-a-half and had lived with her parents for only a short time at the hostel. The imperative for starting her early was the need for childminding during the day while both parents worked. The headmistress asked Natasha, whose command of English was barely adequate at the time, if her daughter could speak the language. Natasha replied 'not really' but added that her daughter could speak Russian, Italian and Polish. The headmistress accepted Eugenie early, on the condition that Natasha spoke English to her daughter at home. They never did—but Natasha sent the headmistress a strawberry cake, as a bribe to keep her on side.

Starting school from a non-English-speaking background was certainly a disadvantage but the Russian child coped well. Mixing with children who spoke only English saw her fluency in the language surge ahead. Despite speaking exclusively Russian at home, she acquired English in a relatively short time and spoke with the Australian accent of the school playground. In reading, writing and spelling she excelled also. It was at school—virtually from day one—that Eugenie's name was anglicised. She had no choice about the matter. Her teacher considered the pronunciation of Eugenie too difficult for the class and decided she would be known as Jennie from then on. Indeed she would change her name formally to

Jennie by deed poll in adulthood. The young Jennie climbed the ladder at Burwood quicker than most. She recalled:

I did well at school. I picked up English pretty quickly. I can remember—you know how things stick out in your memory—the teacher asked if anyone could spell 'hygiene' and I could. So on that basis I was put up from first class to second class, so I always went through school a year and a bit younger than everyone, which in hindsight was a bit stupid. Later on in primary school I was offered to go to Opportunity School on the basis that I would repeat a year and be the same age as the other children. I was not keen to leave my friends at school but I think it was a bit of a liability to be a year or two younger than my peers.

Natasha allowed Jennie to make the choice of putting her friends first and so she declined to move from Burwood Primary School to the Opportunity School at nearby Enfield. In the schoolyard and at home among the British migrant children, young Jennie was a popular tomboy. She would run out the hostel door to be on hand when there were fights between kids and defended her younger friend Irene if she called for help. She remembered those days with fondness:

My times as a girl were happy times. I did not have brothers or sisters but you had a whole host of kids you played with. It was an extended family. We would eat together in the canteen. They were good times.

Jennie lived with her parents for about a year-and-a-half in their flat in Broughton Hostel's E Block, a basic fibro barrack that offered families a private bedroom and sitting room and common showers and toilets. The arrangement changed when Xenia contacted Natasha from Queensland with news that her interstate romance was over and that she was alone and penniless. Distraught, Natasha appealed to Oleg, declaring that her mother was starving. Although he disliked Xenia, Oleg responded to the pressure. 'Send her ten pounds and bring her back,' he said. The next step required a big favour from the hostel manager, Stan Benson. Under the rules, once migrants had left a hostel, they were gone for good. And this was a hostel for British migrants, not Russians. But Benson agreed, when Natasha begged him, to allow Xenia to move in.

Xenia received her own room in E Block but there was a catch: she had to share it with Jennie and look after her. This left Natasha and Oleg together in their room. Natasha and Oleg now had privacy and childminding outside school hours no longer interfered with their shifts at the hostel. Once more, Jennie's primary carer was her grandmother, although she was not really parted from her parents: they were still a family.

Jennie remained an only child. Natasha wanted no more children because of their circumstances—both she and Oleg were poorly paid. After Jennie's birth, she had four abortions with the aid of doctors: two in the camps of Italy when more babies would have proved disastrous, and two in Australia. Natasha wanted the best education possible for Jennie to give her daughter the opportunity to climb out of the poor working-class rut in which the family was trapped in this new country. It would be the sort of education that Natasha had been denied because of the war. She believed that such an education would be financially unattainable if she were to give Jennie a sister or brother.

As Oleg started to drink more heavily, the family atmosphere was also not conducive to having more children. He drank anything he could lay his hands on now. Remarkably he still held down a job but he became impossible to live with, turning increasingly nasty and then violent towards Natasha. In his alcoholic rages, he would make jealous accusations and hit her.

Natasha's best friend, Vera Shihoff, another Russian migrant who worked and lived at the hostel, recalled:

> She had a big problem with Oleg. He used to give her 'left' and 'right'. Natasha's mother would interfere and then Natasha was left

on her own. The next moment, Oleg knocks on the door in the night and starts again. And she gets bruises.

Oleg's moods swung wildly, from euphoria to uncontrollable anger to depression. Natasha remembered him coming down the E Block hallway to their room, late at night, waking up the residents as he banged the walls with his fists shouting: 'Everybody's happy, everybody's happy, let's have a party!' After one binge, he told her that he was dying:

> I said, 'Oleg, what is the matter with you?' He said, 'I want a drink' and I remember he would say, 'If I had a gun I would shoot myself'. But he still craved another drink. That's how he suffered, you know, the next day, because he couldn't get any alcohol. Because he was so sick, I would bring him a bucket. 'Not that, I don't need that, go away from me. I want to have a drink.'

On another occasion, when Natasha was invited to go to Luna Park with Vera and some friends visiting from Adelaide, Oleg threatened to cut his wrists if she joined them. Vera recalled: 'I said to Natasha, "He is not going to do anything of the sort. I say get out because if you don't come with us he is going to bash you up anyhow".'

Returning home to Burwood, they found Oleg had left a suicide note near the door and slit his wrists—but he was still conscious. They pulled him out from under a table where he had hidden himself and called an ambulance. He raced around the room in shock at the sight of blood running down his arms.

When her parents split up the first time in 1955, Jennie was eight years old and too young to know fully what was happening. Oleg had confined his violent outbursts to Natasha, although Jennie remembered one occasion when she played a wrong note during piano practice: 'He grabbed me and threw me against the wall. I was very scared.' Jennie was also sheltered from the worst alcoholic excesses of her father because she slept in her grandmother's room in another part of E Block.

Her grandmother spoke harshly about Oleg in front of her, however, which gave her some idea of what was happening and helped determine her attitude towards him. Jennie's later memories of her father would be few. As a young adult she never talked about him, even with people very close to her. She expunged him from her mind. Jennie remembered:

> They split up and I saw him irregularly—and when I did it was pretty unpleasant. Like I remember him taking me to the movies and leaving me in there while he went to the pub, and then forgetting to pick me up at the end of the movies.

Already Jennie faced taunts from some children that she was a 'wog', a 'dago' or a 'reffo'. Ever the tomboy, she learnt to overcome these slurs by fighting back in skirmishes at school and at the hostel, and gave out as hard as she received. But now that her father was mostly absent, she faced the cruellest taunt of all. Inspired by some of the parents at the hostel who were quick to condemn Oleg's absence or questioned whether he existed at all, she was called a 'bastard' as well. When Jennie complained to her mother that one such parent had called her a bastard, Natasha confronted the person, warning: 'The day you meet Jennie's father will be the day you regret ever calling her a bastard.' Natasha was thinking about how Oleg might have reacted if drunk. But her anger was fuelled by the slander—as much an insult to her as it was to Jennie.

Oleg had left the hostel and found a string of jobs as a cook when he and Natasha separated. Typically he lived-in at the establishments where he worked. But like a yoyo, he kept returning to Natasha and she accepted him. One of these reconciliations was around the time of the 1956 Olympic Games in Melbourne. Oleg had scored a job as a cook in the athletes' village and took Natasha and Jennie with him to enjoy the Olympic spectacle. Such highs were all too brief, however, as pain and anguish overshadowed what was left of the marriage.

Finally Natasha tired of Oleg's returns to Burwood, and the

inevitable bouts of violence. She had to escape. The solution materialised in an offer from the hostel's new manager to transfer Jennie and her as well as Vera, and Vera's child, Irene, from E Block, to live in the hostel's main building. Xenia remained behind in E Block in her own room. A grand old house that contained the manager's office and residence and accommodation for senior staff, the hostel's main building was luxurious compared with the fibro barracks. Inside were apartments with large art deco-style rooms and non-shared bathrooms. But it was now almost vacant as most senior staff and their families had moved west to Housing Commission homes at Blacktown and commuted daily to work at Burwood. With the manager in close proximity and the heavy front doors locked at night, her new home gave Natasha security and protection. Oleg could not come and go as he pleased anymore.

In 1957 Natasha attempted to apply for the then equivalent of an apprehended violence order but the magistrate merely referred her to a solicitor whose fee, even for a consultation, she could not afford. The following year she was divorced. By now Oleg was working as a chef at the American Club in Sydney's CBD. Natasha tried vainly to force Oleg to pay maintenance for Jennie's upbringing, even threatening him with court action (though she still could not afford a solicitor). Oleg made a few half-hearted attempts at reconciliation but eventually stopped coming to Burwood and they lost touch. Peace had descended on their lives at Burwood. Jennie never saw her father again.

In August 1960 Natasha received a telephone call from someone at the American Club. Oleg's body had been found in his dingy inner-city hotel room after he had failed to turn up for work. Divorced for two years, Natasha had had no contact with Oleg for some time but was asked nonetheless to identify the body. Oleg was dead at just 39 years of age, from a heart attack after years of heavy drinking and smoking. Jennie attended her father's funeral but her recollection of it was a blur. Her reaction to Oleg's death at the time, according to her mother, was none at all. Thirteen-year-old Jennie knew something of how her father had treated her mother but kept it to herself and appeared to blot out the memory. However, Xenia confided to Natasha that Jennie had said to her: 'Thank God my father died before he killed my mother.'

While acknowledging his uncontrollable behaviour and her suffering at his hands, years later Natasha still referred to Oleg as a 'good man'. In her forgiveness she accepted that he had suffered too, from the dislocation of the war and from his addiction to alcohol, which Oleg himself had called 'the devil'. The adult Jennie George, emotionally close to her mother, adopted a similar, more charitable view of her father:

> When they split up I was eight. He moved out and I saw him rarely. He died when I was 13. But you could understand—they were coming to a new land and their lives had been stuffed up by the war.

After Oleg died, Natasha had a framed photograph of him made for Jennie, so she could remember her father. But Jennie refused to look at it and hid the picture in her bedroom wardrobe. Natasha told Jennie: 'As long as you put your father's picture in the wardrobe you will never be happy—put him out.' The photograph stayed in the cupboard, out of sight.

3

TEEN REBEL

A t times during her high school years Jennie Sinicky spent more hours in the corridors than inside the classroom. Her teachers threw her out frequently for chatting and playing up. She was caught wagging lessons and smoking behind the toilet blocks. She was chastised for wearing her skirts too short and for putting her hair in a ponytail—even hauled out of school assembly on one occasion for repeating the 'crime' and threatened with being barred from sitting biology honours if she did it again. She played up particularly in mathematics, her weakest subject, prompting her teacher, Pat Dyson, to remark much later: 'You were the cause of much stress in my life.'

After school Jennie did not go straight home. Instead she played pinball machines at the milk bar opposite Burwood Park. It was while playing pinball that she met her first boyfriend, someone she later remembered only as 'Curly'. She told her mother most things, but never mentioned Curly. It would have shocked Natasha to hear about him. Jennie's liaison with Curly was innocent enough—but it became an especially thorny issue when Curly was sent to Long Bay Gaol at Malabar for stealing.

Jennie made one secret and thrilling visit to the gaol with a girlfriend before losing contact with him. She was enthralled by the romance and drama of the teenage adventure as they signed themselves in at the gates to see him. She was also scared lest her mother find out.

This was Jennie Sinicky, the street-wise high school rebel. It was the other side of the well-behaved child of primary school years who did her grandmother's bidding without question. She took piano lessons, studied ballet, attended Sunday school at the Burwood Church of Christ, was tutored in her Russian heritage and learnt the language formally at Russian school on Saturdays. She also joined the Russian Girl Guides and participated in Russian pantomimes held at the Russian Orthodox Cathedral at Strathfield. By the early years of high school, however, Jennie was finished with such things and was more intent on challenging the world around her.

Ultimately Jennie's rebellious behaviour did not count against her because—to the great satisfaction of her mother—she performed well academically at Burwood Girls' High School at Croydon. She later professed to have enjoyed school, even if her behaviour suggested the contrary. Jennie's average mark was 72 per cent and school reports praised her work as 'good' or 'very good' with capacity for better. The teachers appear to have liked her too, despite her rebelliousness. One in particular, her history teacher, Pru Martin, could see her potential. She took Jennie under her wing, impressing upon her the importance of history and talking to her about the more serious side to life.

The rebel in Jennie Sinicky was born partly of peer pressure. She compensated for her academic ability by naughty antics so that she could still relate to her peers and remain popular, not appearing to other children to be bookish or the teacher's pet. Another reason for her rebelliousness was the acting out of the tough exterior she put on display, consciously or not, to cover up a range of insecurities. When her father was on the scene, his alcoholic ramblings and to-and-fro living arrangements had created significant upheaval in Jennie's life. Her home life had certainly improved once her father departed but his absence made her unlike most other children around her. Without the balance of a guiding paternal hand a gap was left in her life. Her mother and grandmother gave her the best loving care they could. But while both women were strong role models, they could not make up entirely for the lack of a father.

As Jennie grew older, her grandmother's commitment to the church and Russian community life was far removed from the world in which Jennie mixed. Her mother, who had similarly become absorbed in the church and Russian community, was devoted to Jennie and the source of great support. But she was also working most of the time. Often Jennie had to cope alone when she faced taunts about being a wog or a bastard or worse—all of which affected her. She had to be strong enough to withstand the teasing, and so developed a front to shield her vulnerabilities and deflect attempts to hurt her.

Ethnic insults were not limited to school and the hostel. When travelling somewhere by bus with her grandmother, Xenia embarrassed her by speaking loudly in Russian. Jennie implored 'Granny'—as she called her—to talk in English or keep her voice down to a whisper in order to avoid rude comments from some passengers. 'You bloody wogs! Why don't you speak English?', they would say.

Jennie Sinicky left behind the Burwood hostel in her final year of school. Natasha had registered the family's name for public housing and approval came through for the move to a small flat on the ninth floor of Block B of the John Northcott Place Housing Commission units in Belvoir Street, Surry Hills. Xenia moved with them, so all three were living together for the first time since the Bonegilla refugee centre. Jennie did not change high schools. Instead she completed her fifth and final year commuting from Surry Hills to Croydon each day, and sitting for the Leaving Certificate examinations in 1963. Jennie's subjects were English, history, French, mathematics, geography and biology. She took honours in history and biology. Mathematics remained her weak point and she had avoided physics and chemistry. At the end of the year, Jennie's reference from the acting principal predictably gave no hint of her rebelliousness:

> For five years Jennie Sinicky has been regular and punctual in her attendance at the above school and has completed the Leaving Certificate course. Jennie's manner, speech and appearance are pleasing and she has shown herself to be co-operative, intelligent, hard working, reliable, and courteous in all her school activities. I can confidently recommend her for any position that requires intelligence, co-operation, industry, reliability and courtesy.

A report by the Vocational Guidance Bureau of the NSW Department of Labour and Industry from the same year said that test results showed Jennie was 'superior' in general intellectual capacity and 'very superior' in clerical speed and accuracy. She demonstrated a high average in spelling and abstract reasoning ability:

> These results, together with your satisfactory academic progress suggest that degree course studies are a feasible aim for you. Your expressed interests and school subject background most strongly favour studies in the faculty of Arts. Social welfare, teaching, librarianship, broadcasting, advertising and the diplomatic service are some of the fields for which this course can provide a basis. The diploma courses in social work and speech therapy (for which the NSW Public Service offers traineeships) are further possibilities.
>
> If your interest in scientific careers remains strong, medical technology and dietetics could be considered, although in view of your lack of background in physics and chemistry the previous recommendations appear to be more suitable.

Nursing had been a passing fad but, Jennie's goal, since middle high school years, had been to teach. She performed well enough in the Leaving Certificate examinations to be offered two bursaries, one a Commonwealth government scholarship, the other a State government-funded teacher's trainee scholarship. She chose the latter because it offered an allowance, as well as university tuition fees. The trainee scholarship made Jennie more independent financially and took some of the pressure off her mother. The catch was in the obligation of her scholarship bond. After graduation she would have to pay it off by working for at least two years in the NSW public education system at a school not of her choice.

Jennie was just sixteen when she started as a teacher's trainee studying for an Arts degree and Diploma of Education at the University of Sydney. A scholarship was the only way she could have contemplated tertiary education because her mother certainly could not afford the fees. Knowing that Natasha could not afford the textbooks either, Pru Martin sent Jennie the books she needed for her first year.

Although street-wise in one sense, it was a naive and immature Jennie Sinicky who began her university studies. The sensually powerful D. H. Lawrence novel *Sons and Lovers* that was required reading for her English 1 course made no impact on her at the time.

No matter what Jennie's school reference had said, she remained rebellious and clashed repeatedly with her grandmother in the Surry Hills flat. They shared the same bedroom while Jennie's mother slept in the other bedroom so she could have a private life of her own.

Jennie was mad about the Beatles, much to her grandmother's horror, and living with this passion and Granny in the same confined space became a major problem for them both. Jennie plastered her walls with posters of the Beatles but as soon as she put them up, Granny tore them down. Paul McCartney—heartthrob to millions of girls around the world—was Jennie's favourite. She was in love with McCartney and was assured he felt the same way after she went to see the Beatles at one of their six Sydney concerts in June 1964 amid thousands of screaming teenage fans. She had won tickets in the second row after entering a competition in *The Sun* newspaper and came home convinced McCartney had been looking at her all night. She also spent hours on the pavement with her friend Brigit Musal and other girls outside the Sheraton Hotel in Potts Point, the usual abode of visiting international pop stars at the time, waiting for the Beatles to appear and wave from the balcony above.

Jennie almost qualified as a rock 'n' roll groupie. In January the following year she ended up at a wild party with the Kinks when they toured Australia with Manfred Mann and the Honeycombs. She was one of the girls hanging around outside the band's Sydney hotel—the Sheraton again—who managed to sneak up the fire-escape to the band's rooms. During the excitement she was led to the bathroom and propositioned, she said, by Dave Davies, band member and younger brother of the Kinks' lead singer, Ray Davies. She managed to escape unscathed, but the incident, in hindsight a foolish thing in which she had not realised the possible implications, scared her. Indeed she was lucky. According to Ray Davies's account of his brother's ravenous sexual appetite in his autobiography *X-RAY*, Dave Davies lived the life of a pop star to the hilt with all-night parties, an 'endless stream of girlfriends' and what their mother called 'sex orgies'.[1] Reflecting on her risk-taking behaviour years later, Jennie put it down to 'youthful exuberance'. She recalled: 'That whole period was so full-on. Gatecrashing that Kinks party was something to brag about to your girlfriends.' Though clearly very interested in boys, Jennie was still inexperienced.

Jennie's mother had kept the peace when the three of them were living at the Surry Hills flat, acting as a circuit-breaker when tensions ran too high. Natasha got on well with her daughter, knowing the way to her heart and having a more relaxed view about her social life and curfew hour. Jennie recalled:

> I was lucky because although my mother was very religious she had a very open mind and I think was quite liberal in her attitude

and treatment of me. Even at sixteen or seventeen I would be going out somewhere and she would not expect me to be home at midnight. She had a lot of trust and confidence in me.

That fragile harmony was shattered when Natasha moved out during Jennie's first year at university to live with her new husband, Vladimir Feodosiu, a Russian ten years her senior whom Natasha had met at the Russian Club at Strathfield. Vladimir was kind and loving to Natasha and they went on to enjoy a healthy, enduring relationship in contrast to Natasha's destructive first marriage.

Vladimir and Natasha tried briefly to share the cramped living conditions at Surry Hills, but it did not work. Vladimir could not cope with Granny Xenia's constant interfering and insistence that she was in charge of the flat. At first Jennie was jealous of her mother leaving her behind, just as she had been when Natasha married Vladimir. 'Why are you marrying someone who is old enough to be your father?', she had snapped. But ultimately she did not blame her mother, accepting that Natasha had a right to live her own life with her second husband and that he could not live with his mother-in-law. Moving out, however, left behind Granny and Jennie, the two most volatile of people. A domineering grandmother and a strong-willed teenage grand-daughter in the Surry Hills flat was a terrifying combination. Jennie had her own room now but Granny tried to impose restrictions: when she went out; where she went; how late she stayed out. Jennie fought her every step.

Jennie's favourite haunt was Beatle Village, a downstairs nightclub near the city-side corner of Oxford Street, Taylor Square, that cashed-in on the famous group's name. At sixteen, during her first year of university, Jennie was a regular every Friday and Saturday night, walking down the flight of stairs to meet her boyfriends. At Beatle Village she got to know the top local group, the Easybeats, and their singer Stevie Wright. She even dated Frank, an occasional substitute guitar player for the band, for a while. If she felt she had nothing to wear, she would shorten some of her mother's dresses left behind in the cupboard at Surry Hills.

Beatle Village was the epitome of the swinging sixties, a time of exploration and rebellion by the post-war generation. The pop musicians and their songs that Jennie adored were part and parcel of more permissive attitudes to sex and censorship. Finished with migrant hostels, out of school, going out late, mixing with exciting people—this life seemed like freedom to her.

Relations between Jennie and her grandmother became worse. One night, when Xenia refused to let her leave the flat, she decided to take a stand. As Granny barred her exit at the door, Jennie pulled a knife out of the kitchen drawer and waved it in front of her grandmother. In an act of defiance against this old woman trying to dominate her life, Jennie declared that she was leaving and no-one was going to stop her. After a bitter row, Granny finally relented. Jennie forced her way out the door and into the night. She was free again. Afterwards, when Natasha told Jennie it was a terrible thing to do to pull a knife, Jennie insisted she never would have hurt her grandmother. Xenia told Natasha: 'Your daughter is a real problem.' Jennie later recalled: 'I loved my grandmother. I don't want anyone to think I was really threatening her. It was a reflex action—I just wanted to go to Beatle Village.'

Natasha decided that Jennie would have to live with her and Vladimir at their rented flat at Bondi. Granny moved from Surry Hills soon after as well, to a pensioner's flat in Waterloo, where she lived until not long before her death at age 89. At Bondi Jennie had far more freedom. She also liked Vladimir, accepting him as her stepfather despite her initial scepticism. Vladimir was a Russian from Shanghai whose family had been among those sent to work in China when the Moscow–Beijing relationship was close after the 1949 Chinese Revolution. When the two brands of communism split, he was among those forced to leave. Instead of returning to the Soviet Union, he moved to Australia, as part of another post-war wave of Russian immigration, and landed a job at the General Motors-Holden's car plant at Page-wood in Sydney's south.

Vladimir was kind and very protective of Jennie but stricter than Natasha. One night to teach Jennie a lesson about staying out too late, he put the chain on the door at 2 a.m. and then returned to bed so that she would be locked out when she came home. When he fell asleep, Natasha got up and unhooked the chain. Sneaking inside a few hours later, Jennie was relieved no-one was waiting for her. She had been out with her girlfriend Brigit, both of them invited onto a boat with some sailors. Unaccustomed to alcohol, she became drunk for the first time in her life, vomiting all over her new black corduroy suit. She had been afraid to face her mother at the door and sneaked inside, hiding the suit in the bottom of her wardrobe.

Another night, when Jennie was supposed to be preparing for her examinations at home but had gone out instead, Vladimir and Natasha went to Beatle Village in Oxford Street. Again Vladimir wanted to make a point to his wayward stepdaughter. But not bold enough to venture inside lest they embarrass themselves or Jennie in front of her friends, he and Natasha parked near the entrance door and waited in the car, hoping to catch Jennie if she happened to be there and came out. Jennie *was* there that evening, blissfully unaware of her parental spies who gave up and drove home after a few hours when she did not show. She was too busy dancing.

Inevitably party life took its toll on Jennie's studies and she failed her first year in English. Being younger than most of her fellow students, she had struggled to grasp meaning in lectures about classics old and modern, from Chaucer and Shakespeare to Chekhov and Lawrence. But her main downfall was spending too much time at nightclubs, immature and arrogant enough to think she could coast as she had at school. 'I had always done well academically. I thought I could sit for exams without reading the text,' she admitted later. To continue at university meant repeating first year—and not just the subject she failed. A short-lived university by-law of the time dictated that students had to repeat all first-year subjects, even in the case of only one subject failure. Jennie's chief problem though was that failure meant losing her scholarship. Natasha was distraught. Jennie used the excuse that she had concentrated on Shakespeare and not studied Chekhov. But what could Natasha do? She could not raise the £60 in fees necessary for her daughter to continue: she and her husband had no extra money after having spent what savings they had on their wedding. By now Natasha had left her kitchen hand's job at the Burwood hostel and was doing similar work at the fledgling Menzies Hotel above Wynyard Station in the city. Although ashamed of herself for doing so, she began borrowing money from the hotel cooks, asking around for £20 loans. Then her friend Vera's second husband came to the rescue. He volunteered a loan for the full £60 because he said he liked 'intelligent people'. It was a grand gesture from someone who was hardly rich but Jennie's fees were paid and she was back on track.

Failing English was a shock to Jennie. The ignominy of having to repeat all her subjects and the added burden it placed on her mother made her think more clearly about what she was doing. She did not give up her love of boys and partying but accepted that her first year out of school had been a wild indulgence.

In her repeat year she toned down her night-life and applied herself, passing all her subjects including English—and winning back her scholarship. She performed so well the year after (technically her second year) that she was issued a university certificate of merit.

Throughout this period, Jennie had a series of part-time jobs to earn pocket money. It gave her an idea of what the real world of work was like. Her first job, in university summer holidays, had been stacking shelves in the Franklins supermarket at Bondi

Junction, not far from where she lived. Then she packed boxes at the Peters ice-cream factory at Redfern, a job she loathed. Her next job was pleasant enough, as a sales assistant in the pharmacy section of the Walton's city department store in Park Street. Her last vacation job was the most closely linked to her future credentials, tutoring Aboriginal children through the university's adult education service.

Jennie always was a very social, boisterous person, yearning to be surrounded by friends and confidantes. Her first year at university, like many novice students, had been a matter of finding her way around and her social life off campus took precedence. During her repeat of first year, in 1965, she became more interested in university life and began exploring the opportunities it offered. There were plenty of clubs and societies on campus that were open to young undergraduates. Not to join one or more of them could have meant a lonely, isolating existence in an institution that would be the focus of Jennie's attention for up to five years. The primary reason for her to join, though, was the opportunity to meet boys. The clubs and societies were a great means of meeting the opposite sex—they created the setting for personal interaction.

She first joined the Trainee Teachers' Club and became fairly involved in its activities, later editing a trainee journal called *Status* and campaigning for better conditions for trainees like herself. During her repeat year also she began attending the campus Labor Club and, apart from meeting some interesting young men, her interest in politics began to take shape. An invitation to a gathering sponsored by the Eureka Youth League was a seminal event in Jennie's life. It came from Jane Rennie, a friend Jennie had known since childhood. Jane's family had lived at the Burwood hostel as British migrants and now Jane and Jennie were studying together at the University of Sydney. Unlike Jennie, Jane came from a highly politicised family. Her parents were members of the Communist Party of Australia and were strongly sympathetic towards the Soviet Union. Jane and her siblings, Phillip and Maxine, all belonged to the Eureka Youth League, the youth organisation established and funded by the Communist Party of Australia.

Just turned eighteen, Jennie had some awareness of news and current events. She also had a solid grounding in history thanks to Pru Martin and was questioning the world around her as part of her natural rebelliousness. Yet she remained unsophisticated politically. Jennie's chief home influence, her mother, had no political connections and, like many of her generation, had a limited interest in politics. Natasha was a conservative on most issues of the day and supported Menzies. Her most dogmatic stance was reserved for avowed opposition to the Soviet regime. When Jennie accepted the Eureka Youth League invitation, it was initially the inherited politics of her mother that she took with her. But, at this stage, political activism was not a priority. The first league gathering Jennie attended was an informal party, held at someone's house, not at the university or one of the league's usual meeting places in the city. Despite the informal setting and the social nature of the occasion, it was still a lure for recruits.

Jennie began attending regular league meetings after Jane Rennie's informal introduction at the party and soon became deeply committed to its campaign against the Vietnam War. But while her league involvement in the war protest was the key to Jennie's politicisation, it was a man in the league who sparked her initial interest—almost straight away. His name was Paddy George. More than anyone else, Paddy George would help to develop Jennie's political consciousness and ideas, and open her eyes to what it meant to be committed to a cause. He became her mentor. He also became the love of her life.

4

PADDY

_____

Everyone loved Paddy George. He was full of enthusiasm, warm-hearted and kind and had a confident, positive aura about him. He was a natural leader. He also had a knockabout charm. His male friends used superlatives to describe their high regard for him. Young women adored him, even flocked around him.

As a card-carrying member of the Communist Party of Australia, Paddy took his political commitment seriously. He was loyal to the party but struggled with its dogma and allegiances. In particular he had difficulty reconciling his Moscow-aligned party faith with the lack of openness in the Soviet Union and later the brutality of Soviet tanks rolling into Czechoslovakia. Despite the level of his commitment, Paddy did not have the intensity of some political operatives—he did not press himself onto others and had a sunny disposition that made him fun company. He balanced his life with a wide circle of friends and a love of sport. As close friend Cathy Bloch put it: 'Being with Paddy made you happy. He was prepared to get into anything and everything. He was a smiler—he wasn't a heavy dude politically even though he had very responsible positions. He was open.'

Paddy had come from a strong Australian communist background. Both parents were diehard members of the party in the post-war period and he was brought up through the Junior Eureka League, a Soviet-style 'Young Pioneers' organisation for Australian children that was a precursor to the youth league. Junior leaguers looked like Boy Scouts or Girl Guides. They wore similar uniforms and scarves, only the outlook was most definitely socialist. Even the emphasis on sports had Soviet overtones. Sports were encouraged in an attempt to replicate the mass culture of the Eastern European States under Stalinism. Behind them lay a non-religious but nonetheless puritanical moral code in which girls and boys were to be distracted as much as possible from sexual thoughts by exhausting sports so they did not touch others or themselves. Paddy excelled at most sports—he liked football, volleyball and swimming. He was competitive but friends recalled he 'did it all very cheerfully'.

Like Jennie, Paddy was an only child. He had grown up in the beach suburb of Maroubra in Sydney's south-east. His father, Michael, a World War II veteran of the Kokoda Trail, was a metal tradesman at ICI's Botany plant. His mother, Gwen, was a trained librarian who worked in the research section of the Amalgamated Metal Workers Union (AMWU). Both parents, influenced by a 'Back to the Factories' campaign of the Communist Party of Australia, urged Paddy to take an apprenticeship as an electrician. He worked for several years for the NSW Electricity Commission at Bunnerong power station near Botany Bay. Gwen George recalled that she once provided a set of saucepans as the prize for a staff running race at the power station. Paddy entered and won—so he had to present his mother with her own saucepans.

By the time Jennie met Paddy in late 1965, he was a full-time political activist for the Communist Party, having risen to become the State secretary of the Eureka Youth League for NSW. The job was a labour of love for Paddy but very demanding and underpaid. His income, funded by the party, was minimal. He was lucky if he came close to the basic wage and the general custom when in the company of young full-time officials such as Paddy was to shout them a drink or a meal, considering they were living on the breadline.

Some regarded Paddy as one of the party's future leaders. He was one of the younger, dynamic members who gained a better chance of advancing through party ranks after 1963 when Maoist separatists formed their own Communist Party of Australia (Marxist-Leninist) in the wake of the falling out between the Soviet Union and China. In his idealism, Paddy was very open-minded but also lacked accurate information about the reality of life in the Eastern Bloc countries. Like many who made trips to Moscow for party schooling or to the Soviet satellite countries for international conferences, Paddy had been sheltered from the political repression and hardship suffered by the people on his own party-sponsored travels through Eastern Europe. He knew something was amiss, which strengthened his belief in the need for the Australian Communist Party to be independent from the Soviet Union. But he never had to experience the queues for basic foods and was not denied the rights and freedoms taken for granted in Australia.

Despite challenging the Soviet Union's direction and questioning some of the local hierarchy's edicts, Paddy remained firmly committed to the Communist Party of Australia. Several key developments had glued him to the cause through the years, chiefly the party's growing acceptance of more democratisation. He also calmed his doubts by welcome signs that the Australian party really was making decisions independent from its Soviet parent. The Eureka Youth League, funded by the Australian Communist Party, regarded itself as having a degree of independence from its local benefactor as well.

The Eureka Youth League had undergone several name changes and transformations since the Communist Party of Australia first recognised the need to form a youth organisation to feed its ranks in the 1920s.[1] Its name was adopted from the famous rebellion on the Ballarat goldfields in 1854, as was its oath: 'We swear by the star of the Southern Cross to stand truly by each other and to fight to defend our rights and liberties.' The league had elements of all its predecessors but was much broader. It was not a strict educator in Marxist–Leninist doctrine like the original Youth Communist League formed in 1923, although it did hold introductory study classes to foster socialist politics in Australian youth. Like the League of Young Democrats formed in 1939, it also accepted communists co-operating with non-communists. One of its primary appeals was built on the ideas developed in the 1930s—by organising sports, well-run holiday camps and public speaking.[2]

Formed in 1941 from the ashes of the League of Young Democrats—which had been banned by the first Menzies government at the outbreak of World War II—what really distinguished the Eureka Youth League from its predecessors was its active role in mass campaigns. Its early mainstay issues were world peace and youth rights. At the time Jennie was introduced to the league, its primary involvement by far was in the fledgling campaign of protest against the Vietnam War. The anti-Vietnam War campaign gave the league a renewed impetus and more common ground with general community sentiment than it had ever enjoyed. The rallying point was growing opposition to Australia sending conscripts to Vietnam, against the background of serious questions about the growing number of casualties and American–Australian involvement in the war in the first place.

Estimates of the league's national membership varied. The most ambitious figure was 5000 'at best' while others rated it by the mid-1960s at between 300 and 400.[3] Certainly numbers were not high. One estimate by the Federal government's Australian Security Organisation (ASIO) based on the number of delegates sent to the league's national congress put the number in NSW at no more than 160. Whether its members later joined the Communist Party, became fellow travellers, drifted to the mainstream Australian Labor Party, or lost interest in politics, the league provided a very useful training ground for a considerable number of young people who were to become prominent in left-wing politics in Australia.

The Eureka Youth League under Paddy's leadership had a succession of meeting places, the first being at 40 Market Street in the city. Members gathered there at the league's gymnasium club, on the floor above the offices of *Tribune*, the Communist Party's weekly newspaper. Later meeting places included a hall owned by the Waterside Workers' Federation in nearby Day Street and Communist Party premises in Glebe. There was a social atmosphere to the league's activities even though the business at hand was serious. Much of the time was spent writing anti-Vietnam newsletters, folding mail-outs, making placards and organising demonstrations. The focus of the league at this point in its history, through Paddy's guidance, was its deep involvement in the Vietnam Action Committee. The committee played a central role in the national anti-Vietnam War movement alongside various competing liberal and leftist anti-war groups, among them the Association for International Cooperation and Disarmament, Youth Against Conscription and Save Our Sons.

Jennie had been attracted to Paddy as soon as she spotted him at a league gathering in late 1965 but was aware that there was another woman in his life. At first Jennie and Paddy met as part of a group—at social get-togethers in pubs or at friends' parties, formal league meetings and anti-war demonstrations. The chemistry between them was becoming obvious but the real impetus for their inevitable romance did not occur until after Paddy left the country in June 1966, to attend the World Federation of Democratic Youth Assembly in Sofia, Bulgaria. During his six-week absence he sent Jennie postcards telling her about his travels. Paddy's correspondence and physical separation from Jennie had a spellbinding effect on her. She could not stop thinking about him. By the time he returned, what was originally Jennie's teenage crush had developed into the single most important thing in her life. Paddy split up with his girlfriend, Megan, and they began dating. Gwen George, Paddy's mother, witnessed Jennie's enthusiasm for her son. She recalled: 'When Jennie first met Paddy, she said, "I know that's the man for me!"'

Doris Jobling, then a union organiser for the NSW Teachers' Federation, was a mentor to Jennie and other young women like her who came through the ranks of the teacher trainees' union. She said: 'Jennie would have done anything to get Paddy. I remember counselling her. I said,"you shouldn't go after him just because he's the secretary of the league. It doesn't mean he's the right one for you".'

By now Jennie had grown out of Beatle Village and her adherence to the traditional pre-revolution Russian culture of her mother was a distant memory. There had been a succession of not-too-serious boyfriends. Jennie was no longer a virgin but typical of her complex and often contradictory personality, she had conducted many of her infatuations with boys in a rather coy, conservative fashion, rarely venturing beyond the hand-holding stage and at odds with the image she presented of herself as a wild partygoer.

Paddy, seven years Jennie's senior, was charismatic, wise and unlike anyone she had met. He was a perfect foil, someone capable of soothing some of her insecurities, and self-assured enough to guide her on a path to independent thinking without him being worried that it would jeopardise their relationship. Jennie explained what stirred her about Paddy: 'He was older than I was and he was different from the silly boys down in Beatle Village. He was intelligent and he had all these girls chasing after him. And he was good at sport.'

Almost as soon as he had arrived home from Bulgaria and they began dating, Paddy had to leave again for Melbourne on Eureka Youth League business. So once again, their romance was conducted by correspondence. In the wake of the foreign postcards it became a stream of interstate letters between the two cities. Contrary to her earlier style, Jennie often waited at home, longing for Paddy's return. Among friends in the league, they came to be regarded as a couple and were open about the nature of their relationship. Paddy's close friend, Rex Hewett, remembered: 'Paddy was madly in love with Jennie and she likewise—it was a sort of meeting of minds in a lot of respects.'

Afraid of her mother's reaction, Jennie did not tell Natasha about Paddy immediately. She knew that Natasha would blanch upon hearing that her daughter had fallen in love with a communist and one deeply involved in the party organisation at that. There were still strong expectations that Jennie—the treasured only child in a Russian Orthodox family—would marry a good Russian boy in the cathedral. Her mother may have accepted a non-Russian but to accept a communist whose political party had a direct line to Moscow as a possible son-in-law was an anathema to a traditional Russian woman who had lived under Stalinism. When Jennie did mention Paddy to Natasha, the expected torrent gushed forth. Had she not listened to her mother all those years? How would it look in the eyes of the Russian community? 'Oh Jennie, you're killing us,' Natasha said. Jennie replied: 'Never mind, I love him. I don't want to follow your footsteps. I am what I am, Mum.' Despite misgivings, Natasha and Vladimir did accept Paddy when they met him and came to like him. They had no choice anyway with a headstrong daughter like Jennie—but as Rex Hewett said:

> You could not have got a better person to break the ice because Paddy was an extremely wonderful person, very kind and considerate while nevertheless committed to left-wing politics. If you were going to get married or hooked up with someone who had the opposite view to your parents, Paddy would have been the one to do it with.

The embarrassment increased for Natasha, however, as it became more widely known among people in the closed, very traditional Russian community with whom Natasha mixed that Jennie's partner was a communist. Jennie was tarnished in their eyes. Some Russians branded Jennie a 'spy' and urged Natasha to disown her daughter. The pressure caused Natasha much heartache but she stood by Jennie and never wavered. Vladimir too stood by Jennie, refusing to hear a bad word against her. One of those who abused Jennie to her face was Vladimir's brother, Sergei, a staunch supporter of the fallen Tsarist monarchy. Vladimir was enraged. 'Jennie's spying on you? She's got so much to do without you!' he snapped, and never spoke to Sergei again.

Amid such family turbulence, Jennie stunned her mother by moving out on Boxing Day 1966 to share a rented flat with several girls at Annandale. Bondi was too far from the university and friends, and she wanted to be independent, she argued. But Paddy figured high in her thinking. Moving out offered her a freedom she had never experienced. Out of parental view in a laissez-faire undergraduate household, Jennie could have a private life with Paddy and fewer prying questions about what she was doing outside university hours at anti-Vietnam demonstrations and league meetings. It did not take long for news of the company Jennie was keeping to reach Natasha. By coincidence, a friend from the Russian community happened to live in the Annandale area and reported back to Natasha that 'Jennie is living with commos'. Natasha was mortified but there was nothing she could do. Jennie did not last long at the Annandale flat. Independence cost money and she moved home again before her twentieth birthday in 1967 because it was cheaper. Back at Bondi, she and Paddy continued to see each other. Paddy lived in a rented flat in Paddington and usually stayed the night if he came to visit Jennie at her parents' home—a rare thing for the times. Natasha would make up a bed for him in the lounge room, although after her parents had gone to sleep Jennie would quietly join him under the covers for part of the night.

As Jennie's relationship with Paddy deepened, so did her involvement in the Eureka Youth League and all the demonstrations, marches, teach-ins and sit-downs held to advance the protest movement's cause. The league, however, while crucial to what direction her political activism would take, had not been her initiation to politics. It was possible for young students such as Jennie to have very fluid political associations at university in the 1960s, hovering around several groups without a specific allegiance to any.

Jennie's first political association—apart from joining the Trainee Teachers' Club—had been to attend the university Labor Club. The club attracted a hotchpotch of ALP members, communists, anarchists, Trotskyists, syndicalists, industrial left-wingers and romantic idealists. Jennie was attracted to one of the club's young idealists, Russell Darnley, a teacher trainee like herself. He had started out as a junior ALP right-winger mixing with the likes of Bob Carr and Paul Keating but then swung to the left, incensed at Australia's involvement with the United States in the Vietnam War. The relationship between Darnley and Jennie Sinicky never went beyond holding hands and kissing at parties, but they cared about each other and, as budding left-wingers, were among those who soon gravitated to the Sydney-based Vietnam Action Committee, which had been started by the young Trotskyist and ALP member, Bob Gould, in late 1965. Detested by the Communist Party hierarchy because of his hardened antipathy to the Soviet regime and promotion of super left-wing socialism, Gould had put all his effort into the anti-war campaign through the Vietnam Action Committee. He stole the initiative in the anti-Vietnam movement from the Communist Party by becoming the early leading force in the organisation of street marches and other demonstrations. But the leadership of the anti-war movement soon became a competition among a range of groups, some of which forged alliances. Under Paddy's leadership, the Eureka Youth League joined forces with Gould's group on the Vietnam Action Committee and played a major role in demonstrations from then on. Ann Curthoys, one of the demonstrators and later professor of history at the Australian National University, explained the complexity of alliances which saw the Communist Party and the Eureka Youth League, as its youth organisation, became important forces in the anti-war movement while not necessarily controlling it:

> A loose coalition was being forged between very different groups which shared a broadly similar attitude to the war and conscription. For many of these people communists were genuine political allies, not political outlaws. Even together, however, these political forces were still very much a minority and clearly unable to threaten the Government's policies or win over large segments of an essentially conservative Australian population. This would change in the following years as the politicisation, even radicalisation, of Australian youth—the maturing 'baby boom' generation—particularly those in tertiary education, mobilised against conscription and the war.[4]

Gould's early strength was his ability to attract a youth audience. He drew on the support base of the Vietnam Action Committee to form a radical breakaway youth group in 1966 called Resistance, which posed some threat to the Eureka Youth League's rival drive to recruit the baby boomers. While a tense contest ensued, both groups communicated and maintained a united front on Vietnam.[5] Darnley explained what drew he and Jennie to Gould:

> We were people who were radicalised by the Vietnam War and under Gould's influence briefly—largely because he was the only person who seemed to have something that was flamboyant and colourful, and focused on the Vietnam War, going. The alternative was a rather more stodgy form, a more conservative form of socialism that was more directly aligned with the Soviet Union.

Gould recalled meeting Jennie when she came to Vietnam Action Committee meetings and seeing her in the company of Jane Rennie and another former schoolfriend whose parents were communists. In times when the prevailing mood among youth in Australia was apolitical, Gould believed that Jennie related to children of Communist Party parents such as Rennie partly because they shared a common interest despite their different backgrounds. While Jennie in her rebellious drive for independence was finding her own way politically after having received a negative rendition of Stalinism from her mother and grandmother, the children of Communist Party parents were challenging the 'High Stalinism' drummed into them from early years.

Like other young men, Gould regarded Jennie as striking. Her appeal was a jumble of her looks, background and radical politics. Unlike many young Australians, Jennie actually *knew* what Stalinism was from her family history. Her Russian ethnicity made her seem sexually exotic and at the same time gave her a quality of left-wing political authenticity that others of her generation yearned for.

Russell Darnley believed that Jennie's politics were 'conservative' compared with the left-wing extremism propounded by Gould and that she only flirted with Gould's Resistance group. She endorsed 'direct action' but not to the same extent as Gould's more militant, confrontational approach, which risked turning peaceful demonstrations into street-fighting violent clashes with authorities. Darnley observed Jennie move further and further towards the Eureka Youth League, but believed that it was Paddy George's presence, more than ideology, that made the difference. Gould agreed about the influence of Paddy George: 'Jennie was in our periphery for maybe six months but then she was drawn into the Eureka Youth League and the critical thing in her change of allegiance was her relationship with Paddy. She fell in love with Paddy and away it went.'

The Communist Party to which Paddy George was aligned had a great deal more influence in the mainstream left-wing of the labour movement than Gould's group could ever aspire to. It reached deep inside trade unions and the Australian Labor Party. Some of its members were leading union officials such as Jack Mundey and Laurie Carmichael and certain ALP parliamentarians who have never been publicly named. Within the ALP, there were many communist 'fellow travellers' and even though the ALP officially forbade it, there were dual card-carriers who were ALP members in public but secretly Communist Party of Australia members as well.

Jennie did not make her decisions according to any set plan for her career in the long term but she was ambitious and always considered her next move. Her switch to the Communist Party-backed Eureka Youth League, while driven mainly by her love for Paddy, was a better career choice for her than remaining under Gould's influence. It gave her a bridge into the mainstream left-wing, rather than remaining far outside. Her Communist Party connections would later help open the doors to the left-wing leadership which ran the union of her profession, the communist-influenced NSW Teachers' Federation, and give her left-wing credentials from an early age for positioning herself in the broader union movement.

The highlight of Jennie's participation in many anti-Vietnam demonstrations was undoubtedly the visit of United States President Lyndon B. Johnson to Australia in October 1966. Enthusiastic crowds, cheering and waving, lined the streets of Sydney to greet the so-called leader of the free world, Australia's great ally in the fight against the communist menace emanating from the North against the South Vietnamese regime of President Ngo Dinh Diem. But there were also the demonstrators from the Vietnam Action Committee holding placards saying 'Go away LBJ' and 'Try LBJ for war crimes'. Jennie was one of several women who ran onto the road and threw themselves in front of the presidential limousine as it passed Hyde Park, on the corner of Liverpool and College Streets. Their protest prompted the Premier of NSW, Bob Askin, sitting next to Johnson, to utter the famous wry remark: 'Run over the bastards'.[6]

Although Jennie was unhurt and mingled safely among the demonstrators on the footpath after the incident, her action had carried some danger. As well as oncoming presidential wheels, the horses of mounted police were within trampling distance and there was the risk of arrest. Police at the scene did drag Jennie and other women off the road but made no arrests. Their chief priority was ensuring Johnson's security along the motorcade route. Police strength at that particular point was also not sufficient to devote time to making arrests once protesters were cleared.

It seemed to friends who knew her well that Jennie's decision to run in front of Johnson's car was out of character. She was becoming a seasoned protester but friends regarded her as normally cautious, someone who acted after due consideration, not with reckless abandon. Doris Jobling remembered Jennie being in her friend Jane Rennie's shadow: 'Jane was the organiser. It was all planned out very carefully—Jennie ran behind her.' Jennie remembered it as a clear-minded judgment on her part to run onto the road. She could not emulate the ultimate protest of men who risked jail as conscientious objectors by refusing conscription; as a woman, sitting in front of Johnson's motorcade was the most forthright personal contribution Jennie felt she could make to the protest movement.

Jennie *was* arrested by police—but it happened only once during her incarnation as a protester. The following year, she and two other women, Pam Tuckwell and Barbara Levy, broke away from the crowd and ran onto the Sydney Showground during the Royal Easter Show carrying anti-war placards just before a United States military band was due to play. After bringing them to the ground with flying tackles, police dragged Jennie and the other young women off the field and arrested them. They faced the rather curious charge of 'offensive behaviour (not prostitution)'. Appearing in court, a magistrate let them go with a first offence warning and no conviction was recorded. The Vietnam Action Committee had a policy of avoiding unnecessary arrests but this was one occasion— three women protesters isolated in the middle of an open field—when arrest seemed unavoidable. Again, Jennie was showing she could do something gutsy—but not without a bout of nerves during the wait before running on. In typical style, according to observers, she debated right up until the moment whether or not to do it.

Jennie seemed to spend her life in protests at this time. Despite the serious business at hand, the protests did have their amusing moments, even with the authorities: so regular were the demonstrations that police and protesters came to know each other. Jennie struck up an amicable relationship with, of all people, the head of NSW police Special Branch, Fred Longbottom. He was always pleasant to her and, so she believed, disliked the political role he was required to fulfil. She recalled: 'Every time I'd go to a demo, Freddy Longbottom would be there, and he'd say "Jennie, you're here to add to my file" and we'd have a laugh about it.'

Jennie had another growing file. Since mid-1966 she had attracted the attention of the Australian Security Intelligence Organisation (ASIO). Her personal ASIO file, marked 'secret' but obtained under government regulations allowing open access after 30 years, runs to more than 80 pages for the first two years of ASIO's interest in her political activities.

Most of the file is innocuous—typically it lists attendances at the Eureka Youth League's weekly meetings, which ASIO gathered from photographic surveillance of the league's Day Street headquarters and from undercover agents present. One entry next to her name says simply, 'arrived late'.

There are some interesting vignettes, nonetheless, that help build a picture of Jennie's relatively speedy political development, and say much about what was regarded as potentially subversive activity in Australia during the Cold War climate of the 1960s. While ASIO's interest focused chiefly on the activities of Jennie and her colleagues at the Eureka Youth League, the first official file entries in May 1966 show that Jennie came to ASIO's attention because of her links with the Rennie family. Jane Rennie's father sent a telegram from the Australian–Soviet Friendship Society to Jennie at her Bondi address that was intercepted by ASIO. Rennie had wanted to use Jennie as an interpreter for a visiting Russian singer following a request from the Soviet Embassy. As it transpired, her services were not needed on this occasion. Jennie was a political novice—just 18 years old—and had no recollection of the incident many years later, but ASIO noted in her file that she 'sometimes assists with translations' for the society. The society was of interest to ASIO because—despite its public image as the pleasant face of Soviet communism—it was really a front for the Soviet government, was infiltrated by the KGB and was intent on recruiting Australians as agents of influence.

ASIO did not begin recording Jennie's attendance at the league in a methodical fashion until October 1966 when she attended a meeting called to work out protest tactics for President Johnson's visit. (One agent at the meeting referred to her phonetically as 'Jenny Senecki', another as 'Jenny Sinnicky'.) 'It all depends on the temperament of the crowd as to whether they will hold a mass sit-down and if they do the EYL will be in the forefront,' reported one agent. In ASIO files the league's role was originally reported under the heading, 'Communist Party of Australia interest in the visit of President Johnson'.

Jennie's official profile said of her:

> Smokes and drinks. Politically minded. Goes to Sydney University. Was one of the girls arrested during Easter 1967. Very active in the League. Parents are Russian. Has rather boyish, rough voice. It is not known where her income comes from.

In January 1967, Jennie was seen by ASIO surveillance at a demonstration against South Vietnam's Prime Minister Ky. Her quick rise up the league hierarchy was noted when, in March 1967, she headed the Eureka Education Committee and, in June 1967, when she was elected State vice-president of the league. According to one ASIO agent, Jennie wrote a covering letter in September 1967 in connection with a possible league 'Campaign to aid North Vietnam and the National Liberation Front in Vietnam'. It was noted subsequently that there was 'nothing really concrete'.

Besides Paddy George, the key influence in Jennie's political development during this period was Mavis Robertson. Friends and foes alike regarded Robertson as a formidable character. Married to Alex Robertson, editor of the Communist Party's national newspaper, *Tribune*, she was the long-time national secretary of the Eureka Youth League and later became one of several joint national secretaries of the party. Bob Gould, an avowed opponent of Robertson's at the time, spoke of her with barbed admiration: 'Mavis was an absolutely ruthless, Stalinist apparatchik of the most capable sort. In her own apparatchik way she was quite a powerful figure.'

Robertson became a role model for women such as Jennie. The male-dominated Moscow-aligned Communist Party hierarchy was not interested in issues such as women's rights. But Robertson, while firmly loyal to the party's discipline, was very astute in harnessing the rhetoric of the emerging Women's Liberation Movement from the United States. A very articulate speaker, she drew upon feminist ideas as part of her nurturing of young women who came through the communist movement. She opened Jennie's mind to sexual inequality endured by women at work and home and to the possibilities in life for women if they were no longer treated as second class to men.

Jennie met Mavis Robertson via Paddy. As the league's national chief, Robertson could see Jennie had potential and took her under her wing as a protégée. She remembered Jennie as a highly intelligent and enthusiastic young woman who supported 'direct action' at that period and whose motto was 'Let's not talk, let's do what we have to do'. While not endorsing violence, Jennie believed that people should stand up and fight for what they wanted. Robertson recalled:

> There aren't any organisations like the Eureka Youth League any more. It was connected to the Communist Party of Australia but it was an independent grouping of people. So as long as we didn't do anything outrageous, here was an opportunity for young people like Jennie to do things in their own right. It was a place where young girls and boys met. It was a place where young girls didn't feel inferior, and so you got a lot of feisty girls, and Jennie was its most outstanding graduate.

Robertson hailed the Eureka Youth League as a useful training ground for important life skills quite apart from its doctrinaire purpose as a potential recruiting point for the Communist Party. It was, she believed, the **first** opportunity for young people such as Jennie to learn organisational skills, developed as they worked on the protest collectives but also on committees formed to run

league-sponsored holiday camps. The change in Jennie's outlook
—compared to just a few years earlier—was stark. By March 1967,
as chair of the Eureka Education Committee, she was organising
weekend classes on 'Basic Marxism' at the Communist Party
compound run by the Aarons family at Minto, a far southwest
suburb of Sydney. The same month, Jennie helped Paddy run the
league's Easter holiday camp at the coastal town of Corrimal, near
Wollongong. She took part in a panel discussion at the camp
chaired by Paddy on 'hooliganism', and listened, along with others,
to an address by Communist Party central committee member Bill
Gollan on 'the difference between Marxism and Socialism'.

Jennie and Paddy announced their engagement in October 1967
and threw a party the following month at the Double Bay
Sailing Club. It was a huge gathering of mainly Eureka Youth
League friends. When Paddy told Natasha that he had proposed
to her daughter, she protested that Jennie was still a university
student. But Jennie stepped into the fray, very determined. She
was 20 and, reflecting attitudes of the times, feared she would
be 'left on the shelf' if she waited any longer. She told her
mother they planned to marry early the following year. By then
Jennie would have completed her Arts degree, majoring in English
and history, but still would have a final year of study for her
diploma of education. The engagement even rated a mention in
an ASIO report from the time, based on a telephone intercept
at the Communist Party's Sydney headquarters. A colleague of
Jennie and Paddy's, thought by ASIO to be Mick Tubbs, was
recorded talking to a woman, saying that Paddy had been 'trapped
at last' and would marry Jennie 'probably in February'.

Jennie and Paddy were married on 10 February 1968 in a quiet
civil wedding at the Sydney Registry Office with only immediate
family members present. In keeping with custom of the time, Jennie
dropped her surname of Sinicky and used Paddy's as her own from
that day forth. The post-wedding celebration was a big event. They

hired a recently opened reception centre in Darlinghurst, inviting family and friends for an exuberant night of food, beer, dancing and speeches. Natasha and Vladimir toasted the couple with vodka, sitting with Paddy's parents, Gwen and Michael. Granny Xenia, whom Jennie rarely saw now, joined in too. The wonderful paradox of the event was the coming together of two such politically opposed cultures: traditional anti-Soviet Russians on Jennie's side and Soviet-aligned communists on Paddy's side. Yet the families were brimming with happiness. Paddy's mother, Gwen, recalled:

> It was a tremendous wedding because there was all this Russian involvement. Paddy had gone to the Soviet Union, and there's the dance that Russians do when they bend on one knee and kick their legs out. It's fairly energetic. On their wedding day, Paddy being Paddy, he did one of those. There he was, kicking his legs out. Boomp! Boomp! Jennie was highly in favour. She had Russian parents. There was Natasha and Vusia [Vladimir's nickname] and all the rest of them. There were lots of Russians there.

The next day, the newlyweds escaped for a week-long honeymoon on Queensland's Whitsundays. It had not been the grand wedding ceremony in the Russian Orthodox Cathedral at Strathfield that Natasha had hoped for her daughter. Far from it. As non-believers, the couple had rejected a church wedding. But they did make a major concession for Natasha's sake. In order to relieve her anxiety that the church would not be blessing the marriage, they agreed to Natasha's idea for a separate, private ceremony. Natasha asked the Cathedral priest to come to her home at Bondi several days before the official wedding. They held a private ceremony in the living room, Jennie and Paddy kneeling before the priest as Natasha and Vladimir reverently looked on. Wearing all his finery, the priest said prayers, read from the Bible, burned incense and led some singing. Jennie's faith had lapsed and Paddy was a communist atheist. Yet both kissed the cross, observing pre-revolution Russian Orthodox tradition. The priest gave their marriage God's blessing.

5

MARRIED TO THE PARTY

Marriage made Jennie feel physically and emotionally grounded. It cast aside the memories of a largely fatherless poor migrant childhood when she was often separated from her mother. It did not blow away her insecurities entirely but she thrived in Paddy's good-natured, energetic company, developing into the independent, outwardly strong person she wanted to be. She even reversed their roles as time went on, encouraging him to rethink his future direction by starting a university education. There was initial resentment directed against Jennie from some young women—they reacted as if she had stolen Paddy from them. Paddy was very highly regarded because of his engaging personality and devotion to the league. It was as if an interloping newcomer had snapped him up. Jennie acknowledged: 'There had been a girlfriend in his life and he was a very attractive young man in the Eureka Youth League. So a few noses were out of joint.'

As people around them became more accustomed to the marriage, these feelings subsided and their official union was accepted—so much so that the marriage of Paddy and Jennie

George attained something approaching mythic proportions over time. Among a wide circle of friends in the Eureka Youth League and beyond they became known as 'The Royal Couple'. They were the two good-looking, glamorous, bright and articulate people thought most likely to succeed.

The couple's first home was a humble rented flat near the beach at Bondi, offered to them by Paddy's friend in the league, Cathy Bloch, when she moved out. Jennie completed her final year at the University of Sydney—a diploma of education at the teachers' college in the university grounds—while Paddy continued as full-time State secretary of the renamed Young Socialist League.

As young socialist idealists, Jennie and Paddy were committed to achieving the 'socialist objective' of complete State ownership in Australia. They also accepted communist dogma that required a revolution to achieve that objective. Their major conundrum— apart from whether or not revolution was likely—was how to follow through without blood-letting and a possible repeat of Stalin's reign with all its sham trials, executions and murders. They were among many socialists who asked whether or not a revolution, according to strict Marxism, was necessary at all to achieve the socialist objective.

The way Jennie and Paddy conducted their relationship in public was both inspiring and odd. They argued—a lot—mainly about politics. For the uninitiated observer it may have appeared that their relationship was in jeopardy but disagreements were part of the dynamic of their partnership without threatening it. They seemed to fire off each other. Jennie in particular used arguments as an opportunity to expand her independent line of political reasoning or to help reach a conclusion about a difficult decision she had to make. She was also challenging the straitjacket of the Communist Party, about which doubts were growing for both her and Paddy. Rex Hewett recalled what it was like to witness Jennie and Paddy in a verbal sparring match:

I think that his type of politics—which was much more fluid and flexible than hard line, and what was the hard-line view at that stage in the Communist Party—helped to influence Jennie, to develop much broader social values and views. They were genuinely at one in their political thinking. Jennie was always very [argumentative]. In one sense Paddy was a mentor, but on the other hand she was an incredibly sceptical person—not sceptical in a negative way but sceptical in order to ensure that she adopted the right position by testing it out. They used to have great arguments in their lounge room about union or political strategies and they were both involved in the Vietnam Action Committee, as I was, and [my wife] Helen was. It was always quite a liberating experience to have, those two, who you would think, while nonetheless they loved each other and were deeply committed politically, they could have quite strong differences about political strategies.

It was all out, it was 'in your face' stuff, it was never hidden. I think it was actually what she was like all the time. Certainly from Jennie's point of view. And I don't know whether you've noticed—she doesn't do it as much now—but she used to, particularly in social situations, often go over something several times. Some people say it's monotonous and boring but for Jennie it's probably thinking about giving the right angles and testing it out on a number of people. She has always been like that. It's part of her critical faculties working through something.

The couple had good cause for political debate in the first year of their marriage. The Tet Offensive, a major attack by the Vietcong forces in the early months of 1968, was enormously costly in terms of North Vietnamese casualties but handed the North a significant tactical victory that proved to be the turning point of the war. It destroyed any notion within the American–Australian allied camp that the conflict was close to ending and led to President Johnson announcing in March that the bombing of North Vietnam would stop for the time being in the hope of negotiations with the enemy. Johnson's presidency was already critically damaged by media opinion and graphic television coverage of American casualties. By April he announced he would not be seeking a second term in that year's presidential elections, interpreted widely as a sign that Johnson believed the war was not winnable.[1]

Negotiations in Paris with the Vietcong got nowhere. But for Jennie and Paddy, public fallout from the Tet Offensive was an important fillip to their anti-war efforts and gave them a sense of optimism to keep campaigning. Local enthusiasm in the protest movement had recently dipped with falls in numbers at demonstrations. Now enthusiasm was fired once more, spilling into wider public debate about the morality and futility of Australia's continued involvement in the war. The growing dissatisfaction following the Tet Offensive prompted Prime Minister John Gorton to declare that Australia would not increase its troop commitment. If the mood continued, there was the prospect that the anti-Vietnam campaign could yield the result Jennie and Paddy wanted. The Communist Party officially backed the moderate position within the Labor Party advocated by the new Opposition Leader, Gough Whitlam, which was withdrawal of Australian troops to holding areas. For frontline protesters such as Jennie and Paddy, the Whitlam position was a good start but they wanted total withdrawal and an end to conscription.

The second big issue of 1968—student riots in France— brought these issues into sharp focus. The French Communist Party was enjoying enormous success, having won enough support at the ballot box to become the second-largest party in the country's assembly. But it enraged Trotskyists, and many within the Australian Communist Party who wanted a straight-out revolution, by adopting a more conservative, gradualist approach to change. They were particularly angry at the response of the French party to widespread student unrest in May. Instead of using the opportunity to seek the overthrow of the political system and seize power, the French party denounced the student revolt.

The official position of the Communist Party of Australia, reported in *Tribune*, was support for its French counterpart. There were two ways of looking at this stand. First, it was a sign of reform in the Australian party, a preparedness to exert its independence and water down revolutionary dogma. Alternatively, it reflected the remaining 'Stalinist' elements in the party who would always defend another Communist Party no matter what. The first view is more consistent with the direction in which the party was heading. Jennie and Paddy supported the party's stand and took it as a positive sign of reform, although the French party's denunciation of student protests troubled them. The notion that reform really was occurring tallied with the favourable reporting *Tribune* was giving at the time to the democratic and economic reforms of the Czechoslovakian Government led by Alexander Dubček, which the Communist Party of Australia's national secretary, Laurie Aarons, also said 'lights the way for us'.[2]

The climactic event of 1968 was the Soviet invasion of Czechoslovakia in August, which sent shock waves through communist parties around the world. It brought to a shattering end Dubček's 'communism with a human face'. For the first time, communist parties, including the Australian organisation, passed resolutions openly condemning the Soviet Union for quashing the new openness and freedom of the Prague Spring in which Dubček had attempted to redefine world socialism. Unlike what occurred after the brutal Soviet suppression of the Hungarian uprising in 1956, the Soviet troop invasion of Czechoslovakia did not spark mass protest resignations from the Communist Party of Australia because of the local party's firm opposition to Soviet intervention this time around. Nevertheless, continuing membership was becoming more difficult for many young socialists. Despite the strong local reaction against its abhorrent behaviour, the Soviet Union was still regarded generally as *the* socialist model and its invasion of Czechoslovakia dramatically increased internal divisions already simmering within the Communist Party of Australia. Many members did become inactive or drifted away over time. Those remaining divided into pro-Soviet and anti-Soviet camps, culminating in another split when the pro-Soviets led by Pat Clancy, Alf Watt and Edgar Ross left the Communist Party of Australia in 1970 and formed the breakaway Socialist Party of Australia a year later.

At a personal level for Jennie and Paddy, the Soviet intervention in Czechoslovakia was a troublesome period during which they tried to reconcile their socialist allegiances. Their closeness to the Communist Party of Australia was sustained by their belief that it was independent from the Soviet Union—confirmed by the quick condemnation of the invasion by a hastily convened meeting of the party's executive.

Jennie and Paddy associated with Communist Party reformists who advocated more democracy in the party and co-operation with other socialist and leftist groups. The reformists had been buoyed by a decision of the Communist Party of Australia's 1967 congress to produce a 'Charter of Democratic Rights'. The charter upset the party's pro-Soviet old guard but was like a breath of fresh air to reformists because it challenged communist dogmas and dumped the notion of single-party rule.[3] The charter provided for citizens—both supporters and opponents of socialism—to have full rights to form political parties and associations of their choice, to stand for elections, to conduct meetings and demonstrations and to issue propaganda. Guarantees including freedom of speech, assembly, press, religion, travel and respect for minorities were to be incorporated in the Australian Constitution once socialism prevailed. The party accepted that the decisive political force 'leading up to and following the establishment of socialism' would be a 'coalition of left-wing parties and groupings'. There were obvious contradictions in the charter, chiefly on the last point. While accepting democracy with full rights given to opponents, the charter still assumed the inevitable end of capitalism and left no room for the democratic support for any system except socialism. There was also the practical reality that the Sydney-based leadership under Laurie Aarons would not tolerate any dissent in the way it functioned. Nevertheless, the charter did offer young people such as Jennie and Paddy a more modern form of socialism that appeared open and humane.

The author Gerard Henderson remarked in his history of the Liberal Party, *Menzies' Child*, that at first glance Australian communists 'seemed mild-mannered enough and, in a sense, they were'.[4] The comment certainly could have applied to Paddy's style of communism. But there was a darker side lurking within the Communist Party hierarchy that raised chilling possibilities about what might occur if the socialist revolution went ahead. Eric Aarons, brother of Laurie, wrote in his memoirs *What's Left?* that he and the majority of the local communist leadership decided to cover up Nikita Khrushchev's secret 1956 speech to the Twentieth Congress of the Communist Party of the Soviet Union which detailed Stalin's murders—even though they knew many of Khrushchev's facts 'to be true'. Aarons wrote:

> I made the point at the Central Committee meeting which decided [to ignore the killings] that our outlook was such that, had we been in power, we too could have executed people we considered to be objectively, even if not subjectively (that is by intention), helping our enemies.[5]

The reformist socialism of Jennie and Paddy, which put emphasis on forming a coalition of left-wing forces to assume power, still meant that at some stage there had to be a revolution of some sort. After all, they did want to dispossess the 'capitalist class', which was hardly likely to give up its power and wealth without a fight. Russell Darnley believed the politics of Jennie and Paddy were very similar. They were not advocating a direct electoral process but their style of left-wing politics played down the notion of a revolutionary bloodbath. He said:

> At certain points, this widening participatory democracy they were advocating might simply circumvent laws that were in effect. But I don't think it was like the Russian Revolution or the Chinese Revolution—not like Mao Tse-tung's summation, which was that

it was 'an act of violence by which one class overthrows another'. It was more a question of whether it could be entirely legal or not, and whether it could follow the parliamentary road or not.

The late Denis Freney, a Trotskyist who defected to the Communist Party of Australia, described in his autobiography, *Map of Days*, how he suggested launching a new coalition called the Revolutionary Socialist Alliance. He wrote:

> I distributed the document to Paddy and Jennie George, Brian Aarons and others at the Young Socialist League office and to Bob Gould and the Percys down at Goulburn Street. All sides agreed, although Bob was less than enthusiastic, particularly when I insisted that the YSL should also participate.[6]

The alliance was formed at a subsequent conference of 120 people in Sydney. The dream of using the alliance as the basis of an influential left-wing coalition fell apart, but Freney's interpretation of its purpose gave an insight into what he, Paddy, Jennie and others hoped to achieve. The alliance was pledged to seek united left action and was supposed to spread 'radical socialist ideas', especially those of 'workers' control and self-management'.[7]

One of the intriguing aspects of Jennie George's persona is why she has sought, over the years, to shroud the true nature of her political background—even when it was obviously no longer controversial. Jennie was always avowedly of 'the Left', but kept her exact credentials deliberately vague, indeed ambiguous. Her standard response, when asked about her political history, was to say she had been a member of the Eureka Youth League, but not the Communist Party.

The distinction was a convenient ploy for Jennie because it placed her in a similar category to dozens of young student activists who came through the league's ranks but declined to make the major commitment of joining the league's adult guide, the Communist Party. In fact, her response was an attempt to downplay the depth of her political involvement and close the door on an entire area of legitimate inquiry.

Jennie maintained, to the surprise—even disbelief—of a number who have heard it since, that she *never* joined the Communist Party. Furthermore, she insisted that while she attended party meetings and other party-sponsored events with Paddy, she was not interested in joining and neither Paddy nor anyone else coaxed her into signing-up. Some friends and former colleagues have said that she was 'definitely a member' while others backed her position. Jennie continued to deny membership, recalling:

> I was never a card-carrying member of the Communist Party. Obviously I was very close to the party. I went along to meetings and social things and I was married to a communist but I was never a member myself.

New research confirms, unequivocally, that Jennie *was* a card-carrying member of the Communist Party. Futhermore, it shows that she was elected to office-bearing and delegate positions in the party, and remained in its ranks for longer than some had previously thought.

Documents from official Communist Party records, which are held in the Mitchell Library in Sydney on restricted access, show that Jennie was elected to the party's Sydney District Committee in 1972. She was 24 at the time. The party list shows that Jennie received 72 votes—one fewer than Brian Aarons—putting her half way down the pecking order of 23 candidates elected to office (52 contested the ballot). Judy Mundey, who topped the ballot with 95 votes, was elected Sydney district committee secretary. Among others voted onto the committee with Jennie were Jack Mundey, Richard Walsham, Joe Palmada, Paula Rix, Denis Freney and Mick Tubbs.

Jennie was also one of 32 Sydney delegates elected to the Communist Party's National Congress. Again, Judy Mundey topped the ballot, this time with 94 votes. Jennie received 73 votes, the same number as Denis Freney and two more than Mavis Robertson. Other delegates elected included Jack Mundey, Bill Gollan, Laurie Carmichael and Joe Palmada.

According to the documents, when it came to a ballot for the National Committee of the Communist Party, both Jennie and Paddy nominated but failed to gain sufficient votes. Jennie probably did not expect to win a place on the party's ruling body, considering her lack of seniority. The big field of candidates included party heavyweights Laurie Aarons, Laurie Carmichael, Jack Mundey, Judy Mundey, Bernie Taft and Mavis Robertson. But at least Jennie's name was put forward, giving her the recognition needed to run for the party's national committee in the future.

One of the effects of Jennie denying her party membership was to give the appearance of a fundamental political gulf between Jennie and Paddy because she was not prepared, supposedly, to share party membership. Though they may have had their differences, in reality a fundamental political gulf did not exist between them.

It is difficult to understand why Jennie has wanted so desperately to perpetuate the lie that she was not a party member (only card-carrying members could nominate for the positions she sought). When Jennie was a member, the Communist Party was still a publicly vilified organisation that was suspicious of outsiders and ran its affairs in secret. But acknowledgement of former party membership does not bear the same stigma it once did. Now, many former communists—despite having moderated their political views like Jennie—are frank about their party roots and look back with nostalgic pride.

When told that her party membership had been confirmed, including her election to party positions, Jennie said that her political association had already been canvassed and she had 'no comment to make beyond that which has already been written'. She doubted her name was on party records, although it most certainly is. At best, she seemed to admit that she could have been one of the party's secret members.

The fact of Jennie's party membership establishes her political lineage more clearly than ever before, showing that she was far more committed than she was prepared to admit. Admission to the Communist Party was not automatic and membership of the Sydney District Committee was a fairly demanding middle-level responsibility during a period of wide-spread political agitation in which the party was actively involved.

One of Jennie's supporters, who had previously denied her membership despite knowing otherwise, later explained away the matter: 'I thought that's what she would want me to say.' The answer betrays what has been a concerted effort by a number of Jennie's circle to protect her. While a sign of the immense loyalty she has inspired over the years, it also indicates a shared belief that there was reason not to be completely open about her political past.

Colleagues of Jennie's prepared to admit she belonged to the party concur that its discipline did not suit her and ultimately she drifted away. Nevertheless, she remained a member longer than many. She was sufficiently devoted to seek party positions more than four years after the upheaval caused by the Soviet Union's intervention in Czechoslovakia (accepting that the Australian party made a complete break with the Soviet Union) and just on the cusp of the election of Gough Whitlam's Labor government.

Jennie firmly rejects that covering up her membership had anything to do with her later position as ACTU president, saying she would be judged on current performance, not 'what I did 30 years ago'. It is tempting, nevertheless, to think that in the forefront of her mind has been a pragmatic judgement that public admission could be damaging to her ongoing political ambitions.

A significant factor behind Jennie's reluctance to be open about her party membership may be sensitivity to the anti-Soviet stance of her family, particularly her mother. This appears to be a hair-splitting exercise, given the strength of her involvement with the Eureka Youth League and marriage to Paddy. As Jennie said: 'Whatever connection I had with the party was in the context that I came from a family whose feelings I had some respect for.'

Jennie had successfully completed her diploma of education in 1968 and started teaching the following year. Her first posting in the NSW teaching service under her two-year scholarship bond was to Bankstown Girls' High School in Sydney's western suburbs. The school was very under-resourced. It catered for students who came from low-income working-class families and who received minimal encouragement from home about the need for a good education.

Even though she was a novice straight out of teachers' college, Jennie was given the fifth and sixth form Higher School Certificate level classes in history, her pet subject, and mainly middle and lower classes in English. She was one of few teachers at the school who had a university degree, others having risen through the ranks with only teachers' college qualifications. Teaching modern history, Jennie followed a curriculum that started at the French Revolution, then ranged through China and Japan and the Tsars of Russia in the nineteenth century, a smattering of philosophers, through to the origins of World War I, the Russian Revolution and the rise of Stalin and Hitler. She also taught the special Level One extension classes for students aspiring to honours in history. These classes were held outside the normal timetable, either early in the morning or after the day's final school bell. They were long days. Jennie took a bus from Bondi to Central and then a train out west to Bankstown for the 8 a.m. classes. At other times she stayed after school for 3.30 p.m. classes, which meant she arrived home late.

Jennie's radicalism did not extend to the way she dressed. In fact, she would not have looked out of place at a Liberal Party fundraiser, let alone a Sydney high school. She was a conservative dresser, her modest attire usually combining a blouse, decent-length skirt, pantyhose and patent-leather shoes. She kept her brown hair neat—parted at the side with a half-fringe—and wore make-up and lipstick. From her early twenties onwards she wore trademark large spectacles for short-sightedness. Her eyes were brown, she stood five feet five inches and watched her weight. Her olive complexion tanned easily and gave her a healthy glow.

According to former students, Jennie's teaching style was one of extraordinary commitment, to the point where those fortunate enough to go on to university found it a let-down after the content and encouragement they had received in her classes. Her most senior students had no inkling that their teacher was a mere five years older. She took her work seriously, staying up late into the night preparing her classes for the next day. In marking essays, she was very particular about spelling and careful about detail, her margins often overflowing with correction notes. Following the lead of Pru Martin, the history teacher from Burwood Girls' High School who had helped her understand why she was studying history, Jennie took her classes beyond the basic syllabus. Her students read the standard Penguin edition of E. H. Carr's *What is History?* and she encouraged them to think about the big questions of history. Jennie empathised with students' problems outside the classroom too. During Christmas holidays one student fell pregnant. When it was becoming obvious, the girl was removed by her mother and missed at least a term of school until the baby was born and put up for adoption. Jennie offered her emotional support and assisted her personally in her integration back into the class.

Jennie's best student was Suzanne Jamieson, school captain at Bankstown Girls' High School and much later a senior lecturer in industrial relations at the University of Sydney. Jamieson recalled that Jennie was an extremely conscientious teacher and 'very neurotic' about how her students might perform in the HSC:

She was obsessive. She used to provide us with notes that we should have done for ourselves. We were her babies—she was incredibly dedicated to the whole thing. She tells me now that she used to go home to Paddy every night and say 'my God, these children, they're brilliant, how will I keep ahead of them'. And we used to think she was just wonderful.

Jamieson also remembered 'Mrs George', as they called her, waiting nervously outside the Higher School Certificate examination room in 1971—Jennie's third year of teaching—waiting for her students to come out:

She was outside, pacing up and down like a first-time father waiting outside a delivery room—a big pile of cigarette butts—because she was a dreadful smoker even then. Walking back and forth nervously, she was terrified about what we were writing in the school hall, and waiting for us to come out and tell her how we had answered all the questions. When we came out, she was really nervous and overwrought—it was like she had been sweating blood for three hours while we had been writing the exam. She was always neurotic when I think about it. She was terrible, a real worrywart. It didn't surprise us though—it was rather endearing.

Another pupil from the Level One history group, Maureen Burns, who later became a lecturer in photography at the University of Sydney, said that Jennie's passion and dedication as a teacher affected her life deeply. In the Level One group, the subject of study was Nazi Germany and students were required to read original source documents as part of their preparation for class. Burns recalled that Jennie set an example, always having her work prepared. One day the class had not done the required reading and Jennie's reaction was a shock to them all. Burns said:

She cancelled the class! This was my first inkling of the contract that students undertake with their education. We were meant to have read these original Hitler documents but it was a day when I don't think anyone had—and the guilt stayed with us.

Jennie became a role model for Burns, encouraging her to leave behind her working-class background in the western suburbs and consider tertiary study. After finishing school and starting her first year at university, Burns maintained contact with Jennie and showed interest in left-wing politics. In turn Jennie introduced Burns into her milieu, including the rollicking social life at hotels such as the Sussex and the Criterion in Sydney's Sussex Street where Jennie mixed with other left-wingers after work on Fridays.

Although Jennie focused on securing good passes for her pupils, they had no doubt about which side of politics their teacher supported. While she did not spread her left-wing views in front of general classes, she did intimate where she stood on issues in front of the smaller Level One history classes where teacher and student had closer contact. The most obvious sign of her politics, however, was her union involvement. At university she had been active in the Trainee Teachers' Club. From the start of her teaching career, Jennie played a strong role in the local teachers' association at Bankstown, a branch of the NSW Teachers' Federation, and was the local union delegate to the council of the federation, based in the city. Agitation throughout the government school system had been heated. The Teachers' Federation, under the leadership of president Jack Whalan and secretary Ivor Lancaster, had organised the first one-day statewide strike of any teachers' union in the country the year before Jennie entered the service. Jennie carried on the fight locally to protest a lack of teachers and funding at her own school and others in the area.

Matters came to a head at Jennie's resource-starved school during 1971 when the top English class studying for its Higher School Certificate was left without a full-time English teacher. The department sent a few temporary replacements but they left within weeks. Staff tried to keep the class running but the gaps were not filled adequately. Classes were often cancelled and the students suffered from lack of constant tuition. The class affected was not Jennie's own but she became deeply involved. As the federation delegate, she called an evening meeting of students and parents in July. Parents coming to the school at night for an education issue in working-class Bankstown then, when the local Parents and Citizens Association was not strong, was a momentous occasion. At the meeting, Jennie gave a rousing speech. But the point that attracted local media criticism—and the department's attention—was her threat that staff at the school would walk out on strike unless the Education Department provided a new teacher immediately. The school got its teacher and Jennie, gaining an early taste of the power of union strength combined with parent and student support, had won one of her first industrial victories.

The activism of the local association in which Jennie played a prominent part attracted the attention of the local weekly newspaper, the *Bankstown-Canterbury Torch*. Its owner–editor, Phil Engisch, adopted a hard anti-communist position against local teachers led by Jennie. In one 1971 editorial he attacked 'these militant, radical teachers—who are suspected of harbouring communists in their well-drilled ranks'.[8] In another editorial, in which he attacked the morality of communism, Engisch wrote:

> It has been obvious in Canterbury, Bankstown and throughout the State, from the ways in which the education system is now being disrupted, that the militant Teachers' Federation is well into its stride in implementing the Communists' educational philosophy.[9]

Becoming more heavily involved in union activities helped Jennie carve out an identity separate from Paddy and a more distinctive presence. She would eventually gain the ascendancy over him as a political operator. If she was in his shadow at the start of their marriage, it was because of obvious reasons such as lack of maturity, experience and skills, which she rapidly redressed. Jennie continued to lack self-assurance at times. But she began to establish, on her own terms, what she stood for. The key to her political values was her outrage at injustice, particularly as it affected people unable to stand up for their rights. Reflecting upon her own migrant, low-income background, she was a staunch defender of funding for public education, housing and health as the means to guarantee living standards and eliminate potential inequality. She detested the guiding conservative principle of 'capacity to pay'.

Feminism became important to Jennie. Already she had learnt from Mavis Robertson about American feminist thinking, largely based on Betty Friedan's classic 1963 book, *The Feminine Mystique*, which argued that women had been duped into thinking that marriage and motherhood were their sole gateway to happiness. She read Germaine Greer's *The Female Eunuch* soon after its publication in 1970 with great interest and later enjoyed the works of feminist authors Marilyn French and Sheila Rowbotham. As for the basis of her social values, however, her advocacy of equal rights and opportunities for women was guided mainly by life experience. She was attracted to feminism from a practical, not theoretical standpoint. She believed that campaigning for an end to inequality from within existing institutions was the best way to change a patriarchal society, rather than attacking its failings from the outside. Jennie recalled:

> I grew up in a household with two strong women. I didn't have the luxury of a mother who didn't have to work and didn't grow up with a male around. So the myth that someone was going to look after me when I grew up was dispelled at an early age. I grew up believing I would be in the paid workforce.

As Jennie's political thinking evolved, she switched from mentored to mentor in her relationship with Paddy. He had to think about his future, she said, while the world changed around them. It was the time of the Communist Party split. Laurie Aarons had led his party in a complete break from the Soviet Union. Pro-Soviets led by Pat Clancy and others had walked out in 1970 and formed the Socialist Party of Australia. The renamed Young Socialist League that Paddy led—now as national secretary in place of Mavis Robertson—was a victim of the party infighting and, caught in the crossfire, was soon wound up.

Jennie impressed on Paddy that he had well and truly 'paid his dues' after slogging for little reward throughout the 1960s and that he was deserving of opportunities outside the communist movement. He was already a qualified electrician and could return to his trade. She urged him to go further. Paddy's schooling stopped at the intermediate level. Encouraged by Jennie, he had gone to night school at the Sydney TAFE and sat for his Higher School Certificate in 1970. He performed well enough to gain a tertiary scholarship and spent the next three years studying for a degree in economics and industrial relations at the University of Sydney. During this time the couple lived on Jennie's salary, although Paddy did some casual tutoring work.

The Vietnam War was about to fade as the all-consuming political issue for Jennie and Paddy as they pondered what course their careers and political direction would take. In the midst of Vietnam Moratorium marches calling for the end of the war, the Federal Government led successively by Liberal Party prime ministers John Gorton and Billy McMahon had announced a series of major troop withdrawals. By December 1971, the last Australian troops had left Vietnam. Upon its election in December 1972, Gough Whitlam's Labor Government then withdrew the few remaining Australian advisers in Vietnam and ended conscription.

Labor's election, after 23 years spent in the wilderness of opposition, was a joyous occasion for left-wingers such as Jennie and Paddy even though they did not hail from its ranks. But it was also a time for reassessment. Some of the reforms they wanted in Australia looked like being achieved, and divisions in the Communist Party to which they belonged were continuing. New campaign issues had emerged such as the anti-apartheid demonstrations against the South African Government—but Jennie and Paddy remained on the fringe of these after having concentrated for so long on the anti-war protest movement. Instead of issue-based politics, their attention focused more on fostering a broader political Left through the Communist Party.

Soon after completing his degree, Paddy joined Sydney TAFE as a teacher in industrial relations and politics and joined Jennie in what by now had become her active pursuit of a career in union politics. Paddy became part-time secretary of the Technical Teachers' Association of Australia as well as teaching. Jennie and he would end up together on the council of the NSW Teachers' Federation—but her career would eclipse his.

R U N N I N G   F O R   O F F I C E

It would become a hallmark of Jennie George's career in union politics that she never did the running herself for the elected positions she sought. Without question, she did some lobbying for support and her strong personality was important to her rise. But there was no brazen grandstanding or counting of votes on her part. Her adroit style was to leave that to her supporters so she could be asked or 'drafted' for the job she sought. That way, she was removed from the grubbier side of politicking. She could test the water and if she failed, it was less of a defeat, keeping open her options for the future.

In 1972, a casual vacancy was to be filled for a full-time assistant welfare officer's position in the NSW Teachers' Federation and Jennie, still a teacher at Bankstown Girls' High School, was keen to stand for the job. It was a position elected by the federation's council, not by teachers at large. Jennie was ambitious and regarded a union career as the most practical way to pursue her political activism, even though she enjoyed classroom teaching. She already had good connections in the federation, having been the local Bankstown representative on its council for several years. Her Communist Party credentials, whilst not known outside the party, put her in good stead with the union's communist leadership. Doris Jobling, a decade older and the second female union organiser in the federation's history, was an important supporter. Her other chief backers were friends employed in central office she had met through the Eureka Youth League, Cathy Bloch and Richard Walsham. The federation's secretary, Ivor Lancaster, also knew of Jennie from her role in the teacher trainees' union, campaigning to have allowances increased and the teachers' bond abolished. As a feminist, Jennie's campaigning strong point was the shortage of women in the federation's organisation. It was a situation she regarded as appalling—especially considering the high proportion of females in the teaching profession compared with most other occupations, bar nursing and clerical work. Fifty-seven per cent of the State's teachers were women. In the council vote, Jennie was defeated, losing to a male teacher, Rock Brockett, who did not last long in the job.

In 1973 Jennie stood again for the position at a council by-election and won. It was a valuable early lesson that she should not be discouraged if defeated on a first attempt. Her second try was boosted by her high profile within the federation shortly before her election win during an area-wide strike over staffing levels by all high schools in the Canterbury–Bankstown district. The strike was the first of its kind by any local teachers' association that had federation endorsement, and attracted much internal debate. Richard Walsham, the federation organiser for the area as well as a key supporter of Jennie's, recalled that she gave a strident speech at the strike meeting held at the Wiley Park Oval. He believed even at that point that she had a bright future ahead of her in the union.

Leaving Bankstown Girls' High School and arriving to her first job in the city head office of the Teachers' Federation in Sussex Street, Jennie was given the rather cumbersome title of 'assistant correspondence and interviewing officer'. She was one of three under the supervision of Ethel Withers, all of whom were later renamed welfare officers. Their role unambiguously was to counsel teachers in personal distress and answer telephone inquiries about teachers' conditions. At other times, the job required acting as an intermediary when teachers resisted transfers or, more seriously, faced disciplinary charges or dismissal. It was the kind of work that could become overwhelming if the welfare officer was too emotionally involved in the problems of members. Jennie recalled: 'Someone would ring in and they would be having a breakdown or they did not get their leave entitlement or they were being underpaid.' The job provided good grassroots experience but Jennie found it 'very demanding'. The other tension in the office was political. While Jennie was an ardent left-winger, the other two, Harry Smith and Pam Hewish, hailed from the union's fading right-wing leadership faction.

The union domain Jennie had just entered was not only rich in history but also a hotbed of ideological division. Formed in 1918 and registered officially as a trade union the following year, the NSW Teachers' Federation presented itself as both a 'professional' and 'industrial' organisation. Often it was torn between the two.[1] Its foundation constitution sought 'to promote the cause of education in NSW'. While there was no explicit mention of industrial objectives, it did claim a right 'to speak authoritatively for teachers'.[2] The federation had claimed to be a non-party political organisation over the years but it did advocate support for parties at elections. While justifying such decisions on policy grounds, more often that not, despite strains, it supported the Labor Party. The federation had a number of active Labor Party members. The most powerful and influential faction within the federation's ranks, however, dating before World War II, was a group of officials who belonged to the Communist Party. Of these, the towering figure was Sam Lewis, president from 1945–51 (when he lost to conservative headmaster Harry Heath) and again from 1964–67. Lewis was the driving force of the federation, promoting 'united action' as the best method of achieving its goals. He worked closely with the federation's other significant figure, Harry Norington (the author's grandfather). Norington was the union's first full-time organiser from 1938–44 and then general secretary from 1944–62. Together with Norington, Lewis presided over a period of major success. The federation's tactics under Lewis excluded the unthinkable option at the time of industrial action by teachers. Instead 'united action' was based on mass-campaigning and community alliances. Lewis enunciated the guiding principle that was to remain at the core of the federation's advocacy of non-sectarian public education. In opposing State aid to private schools, he spoke against division in society. He argued that children who went to public schools should do so irrespective of religion or politics, free of sectarian or class distinction: 'If people want class education, if people want their children treated separately, as somebody separate from other types of children, let them pay for it. If they want sectarian education, let them pay for it.'[3]

Besides Lewis and Norington, other well-placed Communist Party members in the federation's 'old guard' leadership team were Ivor Lancaster, Elizabeth Mattick and Joyce Clarke. A later generation of communists included Tim Hornibrook, David Beswick, Doris Jobling and Les McGowan.[4] Party or former party members who came through the ranks with Jennie George were Barbara Murphy, Col Rennie, Cathy Bloch and Richard Walsham. During the Cold War period, most of the federation old guard was reluctant to advertise their membership of the Communist Party because of its affiliation to the Soviet Union. All had experienced the dark public mood towards communists in the height of the McCarthy era. The irony of the concentration of communists in the Lewis-led old guard of the Teachers' Federation leadership, however, was that, for the most part, they exercised their authority with great caution and their approach would be later regarded as outdated and conservative. Their communist influence gave the federation a focus and discipline that made it an effective organisation but they did not allow the federation to become an instrument of the party. Operating with caution was in line with membership sentiment and in the best interests of presenting the 'united front' with non-communists, including Catholic members, which Lewis and others had worked carefully to build.[5]

By general union standards, the federation exhibited a high level of accountability and industrial democracy. Its supreme governing authority was the annual conference, for which delegates of working teachers were elected by statewide and local teachers' associations. The federation's state council, elected every two years by rank-and-file ballot, met twice a month before 1968 and once a month thereafter. The council held annual elections for the federation's inner executive.

The full-time paid leadership of the federation was divided in two parts: presidential and administrative officers. There were three presidential positions—a president, senior vice-president and deputy president—elected every two years by the federation's council until a rule change in 1951 required that a general ballot of rank and file of teachers thereafter. The president, at the apex of the federation, had an up-front political role leading the organisation and was its public spokesperson.

The general secretary, elected every three years by the council, had the hands-on job of running the union and carrying out decisions made by the federation's decision-making bodies. Administrative officers—such as organisers, welfare officers, research officers and industrial officers—were under the control of the secretary and elected by council in the same way. Combined, the three presidential officers and the secretary were the most senior and powerful officials of the union.

Primary issues at stake for teachers throughout the federation's history tended to be a recurrent crop—typically, education funding levels, the thorny question of State aid to private versus public schools, class sizes, teacher numbers and salaries. Management issues were negotiated with the Department of Education although the department was not responsible for wages for much of the federation's history. Instead, unlike most State unions subject to rulings of the State industrial tribunal, the Industrial Commission of NSW, the federation negotiated directly with the State Public Service Board, which was technically the employer of teachers in the public education system. This meant that much of the industrial conflict was with the board rather than the department or commission. After 1970, however, the federation was brought into line with other unions under the commission's jurisdiction.[6]

The federation preferred to remain outside the mainstream and was generally reluctant to submit to arbitration by the commission. Doing so suited the white-collar 'professional' status of teachers that the federation wanted to portray. It meant that teachers were not locked into accepting commission rulings on modest wage rises for the general workforce covered by industrial awards. Like other professional groups, the federation could run separate cases seeking higher wage rises that were commensurate with the work value of teachers.

The federation's tacit ban on strike action by teachers came under serious internal questioning by the mid-1960s. Strains in relations were already evident between the federation and the State Government led by Labor Premier Jack Renshaw, particularly after he refused to accept the federation's proposal to establish an Education Commission in place of the 'undemocratic' Public Service Board. Relations with the Government went from bad to worse after the 1965 election, won by the Coalition. The new Premier Bob Askin reneged on his promise to set up an Education Commission. Younger union activists were already calling for tougher methods to win what the federation wanted. In October 1968, after considerable debate, and endorsement of the federation leadership, a ballot of teachers supported the leadership's call for a 24-hour statewide strike over staffing shortages and class loads. A strike, although commonplace for manufacturing or transport workers, was an extraordinary step for teachers. As a protest strike—the first statewide strike of any teachers' union in Australia—it worked. The Government made immediate pledges. It also marked the crossing of an important psychological barrier that smoothed the way for successive federation leaderships to gain support among teachers for industrial action. A strike in 1972, which prompted threats of deregistration by the Askin Government, was called off at the last moment. But a 24-hour strike over pay went ahead in September 1974, as did another in September 1975 over the Government's attempt to override laws giving preference of employment to federation members.

Women had always comprised the majority of teachers in NSW—about 57 per cent in the mid-1970s—and were usually a majority in the highly unionised federation as well.[7] However, women did not receive the same voice in the federation's affairs as men and historically they had lagged behind in pay. It was not until 1958 that the NSW Government agreed to the concept of 'equal pay' for teachers. The decision was far ahead of the first major equal pay case run by the ACTU in 1969 to guarantee 'equal pay for equal work' and eliminate the old rule in which women's basic pay was set at 75 per cent of the men's rate.[8] Nevertheless, the acceptance within the federation over many years that women were paid less than men to provide a pool of 'cheap labour', and that their needs were secondary to men, was an indication of how women's influence in the federation was low and did not equate with their numbers. In his history of the Teachers' Federation, John O'Brien wrote that arguments used by the federation to its members were frequently directed at the minority male membership, indicative of 'the strength men possessed within the decision-making structure of the union'.[9]

When Jennie entered the federation, equal pay was not as much a problem for women teachers as it was across the rest of the workforce. But the low proportion of women promoted to senior positions in schools, such as department head and principal, who received higher rates of pay, was a contested issue.

So were disputes with the Education Department related to maternity leave and the mobility of women teachers. Jennie placed women's issues high on her list of priorities in dealing with complaints from teachers in her first federation job. But she was not to remain an assistant welfare officer for long. The federation council gradually reduced the number of assistants' positions from three to one. When federation council elections were imminent in 1974, Jennie had the opportunity to be confirmed in the job—but she declined. Much to the dismay of left-wing colleagues encouraging her to run, she used the excuse that she was not confident enough to manage legal cases arising from alleged misconduct or dismissals. Cathy Bloch recalled:

> We on the Left thought that Jennie was going to run. She said she wouldn't and we said 'why?' and she said she couldn't handle the legal cases. I mean, what a joke! I couldn't believe it! The legal cases, you never did handle them! For anybody with a problem that needed to go to the law, you'd interview them and then you'd make arrangements with the federation solicitors to handle that. But it was often a bit sticky with people who were dismissed and found unsatisfactory or whatever trouble they'd got into.

Jennie was far from abdicating from union life. In fact her motivation for not standing was a better offer. As well as performing her job, she had become involved in the internal politics of the union and gained favour with Ivor Lancaster, the longstanding general secretary of the federation who was nearing retirement. Recognising her ability and endorsing her left-wing credentials, Lancaster thought Jennie would be wasted if she remained where she was. He now played a key role as mentor, urging her to take the job as his assistant with the title of 'administration officer', a position he had created in the mid-1960s to absorb some of his huge workload. Lancaster recalled: 'I called her up to my office and said "you're too good for this. You should consider applying for the administration officer's position".'

Typically, Jennie exhibited the insecurity that would always lurk beneath her hardy exterior. Bob Sharkey, the federation's assistant secretary, was in the room at the time. He recalled: 'Anyone who knew her thought she had a lot of potential—but she felt she didn't have the experience.'

After a lot of talking, they finally convinced her. With support from the top, Jennie was elected to the position unopposed by the federation's council. Winning the administration officer's position, despite its unassuming title, was a major leap. It made no difference to Jennie's seniority compared with other young officials in the federation's flat hierarchical structure beneath the leadership level, and she remained on the same wage. But she was presented with an opportunity as the secretary's right hand. From now on, she would work very closely with him, gaining an insight into the workings of the union. It placed her in a strategic position in readiness for a possible tilt at the general secretary's position later on. She would be able to argue that she had gained much experience from helping the secretary carry out his duties. Serving out his final months as secretary, Lancaster regarded Jennie as a 'godsend'. He was struck by her enthusiasm and conscientiousness. Under his direct authority, Jennie's first task was to conduct training sessions for new union organisers, to acquaint them with teachers' salary structures and superannuation and advise on how to handle individual cases. Lancaster also required her to prepare documentation for deputations to the Education Department and to represent him at meetings he could not attend.

Lancaster soon handed the reins to Max Taylor, who took over officially as the federation's secretary in 1975 and became Jennie's new boss. Besides reporting to Taylor, during the next five years Jennie also worked closely with Cathy Bloch. Their friendship, which had begun through Cathy's association with Paddy, cemented into a lasting bond. Apart from her mother, Bloch became Jennie's closest and most trusted confidante. Bloch had been a research officer for the federation when Jennie was assistant welfare officer and had considered returning to teaching in Wollongong when council elections were due. When Jennie declined to run again for the position, Bloch changed her mind. Unwilling to see it fall to a candidate from the opposing right-wing faction, she decided to stand herself, and won.

One of the most notable cases on which Jennie and Bloch worked together was on behalf of female teachers who took unpaid maternity leave of up to twelve months—to which they were entitled—only to find that they had no job when they returned. The system had worked when there was a high turnover rate in teaching and vacancies were almost always open. But the federation did not accept the department's policy of filling the positions of women teachers on maternity leave with permanent appointees. After the turnover rate slowed, the jobs of teachers on maternity leave were often taken for good and nothing was available to them at their school. Women from country areas were hardest hit, having to relocate their families if they wanted another job.

In the NSW Industrial Commission Jennie and Bloch ran a case that attempted to gain a legal right of return to the *same* job for women teachers on maternity leave, thus forcing the department to fill their positions with casuals. The case was a novelty, not only because it was the first time that the two women had appeared as advocates together. It was also rare for the federation to use the commission this way. The federation still preferred direct negotiations with the board or department or minister's office—but these had proved fruitless on the maternity issue. With Bloch's help, Jennie won the case. The most memorable aspect for both women, however, was not so much the cut and thrust of courtroom proceedings but private disagreement between the two over what they would wear. They were very conscious of promoting an issue for women, which would be aired in a courtroom full of men in the less tolerant 1970s when equal pay was only recently entrenched in Federal law. Neither knew the dress protocol or how perceptions might affect the commissioner presiding. Jennie believed these things were important and insisted that both should dress conservatively, a sign of her innate pragmatism. Although politically radical, she was prepared to opt for moderation on many things for the sake of a desired result. Bloch recalled:

> We had a discussion about what we were going to wear and I said, 'well, I'm going to wear slacks', because I was a bit stroppy at the time. She said, 'I'm going to wear a skirt and I think you ought to wear a skirt too'. I said, 'I'm not going to wear a skirt, I'm going to wear slacks'. She said, 'I think you should wear a skirt'. I said, 'why?' And she said, 'think of the members'. It sounds ridiculous now—do you wear a skirt or trousers in the Industrial Commission? She wore the skirt and I wore the trousers, because I was being more Bolshie than she was. We won the case anyway, it didn't really matter, but to us they were really big issues.

The timing of Jennie's elevation to administration officer was impeccable in terms of thrusting a young ambitious woman into the centre of federation politics. The United Nations designated 1975 as the International Year of Women as the women's movement built momentum. Jennie was among a leading group of feminists in the federation, some full-time officials, some not, who were attempting to manipulate a higher profile for women's issues. Others included Cathy Bloch, Gail Shelston, Barbara Murphy, Josepha Siobsky, Joan Bielski, Pam Allan and Doris Jobling. All belonged to a Women in Education group. Jennie also joined the Working Women's Charter, a group formed in the mid-1970s which called for universal childcare for women.

The childcare debate was becoming a major issue for women in a union movement dominated by males who deemed women responsible for rearing children. Typically men regarded it as an issue of low priority compared with traditional industrial matters such as wages and conditions. In the most hardened conservative quarters, it was argued staunchly that child-rearing should be done exclusively at home. Such logic obviously meant denying mothers participation in the workforce, certainly in full-time jobs, which meant women's jobs remained secondary to those of men. It was part of the wider pervasive attitude in the union movement that family life should still be based around a working man, a dependent wife and children. Jennie was intent on shifting such attitudes. She wanted childcare to become a primary industrial issue. The cost of private childcare proved prohibitive—up to half or more of a woman's weekly wage. Jennie wanted women to have the right to choose whether or not to use childcare, a choice available only if childminding facilities of an acceptably high standard, with some level of public funding, were available to women who wanted, or needed, to work.

During this time, an opportunity to push women's issues in state and national forums appeared. Jennie became one of the few women delegates to the Labor Council of NSW and was elected to the ACTU women's committee. Not surprisingly, she did not get far within the right-wing-dominated Labor Council, but, thanks to her outgoing personality and ability to socialise with almost anyone, she did establish a respectful rapport with the council's often abrupt, unyielding deputy, Barrie Unsworth.

It was hard enough to receive a hearing, even within her faction. Arguing for more female representation at a Left caucus meeting during the 1977 ACTU congress in Melbourne, Jennie and Cathy Bloch were directed from the chair to shut up and sit down. Furious, they stormed out. But they had caught the attention of the noted communist and Amalgamated Metal Workers Union (AMWU) leader, Laurie Carmichael, who raced out behind them in an attempt to appease them. Carmichael, despite his gruff, humourless manner, was attuned to change and believed that the Left needed to finally acknowledge women's rights. He told Jennie and Bloch he thought they had been treated unfairly, and asked them to meet over coffee with him so they could set out their arguments. The ensuing conversation would be important in helping to change attitudes among left-wing male unions, and the union movement generally, once a powerful advocate such as Carmichael was prepared to treat seriously women's concerns about a lack of representation.

Throughout its history, and unlike other unions, the Teachers' Federation had promoted several women to senior positions. Elizabeth Mattick, Lucy Woodcock and Doris Osborne had reached deputy or senior vice-presidential level since the 1950s. Other prominent women in the federation's history included Helen Palmer, Joyce Clarke, Gloria Phelan, Clare Spies and Vera Leggett. No woman, however, had attained the top leadership positions, of secretary or president. The federation, despite its higher proportion of women members, remained like most unions, a distinctly male-dominated domain. Council meetings were a sea of grey suits and a smattering of colour from the women. The mid-1970s, however, were to suit Jennie George. Her strategic position in the union as administration officer coincided with a heightened awareness of women's issues. Together, they were critically important to the next step in her career—making a run for general secretary.

Jennie had become very involved in the internal politicking of the federation while working as Max Taylor's administration officer. She associated with a younger breed of 'New Left' activists in the federation radicalised by the anti-war movement. From the mid-1970s onwards, Paddy was on the federation council with Jennie and they held faction meetings at their home to plan tactics before the council gathered each month. Among those who attended were Van Davy, Richard Walsham, Ray Cavenagh, Greg Smith, John Hughes, Cathy Bloch and her sister Paula. The federation had undergone a period of great turmoil in recent years as the New Left reacted against what remained of the communist old guard, whom they perceived to be stuffy and conservative. A watershed election in the federation had been the victory in September 1973 of a New Left leadership ticket comprising Eric Pearson (president), Col Rennie (deputy president) and Van Davy (senior vice-president). The victory, which

Lancaster (then still secretary) accepted despite some differences of opinion, led to great excitement within the New Left faction about the new possibilities for teacher activism. The pace of political change around them was furious. The Whitlam Government poured much federal money into education. Despite gloom at Whitlam's election defeat in 1975, the New Left took heart from the State election result the following year. With Labor back in power in New South Wales and Neville Wran as premier, the federation's relations with the State Government improved and lingering threats of deregistration left over from Askin evaporated.

The New Left leadership ticket did not remain intact, however. Eric Pearson left the presidency early because of ill health and was succeeded in 1976 by Barry Manefield, a tough-minded primary school principal from the 'Centre Left' faction, regarded as more conservative than the Pearson–Rennie–Davy team. By 1979, when elections were next due, there was a strong view inside the federation that it was time for a woman to take one of the two top leadership positions. Max Taylor, the general secretary, intended to stand down at the end of his term in 1979 and return to teaching—for the time being. It was known that he would not be contesting his position at the council election due in September that year. His imminent departure created an opening.

Jennie had a problem about standing for secretary, however, if it meant she had to work with Manefield in the presidency. A combination of personality differences and her reservations about what she regarded as Manefield's conservative style, stood between them. When Jennie's chief supporters, Richard Walsham and Cathy Bloch, urged her to stand for the general secretary's position, she was enthusiastic but argued that she could not work with Manefield. She was prepared to run only if Van Davy challenged Manefield for the presidency in the hope of toppling him.

Jennie was close to Davy, an old friend she and Paddy had

known from Eureka Youth League days. Davy had moved from senior vice-president to deputy president in 1975 and then left the federation in 1977 to head the national union, the Australian Teachers' Federation (ATF). Just as Jennie hoped, Davy did return to challenge Manefield in 1979, guaranteeing that she would stand for secretary in the council ballot. Compared with Jennie, Davy was taking a risk against Manefield, a formidable president with widespread support that some regarded as unbeatable. Davy's run for president also had the unwanted effect of creating an enduring split in the Left between supporters of both men.

In other circumstances, Jennie may not have been the obvious candidate for secretary. Certainly she was being groomed for higher office one day. She could justifiably boast experience, having worked for Lancaster and Taylor, her competency was undisputed and she was able to demonstrate her talent as an articulate speaker at the federation's monthly council meetings. Above all else, the real momentum of her candidacy was the growing sentiment that it was time for the federation to elect its first woman secretary. This sentiment coalesced behind Jennie and swept her into office. It was like an unstoppable wave. She had overwhelming backing from members of the New Left, who held her in high regard. She also drew support from her friend Mary Boland, who led a more radical left-wing faction with Peter Woods, known with some amusement by their opponents as the 'Left-Overs'.

No other woman candidate stood in Jennie's way. Cathy Bloch was not cut out for the job and was an unequivocal supporter of Jennie's anyway. Barbara Murphy, while much-respected, was re-contesting the senior vice-president's position. Jennie's male opponent in the council ballot was Bob Sharkey, brother of Building Workers' Industrial Union leader Stan Sharkey and the federation's assistant secretary in charge of organisers. The contest that ensued was not bitter as such ballots go. Sharkey took the defeat well. He was the first to congratulate Jennie, and, by competing in this election, had staked his claim for the job at a later date. Jennie won easily after her backers did the rounds of council to maximise support. The result of the council vote was 157 to 58, a big margin indicating the strength of feeling that she was the better candidate. Van Davy, whom Jennie had wanted badly to win, was not so lucky. Manefield defeated him resoundingly in the general ballot of federation members, prompting Davy's return to the presidency of the ATF.

Manefield's victory created a conundrum for Jennie. After claiming she could not work with him, she had to change her tune. In the afterglow of her own win, she suppressed such a ticklish problem. Jennie had a major triumph to celebrate. She was the first woman to hold the position of general secretary of the NSW Teachers' Federation in its 61-year history. With 60 000 members, she would be responsible for the affairs of the largest union in the State and the twelfth largest in the country. Her appointment, as she acknowledged at the time, was significant for women right across the union movement.[10] It was a long-overdue acknowledgement that women deserved greater representation in senior roles, not just in unions but throughout society. It was a pointed reminder to men in power of the need for redress.

7

DEATH OF A MARRIAGE

The marriage of Jennie and Paddy George had lasted for more than a decade. Unlike many other couples who had met in the heady world of left-wing politics and whose internecine marriages ended in early divorce, they had stayed together. But their relationship was showing signs of strain. Jennie had risen rapidly in the union movement, altering the dynamic of her relationship with Paddy. When they met, he was the star. Now the roles were reversed: his career looked promising but he was obviously in Jennie's shadow. As understanding and reasonable as Paddy was compared with many men, he had difficulties coping with her ascendancy. Mavis Robertson, close to both of them, recalled Paddy telling her about their problems: 'There were tensions between them. Paddy said it was hard to adjust to her being in the limelight—but he was enormously proud of her and supportive.'

After several years of renting at Bondi, Jennie and Paddy had moved into a house they bought at Ashfield in Sydney's inner west. It was not to be their home for long though. Close friends Rex and Helen Hewett had been house-hunting in nearby

Haberfield in 1973 and found two semidetached houses up for sale on the same block. The couples talked about sharing and agreed on a 50–50 split to buy the block, making them neighbours as well as friends. One house was in good condition but the other was in a dilapidated state. Tossing a coin to contest which couple would get the better house, Jennie and Paddy lost and had much cleaning up to do. That was the only downside of the venture. As neighbours, their friendship endured despite living in each other's pockets. They tore down the backyard fence between the two places and were often in one house or the other, chatting or partying or hosting backyard barbecues. With the help of friends such as Van Davy, they built an extra storey on top of both homes, which became upstairs bedrooms. Jennie and Helen Hewett became especially close during this period and were in constant contact during Jennie's term as administration officer at the Teachers' Federation from 1974–79. One of the things that struck Helen, the federation's finance officer, was Jennie's incredible stamina:

> She's got an enormous capacity to keep going all night. At Haberfield we would have these incredible card games that would go all weekend. I remember we started one on a Sunday night, early evening, and played through until 4.30 a.m. Then the two of us just talked. Paddy had more sense—he'd gone to bed—but we decided to have a shower and go straight to work. I drove us in. There was no breathalyser then. Just as well. I went to work and survived a few hours and went home. But Jennie kept going and the next night she went out!
>
> She used to go off to ATF conferences and wouldn't go to bed—she'd be up four days non-stop. But you wouldn't go near her when she came back—she'd be so exhausted.

Living so close, the Hewetts could not help but notice marital difficulties that surfaced between Jennie and Paddy. Like Mavis Robertson, they accepted that it was hard for Paddy to adjust to playing second fiddle to Jennie. But there was a deeper problem not so obvious, of the kind experienced in many marriages after a decade or so: Paddy lost interest in the physical side of their relationship and retreated from Jennie. It became a major issue between them. Jennie was hurt to think Paddy might not be attracted to her anymore. In fact, it seemed to Jennie that Paddy was a different person. She was young, gregarious and the life of the party—but he did not show the same enthusiasm of the past. Jennie said: 'The spark had gone. From my point of view Paddy was not like he used to be.' Mavis Robertson recalled that the couple's relationship had 'hit a brick wall' but that they managed to remain good friends despite their troubles.

A possible physical reason for Paddy's distance began to emerge in the early months of 1979. He started complaining to Jennie about feeling unwell. He also experienced discomfort in his lower abdomen. Jennie told Paddy to stop complaining and to consult the local GP for a check-up. He did but the doctor found nothing abnormal. Paddy had been fit with a sturdy physique, reflecting his years of playing sport. But now, for no obvious reason, he was thinning, to the point where his weight loss was noticeable to friends. He continued to complain about feeling unwell and again visited the local doctor. The doctor assured him it was nothing serious and attributed his discomfort to possible prostate pain. When Paddy's symptoms persisted, he was told his problem was either a stress-related or psychosomatic disorder. He saw another doctor, who referred him to Royal Prince Alfred Hospital for minor surgical treatment of polyps in the bowel and, as a precaution, a barium meal X-ray, which showed no cancer in his stomach and upper bowel.

Paddy was urged to relax more and to eat a high-fibre diet. He tried to ignore the symptoms as the best antidote—but still his discomfort and weight loss continued. David McKnight, who knew Paddy from Communist Party circles, remembered attending a get-together one night at the Georges' home and commenting how thin his friend was becoming. 'Doctors don't know what it is, they just don't know,' Paddy told him. Afterwards, when

McKnight was walking home, he wondered what the trouble could be. Because of the sustained weight loss he thought Paddy had cancer, but Paddy was too young and it had been discounted anyway. As well as weight loss, Paddy's lack of energy became more pronounced. Jennie noticed that he tired very easily and seemed to nod off early in the evenings.

Brian Rix, close to Paddy since early Eureka Youth League days in Botany, believed something was definitely amiss, despite the medical opinions. He was also aware that Paddy's marriage was shaky, though the two things were not necessarily connected. 'I knew there was some tension in the family but I didn't know what was behind it. He never talked about it. [Paddy] felt it was up to him to sort it out.'

Jennie bumped into Jack Mundey at the Teachers' Club after work one evening in April 1979 and they shared a drink. She had known Mundey, a prominent communist, from her days in the league and party. Since then he had become a much-romanticised figure in left-wing politics. He was the union hero who had coined the term 'green bans' to describe numerous union boycotts he led as secretary of the NSW branch of the Builders' Labourers Federation (BLF) in the early 1970s. Mundey's green bans pioneered a new form of protest that drew wide community support by stopping development projects on the moral grounds that they would have destroyed buildings or land considered to have major historical or environmental significance. Mundey received huge publicity. Saving historic Sydney buildings from the original colony in the Rocks area near Circular Quay was his greatest triumph. But the most famous and certainly most curious episode of the green-bans era was the campaign to save Kelly's Bush in Hunters Hill. It united an unlikely combination of middle-class housewives who were the local residents and tough BLF unionists who were loyal to the Communist Party.

The Communist Party leadership of Laurie Aarons paraded Mundey's leadership of the BLF's NSW branch as the model for all unions to advance the revolutionary movement.[1] However, Mundey did not last. After failing to shore up support inside the BLF, he was removed from office in 1974 by intervention of the BLF's Maoist–Communist national leadership, run from Melbourne by Norm Gallagher.

When Jennie became reacquainted with Mundey at the Teachers' Club, he had been out of the BLF for five years. He was intermittently unemployed but was still deeply involved in environmental issues. Recently he had been national president of the Communist Party of Australia. At a difficult time in her marriage, when she felt there was a growing gulf between her and Paddy, Jennie turned to Mundey and they began an affair. She described him as charismatic and flamboyant—a 'soul mate'. His rich communist and union history added to his mystique. He had a big ego and a reputation as a big drinker with a larrikin spirit but underneath the tough image Mundey was a gentle man. He filled the emotional void in Jennie's life at that time. She was 31 and there was an age gap of seventeen years between them. Mundey was also married.

This period was a turning point for Jennie. While not her first affair while married to Paddy, the relationship with Mundey was no mere fling—it changed her life. In June 1979, several months into the relationship, Paddy began to pick up on his wife's emotional distance and absences at key times. He finally confronted her: 'Is there something happening between you and Jack?' She replied honestly. Paddy felt there was no choice now—one of them had to move out. He left Haberfield and stayed with his close friend Van Davy in Balmain, while Jennie remained in the house and continued the affair with Mundey. It was very stressful for Jennie and Paddy but remarkably they remained in regular and amicable contact over subsequent months. Paddy came back to Haberfield every weekend to mow the lawn. He spent time in the house and had a favourite chair in which he liked to sit. As a 'couple', he and Jennie still had the odd restaurant meal together and even went to the movies.

Reconciliation was not likely at this stage but the fact that Paddy never removed his belongings from Haberfield kept alive the slim possibility. He only took clothes and personal items he needed to Balmain, a bachelor household consisting of himself, Davy, and Tim Hornibrook, a friend from the Teachers' Federation also residing with Davy following marital difficulties. While never malicious about Jennie's affair, Paddy did make a few critical remarks about Mundey that surprised his Balmain friends considering he usually never said a bad word about anyone. Paddy showed no sexual interest in other women while separated from Jennie, although he had had a brief affair while he and Jennie were still together (unknown to her until many years later).

Paddy's health became worse while he and Jennie were apart. Hornibrook noticed one day that Paddy had passed blood in the toilet bowl at Balmain when some remained after flushing. Both he and Davy chastised Paddy for not looking after himself and insisted he see a doctor. Jennie, meanwhile, had been just elected secretary of the Teachers' Federation in September 1979 but was not due to take up her new position until the following January. Feeling pressure in all aspects of her life, she desperately 'needed some space'. In early November Jennie escaped to Melbourne to spend a few weeks with friends. During the stay, Paddy rang her and said he had become 'really ill'. He said he was suffering heavy night sweats and had lost even more weight. 'I think I'm seriously ill,' he admitted. The news shocked Jennie. She cut short her Melbourne holiday and returned promptly to Sydney. She put her affair with Mundey on hold. After having lived apart for six months, Jennie insisted that Paddy return to Haberfield. She recalled: 'When he got really, really ill I said "forget it, move back home. What are you doing living in Balmain?"'

Back together again at Haberfield, the cause of Paddy's malady was no more obvious. By chance they met a friend at the Teachers' Club in Sussex Street, Maurice Cohen, a TAFE teacher colleague of Paddy's who happened to ask him what was wrong. Paddy replied, 'I don't know but there's got to be something seriously wrong. Every time I go to the doctor they say it's nervous tension or anxiety.' Jennie jumped in, 'I think Paddy's very ill'. Cohen recommended that they consult his cousin, Dr Charles Ovadia, a GP in Newtown. Desperate, they agreed. In the consultation room, Ovadia said he did not know the cause of Paddy's problem but wanted further tests conducted. Jennie recalled:

> For the first time, Charles actually took him seriously and said 'I don't believe it's just nervous tension—there is something seriously wrong'. So he sent him off to someone who specialised in diagnoses. They gave him all sorts of scans and then put him in hospital for exploratory surgery.

The seriousness of Paddy's condition depended on what doctors found during surgery at Royal Prince Alfred Hospital at Camperdown. It was the end of November 1979. Jennie was home at Haberfield, next-door with Rex and Helen Hewett, on a day of great anguish with Paddy on the operating table, when the news was telephoned through from the hospital. Jennie's mother, Natasha, and Paddy's mother, Gwen, were present too. The surgeon's message was devastating—he had found Paddy was suffering from bowel cancer. One of Jennie's first thoughts was trepidation at the prospect of Paddy having to use a colostomy bag. But the disease was too advanced to worry about such things—secondary cancer had spread to his liver. The surgeon made no attempt to remove the malignancy. He told Jennie that there was nothing that could be done for Paddy and that her husband's condition was terminal. Paddy was given six months to live. In the months when he had begun feeling ill Paddy had undergone every test available—except the one that could have detected lower bowel cancer. Doctors treating Paddy in the early stages had declined to recommend a barium enema X-ray because cancer of the bowel was rare in men under 40.

Soon to take up her challenging new position as Teachers' Federation secretary, Jennie was distraught and in a quandary about what to do. She talked to Paddy about giving up the job to care for him but he rejected the idea, urging her to pursue her union career. Jennie did, however, take off large slabs of time over the next months, her position temporarily filled by federation official and friend Vic Baueris.

After a depressing Christmas, Jennie and Paddy again went to see Charles Ovadia, who made it plain that nothing more could be done. Ovadia offered, however, to start visiting Paddy at home and they became friends during this time. They shared a similar outlook on many things. Ovadia was a member of the Doctors' Reform Society, the rival to the establishment Australian Medical Association. Too sick to continue his job as a TAFE teacher or venture far from the house, Paddy began spending most of his days from March 1980 lying in bed. The couple's dog, a German Shepherd-cross called Whisky, lay quietly near him, appearing to sense, some observers said later, that something was amiss.

On his visits Ovadia gave Paddy a cocktail of opiate-based pain-killers in an attempt to control his growing distress. In hindsight, Jennie believed that he could have taken his own life, with access to the multitude of drugs on his bedside table, if he had wanted to do so. She thought he was still in denial, acting as if he could beat the cancer. As the months passed, Ovadia commented on how Paddy appeared to be outliving expectations. 'I don't understand. He's got a strong will to live,' he told her. Paddy became gaunt and frail as his weight loss continued. One day, just when Jennie had turned her back, he slipped and fell in the shower, breaking some ribs. The stress of seeing Paddy's deterioration and knowing he had such limited time left took its toll on Jennie. Emotionally she came close to breaking point, waking up in the morning next to Paddy, not knowing if he would be dead or alive. She asked Ovadia, 'How do I cope with someone dying?'

Cathy Bloch was living in Wollongong at this time. But she travelled back and forth to Sydney as much as possible to see

Paddy, tragically aware that he was close to the end. She also comforted Jennie through her immense difficulties, and recalled the night on which Jennie had first told her of Paddy's illness: 'I don't know how I ended up at Jennie's place but it was one of those nights which I've been through with Jennie, when her way of processing something that's hard to deal with—she just goes on, and on, and on, and on.'

Bloch was among many friends shocked at news of Paddy's cancer, especially the unfairness of its attack on such a good-natured human being, so undeserving of having his life cut short. Among the things that Jennie and their friends did to honour Paddy while he was still alive was to hold an informal reunion of the Eureka Youth League at their home. Although weak, Paddy tried to be sociable. He came downstairs from his bed briefly to join the gathering but could not stay long. One observer described the event as 'macabre'—as if the guests were taking their ceremonial leave of Paddy. For others it carried positive memories of a celebration of Paddy's life while he was still able to speak to them. Mundey was among those who attended the early 'wake'. He grabbed attention, holding court in the living room, which some thought insensitive.

Mindful of the shortage of time, Jennie and Paddy had made plans for a last holiday together to visit some of his relatives in England. But they changed their minds, considering the ordeal of long-distance travel to be too much of a strain on Paddy's wasting body, and opted for New Zealand instead. They travelled with friends, Van Davy and his partner, Vivienne White. Davy mixed a holiday with a speaking engagement he had in Auckland. But he and Vivienne were also there for Paddy in case he needed extra help. The trip during the May 1980 school holidays was a disaster. By now Paddy was jaundiced and so frail he had to be helped on and off the aircraft. After a short stop in Auckland, the two couples drove several hours from Auckland, through Rotorua, to visit the famous caves at Wiatomo near Hamilton. There they joined a party of tourists for a boat ride along one of the gentle cave streams to see the brilliant spectacle of glow-worms lighting up on the ceiling.

Paddy's chest was weak and he could not stop coughing in the cool and airy cave. His coughing disturbed the glow-worms so much that they 'switched off' and left the tourist boat in darkness. Jennie, most embarrassed, pleaded with Paddy to try to contain himself so the glow-worms would turn on again for everyone. But he could not. Vivienne White said: 'We were all laughing in the end—it was a funny moment.' Humour aside, the fiasco of the cave visit became a metaphor for the entire New Zealand trip. The next night, just three days after arriving in New Zealand, Paddy began suffering dreadful pain, his distress so great that the couples were forced to abandon their holiday and return to Sydney early.

Back home Paddy was bedridden. Medication appeared to make no difference. Within a week, he was screaming in agony. There was nothing an anguished Jennie could do except to urge Charles Ovadia to admit Paddy to hospital. Ovadia agreed. He arranged for Paddy to be transferred by ambulance to Royal Prince Alfred Hospital—to die.

So began the last horrible phase of Paddy's life, a sad deterioration over ten days. As higher doses of morphine administered to control his pain began to take effect, Paddy drifted in and out of a coma. In his darkened room, he was never left alone. Jennie, Paddy's mother, Gwen, and relatives, Frances George, Allen Campbell and Bronwen Campbell saw him daily. Van Davy also organised a bedside vigil in rostered four-hour shifts that included Vivienne and close friends Cathy Bloch, Rex Hewett, Helen Hewett, Brian Rix and Mike Keane, so that someone always was ready to answer Paddy's needs, talk to him when he was conscious and ensure that he did not die alone. Early on, Rix believed, Paddy made an effort to remain alert. Although he never said as much, Rix felt Paddy was bidding farewell. It saddened Davy and others in the small circle that for a person with so many friends in his life, so few were prepared to come near at the end. Cathy Bloch, heavy with grief at the thought of losing her long-time friend, moved temporarily into the Georges' home so she could be close by. She recalled how Paddy clung to life in his last days, wasting away while Jennie and others struggled to keep their senses:

> I can remember watching him, he was in hospital, he was lying there—and just nothing. And you could see his heart, he was in a coma, and his heart was just beating, like it was so strong, and everything else was shutting down, and his heart kept on going. It was just awful. It was terrible. It's a terrible thought to think, you know, in a way you'd wish one of your best friends dead. But you want him dead because the suffering was so terrible. So I don't know. I could see all these people around me and I'm trying to be—because I wasn't part of it, I was somebody who was there to be support but who's not family—and of course all these people were crumbling around me because the stress and tension on them was just terrible.

Paddy had wanted to end his days at home and during one of his conscious periods he said to Jennie, 'Please take me home'. She replied, 'I can't. How can I get you home?' He said, 'I just want to die at home'. Paddy's wish sparked some serious talk among those in his bedside circle about sneaking him out of his room and taking him home. But they realised it was not feasible. They could not offer him the level of care he needed and gave up on the idea. Paddy's friend Brian Aarons remembered spending time at the hospital near the end when Paddy was in terrible pain, sometimes conscious, sometimes not. He could barely speak but was appealing for help, just to be put out of his misery. Mavis Robertson, who had been away overseas for almost all of Paddy's illness, visited him in hospital. She recalled: 'It is very difficult to describe. He was fading before your eyes. And his bodily functions were breaking down, which Paddy would have hated. He was very finicky about his health and hygiene.'

Four days before he died, Paddy asked Jennie for some water. She gave him some, pouring from a teapot into a cup that Brian Rix had brought Paddy. Natasha, who was also there, remembered Paddy drinking with pleasure, even in his wasted state. Drawing on her faith, she was reminded of Christ on the cross taking water from a sponge that was held to His lips. 'He is going to die very soon,' Natasha told Jennie. Yet Paddy clung on. Jennie recalled: 'We had someone there for every hour. He had cotton bedsheets and tubes and he had wasted away all those months. He was never alone—it was only the last two days his Mum couldn't handle anymore and I said "go home, this is cruel".'

On Friday 20 June nurses told Jennie that Paddy was not likely to survive another weekend. She tried to adjust to the idea that it would be best for Paddy if he did die—but still his heart kept beating. Cathy Bloch was with Jennie when she contacted the hospital ward sister from Haberfield on Monday morning to check Paddy's condition. Bloch recalled: 'Jennie rang the hospital and they said "he's still alive" and I could just see she was starting to fall apart and I thought, "oh my God, this is going to keep going". Like, I thought they were all going mad, they were all going mad around me.'

His strength gone, Paddy's heart finally stopped beating later the same day. It was 23 June 1980. He had lived for seven months after his cancer was belatedly diagnosed, a month longer than predicted. He was 39 years old, coincidentally the same age at which Jennie's father had died 20 years earlier. Jennie was at home when the hospital rang to inform her of Paddy's death. She telephoned Gwen George at her home in Glebe to tell her and asked if Gwen would come over to Haberfield. Gwen was too upset to go anywhere, so Jennie, though equally upset and drained emotionally, insisted on going to see Gwen in Glebe.

The following night, Jennie hosted a wake for Paddy at home in Haberfield with Cathy Bloch, Van Davy, Mike Keane, Rex and Helen Hewett and a few other friends from their immediate circle. They fetched Paddy's port glass, filled it, and placed it on the mantelpiece. It was a surreal experience amid the sense of tragedy and deep loss that everyone felt. Cathy Bloch recalled: 'We sat around talking and then we started singing and everybody got a bit pissed. And Jennie was, that was Jennie's way [of handling it], she was just getting [drunk], there was more and more of that happening.'

Paddy's funeral at Rookwood crematorium was huge— attended by family and hundreds of his friends over the years from the Sydney network of the Communist Party and beyond. Afterwards, mourners were invited back to Haberfield for a feast of Greek lamb and potatoes. The food, supplied by Diethnes, an inner-city Greek restaurant that was one of Jennie and Paddy's favourites, was washed down with plenty of beer and wine.

Jack Mundey continued to be a presence in Jennie's life—he was at the funeral and offered support to her. Cathy Bloch took charge though. She was among lead speakers at the non-religious service, given licence she believed from a private conversation with Paddy in which he had asked her to look after his affairs. She was there too for Jennie's overwhelming grief.

8

AFTER PADDY

The months after Paddy's death were an emotional blur for Jennie. The grief she felt ran through its many stages, some more accentuated than others. She felt the deep pain of loss for the man she had known as her partner, lover and mentor since almost a teenager. She felt guilt over the breakdown of their relationship coinciding with the onset of his terminal illness and tortured herself over whether or not she had done enough to help Paddy when he needed it most. She felt anger at doctors about Paddy's early misdiagnosis and also at Paddy himself for his reluctance to seek proper medical attention sooner. For years, Jennie would harbour the thought that if Paddy's disease had been detected earlier he could have been treated successfully before the cancer spread and would still be alive. She contemplated lodging a malpractice suit against one doctor for wrongful diagnosis but gave up on the idea, mainly because it would entail reliving the trauma. No amount of money could bring Paddy back.

At times she slipped into denial, triggered by an occasional sense of unreality that all was well, or by her attempts to blot out events with late-night binges, drinking and smoking too much with friends. Jennie's friends remembered the times, in the early hours of the morning, looking after her when it all had become too much. Of all the emotions she experienced, guilt was the hardest for Jennie to live with as she gradually came to terms with Paddy's death. Tim Hornibrook, who had lived at Van Davy's house in Balmain with Paddy when the Georges' marriage crumbled, said: 'Jennie carried guilt around with her for a long time after because of the marriage breakdown coinciding with when Paddy became seriously ill. She shouldn't have really.' Media profiles of Jennie perpetuated the myth—which she did not dissuade—that all had been well with her marriage. The ommission made no difference to Jennie's real sense of loss but it did not present a complete picture of her complex life.

Shortly after Paddy's funeral, Jennie took a holiday to Vanuatu with Cathy Bloch to try to recover. It took up to a year, according to those close to her, before she appeared to be functioning normally. Colleagues at the Teachers' Federation showed great understanding, accepting that she was not fit to give 100 per cent. Officially her term as the new general secretary had started in January 1980, six months before Paddy died. But she had taken a lot of leave in that period, dreading the time when Paddy would not be there and knowing she would have to live with herself afterwards if she believed she had not done all she possibly could.

Jennie's invaluable support at the federation in the last months of Paddy's life and in the months following was Vic Baueris, who filled the administration officer's position that she had vacated when she was elected secretary. Baueris was meant to be her right hand, as she had been to Ivor Lancaster and Max Taylor. But Baueris was much more, covering for Jennie by running the union during her absences and taking much of the burden of her workload when she returned, still suffering and finding concentration difficult. Another important support was Greg Dawson, the federation's Newcastle organiser. Along with his wife, Joan, Dawson was very close to Jennie, on tap to offer friendship and consolation when it mattered.

As months passed, Jennie threw herself into her work as the best antidote to her grief and eventually this method worked. In large part Jennie became driven by Paddy's desire, expressed not long before he died, that she should succeed in the union movement. When she consulted Charles Ovadia for help, complaining of stress and even expressing thoughts of giving up her job, invariably she referred to Paddy's wish as her driving force to carry on. Every visit to Ovadia ended with her weeping and eventually she could no longer see him—their relationship overshadowed too much by memories of Paddy. As years passed, Jennie would succeed on her own terms—but there was always a lingering sense in the background that she was motivated by acting out what Paddy would have wanted for her and what Paddy himself may have wanted to achieve if he had survived.

Jennie's immediate concern at the federation was to build a professional relationship with its president, Barry Manefield, with whom she had previously declared an inability to work. Having no choice but to accept him now, she found Manefield was not as conservative as she had first thought and that he was prepared to lead tough action when necessary. Her personal difficulties with him seemed inconsequential anyway compared with her overwhelming sense of loss.

The serious problems that the federation faced also loomed larger than internal conflicts in the leadership. Jennie had become general secretary when there was the unhappy combination of an oversupply of teachers and cutbacks in education spending. As well, teachers' salary increases had slipped well behind the inflation rate. The oversupply of teachers had built up in the late 1970s, largely through falling birthrates affecting student numbers. As the State Government imposed staff ceilings to match the decline in students, teacher unemployment in NSW reached crisis point for the federation with more than 8000 out of work. The federation planned to embark on a salaries campaign but the environment appeared hardly conducive considering the jobless rate. Rather than direct all her attack at the Labor State Government—partly because of political reasons—Jennie criticised Malcolm Fraser's Federal Government for insufficiently funding the State public education system. At this stage in her career she was not an advocate of the national teachers' union, the ATF, preferring to focus on the State-based federation. But she did endorse a $200 000 advertising campaign by the ATF to place education high on the public agenda in the hope of pressuring the Commonwealth to provide more financial assistance for the State.[1]

The toughest political fight with the State Government during Jennie's term as general secretary was a campaign to improve the salaries of teachers. It culminated in four day-long strikes in early 1981 after the federation rejected the ruling of the NSW Industrial Relations Commission to grant a 6.8 per cent rise. The federation's claim was 20 per cent. Following a referral by the State Minister for Industrial Relations, Pat Hills, an appeal bench of the commission improved the pay increase to 10 per cent.[2]

As general secretary, Jennie acquired the leadership style that would characterise her professional behaviour for years to come. Overall, her modus operandi was to be inclusive. It was similar to the 'consensus' politics promoted by former ACTU president and Labor leader-in-waiting Bob Hawke—although Jennie had no time then for Hawke's right-wing politics. As Hawke advocated though, Jennie consulted widely among a mishmash of competing left-wing factions.

Her first port of call was the dominant 'New Left' faction to which she belonged, a broad left-wing grouping including elements of the Communist Party. But she was never a hostage to this faction, having the ability to move freely among the others. She also canvassed the Labor Party-aligned faction of left-wing Steering Committee members Vic Baueris and Pam Allan, the Socialist Party-aligned faction of Bob Sharkey and the Sutherland Trade Union Club, as well as the hardliner Left-Overs faction of Peter Woods and Mary Boland. One federation official,

Tony Amatto, the union's first Aboriginal organiser, was strongly criticised because of his militant, radical views. Jennie refused to side with Amatto's detractors and was prepared to give him her support. Despite the political nature of these dealings, the regard for Jennie among her colleagues remained just as high as it had been before she became general secretary. She was honest, articulate and tough if necessary. But she was also aided by her friendly, social manner, always asking after people's interests and backgrounds as she worked, enabling her to break the ice with the toughest of political opponents.

The few critics Jennie had inside the federation seized on her early 'Stalinist training' by Mavis Robertson—whom some called uncharitably a 'dragon lady'—to highlight what they regarded as Jennie's bureaucratic manner of refusing to budge after having reached a decision. They cited Jennie's intolerance to criticism and ability to pay back those who offended her. The only reservation about Jennie's generally inclusive style from within her own faction was that her links with the breakaway, purist Left-Overs, and in particular her friendship with the faction's Mary Boland, disturbed some who believed she might be prepared to accept that faction's hardline solutions. But these concerns dissipated once Jennie, having assumed power in her own right, demonstrated that she preferred to work within the broad Left. She gave her own plausible explanation at the time, when under criticism for her pragmatism from the extreme Left in the federation. It showed how she understood the workings of power and the realities of taking industrial action:

> I have to temper my own radicalism because with power comes responsibility. There is nothing more demoralising that taking action which does not achieve anything. I only embark on a campaign when there is a clear possibility of winning. Unfortunately, in the face of Federal cutbacks, strike action doesn't always carry that possibility. We have had to look, instead, at taking action in marginal seats and trying to gain some effect that way.[3]

Immersed in issues such as opposition to cuts in teacher numbers and the fall in teachers' real wages, Jennie became a skilful campaigner, travelling with fellow federation officials to country areas on what they playfully called 'royal tours'. Jennie did not forget her feminist roots either and was more active than any official before her in pursuing women's rights. Her professional discipline as secretary came from the federation's regular monthly conference meetings in which more than 300 teachers from around the State descended on Sydney to make decisions on federation policy. The event of the year was always the annual conferences of 1000 delegates. Jennie already had experience of these from her five years as administration officer under Lancaster and Taylor. Now she was directly responsible for ensuring the council worked and, next to the president, had to be articulate and well versed in all issues of debate at short notice.

One of Jennie's hates was open conflict. In keeping with her consensus style, she went out of her way to avoid fights or all-out contests. The job of secretary was accepted as a difficult one. With the responsibility for the smooth running of the federation, Jennie was subjected to enormous stress and political pressure from all factions at times. Members of the federation's executive recalled a couple of occasions during their cabinet-style meetings of 25 to 30 people when Jennie became emotional over factional differences as she tried to turn a decision her way. Her tears, which some men regarded disparagingly as 'feminine tactics', prompted one executive member, Greg Smith, to speak up, gently but firmly, in an attempt to return debate to order. Colleagues recalled Smith said, 'We understand the stresses and strains but we have to come to a decision based on what's before us'. According to one executive member, Smith's words were necessary. He said: 'It had to be done—people were becoming concerned. It happened a couple of times and she was winning the day with this kind of tactic because we were afraid to speak against her when she was upset.'

Executive meetings generally took place in the urban confines of the federation's Sussex Street headquarters but it was decided on at least one occasion that all would benefit from the relaxed atmosphere of a weekend retreat in the Blue Mountains. All agreed that the weekend at a Leura motel was worthwhile, productive in terms of the union business achieved and also as an opportunity for the group to mix socially. What surprised several of the men on the executive, however, was Jennie's inquisitiveness at the dinner table. When she asked for details about their sex lives, they were taken aback. She asked these questions in a voyeuristic but naive way, they believed, as if she were learning for herself about what made men tick. In social situations removed from the seriousness of professional life, Jennie more than once asked similar questions of federation officials. They found it confronting.

Outside work hours, Jack Mundey remained very important to Jennie and was her greatest source of emotional support as she tried to come to terms with Paddy's death. He was there for her to talk through her blackest thoughts. He was even there for menial chores like mowing the Haberfield lawn. A future for the two of them together, however, seemed out of the question. Jennie gave Mundey six months to make up his mind about leaving his wife. When it was clear he did not intend doing so, she looked elsewhere for a possible partner.

At the national conference of the ATF hosted by the NSW Teachers' Federation at the Crest Hotel in Kings Cross, Sydney, in January 1981, a good-looking young man caught Jennie's eye. She was always attracted by good looks. What's more, the young man responded. Simon Marginson was Assistant Secretary, Research, of the Victorian Secondary Teachers' Association. He was a bright former academic sent from Melbourne by his union to experience the national teachers' scene for the first time. He had never met Jennie George but knew of her from afar. He had met Paddy though, and admired him. A former radical in the Melbourne student movement and briefly a Communist Party member in the mid-1970s, Marginson was a passionate Marxist and further to the Left politically than Jennie. However, they shared many political views. At 29, four years younger than Jennie and from a younger generation in the student movement, Marginson was accustomed to feminists and accepted the idea of relating to a strong woman, or so he thought. Marginson recalled: 'She attracted me as a political leader, as a person, as a successful woman. She was an articulate, competent person who was interested and committed to a lot of things, as I was. So it was fairly common ground.'

In the past Jennie had often been attracted to older men— Paddy George was seven years older, Jack Mundey seventeen years older. The younger Marginson, with his boyish face and wiry body, was a great contrast. The attraction was strong and by the last night of the Sydney conference they were lovers. The challenge then was how to maintain an interstate relationship. Even accounting for the obstacles of distance—the cost of airline travel and time constraints because of work commitments in separate cities—they still managed to spend almost every second weekend together. Marginson flew to Sydney more than Jennie flew to Melbourne. In between, their solace was the telephone. Marginson recalled: 'It wasn't easy in that first year, dealing with the emotional highs and lows of an interstate relationship when you're actually quite serious about each other.' Helen Hewett thought Jennie and Marginson were an 'unlikely couple'. It struck her that he was very boyish and looked a little odd in the early days because of the way he dyed his prematurely graying hair. Jennie's appearance, by comparison, was 'straight'. There were obvious personality differences that occurred to Hewett as well. 'He was pretty intense. She was intense too but then the coin would flip and she would be in a totally relaxed state wanting to hear the gossip.'

Jennie had continued to live at Haberfield after Paddy's death but for Helen and Rex Hewett the memories attached to the adjoining houses became too much. With their new baby Peta, born six weeks before Paddy died, they needed a fresh start. They sold their half of the property and moved. For Jennie, the house in which she and Paddy had lived together felt comfortable. As she tried to adjust to a new life, she preferred its familiar surroundings. One source of minor embarrassment for her was that she had employed a cleaner to do her housework once a week. For a 'good socialist' it seemed to contradict her ideological objections to a master–servant relationship, but she had precious little time for domestic chores as a union general secretary. She rationalised that it was necessary and she was providing work. While many people admit to an inability to preset their own video recorders, Rex Hewett noted with amusement that despite her other attributes, the mechanics of household appliances elude Jennie. At one time she had trouble turning on her new dishwasher so asked Hewett to check it. 'I took one look inside and the problem was obvious—she hadn't removed the foam packaging.'

In the second year of their relationship, 1982, Marginson made a geographical shift that somewhat eased the pain of separation and laid the ground for Jennie to make a move of her own. He was elected research officer of the ATF, a position based in Canberra and just three-and-a-half hours drive from Jennie in Sydney. 'Jennie, I think, always felt to some extent [that] she put me in,' recalled Marginson of his election win. According to him, he was headed for the Canberra job anyway. But he was competing with four other men and scored a thundering victory in the ballot thanks largely to support from the NSW Teachers' Federation, the largest State affiliate of the national union and therefore the largest bloc of votes. Jennie had swung these votes behind Marginson. He recalled the effect her power had on him and their relationship: 'That commenced the kind of relationship between us, I suppose, where she was always the senior figure politically and I was the junior. But that worked okay for us. I think a lot of men would have had trouble with that.'

For more than a year, Marginson drove every weekend from Canberra to Sydney, staying with Jennie at the Haberfield house. He arrived on Friday evenings with his suitcase and left at 5.30 a.m. on Monday for the return drive to work. He felt he knew every pothole on the Hume Highway.

The approaching end of Jennie's first three-year term as general secretary presented her with a crossroad in her career. Would she stand again in council elections due in September 1982 or step aside and return to teaching? One reason to stay was the return to the federation of Max Taylor, who had succeeded Barry Manefield as president at the start of the year. Jennie had worked well with Taylor when he preceded her as general secretary. The formula worked again now she was secretary and he was president. Yet the precedent Taylor had set, in returning as president, was also a powerful reason for Jennie to leave. A strong figure in the federation and a rousing public speaker, Taylor had broken new ground as general secretary in the late 1970s by making the post a more frontline 'presidential' position, with political as well as bureaucratic clout. Jennie was the beneficiary of the changes Taylor introduced because she inherited his stronger political role and accompanying power when she became secretary. Now Taylor had broken new ground again. He was the first general secretary in the federation's history to make the major transition from the traditionally bureaucratic job of secretary—elected by the council, to the presidency— elected directly by the membership. Taylor had done so by returning to teaching for two years and campaigning for support among working teachers to win the presidential ballot. Jennie, ambitious despite nagging insecurities, realised that to become president, she would have to follow Taylor's example and leave too—in order to return later.

Her personal life figured in her thinking and provided a happy coincidence. Departing presented the opportunity of ending the long-distance phase of her relationship with Marginson so they could live together. The catch was that in order for Jennie to be in contention for the presidency of the Teachers' Federation, she would have to score a job in the NSW education system. If she moved to Canberra to be with Marginson and taught in the Australian Capital Territory, she would come under Federal jurisdiction. Outside the NSW system, she would not be able to maintain a profile in the State federation by remaining on its decision-making bodies—the council and executive—and thereby muster the support she needed from member teachers.

The neat compromise Jennie devised was perfect for her career *and* her personal life. She gained a teaching position as the careers adviser at Queanbeyan High School in NSW, just across the ACT border, within easy distance of Canberra's suburbs, enabling her to live with Marginson. For his part, Marginson accepted that Jennie was taking a major step in moving to Canberra to live with him and that she was putting their relationship ahead of her closeness to her mother, whom Jennie reluctantly would leave behind in Sydney. Nevertheless, he considered he had little say in the matter: 'I always felt that it was decided for me—that particular arrangement—but I was prepared to go along with it.'

Jennie used a number of justifications to explain why she was quitting as general secretary of the federation after just one term. One public reason that she gave to the *Sydney Morning Herald* at the time was that she believed 'full-time union positions should be frequently turned over'.[4] Another explanation she gave to colleagues was that lingering grief over Paddy's death had taken its toll on her. Indeed this was a legitimate reason—she was tired and wanted out. Still there was another explanation that Jennie would advance much later as the primary reason for quitting. It was partly true but obscured entirely an underlying career motive and contradicted the kind of feminist principles she had been espousing. She said she was giving up her career for a man: 'I thought, like a lot of women think, the male career is more important than mine. So I actually went back to teaching—I gave up the secretaryship of the union. I followed the person I was in love with to Queanbeyan High School.'

In fact, Jennie never gave up her career even though it appeared she had. She made a sacrifice of sorts by moving to Canberra but always, as Marginson phrased it aptly, remained 'on the track'. It was while living in Canberra with him that she would make several significant advances in her career and firsts for women.

Moving to Canberra—a city with a high standard of living, no peak-hour traffic and plenty of space and fresh country air—gave Jennie the more relaxed lifestyle she needed. It was a break from the pressure she had experienced for several years, even though she remained heavily involved in the politics of the Teachers' Federation and made regular trips to Sydney on union business or to see her mother and friends. The slower pace of the nation's capital gave her time to find out what domesticity was like with Simon Marginson, together every day for the first time after two years of inter-city commuting. Jennie also enjoyed her return to the coalface as careers adviser at Queanbeyan High School and found time for further study. Regarding her university degree as ordinary and passé, she enrolled at the Australian National University in a postgraduate course on a subject dear to her heart, women's studies.

Away from work and study, Jennie acquired bourgeois tastes that reflected her middle-class income, education and broadening cultural horizons. She had always enjoyed going to the cinema when married to Paddy, and now took an interest in serious dramatic films, including film noir, with Marginson. She was already interested in art, particularly paintings and pottery, and enthused Marginson in these things. They visited galleries together. Jennie enjoyed reading but did so mostly out of necessity, imposing self-discipline to focus on material she had to learn. She got up early to read the newspapers or, if she did not have time, read them before going to bed late at night. Reading as a relaxing pastime—novels and the like—was relegated mostly to holidays. However, Jennie always read her stars. 'All my friends joke about it,' she said. Inheriting her interest in astrology from her mother, from time to time, Annie Robertson, an old friend from the Eureka Youth League, prepared her astrological chart. Jennie regarded herself as a typical Leo: 'I'm a bit pushy, a bit bossy, but beneath that harsh exterior the pushiness is often a mask for insecurities.'

Good food and wine were important in Jennie's life. She had become interested in cooking and was much better than Marginson although she preferred eating out. As a couple, they exhausted Canberra's limited supply of restaurants and always dined out on visits to Sydney. They experimented with cuisine but preferred Italian. They dined out so much, in fact, that Marginson reached the point where he felt eating out was no longer special. Of the two, he was more the homebody who liked to collapse on the couch and watch television in the evening. If Marginson wanted to stay at home, he had to be encouraged in the kitchen, so Jennie believed. She bought him a copy of Beverly Sutherland-Smith's cookbook *Taste of Independence* and told him, 'There's no excuses anymore! You've got to cook now!' He did improve and shared more of the load. Unlike Marginson, Jennie did not like lounging about much. She watched television for half an hour or so if she came home tired or after a few drinks, but generally preferred to be active. If she was in the mood, she played one of her favourite records to unwind, usually the same one 'month after month', according to Marginson—'Daniel' by Elton John was a favourite. Her musical taste leant to middle-of-the-road pop from the 1960s and 1970s.

Alcohol was important to the way Jennie relaxed and her preference was for white wine. At parties, she drank much more than Marginson and he usually drove home. Partying never interfered with her professional life. Even after heavy nights, she always turned up on time the next morning, lucid and ready for work. In social situations she was not choosy about wine quality but at home she and Marginson took up wine as a hobby and started a vintage collection together, buying half-a-dozen bottles here and there at cellar-door tastings. Jennie was a good judge of fine wine. Their interest had begun in earnest during an ATF conference in Perth in January 1982, a year after they met, when they toured Margaret River vineyards. Marginson was always the more serious about wine, however, to the obsessive degree of labelling each individual bottle with the date of its purchase and its best time for drinking.

Wining and dining came at a cost, other than financial. Both Jennie and Marginson felt the need to lose weight and started several diets over time. Marginson was the more fanatical about sticking to the detail of a diet regimen, although Jennie had more stamina in terms of shedding the weight she wanted to lose. Sometimes Jennie swam but neither did enough exercise and she tended to smoke too much.

A growing interest of Jennie's was travel. She had had a taste of major international travel when she visited relatives in the Soviet Union with Natasha while Paddy was alive, but her preferred holiday destination was the South Pacific islands and she had tried a number of them. She and Marginson went to Vanuatu twice, including one trip with Natasha and Vladimir, who liked Marginson and vice versa. Jennie and he also went to Noumea. Even on holidays, Marginson noticed that Jennie did not have the capacity to stop. She liked sitting on the beach and swimming but she had what he regarded as three modes of behaviour. She had a full-on work mode, very focused and with a full diary; a playing-hard mode, which was essentially 'dancing, drinking and going out to a show'; and finally a relaxing mode, such as visiting an art gallery or inviting friends for lunch. There was no fourth mode of Jennie 'relaxed, doing nothing'. When they had a long-distance relationship, differences in taste and lifestyle between Jennie and Marginson seemed trivial, even endearing. Now they lived together, any differences were magnified. Both wondered where their relationship was heading and whether it could last a lifetime.

THE ACCORD

Jennie George's shift to Canberra in late 1982 coincided with a crucial time in national politics. Australia was in the grip of economic recession with unemployment at its worst since the Great Depression. Expectations ran high that after seven years in opposition, the Labor Party under Bill Hayden's leadership had a strong chance of winning a Federal election that Prime Minister Malcolm Fraser was expected to call sometime the next year. The political intrigue, aside from Fraser's prospects of winning a fourth term in power, but linked inextricably with it, was whether Fraser would face Hayden or Bob Hawke as his head-to-head opponent for prime minister when it came to the actual poll date. Hawke, the former ACTU president in the 1970s, had been breathing down Hayden's neck for the ALP leadership ever since he entered Parliament at the 1980 Federal election.

Hawke was akin to a national hero. He was enormously popular because of his reputation, acquired when he was ACTU president, for settling what appeared to be intractable strikes. There was intense media speculation about Hawke's political future, which he did nothing to discourage. Indeed he used his own sense of destiny about becoming prime minister to good effect. He had already made his first failed attempt to wrest the ALP leadership from Hayden in July 1982. It was only a matter of time before Hawke tried again. Fraser thought his chances against Labor led by Hayden were reasonable but was desperately worried about the more charismatic Hawke. His best hope was to call a snap early election, forcing Labor to drop the idea of switching leaders and ensuring that it fell solidly behind the non-flamboyant Hayden in a short lead-up to polling day. Fraser made his attempt to outsmart Labor on 3 February—announcing a general election for 5 March. But in an exquisite piece of timing, he was outwitted. Around the same time Fraser met the Governor-General to advise of the election, Hayden succumbed to strong pressure and resigned to make way for Hawke.

Jennie was never a creature of the Labor Party and its traditions. While she had friends such as Pam Allan, Vic Baueris and Van Davy who belonged to the party's left-wing faction, the Steering Committee in Sydney, she was still closer politically to her peers from the Communist Party culture in the Teachers' Federation such as Richard Walsham and Cathy Bloch. Pam Allan and another ALP left-winger, Jan Burnswood, encouraged Jennie to join the ALP but she resisted. According to close observers, Jennie believed that the ALP was a 'sellout' and masqueraded as a workers' party. She regarded the union industrial Left as the gatekeeper of working-class principles to which she aspired, and preferred to work through that rather than the parliamentary process. Nevertheless, like all in the union movement, Jennie wanted the Labor Party to win the election. For her, it was a matter of justice. She abhorred Sir John Kerr's dismissal of the Whitlam Government and had been one of the many protesters at the demonstration in Sydney's Martin Place on 11 November 1975. Labor's likely election also presented the opportunity to roll back some of Fraser's conservative policies and to provide better Commonwealth funding for education. Jennie was no fan of Hawke. She objected to his support for uranium mining in Australia and his right-wing connections with ALP machine figures in Sydney, Paul Keating and Graham Richardson. However, she did appreciate Hawke's union history and Hayden had never been close to the movement. Jennie was also a realist, accepting that Hawke as leader would maximise Labor's chances of winning.

Despite her general enthusiasm for a Labor victory, Jennie had major reservations about a key plank of the party's platform. She was opposed to the centrepiece of Labor's economic policy and what was now an important part of Hawke's campaign theme of *Bringing Australia Together*—the proposed prices and incomes Accord agreement with the union movement. The architect of the Accord concept, and person responsible for much of the early work on its formulation, was Ralph Willis, Labor's economic spokesman in opposition and a former ACTU advocate. In the late 1970s Willis had studied social contracts operating between governments and unions in Europe. His model for Australia hinged on a formal understanding between the ALP and the union movement on prices and incomes to secure general restraint. Hayden also was heavily involved in the Accord's evolution as an official wages policy and in selling the Accord politically to the party. The irony was that Hawke, who took the Accord to the election and later implemented it, gained the credit.

Considering Australia's industrial history, there was much merit in the Accord at the time it was proposed. Economically, the Accord made sense in seeking to avoid a wage-price spiral, which had run uncontrolled when Gough Whitlam was prime minister, and incidentally when Hawke was ACTU president. Unions had used industrial muscle then and since to win big pay claims, at a cost of high inflation and unemployment. If unions accepted wage restraint under the Accord, the quid pro quo would be higher employment and a check on prices. The politics of the Accord, assuming Labor won government, also made sense. Labor was anxious to avoid a repeat of the Whitlam Government's reputation for economic mismanagement, which had contributed heavily to its electoral defeat following the Kerr dismissal. Successive attempts during the Fraser years to moderate pay claims had failed, made worse by the Fraser Government's poor relationship with the ACTU. The recent recession, prompted in part by another round of wage claims led by the successful campaign of the Amalgamated Metal Workers Union (AMWU) for an extra $39-a-week and a shortened 38-hour week, presented a convincing reason for a lasting solution. The fallout of that wage round was a serious downturn with the loss of more than 100 000 manufacturing jobs. All sides tried to remedy the economic climate with a shaky truce. Under the auspices of the Conciliation and Arbitration Commission president, Sir John Moore, the ACTU agreed to a 'wage freeze' with no claims for six months. The freeze was due to expire midway through 1983. Unless it was continued, some sort of wages policy was needed to fill the void.

The essence of the Accord proposed by Labor was to replace the wage freeze with a form of wage indexation. Unions were to agree to moderate their wage demands, so that they did not exceed rises in the cost of living as measured by the Consumer Price Index (CPI). The Accord was strict in its application, however. Moore's commission was to oversee automatic adjustments to minimum award pay rates equal to the CPI number, granted twice a year after the release of quarterly CPI figures by the Australian Bureau of Statistics. Businesses would not be subject to such discipline on prices, nor could they be realistically. There was to be no repeat of the failed Whitlam attempt at a referendum to gain control over the regulation of prices, which the public, and the union movement under Hawke, had rejected in the 1970s. Instead, representatives of business were to be invited to tripartite conferences with the Government and unions. Labor would also seek to impose some moral discipline on business by establishing an authority to monitor prices. Its task would be to assess 'the validity or otherwise of price rises sought by corporations and public authorities'[1]—in other words, expose profiteering. The much broader theme of the Accord was a social contract between Labor and the ACTU that came to be known as 'the social wage'. In return for accepting a planned system in which they moderated their wage demands, unions would gain a guarantee from Labor to provide compensation, by way of improved living standards from welfare, taxation and health concessions.[2] A by-product of the Accord was that if all went well, higher employment would feed union membership levels and arrest their recent decline.

Hawke, when he was ACTU president, had centralised the union movement's negotiating base, to some extent, as the national fireman who extinguished strikes and made union agreements with employers binding.[3] The Accord, if accepted by the union movement, would also entrench the power base of Hawke's successors in the ACTU leadership as never before. Under the Accord, the ACTU would become the focal negotiating party with the Government. It would be at the apex of a wages policy in which all unions had to toe the line. The consequences of dissent could be painful.

Jennie's opposition to the Accord stood in striking contradiction to her stance less than a decade later, as an ACTU officer, when she became one of its primary advocates. Ideologically, her objections at the time of the 1983 election were those of a left-winger who believed that union activism—not the parliamentary process or deals with governments—was the best way to improve living standards in society. She believed, correctly as it turned out, that the Accord would be used as a straitjacket on union behaviour, trapping workers into lower real wages. Jennie also had particular objections related to grievances within the teaching profession that were shared by most of her colleagues. By agreeing to the Accord, she knew her union would forfeit its right to seek salary increases above and beyond future, potentially tiny rises in the inflation rate. For teachers, this was a problem on two fronts. They certainly would be denied a retrospective wage 'catch up' which they argued was deserved because of the past slide in their wages relative to the cost of living. They also stood to be denied the opportunity to differentiate themselves from blue-collar unions and press for increases that reflected the special work value of teachers. There was antagonism already inside the ATF over the refusal of the ACTU secretary, Bill Kelty, to support teachers in a campaign to have the metalworkers' pace-setting $39 wage rise flow-on to their profession. Jennie was not directly involved in this disagreement but other officials, including Van Davy and Simon Marginson, had had stand-up arguments with Kelty about it.

Kelty was chief policy-maker at the ACTU and was accumulating immense authority across the union movement. Recently he had been appointed ACTU secretary after a rise through the ranks of the organisation in the 1970s under the patronage of its then secretary, Harold Souter, and president, Bob Hawke. Kelty had become very close to Hawke and was dubbed 'the Sorcerer's Apprentice' for the selfless support he gave his boss at the 1979 ACTU congress, in attempting to reduce Hawke's humiliation for taking a pro-uranium mining stance that was defeated on the congress floor. When Hawke was ACTU president, he was the organisation's most powerful figure and—aside from the uranium defeat—was revered generally by the union movement. Now Kelty, by the force of his own personality, had emerged as the union movement's pivotal figure, allowed to come to the fore because of the remoteness of Hawke's successor as ACTU president, Cliff Dolan. Dolan was nominally in charge and still had all Hawke's presidential powers but he was distant from the running of the ACTU, not least because he lived in Sydney and commuted weekly, working in the ACTU's Melbourne headquarters from Monday to Thursday. Melbourne-based, Kelty ran ACTU operations behind the scenes and accumulated the power and authority that otherwise could have been wielded by Dolan. There was little public hint of Kelty's supremacy at the time because of his aversion to media attention but in reality he was already one of the most powerful men in the country. His position stood to be enhanced still more if the union movement endorsed the new Accord with Labor and Labor won the election. Kelty would become the Accord's chief enforcer.

Union endorsement was the earliest test for the Accord. There was little doubt that a majority would support it. But the ACTU leadership wanted 'unanimous' support at a special unions conference of more than 200 delegates called to give the official nod in Melbourne's Trades Hall on 21 February, just two weeks before the 1983 election.

Kelty was the main union architect of the 37-page document that was to be put to the vote. As chief advocate, he carried the argument and made it his personal mission to ensure support. The other key intellectual figure in the ACTU tent was Laurie Carmichael, the assistant secretary of the left-wing AMWU and prominent communist. Carmichael had suffered tremendous criticism because of his role in the 1981 wage push by his union that cost so many jobs. He was among those that Paul Keating, soon to be Treasurer, claimed were responsible for decimating manufacturing. These people, Keating said, 'carry the jobs of dead men around their necks'. The label did not appear to haunt Carmichael but, in a sense, a redemption opportunity had presented itself. He was a convert to the Accord idea because he could see that its principle of solidarity was a means of looking after the whole. In a time of economic crisis, the low paid who lacked industrial muscle to bargain would not be left behind as they usually were in wage rounds. Employment growth—not losses of the past—would be an intended by-product of the Accord. Apart from Carmichael's intellectual intensity, the great value to Kelty of having him on side was his stature in the union Left and his ability to use his haranguing style to cajole doubters among those in the Left. Kelty, who deeply respected Carmichael, was nominally from the Victorian union right-wing but was becoming increasingly difficult to pigeonhole. His support for

Jennie George's maternal grandparents were a curious match: Frederich, a Soviet government printer of German descent, was a communist sympathiser; Xenia, whose White Russian aristocratic family was left impoverished by the Russian Revolution, despised Stalin's regime. Xenia's feisty, strong-willed character was paramount to survival after Frederich died suddenly during the famines of the Depression.

Oleg Sinicky, the good-looking Russian Jennie George's mother met and married after his release from a German POW camp, stands outside one of the corrugated-iron huts of the refugee camp at Riccione, Italy. Jennie spent her first three years in Italian refugee camps before the family migrated to Australia.

Jennie with her grandmother, Xenia, in the grounds of the Walgrove migrant camp, a former military barracks at Rooty Hill in western Sydney. The picture gives no hint of a family split by immigration authorities. Her father was sent to work as a cook in a British hostel at Burwood and her mother to work as a nursing aide at Camperdown.

A family reunited. Jennie with her parents at the British migrant hostel at Burwood in Sydney's inner west, where both Oleg and Natasha eventually worked in the kitchen. Jennie spoke Russian, Polish and some Italian—but no English—when she started primary school.

Jennie on her mother Natasha's knee in a family portrait with her grandmother, Xenia, and father, Oleg. Finally together at the Burwood hostel, their life was far from rosy. Oleg drank heavily and was violent towards Natasha.

Jennie, dressed in traditional costume (on the far left), taking part in a pageant organised by the close-knit Russian community of western Sydney. She was tutored in her Russian heritage and learned the language formally. She also joined the Russian girl guides and attended Sunday school.

Besides studying ballet, Jennie also learned the piano. At high school, however, she became a rebel who turned her back on such things—as well as her Russian background.

As a teenager, Jennie was mad about the Beatles and was 'in love' with Paul McCartney. She poses here in the Housing Commission flat she shared with her grandmother at Surry Hills, Sydney. Their relationship was tempestuous—when Jennie plastered her wall with Beatles posters her grandmother tore them down.

Jennie with Paddy George, the committed young communist she met at the Eureka Youth League during her second year at university. She became active in the anti-Vietnam War movement of the 1960s, although her initial involvement had more to do with falling in love with the warm-hearted and easygoing Paddy than an interest in politics.

Paddy George looks on as Jennie signs marriage papers on their wedding day, 20 February 1968. As non-believers, the couple were married at the Sydney Registry Office but agreed to a private traditional ceremony to please Jennie's mother.

Jennie addresses a meeting of teachers at Wiley Park Oval in April 1973 during an area-wide strike over staffing levels. She was still a teacher at Bankstown Girl's High School but developing her skills as a union activist. Within months she left teaching for a full-time position with the NSW Teachers' Federation and began her climb up the union ladder. (Courtesy of NSW Teachers Federation)

Now wearing her trademark glasses, Jennie (centre, foreground) in George Street, Sydney, behind the NSW Teachers' Federation banner during a march for the 1975 International Year of Women. On her left is close friend Cathy Bloch. (Courtesy of NSW Teachers Federation)

The first major publicity splash of Jennie's career. Just as Bob Hawke is on the verge of quitting the ACTU presidency in his quest to become prime minister, his eventual successor at the ACTU enters the union stage when she became the first woman secretary of the NSW Teachers' Federation in its 61-year history. (Courtesy of *Sun-Herald*)

Courageous to the end, Paddy George at home in Haberfield is all smiles with Jennie and his mother, Gwen. He was seriously ill and doctors could do nothing for him after he was diagnosed late with cancer.

Carmichael's central role in advancing the Accord was the beginning of a major effort to unite all the factions.

The ACTU was so confident about the result of the special unions conference that it printed a series of advertisements to publicise the Accord—ahead of the result—trumpeting a unanimous vote. These advertisements had to be changed. Unanimous became 'overwhelming' because of one conference vote registered against the Accord by the secretary of the NSW Nurses' Association, Jenny Haines.[4] What the official vote did not record, however, was the opposition to the Accord of Jennie George. Instead of risking notoriety by registering a vote against the Accord, Jennie abstained from voting altogether by not raising her hand when the chair asked for those for and against. Jennie recalled:

> I did that because the ATF had a position that was quite critical about the underlying assumptions of the Accord. There was disbelief that if we were moderate in our wage demands that the employers would do the right thing. So teaching was quite left of the political spectrum.

Jennie was one of two teachers' delegates sent to the conference by the ATF—the other was Van Davy, the ATF's president. Before the special unions conference, a committee of the ATF consisting of Jennie, Van Davy, Bill Leslie and Simon Marginson met to agree on what tactics the two delegates should use. Their lengthy discussions canvassed Carmichael's position, the only thing that was likely to change their minds. They accepted there was some merit in Carmichael's argument: that the Accord was a working-class document and if the union movement voted for it but the Labor Government failed to respect it, then unions would have complete legitimacy in taking political and industrial action to achieve the Accord's objectives. In the end, however, they could not support the Accord. Jennie and Davy then decided to adopt voting tactics that could only be described as childish: they were ruled not by how to best express the ATF's position but by the likely reaction of Kelty if he happened to notice that the ATF was not voting for the Accord. Kelty was an acerbic, enigmatic character who, even then, could instil fear among union officials because of his capacity for retribution. Therefore, all agreed that Jennie and Davy would not expose their opposition by voting against the Accord. Instead they would abstain. However, the two delegates would vote in favour of the Accord if they were in Kelty's clear view from where he sat on the conference stage or if Kelty was looking directly at them when the vote was taken. Hours of discussion about clever ATF tactics came to naught. Davy voted for the Accord. Jennie, sitting next to Davy, did not. She did not ask to have her abstention recorded.

10

EXECUTIVE STATUS

It was a fine balancing act. Just weeks before Bob Hawke was elected prime minister and the Accord was set in stone as government policy, Jennie had expressed her opposition to the Accord. She believed she had stuck to her union's principles by not supporting it—even if her silence meant tacit co-operation. There was, however, a good reason for Jennie to act discreetly and not provoke a very public falling out with Bill Kelty or gain a reputation, like Jenny Haines, as a left-wing recalcitrant. When she had announced her decision to quit as general secretary of the NSW Teachers' Federation the previous year, Jennie said publicly that she planned to stand as a candidate for the ACTU's ruling executive when positions came up for election at the ACTU biennial congress in September 1983.[1] Notoriety would not have helped her cause. When the Accord vote was taken, Jennie had already sewn up her candidacy on behalf of the ATF, although she still had to compete with officials from other white-collar unions in the September ballot for the particular executive seat she wanted. Until recently white-collar unions had not been affiliated with the ACTU or State trades and labour councils because they had their own peak union organisations to deal with issues at a national level. The NSW Teachers' Federation was an exception.

The federation had been affiliated with the ACTU since the 1940s as well as belonging to a national white-collar union organisation that did not belong to the ACTU called the Australian Council of Salaried and Professional Associations (ACSPA). The sheer size of the NSW Teachers' Federation, the twelfth largest union in the country with 60 000 members, meant that it sent a significant number of delegates to ACTU congresses. It commanded a powerful bloc of left-wing votes and was a union with national influence. Nevertheless, as a State union the federation was not entitled to a seat on the ACTU executive. Under the ACTU's rules, the 27-person executive consisted of its most senior full-time officials and about fifteen industry representatives from among federally registered unions. As well, each state had one seat from their trades and labour councils, these being the only state representatives permitted.

Van Davy was influential in gaining a greater say for teaching unions in the ACTU in 1979 during his first stint as president of the ATF. He helped to secure the ATF's affiliation with the ACTU when the white-collar union group ACSPA, in which Davy was a leading figure, joined the ACTU. Once the ACSPA became an ACTU affiliate, the big question was who would take a newly created seat for the organisation on the ACTU executive. Davy wanted the seat himself but failed to win the backing of the NSW Teachers' Federation, which nominated Richard Walsham as the NSW candidate. In the final vote, neither Davy nor Walsham got to the executive. Keith Lawlor from South Australia won the seat.

Jennie was well-qualified to become the ACSPA representative on the ACTU executive when the position came up for election at the 1983 congress. Also, the general feeling at the time, particularly among teaching unions, was similar to when she was elected general secretary of the federation—that it was time for a woman to sit on the executive. This sentiment helped Jennie gain support as the ATF's candidate. Women's rights were high on the public agenda. One million women—just under a third of the total membership—belonged to unions. Their numbers were high among teachers, nurses, clerical workers, caterers and flight attendants. The proportion in other occupations was growing as the female participation rate in the labour market grew. The ACTU even had an official 'affirmative action' policy. But eight years after the United Nations' International Year of Women it was a source of great embarrassment to the ACTU leadership, and reflected poorly on male-controlled unions generally, that only one-tenth of congress delegates were women and not one member of the ACTU executive was a woman. Jennie was poised to be *the* woman with the right credentials, in the right place, at the right time, to lead the way.

Usually the ACTU operated so that the men standing for positions on its executive did deals to settle positions behind closed doors in advance of the vote at the biennial September congress. By the time of the 1983 congress vote in Melbourne's Dallas Brooks Hall, only two executive positions were still to be contested. One was for the building trades group, which Tom McDonald lost to Norm Gallagher. The other was for the ACSPA group. Jennie was already the ATF candidate but she was running in a three-way contest for one position against Barry Durham, federal secretary of the Municipal Officers' Association, and Heather Johnson from the Australian Nurses' Federation. Durham was Jennie's serious opponent. Johnson was from a right-wing union, smaller than the left-wing ATF and unable to gain enough support from the Left-dominated ACSPA group to win. Jennie's campaign team of Cathy Bloch, Meredith Burgmann, Marie Muir, Brenda Forbath and Lyn Beaton knew that Durham's support was so great that they had to do last-minute lobbying. The night before the vote, they buttonholed left-wing men in the ACSPA group to try to swing the result Jennie's way. Burgmann explained, facetiously, the attitude of the men: 'Women saw that voting for Jennie was really important but the men didn't. Some of them didn't really want a woman on the executive—we just about had to sell them our bodies to get them on side!'

Jennie's team was brimming with excitement as the moment neared for the election returning officer, Lindsay North, to read the ballot results from the congress stage. When he called Jennie's name, loud applause and cheering erupted through the congress hall of 1100 delegates. It was the strongest response to any of the names announced from the stage—although some men were not so enthusiastic. As expected, the vote was close. Jennie had won by just six votes out of 57 cast in the ACSPA group. The women jumped and shouted for joy, tossing into the air purple and green streamers, which they had made the previous night out of crepe paper, especially for the occasion. Brenda Forbath also handed out big purple, green and white rosettes to Jennie's team and other women congress delegates to celebrate this first for women. So exuberant was Cathy Bloch that she rushed onto the stage and pinned her rosette on Cliff Dolan's collar. Burgmann, who felt an enormous sense of history being made, recalled: 'It was wonderful! Cliff was such a lovely person. He just sat there wearing this rosette like a prize bull with a puzzled look on his face!'

Jennie too was euphoric and held a celebratory dinner that night. But she quickly put her victory into perspective and gave an outline of the issues she wanted to pursue, focusing on women. She wanted to raise special difficulties experienced by women in the workforce at the ACTU executive, such as exploitation and lack of job security. Although the battle for equal pay was ostensibly won, she stressed that women's average weekly earnings were still only three-quarters of men's earnings. Universal childcare for working women remained vitally important to her.[2] Jennie was also struck by the symbolism of her new position and the responsibility she would carry when she attended her first executive meeting with 26 men. She said at the time:

There is nothing worse than getting there and adopting the 'Queen Bee Syndrome'—in that people say, 'if I made it, there is no reason why anyone else cannot do the same'. I have to make sure that people on the executive do not use the argument that because Jennie George made it, there is no reason why anyone else cannot do the same. I have to make sure that people on the executive do not use the argument that because Jennie George made it, there is no need to do anything for other women. Some people said to me 'congratulations on your election, not just because you are a woman but also because you are a good trade unionist'. That is very gratifying in a sense, but my election to me is not just a personal statement. It means that women are finally going to be accepted. Women have a great responsibility. If they botch the job, men are going to use it as a reason to say women are no good, they can't cope. You have that pressure that through your work you are going to make it easier for other women.[3]

Entrenched male attitudes were the first thing Jennie had to encounter on the ACTU executive. Cliff Dolan had expected her victory because his numbers man, Ray Gietzelt, had told him that Jennie would win by about ten votes. When Dolan informed the all-male executive of the likely new arrival, the secretary of Queensland's Trades and Labor Council, Harry Hauenschild, remarked: 'Oh shit! A sheila! We won't be able to fart now!'

The ACTU's quarterly executive meetings ran for a full five days then. Jennie sat quietly at the first executive she attended in late 1983, taking notes on resolutions so she could report back to her members. Some men became nervous about her jottings, which she made in a little blue book. During a morning-tea break, one executive member asked her if she was noting all their sexist remarks. 'Oh yes,' Jennie replied. 'One day I'm going to write my memoirs and you're going to feature in them.'

Despite having welcomed the arrival of a woman to the all-male executive, it was still hard for Cliff Dolan to lose old habits. At 3 p.m. on the final day of Jennie's first executive, he closed the meeting saying, 'well gentlemen, I will see you again in about three months' time'. Jennie had said nothing all week but could not let his statement stand. 'Cliff, we are not all gentlemen,' she reminded him. 'Quite right,' said Dolan. 'As a matter of fact I'm glad you raised it, Jennie. I don't think there is even one here.'

Cliff Dolan told the author that while he could not claim any credit for Jennie's election to the ACTU executive he had accepted her wholeheartedly. Therefore it rankled when, soon after Jennie had attended her first meeting of the executive, he heard her launch into an attack on its chauvinistic ways when he arrived early at a conference of the NSW Teachers' Federation he was supposed to address. Dolan recalled: 'I just had got there when she was telling all the delegates how it was a "boys' club" and was berating the organisation. I did think she was a bit rough and I said so. But from then on our relationship was a good one.'

While Jennie was on good terms with the genial Dolan, her relations with Kelty were strained. Although he later changed, Kelty had many narrow views and tended to focus squarely on things in which he was expert, such as award wages and conditions. Despite his accumulating power and authority within the union movement, he was shy socially, especially in personal contact with the opposite sex. He sided with traditional male blue-collar unions representing wharfies and metalworkers ahead of white-collar unions, and was not particularly interested in women's issues. Jennie recalled:

> I didn't know Bill all that well. In fact some of my early recollections with Bill were that we clashed about women's issues. Bill was like all of them. They had come from a culture that was male-oriented, male-dominated, and I think his political views changed over the course of time.

Kelty also recalled that he knew Jennie hardly at all. He had met her at the NSW Teachers' Federation's Sussex Street headquarters in the 1970s through the late Merv Nixon, a friend of

Jennie's who was then secretary of the South Coast Labor Council in NSW and a prominent communist. He had some contact with her after she became secretary of the NSW Teachers' Federation but it was mostly at a distance. That was to change in 1983 when she arrived as the first woman on the ACTU executive. Kelty soon came to appreciate the difficulties she encountered and the way in which she was determined to lead the way for better female representation:

> It's hard to be one-out but she *was* one-out. The ACTU was old-fashioned and male-dominated, conservative and in some sense Neanderthal. It's all right for people to look at today's society and say 'look at these standards today'. But it's much harder when you are one-out, fighting alone as she was.

Initially Jennie remained a critic of the Accord in keeping with her Leftist preference for activism and her union's particular concerns about teachers. But over time her views changed. Sitting on the ACTU executive and absorbing its wider concerns altered her perspective. Typical of the way her mind worked, it was not an overnight conversion. She recalled:

> I think my attitude changed when you actually saw the benefits the Accord gave to those who had no bargaining power. I think what happened, when I got on the executive, was that I was forced to take a much broader view of the world. So while I represented teachers I could say there was not much in the Accord for us. But when you actually sat there and looked at things, well, it was all right for teachers because they had superannuation. But when you looked at the rest of the workforce with no super at all, and realised that the only way people in retail or clerical work would make gains was through the political process, you started to see the world in a much bigger picture way.

Among the key personalities involved in Jennie's rise through union ranks, Van Davy was one of the most important. He and Jennie had been friends since the 1960s but Davy was really much closer to Paddy George, having known Paddy since child-hood, growing up under the influence of communist parents who sent him to the Junior Eureka League. Paddy had provided the link between Jennie and Davy. Once Paddy was gone, the glue that bound Jennie's friendship with Davy started to come unstuck as issues came between them. Their main differences were over matters of union policy, but supporters of Davy said that he also felt Jennie did not give him personal political support when he needed it. Davy had moved to Canberra in 1983 as full-time president of the ATF. Jennie too was living in Canberra and Simon Marginson, her partner, worked for Davy as the ATF's research officer. As strains developed between Jennie and Davy, so too did Davy's professional relationship with Marginson sour.

Davy's critics regarded him as an egotist who was difficult to work with: they were put offside by his determination to do things his way. He was also leaning increasingly towards the ALP, which upset Teachers' Federation officials with Communist Party backgrounds and those who pleaded the need for no alignment with political parties. Among Davy's virtues, however, was his vision for the future of education and teachers' unions. He believed that a strong national union was necessary to give public education, under threat from the private sector, more political and industrial punch. As the Federal Government pro-vided significant funds to school education, Davy argued that there was a need for ten-year plans and that the future lay in joint responsibility with the states, including agreements on resources and staffing. Jennie agreed up to a point—but she was very state focused and had differences with Davy about the direction of the NSW Teachers' Federation. As his frustrations grew, Davy quit. He had had enough as ATF president and his partner, Vivienne, was unhappy in Canberra anyway. He and Jennie never spoke again. One observer said of Davy: 'He felt he'd been knifed in the back by Jennie.' Jennie's own recollection of her falling out with Davy was that they grew apart while he was ATF president mainly because of problems in the working relationship between Davy and Marginson. She recalled:

> Van and I had been good friends and Paddy and I had even gone to New Zealand with him and Viv in the May 1980 school holidays. But he and Simon didn't get on and that drove a wedge between us. Simon, being the kind of person he was, made it difficult to have a friendship with Van. He [Van] left Canberra and then our paths didn't cross.

Davy's resignation created an opening for Jennie. She already lived in Canberra where the ATF presidency was based. Despite her previous lack of enthusiasm for the national union, she stood for Davy's position in March 1985—and won with support from the NSW federation, the ATF's largest affiliate. She resigned from Queanbeyan High School and suddenly became not only Marginson's lover but his boss as well. In the process Jennie scored another breakthrough in becoming the first woman to head the national teachers' union. It was another asset, along with her membership of the ACTU executive, assisting her to stake a claim on the job she really wanted—the presidency of the NSW Teachers' Federation.

There was a happy coincidence of timing for Jennie's planned return to the federation. The way she liked to portray it, colleagues in Sydney sent her an SOS to stand as president and rescue the union. Indeed this was true—up to a point. She was urged to stand. But the notion that she was drafted was a myth if it was accepted in isolation and failed to take into account the fact that Jennie's personal ambition had already turned in that direction. In the federation's November 1983 elections, a freakish result had delivered the top leadership positions of the federation to a right-wing team for the first time in 30 years. The defeat of the president, Max Taylor, whom most people regarded as unassailable, and his left-wing team of Barbara Murphy, deputy president, and Alan Cross, senior vice-president, shocked the federation to its core. In an unexpected win, thanks to good campaign material and arrogance by the former leadership, Ivan Pagett, an ALP right-winger, took over as president with his team of Cheryl Screech and Alan Layt.

Almost as soon as the Pagett team took up their positions in January 1984, relations between the federation and the State Government became poisonous. The first deputation of federation officials which Pagett took to see the then Minister for Education, ALP left-winger Rodney Cavalier, was a complete failure after a misunderstanding over what was said at the meeting. Neither side trusted each other after that. Relations worsened over a lengthy saga in which Cavalier insisted that a high school teacher, Dick O'Neill, must accept his transfer to another school, contrary to the federation's policy which opposed forced transfers. While Pagett officially led the federation, he lacked the numbers on the federation's ruling council. He found himself isolated for the two years he was in the job while the full-time left-wing hierarchy united to run the union. The Left wanted to ensure Pagett's defeat in presidential elections due in November 1985 so it could restore its complete dominance and revert to its previous style of leadership. There was an opening for president—and the faction wanted Jennie. She recalled: 'I started getting pressure from the federation about "would I come back" as I was the only one who was thought to have a chance of beating the Right.'

Jennie's run for president was not built on a pledge of union activism or inspiring policies so much as the need of her backers to defeat Pagett and put the federation back on the rails. Were Max Taylor still in the position, she would not have stood. She announced her candidacy in April—eight months before the ballot—as part of a well-organised campaign begun the year before.[4] She had been ATF president for less than a month at the time of her announcement. If she were successful, her leadership of the national union would be very short-lived. Always considering her moves carefully, Jennie was honing her technique of standing as the 'obvious' candidate, who was 'asked' by others to stand for positions she wanted. Usually the pieces fell into place for her, thanks to a combination of her own efforts, working through supporters, and fortuitous circumstances. If the possibility of running for federation president had not come her way then, she would have pursued another option. As Simon Marginson put it:

I don't think she ever sat down and said 'I want to be president of the ACTU'. I think, frankly, that was beyond her reach when she started. But she's always had a next-step plan, and probably a two-step plan, and she's always preferred to work through others, drafting her and encouraging her and becoming the consensus candidate. She doesn't like a hard-fought, straight tussle. Some people thrive and conquer in a split—Jennie's the opposite. She likes consensus and likes to be the obvious candidate. She tries to put herself in a position where everyone's on side by the time the decision is made and generally that's been very successful.

Jennie's running mates in the November 1985 federation elections were Ray Cavenagh, who contested the deputy presidency, and Phil Cross, who contested the senior vice-presidency. Cavenagh recalled how they ran their campaign to unseat the Pagett team:

We didn't campaign too much in terms of an agenda. It was basically a question of leadership and Jennie was a wonderful article to sell. We started early in 1984, seeking the backing of most of the officers [of the federation] and had it sewn up by late 1984. We spent $30 000 on our campaign, sending mail-outs to every member. It was the most expensive campaign ever run—but we were able to raise the money very easily from donations and spent hardly any of our own. Jennie was a credible figure because she had tremendous influence in the decision-making bodies of the federation—that's where she shone.

Jennie easily defeated Ivan Pagett in the general ballot of State teachers by 14 238 votes to 6701, becoming the first woman president of the Teachers' Federation.[5] The voter turnout was only 35 per cent of the federation's 70 000 members. Cavenagh and Cross also defeated their opponents easily. Although elated, Jennie knew her first job when she officially assumed office in the new year was the serious business of repairing the union's poor standing with the State Government. A low point in her personal life—which was the cause of much emotional distraction—also dented the elation she was entitled to feel.

The timing of the push to make Jennie president of the NSW Teachers' Federation was prescient in significant ways other than the desire of her faction to defeat Ivan Pagett. Plans had been afoot to relocate the ATF's headquarters from Canberra to Melbourne. If Jennie had chosen to remain ATF president, she faced a move to Melbourne too. Yet if she and Simon Marginson stayed a couple, with Jennie as federation president in Sydney and Marginson as ATF research officer in Melbourne, they were destined to be apart once more in a long-distance relationship. It seemed that a pattern had been established. Just as her career leapt ahead when her marriage to Paddy crumbled, the overriding factor in Jennie's personal life at this point was her gradually disintegrating relationship with Simon Marginson. Imminent career relocations for both of them became a convenient time to consider separating—but not without huge emotional upheaval on both sides. Marginson had begun to have doubts about their relationship throughout 1985. His main problem was coping with Jennie's much higher status. He recalled: 'The relationship broke down because essentially Jennie couldn't give me enough space to [be] an equal and on the same plane as her. And the fact that I was four years younger was always a difficulty in that sense.'

Marginson knew Jennie well—they had been a couple for almost five years and lived together for three of them. Yet suddenly he realised to what degree their personal interests diverged and he began to have difficulty with Jennie's need to control the relationship. Motivated in part by her personal insecurity, Jennie demonstrated her controlling nature by structuring most of what they did as a couple. Early on, Marginson had accepted it. But he preferred to busy himself with academic-style work and over time came to resent Jennie exerting pressure to do what she wanted. For her part, Jennie admitted her need to control but found life with Marginson was in turn suffocating her. She recalled: 'I'm controlling, I want things my way, but I don't think I smother. I used to feel with him really, really smothered.' Increasingly unhappy, Jennie began questioning their life together too. She had found her early relationship with Marginson 'at a distance' more exciting than their existence together all the time. She noticed things that she had discounted previously—their age gap and different interests, and her own alienation from career and friends in Sydney.

As tensions worsened, the atmosphere at home between the couple appeared to be continually stressed. Marginson remarked to Jennie's mother that the only time Jennie was happy was when they saw her and Vladimir. The issue of marriage had come up, though not until late in the relationship and by then it was too late. Marginson did not want children, at that stage of his life, and Jennie expressed no interest in having a child either, although friends remarked how motherly and caring she was when she minded their children.

With their careers pointing them in different directions in any case, Marginson, despite doubts, instigated the break-up with Jennie. In late 1985, he moved to Melbourne with the ATF while Jennie, anticipating her move to Sydney, bought a flat in the inner-city suburb of Glebe and moved her possessions there. They agreed on complete separation of three months. Marginson came to Sydney in May 1986 to attend the funeral of Jennie's grandmother, Xenia, who had ended her days in a nursing home aged 89. Outwardly, Jennie had been keeping up appearances that she and Marginson were still a couple, perhaps in the slim hope of reconciliation. She did so at the funeral service, standing with Marginson and acting like couples do, so as not to add another burden to the grief of her mother, who liked Marginson and had hoped they would marry. In fact, the relationship had ended by then. Declining to attend the wake afterwards, Marginson went straight back to Melbourne on this 'catastrophic day'. Several months later he returned to Sydney to divide shared possessions. For Marginson, splitting their wine collection was the most painful aspect because of what it symbolised. He said:

> I remember coming up to her flat in Glebe after a couple of months, and we divided up the wine and I took a few other things away. I slept on the couch naturally, since we'd broken up. We found that we could be civil to each other and actually had a conversation for a couple of hours. Then you suddenly find yourself being civil and you think, what's going on here? And you clam up, both of you. It was very strange.

According to Marginson, Jennie went cold on him after he had resettled in Melbourne. She was no longer his boss as in Canberra. However, his job at the ATF and her position as the head of the ATF's largest union affiliate meant that she could exert political influence. When he flagged a possible run for the ATF presidency she refused to endorse him. He took four months' long service leave to get over the break-up and later quit the union for a successful career in academia. He recalled:

> When we fell out personally Jennie paid out on me politically, unfortunately, and it was pretty tough. I could survive it, but I was in my own backyard and Jennie was a big shadow in that backyard. She was upset with me personally and she withdrew support from me politically—but I didn't from her—and that was quite difficult. Those things happen when you mix up political and personal life.

Jennie recalled the relationship with Marginson as a significant part of her life. She denied interfering politically in his professional life after the split and said she had reached a point where she could no longer talk to Marginson, unable to rake over things. 'There was too much tension between us,' Jennie said. The break-up clearly scarred her, throwing her into emotional turmoil just as she made her greatest career step to date. In future she would look for a new way to control her personal life and not get hurt.

11

CAVALIER POLITICS

R elations between the NSW Teachers' Federation and the
State Government had sunk to an all-time low when Ivan
Pagett was federation president—but they improved immediately
when Jennie took over. She established a good working relationship with Rodney Cavalier, the Education Minister from the
ALP's Left faction, and the two of them remained, for the most
part, on friendly terms. Nevertheless, there were many disputes
with Cavalier in the two years that he was minister and she was
president—and sometimes sparks flew.

Even Cavalier's welcoming words to Jennie carried a twist,
the portent of tensions between them. In public remarks just
days before Jennie was officially due to start in the job in January
1986, Cavalier sent positive signals to the Teachers' Federation
about her leadership. But his praise proved too lavish and was
plainly patronising. In a burst of overstatement, Cavalier said that
Jennie was 'one of the most talented people in the entire trade
union movement', a 'great stateswoman' and 'one of the most
capable presidents since Barry Manefield'. He added: 'Much as
it might stick in her craw, she probably finds herself closer

politically to me than to the majority of her executive.'¹ Cavalier's last comment *did* stick in her craw.

Away on annual leave over summer at the time, Jennie was annoyed that his cheekiness about where her loyalties lay could do great damage to her credibility—even before she had started in the job. While wanting to improve relations with the Government, she could not afford to be regarded as a Labor stooge or alienated from her union executive (she was neither). When she returned a few days later, on the eve of starting work on the first day of the school year, Jennie pointed out publicly, albeit in a low-key fashion on Ray Cavenagh's advice, that Cavalier was wrong. She forecast at least one potential dispute over the transfer of a teacher.² The implications of Cavalier's comment about her 'political closeness' to him continued to gnaw at Jennie. Five months later, she again felt the need to address his initial comment about their 'political closeness' and to re-assert her independence. She said:

> That creates the impression that Mr Cavalier and I have known each other for a long time, and creates a mystique not based on any fact. I had only met him once and I don't know what makes him think we're on the same wavelength. I made it clear to him that I had more to do than point scoring in the press. He got used to that pattern over the last two years. A lot of the problems over the last two years may have been internal faction-fighting within the ALP, with Ivan being identified at one stage with the Right and Cavalier with the Left.³

Cavalier freely admitted that his original remark about Jennie's political closeness to him was mischievous. He recalled:

> What I did was deliberate mischief-making, which obviously struck home. The point of what I was saying was that she was surrounded by ratbags, she was a rational person, she was closer to me than them. I had only met her once before I became minister and that was only to say 'hello'. I certainly didn't know her, though I knew her politics, which she'd dramatically moderated since her Eureka

Youth League days. I had known Paddy George. I'd been tutored by Paddy at university—he was a fine fellow.

Among rumours about the supposed closeness between Jennie and Cavalier that began circulating in union and ALP Left circles was one that they were romantically entangled. The rumour was nonsense but had the potential to damage the political reputation of both of them. Beside being a minister, Cavalier was—along with the Miscellaneous Workers' Union national secretary Martin Ferguson—a leader of the moderate Left faction within the Steering Committee, the official Left faction of the NSW ALP. Attacks on Cavalier's credibility threatened not only his ministerial standing but also his position in a bitter internal political tussle he and Ferguson were waging with the party's industrial hard Left faction, led by fellow state minister Frank Walker and union leader George Campbell.

While Cavalier chose to laugh off the ill-founded gossip as the best way of handling it, Jennie vehemently denied it to friends, saying, 'when you're a single woman, people make up so many things about you that you wouldn't have time to do your job if they were true'. It became such a concern for her that she decided to put the matter to rest for good in her 'President writes' column in *Education*, the federation journal sent to all members:

> While obviously within our union there will always be political differences about policies and strategies which reflect in lively and open debate, the line has to be drawn when people who oppose the leadership resort to innuendo, rumour-mongering and personal vilification. At a personal level I reject completely the rumours of promised political patronage and sexual innuendo. Those who are involved in peddling such rubbish deserve to be condemned by all for not only are they aimed at damaging my credibility but the integrity of the federation as well.[4]

Cavalier was a socialist intellectual and astute minister, although his critics regarded him as overbearing and egotistical.

He argued that by the time Jennie assumed the presidency of the Teachers' Federation its influence in his education portfolio had waned. He welcomed the federation's agreement on matters but regarded it as no longer important. A significant clamp on available public funds for all government services meant that Cavalier decided to fight hard, not bow to the federation's claims as had happened in the past. He recalled:

> The most important thing to do was to destroy the claimant mentality. You had to stop the notion that in education resources were limitless and if [the federation] made a large enough clamour, bunged on a stunt here and there, then the Government would concede, throw money at the problem, and buy some industrial peace. We demonstrated, as each government since has done, that industrial peace is nice but it doesn't really matter because teachers are incapable of disrupting what you are going to do for any length of time.

In this climate, confronting such an obstinate minister, Jennie was bound to have disputes. A major concern to her was the decades-old issue of funding of government schools and her expressed worry that public education would become a residual system for the working class if the drift of students to non-government private schools continued.[5] However, she had to accept that the Federal Education Minister, Susan Ryan, had frozen funding levels for another two years and that in NSW, the State Government's resources were limited. If funding was a no-go area, the question of whose right it was to manage the education system was very much at the forefront. Jennie's first major difference of opinion with Cavalier was about his plan to introduce a form of teacher assessment. Ray Cavenagh said: 'It was ludicrous! Was the department going to interview 70 000 teachers?' Jennie persuaded Cavalier to drop the idea, after some argument, handing the federation an early victory. She recalled: 'I just said "it's not going to happen Rodney".'

Another, much more bitter conflict was not so easy to

resolve. Jennie inherited a chronic dispute with Cavalier about a mathematics teacher from Bega High School, Dick O'Neill, sacked for refusing to accept a transfer to a school that was not close to his home. After poor tactics by the federation including a series of pointless strikes, the dispute had become such a mess that it was seriously damaging the federation's capacity to contribute to other education policy matters.

Cavalier insisted upon his right to determine school-staffing formulas. The dispute festered throughout Jennie's first year in office. Finally, under a compromise negotiated by her and federation secretary, Vic Baueris, with Cavalier and Premier Barrie Unsworth, O'Neill accepted an offer to resume teaching. Jennie won O'Neill's reinstatement but Cavalier, not Jennie, won the principle. O'Neill had refused to be transferred to Bombala, about 130 kilometres from his home. Now he accepted a job at Narooma—50 kilometres from home.

Most of Jennie's negotiations with Cavalier did not revolve around salary disputes because the federation's subservience to the Accord had neutralised pay as an industrial issue. Teachers were among a majority of workers in NSW covered by state, not federal awards, so their minimum wages and conditions were determined by the State Industrial Commission. During the Accord years the State commission generally followed its national counterpart, the Australian Conciliation and Arbitration Commission, which ratified, with some modifications, the Accord deals agreed between the Federal Government and the ACTU for workers on Federal awards.

One pay dispute did arise between Cavalier and the federation, however, over the offsets that teachers would have to give in order to receive the so-called 'two-tier' national wage increase in 1987. Cavalier blocked a deal that had been approved by the Public Service Board before it was sent to the State commission for a formal tick because he believed 'it didn't add up' and that the board's president, former Labor Council boss John Ducker, had been too lenient. With backing from Premier Unsworth,

Cavalier held a meeting with Jennie to make his point. Also present were Ducker and John MacBean, the successor after Ducker and Unsworth as secretary of the NSW Labor Council. Cavalier recalled:

> Jennie took this as a colossal personal assault on her by me and just exploded several times. I said to MacBean, 'comrade, it's got nothing to do with this—I'm trying to balance a budget'. MacBean understood, Ducker understood—in fact he was amazed at it. They couldn't believe that she had taken it personally. It had nothing to do with personalities but she took it as a personal affront. An adviser who knew her said she had been like that since she was very young. He said, 'if you stand up to her she takes it personally'. I remember saying that she's never going to make it in the big time with that sort of attitude.

While not denying the incident, Jennie remarked that, 'the number of times I exploded would have been nothing compared with Rodney's reputation for exploding'. Despite such conflicts, she recalled that her dealings with Cavalier were generally intellectually stimulating and she liked him. Cavalier hailed the period when he was minister and Jennie was federation president as the most industrially peaceful since the early 1960s—there were none of the strikes while Jennie was in office that had characterised the federation's Pagett era. Cavalier also appointed Jennie to her alma mater, as a member of the University of Sydney senate, together with Gough Whitlam and Mitchell librarian Baiba Berzins. It had been many years since Jennie's first connection with the university and she accepted the appointment as an honour.

Being president of the Teachers' Federation placed extreme demands upon Jennie at times—but she was fortunate to have a strong back-up team behind her and was able to delegate most of the administrative work to Baueris, as the union's general secretary. Jennie thrived on the variety of her presidential role; all problems confronting the union crossed her desk and she was involved in every major decision. She started before 8.30 a.m. in the federation's Sussex Street office and it was not uncommon for her to finish late with meetings dragging on into the evening. While no day was the same, she often spent her mornings handling factional or political issues, involving plenty of office discussions with fellow officials. Through the day the telephone calls were relentless—contact with officers from the Education Department or with journalists wanting to speak to Jennie in her capacity as the federation's leading spokesperson. When industrial conflicts erupted into major public issues, Jennie's media work took precedence over other chores.

The standing joke inside the federation was that it 'held more meetings that any other union in the world'. There appeared some truth in the comment. Apart from daily meetings for running industrial issues, the federation convened fortnightly meetings of its executive, eight meetings a year of its larger council and an annual conference lasting three days. As president, Jennie chaired them all. Several times a year Jennie toured schools to meet teachers face-to-face in what were commonly called 'Royal Tours'. She was regularly invited to give after-dinner speeches. While accepting some, she handed this job to Ray Cavenagh when the pressure became too much.

While Jennie tried to re-assert the federation's influence on the NSW Government's education policy, she also made her way up the ladder in national union politics. She belonged to an influential group of left-wing union officials—all Sydney-siders and male apart from herself—known irreverently as the 'Kent Street Mafia'. The group came together after a Broad Left union conference held in Sydney in October 1986. Its early initiative was a 20-point plan that sought government intervention in the economy, including a specific policy for industry assistance. The ACTU executive endorsed the plan and incorporated it in *Australia Reconstructed*, an ACTU strategy document for industry authored chiefly by Laurie Carmichael and released the following year.

The Kent Street Mafia label stuck over time because the group held regular lunchtime meetings at the headquarters of the Building Workers' Industrial Union (BWIU) in Sydney's Kent Street to thrash out the direction the country's union Left should take. The BWIU headquarters was chosen as the venue because it was the home turf of the group's tribal elder, BWIU national secretary Tom McDonald.

What began as a larger collection of union leaders who belonged to the 'Mafia' soon reduced to a core of just four people: Tom McDonald, Peter Robson, George Campbell and Jennie George. Although small in number, this foursome wielded considerable influence in Sydney's union Left. They also developed strong friendships as a consequence of their regular meetings, although Jennie already had longstanding connections with McDonald—Helen Hewett was his sister and Cathy Bloch was once married to his brother Don.

All except Campbell were members of the ACTU executive. Jennie and the others were most identifiable as a voting bloc when they arrived in Melbourne for three-day meetings of the executive at ACTU House. They stayed in the same hotels and often dined together at the end of a day's proceedings at one of the many Italian restaurants dotted along Lygon Street in nearby Carlton. Aside from the bonhomie, the importance of the Kent Street Mafia was its generation of ideas on union policy. It became a powerful voice with the union Left in the late 1980s. The Left faction had a majority on the ACTU executive and so Kelty (originally from the Right but now non-aligned and labelled Centre) had to take notice.

Jennie's association with the Kent Street Mafia, and in particular the benevolent attitude McDonald demonstrated towards her, was a crucial factor in the next step of her union career. Since 1983 when Jennie was elected to the ACTU executive, recognition for women at the highest echelon of the union movement had advanced not one bit. Of a total of 31 people sitting on the executive at the start of 1987, she remained the only woman. It was clear that securing equality of representation for women in such a major union forum would never happen at this rate without a forced attempt by the leadership to redress the glaring imbalance. At the behest of Kelty, responding to pressure from women such as Jennie, the ACTU congress held in Melbourne in September 1987 imposed a policy of affirmative action creating three additional positions on the executive that had to be filled by women. Under a factional deal, the Right, the Left and the Centre factions each would choose one woman (the Centre being a euphemism for Kelty's choice).

The challenge for Jennie, already an experienced member of the ACTU executive, was to go the next step and become the first woman ACTU vice-president. A potential opening had arisen because of Kelty's plan to create not only the three new affirmative action positions on the executive but three new vice-presidential positions as well, taking the total number of vice-presidencies from three to six.

By virtue of her executive membership, Jennie was already the highest-ranking woman union official in the country. Winning one of the honorary vice-presidential positions would put her in the frontline of the ACTU's leadership team and shoot her to the top in union ranks—male or female. It would give her a platform from which to comment authoritatively on a wide range of national issues and would add weight to the speculation at the start of the year in a *National Times* newspaper article that 'come the nineties, becoming the ACTU's first woman president is not beyond her'.[6]

In the lead-up to the congress, the women's Left caucus within the union Left faction put forward Judy Bornstein as its preferred candidate for the faction's affirmative action candidate on the executive. The women's caucus was also the prime mover behind a campaign to elect the first woman ACTU vice-president—and Jennie in particular. Among Jennie's caucus backers were Bornstein, Cathy Bloch, Gail Cotton and Pat Giles. Jennie was enthusiastic but deep inside herself had what were familiar doubts to those who knew her. 'I was a bit diffident because I wasn't sure I could handle it,' she recalled.

Jennie was far from guaranteed winning one of the new vice-presidential positions in any case. According to the factional divide, her Left faction had a claim to two out of the total six. One Left position was held already by Dick Scott, national president of the AMWU, and the Left's new position was earmarked for Tom McDonald. If Jennie were to become a vice-president, either Scott or McDonald had to stand aside for her or she had to beat one of them in a ballot. A contest on the floor of the congress would have caused great discord and Jennie probably would have lost, lacking numbers in the male-dominated Left faction. McDonald had won his way onto the executive only two years earlier in 1985 after having lost unexpectedly to the BLF's Norm Gallagher in 1983. As the 'tribal elder', he had a reasonable expectation that the new vice-presidency was his, just as Scott expected to stay on.

Conscious of pressure from the Left women's caucus, McDonald chose to stand aside so that Jennie could be elected unopposed. But while he accepted the principle of a need for better female representation, McDonald did not believe a woman had a *right* to an ACTU vice-presidency. He also had reservations about some of the possible women candidates. He paved the way for Jennie only because he considered her an exception—though his patience was tested when her lack of confidence drew out deliberations to finalise her candidacy. McDonald recalled:

> Within the Left women's caucus there was a big push for a woman. The position I took was that I would not stand aside for *any* woman—I didn't believe in being paternalistic. But if a woman of quality stood, such as Jennie, then I would step aside. Jennie 'ummed' and 'aahed' about whether to accept it and she needed to be reassured. I said, 'For Christ's sake, make up your mind! I would like to see you stand'. There were a couple of people giving her a push.

McDonald's gesture enabled Jennie to score another first—elected unopposed as the first woman ACTU vice-president. The new position proved a huge boost to her prominence in the union movement and was another step towards giving due recognition to women. Its timing was also handy for Jennie's profile as she faced a general ballot of her union members for election to a second two-year term as president of the Teachers' Federation. This time, her election was relatively easy. One challenger, Jim O'Connor, a teacher from the country, nominated for her position but withdrew before the ballot. In what proved a mark of her immense popularity among teachers and ability to unite the federation, she was re-elected unopposed after years in which the presidency had been a hotly contested property.

It was little known that Jennie had already contested an ACTU vice-presidential position as long ago as the ACTU congress in Sydney in 1981—two years before she made it to the executive. Farcical circumstances surrounded her failed candidacy. Jennie's inner circle of women supporters dearly wanted her to win but that was not the faction's intention and none were allowed to vote for her. Jennie was number three on a Left ticket for the vice-presidency behind John Halfpenny, Victorian secretary of the AMWU, and Peter Cook, secretary of the West Australian Trades and Labor Council. The point of the exercise was a tactic by the Left faction to ensure Cook was elected. Jennie was asked onto the ticket in the hope that she might attract preference votes to Cook from congress delegates belonging to white-collar unions or who were not aligned with the rival Left–Right factions.

Swallowing her pride, Jennie accepted out of loyalty to her faction. She recalled, with amusement, telling all her supporters in the Left to observe strict factional discipline. Resisting all temptation, they had to vote Cook number one. Under no circumstances were they to vote for Jennie. Her friend Cathy Bloch remembered Jennie lamenting that she would 'get no votes at all and look like a goose' but was prepared to play along. Cook, who won the ballot as planned, recalled that Jennie received just one vote. Unless the result is understood for what it was, ACTU records convey the impression that Jennie's support base was hopeless.

12

THE METHERELL
CAMPAIGN

A sense of dread pervaded the Labor Party about the NSW State election due in March 1988. The Government would be twelve-years old by then and, according to opinion polls, the 'it's time' factor was a most compelling reason for voters to make a change. But other factors indicated that the Government was headed for electoral disaster on a colossal scale: Neville Wran's successor as premier, Barrie Unsworth, was deeply unpopular in the electorate; there was strong opposition in country seats to Unsworth's anti-guns policy; and there was a lingering smell of cronyism after Labor had been in power so long.

Jennie shared the sense of dread of Labor supporters. She was opposed to the economic rationalism of the Liberal Party's Pre-mier-in-waiting, Nick Greiner but especially disliked the alternative policy advocated by the State Opposition's education spokesman, Terry Metherell. What Metherell proposed was the most radical shake-up of education the State had ever seen. Jennie was encouraged by his promise to stop the drift of students to non-government schools but troubled by the detail of his plan, based on providing more 'choice' and redirecting existing funding.

To her, choice was a euphemism for privilege and redirecting funds was a cover-up for cuts to existing services.

Among changes Metherell proposed were trial dezoning of government schools, more selective schools for gifted children, the trial establishment of school councils similar to private school boards, a 5 per cent increase in funding to private schools, reintroduction of the School Certificate after Year 10 and re-introduction of the cane. Though opposed to many of these proposals, Jennie could not afford politically to campaign hard against Metherell in the State election run-up because many federation members disliked Rodney Cavalier and believed the Coalition could be no worse. Cavalier seemed headed in a similar direction to Metherell anyway, having advocated changes to the staffing formula of schools, promotion of teachers on merit and localised school management, among other things. Jennie's hope was that Metherell would be like former ministers who did not implement their stated policies. She underestimated her opponent.

It was not until after the election, which the Greiner-led Coalition won handsomely, that the full import of Metherell's plans became clear. As Metherell put it, he woke up the next day and decided to remake education. His first act as Education Minister, sacking the new, well-respected Director-General of Education, Gregor Ramsey, was a sign of things to come. Over the next few months, Metherell set in train cuts to 2500 teaching positions. He claimed that the State had an excess of teachers and required those in service to do extra classroom hours. Class sizes were to be increased. Promotion of teachers based historically on seniority was to be replaced by promotion based on merit. The city-based bureaucracy of the Department of Education was to be carved up and decentralised into regional directorates. Schools were to become responsible for their economic affairs under a new corporate management régime.

Much of the problem for Metherell in promoting his education reforms—many of which were worthwhile but were overlooked in the sea of opposition—stemmed from his refusal to adequately consult the main stakeholders, the organisations representing teachers, principals, parents and students. He also had a very quirky personal style. He was arrogant and eccentric—some opponents thought he was mad. Even colleagues described his social demeanour as 'detached' and 'spacey'. He was so absorbed in his own projects—or 'inner-directed'—that he easily drifted away if conversation descended into small talk.[1] He was also most authoritarian, refusing to tolerate any deviation from his opinions once he had made up his mind.

Metherell had been a student radical who swung back to conservatism. Fellow students from his university days recalled his eccentricity even then, such as wearing a duffle coat in summer and sometimes a kaftan. Highly intelligent and determined, Metherell had, according to Neville Wran, 'more degrees than a dog has fleas', among them a Ph.D. in town planning. He also had much experience from having worked for former Liberal Federal ministers John Carrick and Bob Ellicott.

Metherell sparked a minor controversy the year before he became a minister when he was caught nude, swimming backstroke, in the parliamentary swimming pool. But the embarrassing revelation did nothing to hinder his career. He had the confidence and friendship of the new Premier and pressed ahead with his vision for education.

The Metherell style, particularly his detachment, was bound to prove difficult for Jennie. She could be tough but her trademark in one-to-one dealings was to attempt to build a personal rapport. With Metherell, she got nowhere—but she never gained much opportunity to try. Greg Smith, an aide to Jennie as the federation's researcher, recalled the stress for her, as she led a delegation to see the minister soon after the election to discuss concerns about his education plans. According to Smith, after everyone had posed happily for media photographs and the doors were closed for privacy, Metherell suddenly changed. He recalled, 'Metherell sat, staring straight ahead, not engaging in the issues at all. It was extraordinarily difficult for Jennie. The meeting ended before it really began.'

Jennie also said Metherell generally behaved oddly towards her:

> When I'd meet Metherell, he couldn't cope with me at all. He'd be very, very strange. Rodney Cavalier, who was the Labor minister, used to have a lot of disputes with us as well. But we coped with one another because, while we didn't agree, we liked and respected one another. But Metherell—it was the first time in his life he had to cope with a strong, assertive, stroppy woman—and he just could not handle it. So I'd come and say 'I want to raise these issues on behalf of teachers', and he'd say, 'you've got no right to determine the agenda of our meeting'. The other thing about Metherell was that he treated me really badly in the public debate. He alleged that I lied to teachers—and the one thing I won't hack from anybody is that I lie.

Metherell recalled meeting Jennie in the lead-up to winning office and only once as Education Minister, not long after he was appointed. On both occasions Jennie led federation delegations to see him. What Metherell found peculiar about his ministerial meeting with Jennie—to which she referred above—was that she arrived with a handwritten speech that went on for many pages. She proceeded to read it all, like a formal address, rather than discuss a previously agreed agenda in a two-way conversation. After a while Metherell stopped her. Concerned that she was taking up the meeting time and disliking her tone, he asked if she had much more to go. She read on, prompting him to say there was not much point continuing if she was going to read a speech. He terminated the meeting.

Ray Cavenagh, Jennie's vice-presidential team-mate, said that Jennie's approach was not unusual for a first formal meeting with a minister and that Metherell was the difficult party. But advisers to Metherell who were in the room said he resented her taking an instantly confrontational stand, presenting a log of claims and making threats, couched in ideological rhetoric, even before he had had the chance to make any changes to the education system. They also argued that he had no qualms about negotiating with a woman such as Jennie, contrary to her claims. He promoted women to senior positions in his own department and planned, but never had the opportunity, to appoint the first woman Director-General of Education.

Regardless of who was the more discourteous, the one meeting she held with Metherell as minister made a lasting impression on Jennie. She said he could not cope with her, yet it appeared the reverse. She never led another delegation to see him and told former minister Rodney Cavalier soon after that she would never attend another meeting with Metherell. She told confidante Cathy Bloch a similar thing, saying how 'emotionally draining' she found Metherell. It was understandable that she hated to be treated with contempt or ignored. That Metherell got under her skin so easily after just one ministerial meeting, however, said much about Jennie's hypersensitivity and insecurity beneath her surface toughness. It was as though one short-lived meeting became a marathon. Single incidents such as this often became magnified in her mind to gigantic proportions, consuming too much of her emotional energy even if they also helped drive her to fight on. Ray Cavenagh made allowances for Jennie's emotional response. He said: 'You're dealing with a woman of passion—you're not dealing with a political animal.'

Indeed, Jennie's response to Metherell revealed a key feature of her leadership style. She was usually not a 'hands-on' practitioner of industrial relations in terms of being the person who sat through hours of negotiations to resolve tricky disputes and work out the minutiae of settlements. While keeping abreast of the issues, she tended to be the presidential figure, responsible for putting her authoritative stamp on deals cut by others and for giving the public face to those deals. She was not party to the heated exchanges that often occurred in the course of negotiating industrial arrangements. Consequently, on those rare occasions when she did become involved at the bargaining table she was not accustomed to the way the seasoned bargainers could switch with relative ease from apparent animosity to amicable relations in the aftermath. Jennie tended to take conflicts personally, sometimes with lingering resentments towards individuals, instead of accepting the stoushes as part of the process. So it was for her encounter with Metherell.

It was Jennie's lack of experience in hands-on industrial negotiations that would later attract critics from within the union movement when she joined the ACTU. Jennie, however, perceived her role differently, insisting that she *was* involved legitimately in industrial disputes—but at a level distinct from those who were responsible for haggling over detail.

Future negotiations Metherell had with the federation were conducted with Ray Cavenagh, federation secretary Vic Baueris and Jennie's other team-mate and eventual successor, Phil Cross. Jennie and Metherell remained strangers to each other but did communicate—courtesy of the very impersonal method of public comments in the media, where unkind words could be distorted or amplified several times over. Metherell accused Jennie of 'misleading' her members over class sizes and engaging in a 'campaign of lies'. She took it personally and hit back, offended at the challenge to her integrity.

The only other personal dealing Jennie had with Metherell was by letter, when he sacked her from her Labor-appointed seat on the University of Sydney senate just over halfway through her four-year term. Indeed the sacking appeared vindictive. Jennie challenged Metherell in court but lost.

A Teachers' Federation campaign led by Jennie against the Metherell education reforms began in earnest after a mini-Budget delivered by the State Government on 3 June 1988, less than three months after the Greiner election victory. Greg Smith, whose task was to analyse the Government's education expenditure for the federation and brief Jennie, was puzzled at first because no matter how many times he tried, the figures would not balance. It soon became clear that Metherell intended to gain budget savings necessary to fund the new measures by redirecting existing funds. The shortfall would be made up by reducing the number of teaching positions and increasing class sizes and the number of classroom hours supervised by teachers.

Smith was impressed at how quickly Jennie absorbed details of his briefing on the mini-Budget and was able to confront the media, answering questions authoritatively about its content. It was an ability that set her apart from others, he believed. After her initial public response, in which she called the mini-Budget 'the most devastating attack on public schools and TAFE in my recollection',[2] Jennie opened battle in earnest with Metherell the following week. She led the first 24-hour strike by teachers since the Government was elected, ostensibly over teachers' pay but also an opportunity to stage a protest against the changes.

The anti-Metherell climate worsened. Ever since she joined the Teachers' Federation, Jennie had advocated the need to develop good working relationships with natural allies, such as parents. It was a strategy she had used successfully as far back as her days teaching at Bankstown Girls' High School, when she brought parents on side in local campaigns against the Department of Education, calling for more teachers.

Jennie's enthusiasm for alliances, however, could be traced further back in her personal political history. It was reminiscent of the thinking of the Communist Party circles in which she mixed at the time of upheaval caused by the Soviet invasion of Czechoslovakia, when young reformers began urging for a coalition of Broad Left forces rather than relying on the Party alone. Now Jennie saw the opportunity to forge a high-level alliance with parent and community groups on an unprecedented scale to press her fight with Metherell.

The problem in the past, as she had acknowledged during disputes with Cavalier, was that wider support for the union had failed because of an inability to link the working conditions of teachers with learning conditions, or the quality of education provided to children. But Metherell's take-it-or-leave-it approach and the sheer complexity of what he proposed was a gift in terms of galvanising the alliance Jennie needed now.

Neither teachers nor parents fully understood Metherell's corporate managerial model, or some of its benefits, chiefly because he failed to market his vision. Suddenly both teachers and parents had the common link that Jennie needed. They both focused on the effect of increasing the cuts to teacher numbers, joining forces in outrage at the impact that cuts of more than 2000 teaching jobs over the next year would have in increasing class sizes and teaching hours and reducing subject choices.

Bringing parents on side was indeed a necessity if the campaign was to be sustained or have any hope of succeeding. For all her enthusiasm, however, Jennie was not acquainted with the people who led the parent organisations. That meant she had to rely on Ray Cavenagh, the federation's vice-president, to do the groundwork. Cavenagh explained, 'Her contacts were good in the union movement but that was all. I did it because I knew them from having spent four years on the Education Commission with them.'

Thanks to Cavenagh, Jennie gained important support from Shirley Berg, president of the Federation of Parents and Citizens' Associations and Janet Maher, president of the Federation of School Community Organisations. When Berg stepped aside midway through the campaign, her successor, Lesley McPaul, remained on side. Metherell assisted ably in keeping Jennie's alliance intact. He prevented any sympathy that the leaders of the two parents' groups might have had for him by branding them Jennie's 'alter ego'.

The fight against Metherell's reforms became extremely intense and highly personalised, in effect a 'hate Metherell' campaign across the State. He received death threats and complained of personal vilification, but still braved protests during school visits and public meetings. Wherever he went he was met by angry demonstrators carrying placards and shouting 'Metherell out'.

Less than three weeks after the statewide strike of teachers led by Jennie in June, Metherell still shunned the Teachers' Federation but appeared to moderate his style, at least temporarily, by inviting community response to spending on special education over the next four years.[3] However, it was too late.

The political damage that Metherell was causing the Government worried Premier Greiner. In early July, Greiner removed his Education Minister's control over a range of controversial education changes and handed them to the policies and priorities committee of Cabinet on which Metherell did not sit.[4] Jennie, along with leaders of the other groups, welcomed Greiner's decision, but stressed it made no difference if the Government policies remained the same. She said, 'This is a recognition by the Government of the turmoil in education. We need to start again on everything, with proper input from the union. We have one desire—to start all over again and go back to step one.'[5]

The uncompromising stand by Jennie was admirable for the way she stood by her principle of absolute opposition. She was equally as stubborn as Metherell. As a strategy, however, Jennie was taking an immense risk. She raised the stakes too high by leaving no room for anything but a complete backdown by the Government. When the Government refused to change direction at all, and Metherell remained the driving force in education policy despite some stripping of his powers, it was Jennie who had no room to manoeuvre. Her choices were either to retreat or radically escalate the campaign.

The inspiration for the next step of the campaign was all hers. Jennie drew on her own experience of demonstrations during student activist days protesting against the Vietnam War to conceive what she hoped would be the turning point of the campaign against the Metherell reforms—a giant rally in the open space of Sydney's Domain.

Her plan was to hold a strike of teachers across NSW timed

to coincide with the opening day of the next session of State Parliament on 17 August. Teachers, parents and students from as far as Bega in the south, Coffs Harbour in the north and Mudgee in the west would be asked to join those from metropolitan schools. People in regional centres too far to make the trip would hold local rallies. After speeches in the Domain, ideally located behind MPs' offices attached to the historic Parliament House building, Jennie proposed to march into Macquarie Street to the front of Parliament House and demand to see Metherell.

As always, Jennie had her doubts. But she hoped that a show of public anger on a large scale—in front of the politicians' own eyes—would force the Government to accept that opposition was widespread in the community and that Metherell's education agenda should be reconsidered. To put her plan into action, she needed the support of the federation's executive, which she gained easily. Ray Cavenagh recalled: 'If Jennie had an idea, we'd go along with it. There was no way anyone was going to say it was a stupid idea.'

On the morning of the rally, Jennie was nervous about how big the turnout would be. Before joining demonstrators she went to the ABC Radio studios in William Street, with several federation officials, for an interview with 2BL host Margaret Throsby. The interview over, she and her companions walked the short distance to the Domain rather than take a taxi so Jennie could prepare herself mentally for the day ahead and survey the size of the crowd as they neared.

The sea of people that greeted Jennie was beyond her expectations. It was a huge crowd of teachers, parents and children, the biggest city demonstration in more than a decade, shouting 'Metherell out' and waving placards such as 'Come back Rodney, all is forgiven'. Reliable estimates put the numbers at 50 000. Optimists in the federation thought it was closer to 100 000. The strike also was a success—a record participation as 94 per cent of the State's 70 000 teachers walked out.

Jennie knew that she was riding high that day. But she was suddenly struck by the difficulty she would have trying to surpass this high point in the campaign. 'How do we top this?' she said quietly, as she headed for the stage to join the guest speakers. To cheers and applause, Jennie told the crowd that the rally was just the start of a long battle to prevent public education being dismantled. After about two hours of speeches, she led the crowd on a march into Macquarie Street towards the Parliament House gates—locked and guarded by police four deep. The crowd—chanting 'we want Terry'—did see the man they wanted but only briefly.

At the appointed hour, Metherell made the traditional opening-day walk along the balcony facing Macquarie Street from the Legislative Council to the Legislative Assembly with Premier Greiner and other MPs. Greiner turned, for a moment, to look at the crowd. Metherell did not and refused demands to address them.[6] Colleagues had advised him against it in case the demonstration became unruly.

Teachers did not win their fight on 17 August, or afterwards. Greiner stood by Metherell, saying there was nothing to negotiate with teachers and the reforms would proceed. However, the sheer size of the protest made ridiculous Metherell's claim that the community was swinging behind him in the debate and put him under even more political pressure.

The next day's editorial in the *Sydney Morning Herald* captured precisely Jennie's dilemma with its heading, 'After the strike, what next?'. Some in the federation suggested to her that another rally on the same scale should be run the following year—but she rejected the idea. Instead she opted for a low-key but possibly more effective campaign of meeting local members of Parliament to press the federation's case. She also advocated a political protest at the next election, although it was not due until 1991. The teachers' campaign went off the boil the following year, despite Metherell doggedly pressing ahead with his changes.

The campaign against Metherell was a huge boost to Jennie's public profile. She received media attention like no president before her, such were the daily demands for her to comment on the Education Minister's policies and the latest turns in the debate.

The first publicity of note in her career had been her election as the first woman secretary of the federation in 1979, when she happened to share front-page space in the *Sun Herald* newspaper—interestingly with Bob Hawke as he agonised about quitting the ACTU and running for Parliament. She also received a small burst of publicity when she became the first woman to join the ACTU executive in 1983. But now she was a well-known public figure—though mainly in NSW—as she gave interviews or was quoted frequently in the electronic and print media.

Jennie found the constant attention demanding but celebrity had its positive side and privately she enjoyed it (providing she was mentioned in a favourable light). She poured over newspaper clippings to check how she was perceived. Positive reports were a boost to her ego and helped assuage her niggling lack of self-assurance. Highly sensitive to criticism, however, she seethed over reported comments from political opponents that she regarded as harsh or a challenge to her integrity. Jennie kept a mental note of the sources and authors of articles that she believed were unfairly slanted. She blackballed journalists she believed had a track record of crossing her, by declining to return their telephone calls.

During this period, Jennie also learnt the politician's art of manipulating the media by speaking to favourite journalists and planting stories if it suited her cause. Although she remained suspicious of a number of journalists and questioned the motives behind their queries—in part a throwback to her leftist orientation that the press was an arm of the capitalist class—she socialised with others, comfortable in their company once she had their measure.

Jennie's love of partying matched perfectly the late-night milieu of industrial relations journalists, as she joined them drinking and smoking for hours after union gatherings. Typical occasions were quarterly meetings of the ACTU executive, normally held in Melbourne. Jennie formed a lasting friendship with one particular journalist, the *Sydney Morning Herald* education writer, Anne Susskind, which also proved very handy in communicating the federation's point of view, even if the newspaper's editorials backed the Metherell reforms.

The positive side to media publicity for Jennie was that it aided her standing in the union movement should she decide to shift outside her established union domain. Her public recognition was essentially confined to NSW and limited to her role in the federation. But she was acquiring something of a national profile—outside the teaching profession—as a member of the ACTU executive and as the ACTU's recently elected first woman vice-president.

Personally the campaign against Metherell exacted a great toll on her. She had been immersed in her work but was also living on an emotional edge, coping with the stress of the job and carrying with her a deep unhappiness. She still suffered residual grief from the loss of Paddy George and the break-up with Simon Marginson.

Thinking ahead, she did not want to be in her present position for much longer. The pace was hectic and Metherell showed no sign of relenting. If she left soon, she could do so with her record of success appearing intact. Lingering in the presidency meant that her record could be tarnished with failure. She lacked the endurance to last the distance until what appeared to be the first practical opportunity to vanquish Metherell's agenda—the election of a future Labor Government, possibly in the State poll due in 1991 but more likely (considering Greiner's majority) the next due in 1995.

Privately Jennie *had* been working on plans for a career after the federation. In May 1988, before the anti-Metherell campaign had begun in earnest, Jennie had discussed a career move with the ACTU secretary, Bill Kelty, and Martin Ferguson, national secretary of the Miscellaneous Workers' Union. Of the two, she was friendlier with Ferguson and regarded him as an important factional ally.

Jennie and Ferguson had known each other from their days in the left-wing minority facing a Right-controlled Labor Council in NSW. They continued to have good relations as part of the younger generation on the ACTU executive, latterly both of them as ACTU vice-presidents. Ferguson was an influential figure in the Left as the national leader of one of the country's biggest unions. He was also a senior figure in the ALP's left-wing faction in NSW, the Steering Committee, as the leader of the more moderate of its two competing internal factions. From Jennie's career standpoint, Ferguson's influence was relevant because he had been anointed by Kelty to succeed Simon Crean as the next ACTU president when Crean made his anticipated move to parliamentary politics. Ferguson was well-placed to help Jennie move from the Teachers' Federation to a full-time position in the broader union movement if she wanted to make the leap.

Informal discussions involving Kelty and Ferguson about Jennie's future happened at an unlikely place, Surfers Paradise on Queensland's south coast, chosen as the venue for an away-from-home meeting of the ACTU executive. All were staying at the Ramada Hotel, their accommodation arranged by contro-versial businessman Eddie Kornhauser, a friend of Crean's and Hawke's. The proposal Kelty and Ferguson put to Jennie was that she should consider a move to Melbourne to become the deputy director of the Trade Union Training Authority (TUTA), an organisation under the ACTU's influence to train union officials that was started with public funding by the Whitlam Government.

Although Jennie was just five months into her second term as federation president and had the Metherell battle ahead of her, she warmed to the idea. Moving to Melbourne would require serious thought, however, because it meant leaving behind in Sydney her inner circle of friends and her mother.

As the year ended, the Metherell campaign having peaked after the Domain rally, Jennie revived the issue of her future. It was agreed in further talks with Kelty and Ferguson that she would not stand again for federation president at the end of 1989. The plan was for her to leave the federation mid-year to join TUTA as deputy, readying her to take over as head of the organisation when its national director, Ken Stone, departed in three years.

Taking the TUTA job meant that Jennie would have to quit not only the federation but also her elected positions on the ACTU executive and as an honorary ACTU vice-president. She would be removed from the hub of union activity at ACTU headquarters in Melbourne's CBD, instead working at TUTA offices in outlying St Kilda. Her public life, it seemed, was about to end.

Jennie waited until February 1989 to announce that she intended to quit union politics, giving plenty of notice so her intended successor as federation president, Phil Cross, could run a strong campaign for elections later in the year. She gave the story of her plans to major newspapers on the same day, her fullest reflections reported by Anne Susskind in the *Sydney Morning Herald*:

> Everyone knows when it's time for them to go. The problem is the job is so encompassing. There's no time for the ordinary things in life which other people take for granted, like having a free weekend to go to the theatre, read books and go to the beach. There's not very much anonymity. People who don't know you can make all kinds of judgments about you. They can make personal innuendoes, can call you—in a pejorative sense—a mad militant and accuse you of manipulating students and attacking Metherell because you want a political career. That hurts. People can ascribe all sorts of motives to you without knowing you or giving you the benefit of the doubt. I suppose it's the price you pay in jobs like this. I have, of course, regrets about leaving the people I've worked with, but I have no regrets about unfulfilled ambitions. I have been

secretary and president of the largest State union and there are no
other high-flying ambitions waiting to be filled.[7]

Most interesting of all, Susskind also reported that Jennie
ruled out the possibility of 'going higher in the trade union
movement, putting paid to speculation that she would aim for
the ACTU presidency, should Mr Simon Crean decide to run
for Parliament'. There was no such speculation because, as Jennie
knew, Kelty had ensured that Martin Ferguson was in line to
succeed Crean as ACTU president. Before Susskind's report, a
few newspaper articles had speculated that Jennie could be the
first woman ACTU president but no-one holding influential
positions in the union movement was floating the idea seriously.

The reality was that factional wars between the Left and
Right, continuing despite Kelty's efforts to bridge the two sides,
prevented someone attached to the hard industrial Left, such as
Jennie, gaining necessary support. She also lacked the standing,
at this point of her career, to be handed what was still regarded
by many as the principal position in the Australian union movement. These obstacles were in addition to any she might face
because of her gender.

In 1989, the suggestion was especially academic when Ferguson, Kelty's consensus nominee from the moderate Left, was
still to take up the ACTU presidency and stood to remain there
for many years. None of this is to say that raising in print the
idea that Jennie could be a future ACTU president hindered her
cause (apart from creating potential strain with Ferguson). Indeed
it helped sew the seeds of an idea in the minds of the union
movement's powerbrokers—for some point in the future—if the
right pieces fell into place.

Like many of Jennie's celebrations in the big moments of
her life, her farewell as federation president on 26 June 1989
was a huge gathering. She made a very warm and endearing
speech to 400 colleagues and friends in the function room of
Randwick Racecourse, recalling the highs and lows of her career

so far. Ray Cavenagh, her loyal deputy, prompted mirth aplenty with a performance of what he dubbed 'The Jennie George Leavin' Blues'. He recalled later, 'There was regret that she was leaving but we understood here was someone with a bigger future'.

Among the guests Jennie had asked to speak at her farewell was Bill Kelty. It was a surprise choice for many in the room. Kelty had worked with Jennie on the ACTU executive and had just arranged her TUTA job—but the two were not close. While tensions had eased, they had clashed over the years.

Kelty was unpopular in the federation because of teachers' dislike of the Accord—in particular the two-tier wage system he designed in 1987 that had forced them to accept productivity offsets in return for a pay rise. Jennie had penned a series of editorials in the federation's journal officially rejecting the two-tier system. When it was imposed on teachers, she labelled the offsets 'unacceptable'.[8]

In his speech, Kelty turned the situation to his advantage. He paid a handsome tribute to Jennie and declared that her move to TUTA was 'a first step, perhaps there will be other steps'. He also took the opportunity to win the support of his sceptical audience (some of whom booed) by resorting to humour at his own expense. He said:

> I have some very clear instructions here in terms of the invitation I got. It said that 'the fee is $30 but for you it is offset—you don't have to pay because you're a guest. The productivity offset for speaking at Jennie's farewell is $3 a minute'. I thought that was a very subtle way for Cathy Bloch to say, one, well, 'you got your meal for nothing, and remember that'; two, 'remind us that I was responsible for the two-tier system'. Also to say that 'you're only going to talk for ten minutes'.

Jennie's time in the federation leadership—one term as secretary and almost two as president—amounted to six-and-a-half years of service. Collectively she had more than paid her dues with 20 years' involvement in the union's politics. The highpoint of her presidency was undoubtedly the Domain rally. While it did not win the war, the rally was crucial in the fight against Metherell's reforms and was her foremost accomplishment as president in the way she was able to unite public sentiment. Metherell pressed ahead with his changes but he never recovered politically.

Metherell was not long in the job after Jennie quit—but his demise had nothing to do with his education agenda—or Jennie. He resigned as Education Minister in July 1990 when he was charged over making a false statement on his tax return. Later he was convicted and fined almost $12 000.

In a cataclysm of events, Metherell was then directly involved in the downfall of Premier Greiner. When Greiner refused to give him another ministry after the 1991 election, Metherell shocked colleagues by resigning from the Liberal Party and sitting on the cross benches as an Independent, claiming the Government had lost its way and Greiner 'offered no clear vision'. Greiner's numbers in Parliament were precarious after he had almost lost the 1991 election (in large part because of community disquiet over education).

When he offered Metherell a government job in order to secure Metherell's resignation from Parliament so his seat of Davidson could return to the Liberal Party in a by-election, Greiner was found 'corrupt' by his own creation, the Independent Commission Against Corruption, and forced to resign. While an appeal court later overturned the corruption finding, it was too late. Greiner had already resigned.

Martin Ferguson had first alerted Jennie to Metherell's tax charges and resignation when he sent her a fax of newspaper reports while she was on holiday in Vanuatu. From afar, she relished Metherell's fall with a sense of justice in view of her experience with him. The campaign she had led was also instrumental in Metherell's Liberal Party successor, Virginia Chadwick, adopting a more conciliatory stance towards the Teachers' Federation and agreeing to restore most of the 2500 teaching jobs Metherell had slashed from government schools.

One of Jennie's final acts as federation president was to secure an important concession for teachers that struck at the heart of her early reservations, and those of most federation members, about the ACTU Accord. As Jennie predicted, teachers had not done well out of the Accord.

The initial Accord concept of full wage indexation—compensating workers for increases in the CPI with equivalent pay rises—was abandoned in favour of sustained wage restraint as the Government forced Australians to come to terms with opening the economy to world markets. Accord deals hatched by Kelty and his increasingly close friend, Treasurer Paul Keating, centred on small percentage pay rises or flat dollar amounts, ratified by the Conciliation and Arbitration Commission. These rises provided great assistance to low-income earners but did little for teachers, among others.

It was frustration with this system that led to an almighty conflict between the domestic airline pilots and the Government, ending in disaster after pilots quit their jobs during a bitter industrial conflict and most failed to win them back.[9]

The Teachers' Federation did keep the Accord faith, despite serious misgivings, but was buoyed by a deal Jennie managed to cut with Kelty in 1989 to give teachers an exemption from the latest round of 6 per cent rises that prompted the pilots to rebel. Teachers were among several 'special cases' Kelty sanctioned while he ensured that overall wage restraint continued. The deal involved Kelty's support for readjusting base pay rates so that teachers could receive much more than the maximum allowed to most workers.

It took until the following year, after Jennie had departed, before the State Industrial Commission handed down its decision on the federation's claim and the teaching profession in NSW saw any benefit. Teachers gained a significant boost to pay with rises in a range of 12–16 per cent. For executive positions of head teacher or higher, the range was a massive 21–44 per cent. These rises left teachers considerably better off compared with the general workforce. As if it were a parting gift, they had Jennie to thank for persuading Kelty to relax the Accord's rules.

13

MELBOURNE CALLING

It was a recurrent theme of Jennie's that she could not have achieved what she had if she also bore the responsibility of raising a family. She believed it was easier for her to pursue a high-powered career and make the pioneering gains that led the way for other women, without children of her own. Easier her rise may have been—but she also thought that having a high-powered career had sabotaged her personal life. When Jennie became president of the ACTU, she articulated in stark terms the choice she believed women faced in life. They were the same kind of words she had used since having led the Teachers' Federation to explain why she had no long-term partner and no family:

> I've said this to lots of women—and it was actually a quote that had some resonance in the movement for young women—don't pretend. You can do anything, but you can't have everything. So you have got to make really hard decisions in your life. If you want to succeed publicly then that comes at a big personal sacrifice. I mean, my public life has meant that personal relationships have gone by the board. Personal relationships that were meaningful

haven't been able to be sustained. So you can't be president of the ACTU and have a family and children. You can have one or the other.

The difficulty confronting women such as Jennie cannot be understated, nor can the example she set in providing a great public boost to women in unions and the women's movement as a whole. The men who preceded her usually had supportive wives, possibly not engaged in paid work, to be primary caregivers to their children. They also did not have the fear that potential partners might have of a woman like Jennie, outwardly strong, not afraid to express what she thought and the more dominant figure in a relationship—qualities that would scare some men away. All the same, Jennie's black-and-white assessment that 'you can have one or the other'—either career or family—was not helpful to the cause of other feminists striving for equality in a male-oriented world.

The implication of what she said was that women would never make significant gains unless they were prepared to make sacrifices in their lives, equivalent to her own, that most were not prepared to make: to forgo deep personal relationships and any idea of having children. Yet she had never put her views to the test and her strident declaration reinforced old obstacles to women rather than tearing them down.

In doing so, Jennie also ignored the success stories of other Australian women in high-profile, high-pressure positions (and thousands of anonymous women struggling with families and jobs for that matter). These women had found the going tough in a man's world but nevertheless—through good management or supportive partners or both—did their best to strike a balance between professional careers and family lives. Some of them had reached great heights, such as Mary Gaudron, Cheryl Kernot, Carmen Lawrence, Joan Kirner, Ros Kelly, Quentin Bryce, Pat O'Shane and Ita Buttrose. They had achieved, in varying circumstances and under stress, what Jennie said could not be done.

Even in Jennie's world of union politics, some of her women friends had combined a career and family successfully at a senior level. Pam Allan, who worked with Jennie in the Teachers' Federation, entered State Parliament and had her second child while she was Minister for Environment. Anna Booth had a child while she led the Clothing and Allied Trades Union, although she later stepped aside and declined to move to the ACTU citing family responsibilities. Meredith Burgmann moved out of academic union politics in NSW and into an Upper House seat in Parliament while raising her son, Paddy (named after Jennie's late husband). Burgmann stressed, however, that national politics, involving stays in Canberra away from home was particularly difficult for women, and a transition to Federal Parliament was impossible for her because of her 'small child'.

Jennie had made sacrifices, as she said. However, attributing her inability to sustain relationships with men to the personal sacrifice of her 'public life' was, in the end, an excuse to explain away the failure of those relationships. Her relationships with Paddy George, Simon Marginson and others had not failed just because of her public life. Paddy had some problems adjusting to her high-powered career but their marriage breakdown was like many others where couples drift apart. Her relationship with Jack Mundey never worked because he would not commit to her. Her split with Simon Marginson was caused partly by his inability to cope with her as the senior figure in an unequal relationship but also by other factors related to their conflicting personal make-ups and increasingly divergent interests revealed while living together in Canberra. Still other relationships did not work for an entirely different reason—distance.

While Jennie was certainly very unlucky in her relationships with men, she adopted a pattern after her break-up with Marginson (and indeed for part of that relationship too) in which she formed relationships with men who lived in other states or even other countries. Her friends joked, affectionately, about Jennie's complex love life and particularly about these 'long-distance relationships'. They were emotionally tortured affairs in which Jennie met several men over the years from distant locations and continued a romance by occasional meetings but mainly by correspondence. Some were more cerebral than real. She spent more time talking to her close circle of women friends about the maybes of these romances than engaging in their physical enjoyment.

The beauty of a romance from afar for Jennie, though she was reluctant to admit it, was the convenience of not having to become too involved. She could maintain an obscure form of control over the relationship and keep open her options, avoiding a commitment that might leave her hurt, as she had been in the past.

The men were also at such a distance and the meetings so infrequent that fidelity was not really an issue—she was free to pursue casual liaisons at home—despite passionate words written in reams of letters sent back and forth between them. The letters were a romantic throwback to the innocent days of Jennie's youth, reminiscent of correspondence she shared with Paddy before they married when he was often absent on Communist Party business. Above all, from the start, Jennie's long-distance relationships with men were fraught with difficulty and doomed to failure. She acknowledged as much when she said of them:

> Does this indicate that I'm scared of commitment? I've reflected on that a few times and thought, 'why is it that what's available and achievable is not as interesting as that which is a bit distant and romantic?'

Among the most notable of these long-distance romances was her affair with Joses Tuhanuku, secretary of the Solomon Islands' General Workers' Union, whom she met at a conference of unions from the South Pacific Basin held in Fiji in 1986. Jennie had not fully recovered emotionally from her recent break-up with Simon Marginson but was attracted to this bright, good looking young man as soon as they met. It was a whirlwind liaison, away from the realities of life, and each returned to their respective homes after the conference. The romance continued in an old-fashioned way—with an abundance of letters. The Solomon Islands was too far from Australia for frequent visits considering the cost and professional demands placed on each of them: apart from talking on the telephone, Jennie and Tuhanuku managed to see each other only every six months. All the same Jennie remarked, that 'Joses was quite a serious relationship'. Eventually distance defeated them. Neither was prepared to move so they could be together permanently and they drifted apart. Tuhanuku married a noted Australian journalist, Mary Louise O'Callaghan, but he and Jennie remained good friends.

Jennie's other significant long-distance romance was with Dimitri Boltovskoy, a professor of marine biology from Argentina whom Jennie met during 1988—the year of her Metherell fight. They met through family connections when Boltovskoy made a visit to Sydney for a scientific conference. Of Russian descent like Jennie, he was the son of one of her mother's schoolteachers who had emigrated from Russia to Buenos Aires after the war. Their Russian ancestry and family link helped create a bond between them.

Boltovskoy's stay in Sydney was brief and they met only once after that, when Jennie had a Buenos Aires stopover while in South America to attend an international union conference in Venezuela in 1992. Yet remarkably, stretching across those years, Jennie and he conducted an intense love affair of sorts, entirely by correspondence, in dozens of lengthy handwritten letters, many expressing strong feelings and desires that were sadly never consummated. While deep down Jennie harboured no expectations of Boltovskoy, she kept his voluminous letters. 'It was not really a relationship—more an infatuation,' she said in hindsight. By their second meeting, the communication between them had slowed and the romance had lapsed: Boltovskoy had met someone else—soon to have his child—and Jennie dined with the two of them.

Jennie was never fiercely driven by the need to have children. Nevertheless, she did go through a period in her late thirties, like many women, wrestling with the idea of having a permanent man in her life and having a child with him. Her maternal instincts were stirred as she watched her friends' children enter the world and grow and she was conscious of menopause approaching. When the opportunity passed her by, she did not dwell too long with regret. She tended to live very much in the present and immersed herself in her gregarious lifestyle. If she was lonely without an intimate relationship, or if her thoughts turned to her childless state and the lack of a potential father, she preferred to go out and party rather than stay at home and mope. She talked out her feelings with close friends rather than bottle them up. Publicly, she clung to her rationalisation that she could not have reached her career heights but for her sacrifice.

In the first few years of Jennie's marriage to Paddy, Natasha had nagged her about when she might have a grandchild. 'Soon, Mum, soon,' she said at first. When Natasha spoke to Paddy about it, he reassured her that 'there is plenty of time'. Jennie later told her mother that Paddy had misgivings and their dog, Whisky, was the closest they were likely to come to having a child. Lymphoma had claimed the life of Paddy's father and he was worried, according to Natasha, about the heredity risk if Jennie were to conceive his child. It was too late when their marriage collapsed and Paddy died from cancer too. Paddy's mother, Gwen, was also sorry she had no grandchild:

> They didn't have any children of course. I think it was because Jennie was pretty active in the Teachers' Federation at the time and Paddy was very involved in all sorts of things. They just hadn't got round to becoming domesticated and thinking 'I'll stay home and have a child'—unfortunately. I'm sure that's what happened.

Having children was not a big issue during Jennie's relationship with Marginson either. She did not express a strong desire to have a child with him during their time together but it seemed pointless discussing the matter. Marginson was more than just reluctant about children. Before they met, he had had a vasectomy. Jennie recalled:

> I was with Simon in my early to late thirties. I can't ever recall being serious about having children at that part of my life. There's not much point in having regrets—you can't do anything about it. I'm sure, though, that the older I get the more I am going to miss—particularly after Mum dies—that I don't have a family. I think the older in life you get you would look back and think it was all really worthwhile. But there's no point crying over lost opportunities. If I really wanted to have a family and a settled existence I wouldn't have chosen to be a union official. I mean, you make those choices. It's hard enough in this job meeting somebody and sustaining a relationship. I have met lots of people over my time but sustaining something is different. You're never in one city long enough to make a go of it.

The irony for Jennie was that after she and Marginson parted, the prospect of having a child that appeared physically denied to her by his vasectomy changed quickly for him. He married and had the vasectomy reversed so he and his new wife could have a baby. At the end of her relationship with Marginson, Jennie was close to 40 and no permanent man in her life was on the horizon. She talked through the issue of having children a number of times with friends such as Helen Hewett and Pam Allan. 'There were a few times in her life when Jennie thought "should I?"' recalled Hewett. By her mid-forties, however, Jennie was resigned to the idea that she would remain childless. In place of any of her own, she loved her friends' and neighbours' children and played out the maternal side of her nature when in their company. She was particularly devoted to her godchild, Peta Hewett, daughter of friends Helen and Rex. The bond was founded partly on an emotional link with Paddy—Peta was born six weeks before he died and so in Jennie's mind her birth was a strong symbol of life. It was something wonderful to reflect upon from that otherwise awful time. As Peta grew, Jennie shared in her godchild's development and established a close rapport with her, although their early relationship was the source of much amusement in the Hewett household. Helen Hewett recounted how she asked Jennie to mind Peta as a baby one night so she could attend an evening lecture:

> Jennie didn't have much experience with very young babies. I thought I'd shown her how to put a nappy on but when I got home you should have seen it—there was shit all over the place. It was hilarious! Jennie said, 'I tried everything and it just didn't work. So I just left her there on the change table and watched her'. Peta was lying there happy as anything.

In her own family life Jennie focused all her energy on her mother Natasha, to whom she remained extremely close. She was sorry to leave her mother behind when she moved from Sydney to Melbourne in mid-1989 for her new job at TUTA, but they spoke daily on the telephone and Jennie made semi-regular return visits. It took little time for Jennie to find somewhere to live. She bought a flat in Elwood, a small middle-class suburb on Port Phillip Bay very close to her place of work at TUTA's national headquarters in St Kilda.

Establishing new friends in Melbourne came easily to someone as gregarious as Jennie. And she also had the opportunity to re-establish her closeness to two of her oldest friends. In a remarkable coincidence, Rex and Helen Hewett, next-door neighbours in the semidetached house at Haberfield, followed her to Melbourne soon after when Rex was appointed TAFE secretary of the renamed Australian Education Union. They moved into the same street as Jennie in Elwood and became a source of vital personal comfort to her. 'It was sort of like a regrouping of the family,' said Helen.

Although appointed officially as TUTA's deputy director, Jennie's brief from Kelty was to breathe new life into the organisation and become its driving force. TUTA's heyday as a government-funded authority established during the Whitlam years to train union officials had passed. It was considered to be in a rut and needed overhauling if it was to be relevant in the nineties. As Jennie said: 'TUTA needed a new direction—it was floundering a bit.' Tom McDonald, the senior Left figure and BWIU national secretary who took an interest in Jennie's career, said she succeeded in revitalising the organisation.

There were also other compelling reasons, however, to install Jennie there. Located at St Kilda she was away from the hub of union activity and effectively sidelined. But she was still within easy reach if the ACTU leadership decided to call her back to the fray and give her a full-time position among its ranks. Any shift to the ACTU would rely on Bill Kelty's blessing, given that he was now at his zenith as the union movement's most powerful figure. Kelty had not been close to Jennie in the politics of the ACTU throughout the 1980s. They had disagreed on issues ranging from the Accord to Labor's failed attempt, backed by Kelty but opposed by Jennie, to introduce a national ID card in 1987.

There was no vacancy in the upper echelon of the ACTU and no prior arrangement to 'warehouse' Jennie at TUTA for a switch to the ACTU. Nevertheless, it was Kelty who secured the TUTA job for Jennie in the first instance and signalled 'perhaps there will be other steps'. Personal relations between them were warm even if they were not close. As chief strategist at the ACTU, Kelty was an astute operator who listened to advice and usually left open a range of possibilities at his disposal, depending on future circumstances. Jennie said, 'Maybe Bill had in the back of his mind that if I came to Melbourne, and an opportunity came up, I would be there to move to the ACTU at some appropriate time—although that was not talked about at the time'.

Another less-obvious reason to install Jennie at TUTA around mid-1989, she recalled much later, was that 'it was just an opportunity to get me out of the road potentially for the ACTU presidency'. Jennie was not in the race to become ACTU president then, having neither the factional numbers nor Kelty's necessary support. She had not thought about it seriously and Kelty had already anointed Martin Ferguson anyway. Ferguson was to take over from Simon Crean as ACTU president when Crean entered Federal Parliament at the March 1990 election. Yet Jennie believed that Ferguson, with whom she had been friendly, was 'very keen to make sure there were no potential rivals'. Besides Kelty, Ferguson had been the first to raise the question of her move to TUTA. In hindsight she believed it was convenient for Ferguson to have her out of the Teachers' Federation and out of the limelight, ensconced at TUTA, so any talk of Jennie as a potential successor to Crean would cease. Ferguson was not prepared to make any comment about Jennie to the author and so her opinion stands unchallenged. What can be said with certainty is that after Ferguson became president of the ACTU, relations between he and Jennie deteriorated significantly and any friendship between them dissolved.

Jennie remained physically remote from the action at the ACTU for just a year, working in the suburbs at St Kilda or visiting TUTA's national training centre in Albury. Thereafter, she had the opportunity to bump into Kelty and Ferguson, now the ACTU president, merely in the course of her work when, for cost reasons, TUTA head office was shifted to a floor in the building occupied by the ACTU leadership in Swanston Street, Melbourne. Jennie also maintained connections with union officials who relayed to her what was happening in the corridors of union power. One of them was a good friend, Di Foggo, president of the Australian Education Union (AEU), who had replaced her as the education representative on the ACTU executive. Her main connection, however, was contact with what remained of the Sydney-based group of influential left-wing union officials, the Kent Street Mafia of Tom McDonald, Peter Robson and George Campbell.

Jennie's lingering comradeship with the Kent Street Mafia proved vital in the next step of her career. It was known well in advance that Laurie Carmichael intended to retire as an assistant secretary of the ACTU at the scheduled ACTU congress in September 1991. Carmichael's position was claimed by the Left faction, just as the Right had a claim over the position of another recently appointed assistant secretary, Iain Ross.

The names of several people were put on the table when the Left considered who should replace Carmichael. An early name was Greg Harrison, an assistant secretary of the AMWU who was close to Kelty and regarded highly. His elevation to the ACTU also would have ended tensions within his own union between him and the AMWU's national secretary, George Campbell. But Harrison did not want to move his family from Sydney to the ACTU in Melbourne and instead accepted, on Kelty's recommendation to the Government, a Sydney-based appointment to the Industrial Relations Commission.[1] At one stage, Kelty considered abolishing Carmichael's position altogether but the Left prevailed upon him to keep it. The thinking of the Kent Street Mafia was that it was about time a woman held a full-time senior officer's position in the male-dominated ACTU. The five men in the ACTU's top full-time positions were Kelty, Ferguson, Carmichael, Ross and Bill Mansfield.

Again, a number of names were mooted. Among them was Jenny Doran, an ACTU industrial officer, Trish Caswell from the Victorian Trades Hall, and Jennie's friend Di Foggo. But none of these women, for a variety of reasons, had widespread Left support for the job. Yet another was Anna Booth, national secretary of the Clothing Trades Union. Kelty had become close to Booth and pushed hard for her to take the job—but she had qualms about leaving Sydney. The Left was not inclined to support Booth anyway. Despite being on friendly terms with her, the Left was reluctant to deliver Booth the numbers for Carmichael's position because the union she led came from a different faction—the Centre. The logic of faction politics dictated that—except in extraordinary circumstances—it was crazy to give up a prime position in the ACTU leadership mix.

For McDonald, Robson and Campbell—having fixed their minds on nominating a woman from their own faction—the person who stood out above the rest was Jennie. Even by the end of 1990, she seemed the obvious candidate and the odd media report floated her name. The remaining trio of the Kent Street Mafia knew she was competent, familiar with the policy agenda, understood the political dynamic of the union Left and would do a good job as an assistant ACTU secretary. She had different strengths to the haranguing, domineering Carmichael. Endorsing her also meant a further break in the traditional link at the top of the ACTU, away from shop-floor self-educated officials from blue-collar unions, such as Carmichael, to university-educated officials from white-collar unions.

Jennie was precisely the person the ACTU needed as unions confronted a serious decline in overall membership. She had enough grassroots appeal to reach out to all workers but she could appeal particularly to women in white-collar jobs, where the fall was worst-felt despite a steady increase in the participation rate of women in the workforce. Already living in Melbourne, Jennie was ideally positioned to make the transition. Her backers believed she had been away from the pressure of union leadership long enough. Despite her responsibility overseeing a statutory authority with a $10 million-a-year budget and a staff of 90, they thought she held a job that was 'going nowhere'.

Kelty—as the ACTU's kingpin—still had to be persuaded to accept Jennie but the Left's faction leaders did not need to expend much effort. Although Booth remained his preference, Kelty had to accept she was out of contention. Despite his political differences with Jennie in the 1980s, Kelty had a high regard for her as an articulate, gutsy trade unionist with undeniable experience. Another of Jennie's virtues was that she appeared to have toned down her politics, loyal as always to the Left but closer, compared with earlier days, to Kelty's style of pragmatic leadership. Her conversion to the Accord provided vital assistance to her career, enabling her to work with Kelty. Peter Robson recalled that Jennie's relationship with Kelty was not very strong at the time but that he accepted her at the ACTU 'with open arms'. Robson said:

> In those days Bill was king of the castle—he thought he could manipulate events. There were other candidates, others being floated around at the time, but he was very supportive of Jennie. Anna Booth was a possibility but she would not have allowed herself to be put in a competitive position against Jennie.

Tom McDonald was the first to approach Jennie about the assistant secretary's job. As in the past, she hesitated, nervous this time about whose shoes she would be filling. After all, Carmichael had a mighty reputation in the union movement. He had joined the ACTU late in his career. After starting as a tradesman on the Williamstown dockyards, he had worked his way up the Amalgamated Engineering Union in Victoria and, in 1972, became assistant national secretary of the union, renamed the AMWU after a series of mergers. Carmichael had been a key figure on the central committee of the Communist Party of Australia, including president of the party, but he always pursued his industrial goals within the union mainstream and remained one of its most influential thinkers.

Over the years Carmichael had spearheaded many strike campaigns over pay. Billy McMahon had even branded him 'one of the most evil men in the trade union movement' in the 1960s. But he was chastened by the loss of thousands of jobs in the union wage push of 1981—in which he was a leading figure—and remade himself thereafter, joining Kelty as a prime mover of the ACTU's Accord with Labor. Rather than relying on traditional union militancy, he foresaw the opportunity available with Labor's election. The union movement could influence macroeconomic policy, for the sake of employment growth, and negotiate with the Federal Government over tax and welfare, accepting that they affected living standards just as much as wages.[2]

Forging a close working relationship with Kelty, for whom he was an ideas man and important support, Carmichael was involved intimately in all the trade-off deals negotiated between the ACTU and Labor Treasurer Paul Keating that had followed the original Accord—its successors Marks II to VI. The latest model he had devised with Kelty, Mark VI, advocated a move away from the highly centralised wage system of early Accords to enterprise bargaining, less regulated but still managed because unions would commit to yearly average wage targets.

Carmichael had stood down from his AMWU position as early as 1984 but continued to work in the union's backrooms until 1987, when Kelty wooed him officially to the ACTU, giving him a job as an assistant secretary. That was also the year that the ACTU released a document called *Australia Reconstructed*, co-authored by Carmichael, which set out a vision for the union movement emphasising industry policy and skills formation. Among other ideas advanced by Carmichael and adopted by Kelty was reducing the multiplicity of craft-based unions in Australia to about 20 unions defined along broad industry lines. His ongoing passion was education and training and his ACTU swansong, to be endorsed by the 1991 congress in the midst of the recession, was a *Charter for Jobs*.

When Jennie's doubts about taking Carmichael's position persisted over the first few months of 1991, the Kent Street Mafia went to extra lengths to bolster her confidence. Trying to persuade Jennie to accept the ACTU job was one of McDonald's last actions before he, like Carmichael, bowed out. McDonald recalled:

> Jennie is a woman who, in her early period, deep down, lacked a bit of confidence in herself. She has come through and gained confidence since then but she still needed people to reassure her when the ACTU assistant secretary's position came up that she

could do the job—and I was one of those who reassured her that she could do a good job.

Peter Robson also tried to cheer her along. He said:

There are these doubts when high positions come to Jennie. I think also that Laurie being the assistant secretary before didn't help. He was a broadly respected, domineering, intellectually brilliant character. It was going to be very hard to step into his shoes—and I think that had an effect on Jennie's mind.

One of the key psychological reasons for Jennie's doubts could be traced back to her turbulent early life. She needed to hear, again and again, that she was 'wanted'. Expressing her doubts was also a deft means of ruling out the possibility that there might be alternatives considered for a position that—deep down—she coveted. It forced her backers to ensure that no-one else was in the running or rated as serious opposition. Jennie had her own explanation about the insecurity she felt when confronted with assuming positions of power. Her view expressed the conundrum of many women who climbed the career ladder and suddenly found themselves in jobs formerly held by men. She said:

For women it's never been a defining part of your existence. You never imagine that you are going to have any power anyway, and when you get it, you're a bit nervous about what it all means and whether you're up to it.

The most important influence in Jennie's decision to accept the ACTU assistant secretary's job was George Campbell, the brash Irish-born leader of the AMWU. He and Jennie had enjoyed a love–hate friendship over the years, sharing political ideals in the union Left but sometimes descending into conflict after late-night drinking bouts when both became argumentative or when Jennie became maudlin about whatever was worrying her at the time. Their most notable public spat was one evening in a Melbourne restaurant in 1988 when Jennie gave Campbell a huge dressing-down for berating her and others about the stance they took in a wages policy debate at that day's ACTU executive meeting. Campbell was not yet an executive member but was in Melbourne that day and joined Jennie's table for dinner. One observer recalled: 'George Campbell comes in and he calls everyone "bloody sellouts", and then Jennie gets up and she goes at him, a real public airing. It was fantastic! It was sensational!'

Campbell was a trenchant critic of the ACTU leadership at the time of the restaurant incident but later became one of its prime defenders when he was elected to the ACTU executive and drawn close to Kelty. Whether Jennie's friendship with Campbell was in 'love' or 'hate' phase, the bond between them was strong. According to Campbell, Jennie experienced a lot of uncertainty about joining the ACTU full-time and her capacity to handle Kelty. She had already witnessed Kelty's testiness. Campbell reassured her:

> I said, 'Look, I'm there and if there's difficulties with Bill I can be involved so you won't have to be handling it on your own. You've got the support of the Metal Workers, you got the support of the major Left unions, so it's not as if you're in isolation'. Because I think the concern was that McDonald was retiring, Carmichael was retiring and she was going to be thrust into a kind of following-the-leader role. And I think that was probably the point that influenced her the most. Certainly it stands out in my mind because we talked about it on a lot of long, late nights.

Jennie spent little more than two years in her TUTA position. By the time of the 1991 ACTU congress her switch to the assistant secretary's position was sewn up, she had overcome her lack of confidence and was elected unopposed. There was much fanfare in the print media about the changeover but it focused more on Carmichael, reflecting upon his immense influence spanning more than three decades, as he bowed out.

One newspaper article about Jennie stood out, however, a profile titled 'Ms GEORGE the FIRST' by her journalist friend

Anne Susskind of the *Sydney Morning Herald*. What was most striking about the article was the way it reported Jennie playing down suggestions that she was on track to become the first woman ACTU president and yet fanned the flames of speculation. Jennie insisted that her new job was 'definitely the last of her firsts' and said it annoyed her that people wanted to push her further. She claimed that by lacking the grace not to ask, 'where next?' these people denied her the satisfaction of her latest achievement. According to Jennie, a younger woman with more enthusiasm than herself would be the first woman ACTU president. Yet paradoxically she admitted, 'it's the question inevitably asked'.[3]

The photograph accompanying the story only heightened the speculation. It presented Jennie, smiling warmly, posing with her elbow leaning next to a life-size bust of Bob Hawke commissioned specially to celebrate his ACTU presidency. If she was not running for ACTU president, what was Jennie doing? The current president, Martin Ferguson, was entitled to draw some uncomfortable conclusions. All through her career, Jennie liked to pose the question, 'where next?'. As someone who liked to flirt with possibilities, she was again keeping her options open.

When Jennie arrived at the ACTU to take up her new position, Kelty never determined a fixed brief for her beyond a few areas of responsibility. As she explained it, 'the place operated on the basis of us all having a free rein to do what you wanted as long as you did a good job'. The primary industrial responsibility Kelty gave her was to look after unions in the Commonwealth Public Service, including co-ordinating the first negotiations in that sector under the emerging new system of enterprise bargaining. Jennie also rejoined the ACTU's women's committee and oversaw TUTA operations from her more senior vantage point. Automatically, as an ACTU assistant secretary, her position on the ACTU executive was restored. In fact, she became not only the first woman assistant secretary of the ACTU but coincidentally the first woman to hold one of five full-time positions on the ACTU executive.

Kelty had had the foresight (though not without pressure) to put women's representation and female union membership firmly on the ACTU's agenda. By now, ten of the ACTU executive's 38 members were women, a significant advance but still far short of fair representation. Jennie accepted her new position with pleasure but also regarded it as a symbolic statement for women. 'In the 1970s,' she said, 'women's policies would be the last item on the agenda, and when you got to it half the [ACTU] congress would have gone out for afternoon tea.'[4]

Unfortunately Jennie's high spirits as she began her new job did not match the mood of her ACTU colleagues. It was not a pleasant atmosphere awaiting her when she found her modest new office on the sixth floor of ACTU House, wedged between those of Bill Kelty and Martin Ferguson. A battle was raging—and Jennie was about to become deeply involved.

TAKING SIDES

Jennie George joined the hierarchy of the ACTU during one of the most tumultuous periods in the organisation's history. The president, Martin Ferguson, and the secretary, Bill Kelty, were waging what amounted to an internal war against each other. They had begun as friends and allies when Kelty had orchestrated Ferguson's promotion to the ACTU presidency just a few years earlier. Now they appeared to be enemies. Some observers who witnessed events described office politics between the two as 'disgraceful'.

The war was being fought on two related fronts. Ferguson did not accept that he was there to be Kelty's puppet. He was intensely unhappy with the power arrangement at the ACTU that made him its public face but handed almost total control over policy direction to Kelty. Ferguson wanted to exert his own independent influence in the union movement. He was accustomed to running a union himself—where he was in control—in his previous position as national secretary of the giant Miscellaneous Workers' Union. Tensions at the ACTU reached boiling point during 1991 when Kelty and Ferguson disagreed fiercely about the conflict that was dominating the Australian political landscape—the relentless drive of Paul Keating to topple Bob Hawke and become prime minister himself. Kelty was fervently pro-Keating. Ferguson was just as fervently pro-Hawke.

Kelty's assessment was that the Labor Government's direction had flagged in recent years under Hawke and that he should stand aside for Keating, who had the ideas and energy that could revive Labor's public standing and win the next election. At a personal level, he had also grown close to Keating. After Keating's initial lack of enthusiasm for the Accord and Kelty's initial impression that Keating was an opportunist, they had become a dynamic duo. Together they had steered the Accord through the 1980s, as an instrument of macroeconomic policy for the Government and as a mechanism for unions to secure social gains on employment, superannuation, health and welfare. The basis of their friendship was professional trust. Kelty explained it thus: 'When he trusted us we always delivered and, in return, he always delivered.'[1]

Further proof of Kelty's closeness to Keating was that he served as Keating's witness to the secret Kirribilli pact in 1988 when Hawke agreed to stand aside for Keating after the next election. Sir Peter Abeles was the witness for Hawke, who broke his word after winning the 1990 election.

Ferguson never was close to Keating and his assessment was the reverse of Kelty's. He believed that—despite the achievements of the Accord—Keating was now wrecking the party by mounting a challenge against Hawke. To Ferguson, Keating was creating unnecessary disunity within the ALP at a particularly difficult time in the political and economic cycle when the country was in a deep recession. Like most of Hawke's supporters, he scoffed at what he regarded as Keating's hypocritical attempt to promote himself as the potential saviour of the economy when the high-interest rate policy Keating had endorsed as Treasurer helped tip Australia into recession. Ferguson believed that Labor was unelectable with Keating as prime minister because of his immense unpopularity. Sticking with Hawke was the best way for the party to win the next election.

The views of Kelty and Ferguson and the union loyalties they inspired were important to backers of the ALP leadership rivals. Unions influential in the party's Left, Right and Centre factions could exert direct pressure on Labor MPs and so swing the numbers necessary to win a ballot of the parliamentary party caucus that ultimately would decide whether Hawke or Keating triumphed. Both Kelty and Ferguson were careful not to express direct views on the ALP leadership issue in public—at first.[2] Their subsequent behaviour, however, left no doubt where they stood and carried influence.

Since moving from Sydney to Melbourne to become ACTU president in 1990, Martin Ferguson was cut off from his original power base in the ALP Left. He did engage in active politicking, however, to try to ensure Hawke maintained the parliamentary numbers to block Keating, by trying to persuade everyone in his reach that only Hawke could win a historic fifth term for Labor. Ferguson's main political contacts remained those from the ALP Left in NSW, including his brother Laurie, a Federal parliamentarian. As the climax of the battle neared, Ferguson revealed his allegiance publicly by saying it was clear Keating had lost his leadership challenge and should 'face up to the fact that there is one leader'.[3] In his memoirs, Hawke also confirmed that he was helped in last-minute lobbying by Ferguson, who, along with several others, 'worked on those in the Left whom they regarded as doubtful'.[4]

Kelty never did any vote counting for Keating or direct lobbying of ALP caucus members for Keating's first unsuccessful leadership challenge in June and ultimate victory in a second ballot in December. He was not tuned into ALP politics at that level. He had once been on the ALP's administrative committee in Victoria but quit because he disliked its factional squabbling. Keating did not need assistance from Kelty in this regard anyway— he had his own supporters in Canberra to tally his numbers. The support Kelty gave Keating was important in other ways. Keating began his push in earnest for a second try for Hawke's leadership in July from the backbench, having resigned as Treasurer after he made his first unsuccessful challenge. That month Kelty gave a flattering public endorsement of Keating during an interview with radio host John Laws, describing his friend as 'one of the greatest political figures of the generation'. Hawke was annoyed. Retaliating, he told Kelty, 'I run the Government' and urged Kelty to look after the unions.[5]

Where Kelty was most effective in assisting Keating's leadership ambitions was not public comments, however, but rather the application of political pressure on Hawke. This pressure had the effect of undermining government policy under Hawke's leadership and highlighting differences, to those who mattered inside the Labor Party, between the 'pro-active' challenger and 'tired' incumbent.

Kelty's main target was John Kerin, whom Hawke had appointed to replace Keating as Treasurer. The same month Keating's second challenge gathered pace—just two months before Jennie joined the ACTU as an assistant secretary—Kelty put Kerin on notice. He said that Kerin must agree to legislate for a target of 12 per cent of workers' income going to superannuation funds as compulsory employer contributions—a doubling of the agreed schedule—following an Industrial Relations Commission refusal to meet the ACTU's demands. Kelty warned that if Kerin refused, the Accord was finished. Faced with little room to manoeuvre, Kerin agreed to Kelty's demand in the August Budget.

Kelty then had a major falling out with Kerin over the wages growth target for the Budget, which he threatened to go public about. Even after the Budget's release, Kelty sustained his attack with a tirade in front of astonished members of the ACTU executive. He strongly criticised the Budget's failure to adopt a more expansionary economic policy with big-spending programs to reduce unemployment and boost industry—precisely the policies Keating was now calling for. One of his final divisive actions during this period was to override Ferguson in government negotiations, blocking legislation at the last minute that was being prepared by Hawke's Industrial Relations Minister, Peter Cook.[6]

All of these actions by Kelty embroiled the ACTU leadership directly in the Hawke–Keating leadership battle. Kelty had never run the Accord with Keating in such a hostile fashion. Now he created the potential for a wedge to be driven among Hawke's supporters in the union Left that could entice them to switch sides and back Keating for the sake of a more interventionist economic policy to which they were predisposed. The absurdity of Kelty's attack on the Budget in particular was that Keating, before he resigned as Treasurer, had done most of the work on the 1991 Budget that Kerin delivered.

Another source of ongoing trouble, which became entangled with his stance in the leadership battle, was Kelty's fight with the Industrial Relations Commission over that year's national wage decision. For the first time the wage bench of the commission, headed by Barry Maddern, had rejected almost every element of the Accord Mark VI agreed between the Government and the ACTU. Maddern's bench ruled that unions and employers were not yet 'mature' enough to move from the centralised wage fixing system regulated by the commission in the 1980s to a form of less-regulated enterprise bargaining that Kelty and Keating wanted for the 1990s. Kelty refused to accept Maddern's ruling and pushed the union movement into campaigning for the Accord's terms in direct bargaining with employers. Keating went along with Kelty. So did Hawke, albeit with reservations. However, the ensuing furore, which included vitriolic attacks on the commission by Kelty and his absurd comparison of Maddern with the communist dictator Fidel Castro, was a political disturbance that was unhelpful to Hawke at a delicate time for his leadership.

Although Kelty and Ferguson agreed on many ACTU policies such as the Accord, union amalgamations and stronger government intervention in the economy, their feud over the Hawke–Keating leadership battle revealed their tensions over who held the real power in the ACTU. It also paralysed the smooth running of the organisation. The two ACTU leaders had good professional reasons to communicate and had easy access to one another—their offices were just metres apart on the same floor. Yet the breakdown in their relations meant that there was negligible dialogue between them. Some observers of Ferguson said he became 'paranoid' about Kelty during this period. However, they also thought that Kelty contributed to Ferguson's state of mind by increasing his tendency to operate solo and be secretive about his plans.

When Jennie became part of this strained environment at the ACTU, she had a choice to make. Such was the intensity of the conflict between the ACTU's two most senior figures that she was forced to choose between them. She quickly sided with Kelty. He was at the height of his powers and had a mesmerising effect on those who came into close contact with him. It was not uncommon for newcomers to the ACTU fold like Jennie to hero-worship Kelty. He was also her route to success.

Jennie did not take a prominent role in backing Keating—she was not even a member of the ALP. Former ACTU industrial officer Les Ayres recalled: 'Jennie was betwixt and between at first on the leadership question. She didn't know which way to jump—she just backed Bill.' Eventually she warmed to Keating's change of heart about government intervention in the economy after years of his having played to the market with tight budgetary and wages policies. While admitting 'a degree of ignorance on economic matters',[7] Jennie believed in the substance of Keating's push for pump-priming the economy—his call for tax incentives, more public infrastructure and programs for the long-term unemployed.

Such an activist political agenda was not too remote from the convictions she had held when she was one of the Communist Party reformists in the early 1970s casting around unsuccessfully for a coalition of Left forces. The difference now was that Jennie's politics had mellowed as she had matured. It also had taken Australia's need for recovery from a deep economic recession and a desperately ambitious Paul Keating to give such ideas political and economic respectability. Jennie was convinced that Kelty had no role in the internal machinations of the Labor Party over the leadership. She gave Ferguson credit for his loyalty to Hawke but found his method of support distasteful. She recalled:

> There was definitely tension. That would manifest about who was supporting who. I mean, Martin was very public in his support for Hawke. Bill was a supporter of Paul's but not in the same way that Martin was. In fact, I remember Pat Staunton [then secretary of the NSW Nurses' Association] ringing me the day of the ballot or the day before, asking was I aware that the president of the ACTU was in Canberra lobbying for Bob Hawke. And I said, 'no I wasn't', and I spoke to Martin about it. I said I didn't think it was appropriate for the president of the ACTU to be acting in such a partisan way because there were obviously different views within the union movement.
>
> There is a difference between someone who is a key numbers person [Ferguson] and someone who has influence in factional terms by word of mouth [Kelty]. Bill is obviously someone who could carry weight—he could say something. The thing that is admirable about Martin is his absolute loyalty to people who are on his side of the fence. The converse side of that is that if you are not, it can be less than fair. In my judgment as an ACTU assistant secretary at the time I thought it was improper and wrong for Martin to be totally and intimately involved with Bob.

The power struggle in the Labor Party was resolved the week before Christmas 1991 when Keating defeated Hawke in a caucus ballot by a narrow margin of 56 to 51. The result also reinforced Kelty's supremacy inside the ACTU. Over time, Kelty and Ferguson improved their working relationship although it remained uneasy. Ferguson's original desire to exert stronger influence over ACTU policy-making remained unfulfilled although he did carve out a strong industrial role for himself settling a number of difficult strikes.

Ultimately Jennie's decision to side with Kelty had less to do with her views on the distracting Hawke–Keating leadership challenge and more to do with her respect for Kelty himself. She appreciated that Kelty was the ACTU's towering figure, intellectually as well as influentially. Kelty's public image was poor, worse than Ferguson's. But his substance, as the prime mover of all major ACTU initiatives for close to a decade, from the Accord and universal superannuation and union amalgamations to acceptance of the need for greater female representation, persuaded her to back him.

Jennie's respect for Kelty turned into unswerving loyalty and they formed a strong trusting bond. Two years after she joined the ACTU, and after one emotion-charged speech by Kelty in which he was close to tears, Jennie turned to the person next to her during the applause, gripped with enthusiasm. 'You can see why I work for the man,' she said.

The collateral effect of Jennie's siding with Kelty was harm to her relationship with Ferguson. Their loose friendship of earlier years was now finished and Ferguson viewed her with suspicion. In the poisonous divide of the ACTU leadership, Jennie's backing of Kelty meant none of the senior ACTU officers supported Ferguson against Kelty. Ferguson received some support from ACTU industrial staff and remained on good terms with assistant secretary Bill Mansfield. His chief internal ally was Andrew Casey, the ACTU media officer, who had no rank in the hierarchy and thus made no difference to power plays within the organisation.

Jennie believed that a contributing factor to the deterioration of her relationship with Ferguson was that he regarded her as a threat to his position. Indeed she was more articulate and presented better in the media. By comparison, Ferguson appeared wooden on television or radio, stumbling over his words and using stock phrases and clichés that made him sound like an old-styled union bureaucrat. Jennie's close friend Peter Robson recalled, 'I think

Ferguson always saw her as a threat—I think that was the major cause—and I suppose in the end she was. There was some uncertainty about Martin when Jennie was coming through as assistant secretary.'

Some ventured so far as to say Ferguson's suspicions were justified. They claimed that in a quest for his position Jennie missed few opportunities to 'whiteant' Ferguson among colleagues. Jennie denied this and said she was never disloyal: 'I don't know what it was that caused me to get up Martin's nose.'

Nevertheless, she postulated other causes for the breakdown in relations. Among them, she believed, were problems Ferguson may have had working for the first time with a senior woman, following his leadership of the male-oriented Miscellaneous Workers' Union. 'He may have found it difficult accepting that I had something worthwhile to offer,' she said.

Yet another reason was Jennie's friendship with George Campbell, national secretary of the AMWU and comrade from the Kent Street Mafia. Campbell and Ferguson had been political enemies for years because they hailed from rival factions inside the left-wing Steering Committee of the NSW ALP. In the 1980s Campbell also had been an avowed critic of Kelty and Keating. But he changed his tune after finally gaining a position on the ACTU executive. Kelty wooed him and brought him close to Keating, which effectively pushed Campbell and Ferguson further apart politically. Despite Jennie's own disagreements with Campbell over the years, she was loyal and always closer to him than Ferguson. She would not let Ferguson's antagonism towards Campbell come between the stronger personal friendship she enjoyed with Campbell. As a consequence, her relations with Ferguson suffered further.

These strained relations between Jennie and Ferguson, an ongoing dynamic of internal ACTU politics, reached a nadir after the five-day ACTU Congress in Sydney in September 1993. Rex Hewett, waiting in a Sydney airport lounge on his way home to Melbourne, overheard ACTU media officer Andrew Casey commenting about the performance of the organisation's leaders. 'I mentioned it to Jennie,' Hewett recalled. Jennie, believing Casey to have made indiscreet remarks, reported what she was told to Kelty. Thereafter, she said, what transpired was between Kelty and Casey. 'It had nothing to do with me.' In an unpleasant conversation Kelty is understood to have blamed Casey for providing sensitive information to journalist Peter Wilson that was used in an article in the *Australian* critical of Kelty. Casey, who declined to be interviewed for this book, is understood to have denied that he told Wilson anything and pointed out to Kelty that the article in question was already in print at the time he was sighted in the airport lounge. Kelty, however, was not interested. Having control over non-executive staff and having expressed his view on other occasions that there was no need for a media officer, he now put enormous pressure on Casey, making it clear he was not wanted. Wilson recalled Casey rang him in an agitated state, telling him he might need 'back-up' because he could lose his job. 'Casey said Kelty believed he'd leaked the stuff to me for my story. He was not the source and I felt bad about it because he was pinged for something he didn't do. If he didn't leave immediately, he was dead in the water after that.'

Not long after, Casey did quit the ACTU. 'In all the circumstances he decided to resign,' recalled ACTU assistant secretary Bill Mansfield. Casey's departure was a blow to Ferguson. They had known each other for many years and were very loyal to each other. Casey had essentially worked for Ferguson, over and above anyone else at the ACTU, like a ministerial press secretary. Jennie's action in reporting Casey and Casey's subsequent departure caused much ill-feeling among staff, according to former ACTU industrial officer Les Ayres. 'It was an act of paranoia on Jennie's part. Internally a number of us felt he was dealt with fairly harshly. People outside the building would ring up and say "Is he gone? How did that happen?".'

Jennie's action could be seen as unreasonable and as dumping a long-time friend. Like Ferguson, she had known Casey for many years, from the time he was education writer for the *Sydney Morning Herald* in the early 1980s. He had also helped her during a tour of marginal Federal seats she made earlier in the year. Even if Casey had leaked the information—which he did not—it was not necessarily an unforgivable act. (Many other current and former ACTU officials would be in a curious predicament if it were.) In her defence, Jennie denied she had behaved unreasonably. She argued that Casey's comments were inappropriate and that reporting him reflected her ability to make difficult decisions 'in the best interest of the ACTU'.

The conflict over Casey's departure blew over quickly. But it is understood to have permanently blackened Ferguson and Casey's views of Jennie. It also served as a minor proxy victory for Kelty. Casey was a pawn in the larger contest over power between Kelty and Ferguson.

Jennie spent most of 1992 settling into her new job as an assistant secretary, coming to terms with the responsibility Kelty gave her for wage bargaining in the public sector and negotiations to bed-down several mergers to create the giant Finance Sector Union. Her greatest regret was that her ACTU position forced her to live in another city while her mother experienced a time of special need in her life. Vladimir, Jennie's stepfather, died on 31 August. Remarkably it was the same date on which Jennie's father, Oleg, died in 1960. Vladimir had been suffering ill health for some time and caring for him had placed great demands on Jennie's mother towards the end. Jennie's grief was eased somewhat by Vladimir's age—he was 78 and had lived a full life compared with Oleg and Paddy George. Her main worry was for the future of her mother, to whom she remained deeply devoted. Jennie fretted about Natasha living a lonely existence for the rest of her days in the Housing Commission flat in inner-city Waterloo to which she and Vladimir had moved in 1973. For now, however, daily telephone contact and regular interstate visits were the most Jennie could do for Natasha.

Professionally, Jennie was about to assume a very important frontline position for the ACTU that would test her ability. The union movement was most disturbed about the inevitable defeat of Victoria's Labor Government in an impending State election on 3 October and the resultant radical cuts to services and union power anticipated from the aggressive incoming Liberal Premier, Jeff Kennett. Labor was expected to lose after a decade in office because of rock-bottom public support, its reputation ruined by obvious economic mismanagement and incompetence. The Labor Premier, John Cain, resigned more than a year before the election was due. Desperate for public appeal, the party's male-dominated hierarchy thought that replacing Cain with a woman, Joan Kirner, might help. It did not and Labor was trounced in the October poll.

Confronting massive State debt and distasteful of the level of union influence in the former government, Kennett leapt into action. He cut back funding in health, education and transport as part of a rapid debt reduction plan. He also set about dismantling the State's industrial relations system. He abolished the State awards that regulated minimum wages and conditions for about a third of Victoria's workforce (the rest were covered by Federal awards) and scrapped the State's industrial tribunal that governed the system, replacing it with a toothless substitute. He also announced an end to the decades old $17\frac{1}{2}$ per cent holiday leave loading and weekend penalty rates. The right to strike was curbed and police were handed new powers to limit pickets to six or less. Kennett's changes were limited to Victoria but had national implications. He provided a testing ground for the Coalition parties at a national level if their leader, John Hewson, beat Keating in the Federal election due in 1993. Hewson's industrial relations spokesman, former Opposition leader John Howard, was watching events keenly in Victoria and had similar plans.

Despite lacking widespread public support after Labor's huge loss, Victorian unions decided they had to fight the Kennett agenda. But they were divided along factional lines over the best strategy and who should lead them. The Right was particularly disenchanted with the left-wing leadership of the secretary of the Victorian Trades Hall Council, John Halfpenny. A former communist and union militant from his days as Victorian secretary of the AMWU, Halfpenny made a hasty decision without wide consultation after the election to announce a statewide strike on 10 November. It was to be part of an ongoing campaign of strikes. Without support from the Right, Halfpenny's anti-Kennett campaign threatened to collapse.

Then Kelty intervened. He successfully offered ACTU co-ordination as the price of securing the Right's participation and put Jennie in charge. Halfpenny remained the main public focus of the campaign but Jennie was thrust into the role of co-ordinator and became an effective counter to Halfpenny's extremes. She took a public role in speaking out against Kennett. Her main role, however, in which she demonstrated great acumen, was to bridge the factional divide. Although a left-winger herself, she succeeded in uniting formerly reluctant right-wing unions in manufacturing, retail, warehousing, nursing and clerical areas by talking their leaders into joining the fight. The pattern of events was similar to Jennie's conflict with Metherell—a series of strikes with an early climax in the form of a huge rally that accompanied the 10 November strike. As a show of protest, the rally was a success, dramatically exceeding expectations. The streets of Melbourne filled with 100 000 people, the largest public demonstration the city had seen since the Vietnam moratorium. Halfpenny's high-risk strategy was vindicated by the massive turnout. He was ably assisted by Jennie having brought the right-wing unions on side.

Jennie was proud about her role in the campaign even though Kennett rushed through legislation to effect the changes he wanted and refused to relent. Importantly, she also impressed Kelty, who increasingly came to admire her dogged fighting spirit and ability to communicate to a wide audience.

Jennie's proven capacity as a campaigner was next put to use by the ACTU in the lead-up to the Federal election in March 1993. The ACTU had an obvious stake in securing a Labor victory because of union affiliations with the party and as its partner in the Accord. Jennie was placed in the frontline during the campaign to emphasise the benefits of the award system that guaranteed workers' minimum entitlements and what they stood to lose if the Federal Coalition won and then followed Kennett's lead in Victoria. The Coalition's blueprint for industrial relations reform, *Jobsback!*, released by John Howard the same month as the Victorian election, proposed the most radical shake-up of Australia's national industrial relations since the Harvester Judgment of 1907 led to the creation of the basic wage.

Howard advocated abolishing Federal awards. His plan was to have them all expire so workers would be forced into bargaining with their employer. If workers failed to reach an agreement, the terms of their old award would continue but would be frozen without opportunity for improvement. Agreements bargained between employers and individual workers or groups of workers would have to meet minimum conditions: an adult hourly pay rate linked to a relevant award, a youth hourly pay rate of $3.50, four weeks' annual leave, two weeks' sick leave and unpaid maternity leave after twelve months' service. Suffice to say, Howard's minimum conditions were parsimonious compared with those contained in awards.

Over the weeks of the official election campaign, Jennie travelled to marginal electorates in several states, including outlying areas, where she gave speeches to community groups and in workplaces and had the opportunity to talk personally to locals. Unlike the anti-Kennett campaign, it was not Kelty who assigned Jennie this prominent role in the election campaign, although he fully endorsed it. The idea that she should be involved on behalf of the ACTU came from its women's committee, of which Jennie was a key member. The committee was desperately worried, particularly about the plight of women, if the Federal Coalition had the chance to deregulate the labour market as had happened in Victoria and New Zealand. The concept of Jennie embarking on a 'speaking tour' came from Dr Anne Summers, the women's affairs adviser on Paul Keating's staff.[8]

Jennie's chief message on her speaking tour was that a vote for the Coalition would put people's guaranteed wages and working conditions in jeopardy. The ACTU bolstered her campaign by funding a dramatic television advertisement showing people falling from the sky if they lacked the protection of awards. It also placed advertisements in mass-market women's magazines, including *The Australian Women's Weekly* and *New Idea*. Jennie emphasised that women in low-paid jobs without bargaining power would be worst affected without awards. She also attacked what she regarded as the anti-union thrust of the Coalition's policy, which, by promoting negotiations between employers and individuals rather than the collective, undermined the principle of unionism.

When Labor won on 13 March to the great surprise of many, Keating claimed personal credit and exhibited great hubris after many doubters said he was too unpopular to score the party a fifth term. While not denying that Keating campaigned effectively, the election turned mainly on voters' rejection of a 15 per cent goods and services tax (GST), the most controversial aspect of Hewson's comprehensive *Fightback!* strategy. After the GST, the ACTU campaign in defence of the award system was a strong secondary issue. Another strong campaign issue, in which the ACTU played a part, was Labor's commitment to retain Medicare amid fears that Hewson would dismantle it. Jennie's efforts helped swing voters back to Labor. But like many in ALP and union circles, she had her doubts about the likely result. On election night, she was at the home of a Melbourne friend from the Australian Education Union, Dave Robson, brother of Peter Robson, watching television nervously for news after voting finished. 'I remember the Tasmanian results coming in very early in the night and it was very exciting. I had a dreadful hangover the next morning.'

The Keating victory gave unions another three y̶ or so they thought—before having to confront a Coalition agenda that would put them in a hostile environment. In what was interpreted as a signpost of his government's future directions, Keating gave his first major speech since re-election to the Institute of Company Directors in Melbourne on 21 April. He spoke about high principles that pleased unions, such as linking economic policy to programs that produced 'not just social justice but social cohesion and strength'. The last part of Keating's speech, however, devoted to industrial relations, prompted an outcry in the union movement, particularly considering the enormous amount of union effort and money spent to secure Labor's re-election. The unions had backed the Accord's embrace of enterprise bargaining, but not at the expense of diminishing awards. Keating appeared to declare that he wanted enterprise bargaining to *replace* awards. He said, 'We need to find a way of extending coverage of agreements from being add-ons to awards, as they are today, to being full substitutes for awards.'

In the 1980s Jennie had been an opponent of Keating's Right ALP politics and Treasury-line economics. She had become a fan of late, knowing and liking Keating from her experiences during the election campaign and through insights given to her by Kelty. Nevertheless, she found Keating's words troubling, so soon after Labor's election win. Did this mean Keating was advocating wholesale deregulation of the labour market, not dissimilar to Howard's blueprint, as some commentators believed? Concerned, Jennie telephoned Keating's office for an explanation and was assured that the Prime Minister wanted enterprise bargains to be 'more comprehensive' and did not really mean that they should replace awards.[9]

Jennie was satisfied with the response but a rash of similar assurances from the Prime Minister's office did not placate a general sense of suspicion among unions about Labor's intentions. Strains had developed after a decade of the Accord partnership. Officials, such as the NSW Labor Council's Peter Sams, were worried that a downgrading of the Industrial Relations Commission's powers and a greater emphasis on enterprise bargaining was tantamount to implementing the Coalition's agenda on its behalf. These strains worsened within months. Keating's gung-ho Minister for Industrial Relations, Laurie Brereton, proposed legislation for the Budget session of Parliament, which, among other changes, created for the first time a system of non-union enterprise agreements certified by the commission. It was meant to run parallel to existing union enterprise agreements, also certified by the commission. Keating had hinted at such a change in his April speech when he referred to the many workers who 'for one reason or another don't have a union to represent them'.

What Brereton proposed was mandatory for any government that claimed to rule for all people. In the private sector, almost three-quarters of the workforce did not belong to a union. This big non-unionised majority could negotiate informal over-award arrangements on pay and conditions but were denied the right union members had to register their agreements as binding contracts in the commission. Union officials disliked the change and had fiery arguments with Brereton about it. They claimed that legitimising non-union deals would lead to the exploitation of all workers in weak bargaining positions. Brereton had a long history as a policy bulldozer and indeed pressed ahead with his plans. But he attracted such union contempt that he was booed during his speech to the September 1993 ACTU congress in Sydney.

Jennie shared concerns about sanctioning enterprise bargaining in non-union areas. She was worried about possible cuts to wages and conditions across-the-board if unions lost the right to veto all agreements. There was little she could do, however, because the issue was outside her area of responsibility. She took some comfort knowing that Iain Ross, a fellow ACTU assistant secretary anointed by Kelty as his possible successor, was conducting negotiations with Brereton on the basis that enterprise bargaining rights were 'already flexible enough'.

Jennie had enough problems in the lead-up to the September congress trying to defend the ACTU position on enterprise bargaining against a barrage of criticism from—of all quarters— women. She was caught in a difficult position. As part of the ACTU leadership team, one of her responsibilities was to handle women's issues. If the ACTU came under fire, as it was now, she was bound by solidarity to defend ACTU official policy. Much like the principle of Cabinet solidarity, she was obliged to do so no matter how uncomfortable she was made to feel or how the facts might contradict her position. Resignation was her only real alternative.

The complaint expressed to Jennie over a series of months by women's groups such as the Pay Equity Coalition and by individual women who supported her in normal circumstances was that enterprise bargaining was leaving women worse off by increasing the gap between male and female earnings. For Jennie to agree with this proposition meant undermining ACTU policy.

The ACTU had determined that the highly centralised system of the 1980s, when general wage movements were tightly controlled through increases to award pay rates, was defunct. Accords of the 1990s ruled that enterprise bargaining was to be the primary method of delivering pay rises for all in the future and that very small increases in minimum wage rates set by awards were a 'safety net' only for workers unable to strike workplace bargains. The dilemma for Jennie was that sticking to the ACTU line put her at odds with what was now an orthodox view in the women's movement that women were not faring well under the new system.

Protests against ACTU policy on enterprise bargaining culminated in a demonstration staged by women from the Pay Equity Coalition, including Meredith Burgmann, during the 1993 ACTU congress held at the Darling Harbour convention centre. In a move clearly designed to embarrass the ACTU leadership, to which Jennie belonged, the women assembled directly outside the congress doors. For the sake of television and radio exposure, they chanted 'Equal pay! Equal pay!' and carried placards denouncing bargaining for women. Burgmann, while disagreeing with the ACTU, said she was never angry with Jennie personally and sensed that it must have been difficult for her friend to toe the ACTU line. Burgmann recalled:

> My feeling was that Jennie was always uncomfortable about enterprise bargaining because her dear friends like Cathy Bloch and me and other people she knew were telling her it was very dangerous. You see, [the ACTU] argument always was 'the Libs are going to do it, so we've got to do it'.

Jennie's recollection was that she never said that enterprise bargaining was good for women, only that women in unionised sectors who bargained with their employer tended to do better than those not in a union. Twenty months after the official introduction of the new bargaining system, she argued that the jury was still out on the question because of a lack of concrete evidence and, if anything, early figures showed that the capacity of women in unions to bargain compared with men was fairly equal. The tragedy, she said, was that too many women (the vast majority) were not in unions and therefore 'not getting to first base' when it came to bargaining with their employers. She accepted that the more the wage system moved away from being centralised, the worse off women would become. Jennie explained:

> I was an officer of the ACTU and I was bound to support decisions of ACTU congress policy and try to put the best construction on them while always pointing to the inherent difficulties. So I do not feel any qualms about the position I adopted.

Typical of unions and organisations generally, different factions had evolved within the women's movement and among women in unions. They were not just of the Left-versus-Right variety, however. The approach Jennie had always adopted, as an activist for women's rights, was that it was far better to fight for change from within the male-dominated orthodoxy. Her rise through union ranks and the pressure she exerted on men to accept change—by her practical example as a solitary woman on the ACTU executive—was proof that her brand of practical politics worked. But it meant that she was pitted often against a harder-line faction of women, such as the Pay Equity Coalition, who preferred to campaign for change from outside the mainstream. These women were much freer than Jennie to launch fierce attacks on the shortcomings of the male orthodoxy. What they lacked was Jennie's access to power. She was in a position to exert direct influence on men in authority, especially Kelty, who could help drive the change women sought.

Jenny Doran, an ACTU industrial officer on the organisation's women's committee had become a solid friend and supporter of Jennie's. She recalled that there had been concerns about Jennie's closeness to some women on the extreme Left when she arrived at the ACTU in 1991, but that these had soon dissipated. In fact Doran marvelled at the way Jennie was able to communicate across the spectrum of factions in ways that other people could not:

> Jennie can speak the language that enables her to get along with [people from] the loopy Left. We were worried at first, on the women's committee, that she would speak to the loopy Left and start trying to implement their ideas. But she never did—she could get on with them but every call she made was with the powerbrokers [of the ACTU].

Ever persistent, Jennie continued to defend the ACTU's policy on enterprise bargaining for women, even issuing a detailed analysis the following year to back her position.[10] She could legitimately claim a triumph for her approach of activism-from-within when the ACTU made an historic rule change at the 1993 congress, which introduced a new quota to guarantee fair representation of women in the organisation's main forum. The congress passed a rule change mooted by Kelty to ensure that 25 per cent of ACTU executive positions were held by women immediately, rising to 50 per cent by the year 1999. The immediate target was on course because the number of women on the 34-member executive (Kelty had reduced the total from 38) now stood at eight. Equal representation was already close to being achieved in the senior ranks. Besides Jennie as an assistant secretary, there were three women vice-presidents—Anna Booth, Pat Staunton and Wendy Caird (national secretary of the Community and Public Sector Union).

As the person responsible for women's issues at the ACTU, the 50 per cent quota was a major victory for Jennie after years of lobbying for better representation. It was also a year ahead of any move by the ALP to adopt a quota system aimed at guaranteeing equality of representation in its ranks. Pointing out that half of the 'prime age' workforce by the end of the decade would be women whose concerns could no longer be ignored, she said the quota was a necessary reform. Interestingly, she also told the *Australian Financial Review* journalist Sheryle Bagwell that she had rejected the idea of switching to a career in politics given Canberra's poor record of promoting women, 'It's impossible to put a timeframe on it. But I think, by the turn of the century, we could see a woman as president or secretary of the ACTU.'[11]

Jennie was not putting her own name forward but she was stirring *that* issue again. Speculation surrounding her ambitions showed no sign of ending.

15

THE CANDIDATE

A tragic pedestrian accident on 12 February 1995 changed Jennie George's life. Olive Zakharov was hit by a car as she crossed St Kilda Road, Melbourne, after attending a gay and lesbian festival. She never regained consciousness and died from her injuries in nearby Alfred Hospital three weeks later. The accident not only took the life of Zakharov, an ALP Senator for Victoria; it proved to be a turning point for Jennie.

Jennie had joined the ALP quietly in late 1992, about a year after she became an ACTU assistant secretary. It came as a shock to some of her close personal friends when she told them. Her closest, Cathy Bloch, was staggered. So late in Jennie's career, after having repeatedly rejected over the years the urgings of friends such as Pam Allan and Vic Baueris to sign-up, why had she made this unexpected move—and apparently without the agonising that usually accompanied major decisions in her life? It was especially difficult for Bloch to fathom at first because Jennie, like herself, was steeped in the political influences of the Communist Party, not the ALP. Jennie had shunned the ALP in her youth because she did not believe it was a true workers' party. Her early political thinking had been shaped by strong figures in the communist movement, such as Mavis Robertson, and by communist reformists, such as Paddy George, who, like Jennie, wanted to form a coalition of Left forces— excluding the ALP.

Much had changed in the 25 years since Jennie's political associations began. She and others drifted away from the Communist Party in the 1970s. Beset by division and lack of clear direction, the final blow to the Party was the fall of the Berlin Wall in 1989 and the collapse of the Soviet Union and its rule over Eastern Europe under Mikhail Gorbachev. The end of the Soviet empire did much more than kill communism. It challenged the ethos of the Broad Left, of which Jennie was part, throwing into serious doubt its *raison d'être*. As Jennie grew older, her politics had become more pragmatic too. The ALP was no longer the 'sellout' she and her friends once thought it was. In spite of its middle-class aspirations, the ALP was now the only viable political alternative to combat the rise of a New Right agenda, to which Jennie was most firmly opposed.

Jennie had told many people that one reason for not belonging to the ALP when she was president of the Teachers' Federation was that she had to deal on a professional level with Labor governments and wanted to maintain her independence. Other senior federation officials, such as her friends Sharan Burrow and Vic Baueris, had no such qualms about their ALP membership. Jennie could argue that once she had left the federation, this question of independence faded for her. It seemed that finally, after years of deliberate ambiguity about her politics in the public domain, Jennie felt comfortable about openly belonging. She was considering her next move.

The primary reason for finally joining the ALP, Jennie explained to friends, was the Kennett Government's election in Victoria and its harsh measures to cut services and curtail union rights. Cathy Bloch recalled, 'She said to me, "you know, you really can't *not* be in the Labor Party in Victoria with Kennett having been elected".'

Bloch remembered Jennie saying that Martin Ferguson had whipped around ACTU officials at the time, asking everyone who was not a party member to join. 'I think it would have been pretty hard to say no,' said Bloch. Others dispute that Ferguson applied pressure on Jennie or anyone else in the ACTU to sign-up.

Rumours that Jennie was interested in quitting the ACTU for a safe seat in Federal Parliament began soon after Keating's re-election in March 1993, less than twelve months after she had joined the ALP. Speculation focused on the Labor seat of Melbourne Ports, held by Clyde Holding, who was expected to retire soon. It spilled into the public arena when the *Age* published a front-page story confirming that the search for a seat for Jennie, as well as for fellow assistant ACTU secretary Iain Ross, had begun. Jennie denied publicly that she had sought or been offered any seat. But the rumours became so strong that one of the pre-selection candidates for Melbourne Ports, Michael Danby, the former head of Australian–Israel Publications, started writing to ALP members attacking her.[1]

The speculation was caused partly by the role Jennie had taken in Labor's re-election campaign. Keating made known his admiration for her efforts touring marginal seats to help win the women's vote. He also said he wanted more women, such as Jennie George, to enter Parliament, as part of his quest for high-profile talented women to address the gender imbalance on the government benches. Jennie reciprocated Keating's admiration and kept in her office a framed copy of a Melbourne newspaper's premature election-night front page that declared a Hewson victory. It was signed, 'Paul Keating, with appreciation and affection'.[2]

While downplaying speculation that she wanted a parliamentary future, Jennie *was* considering her options and had discussed her political ambitions with several union officials. The seat of

Melbourne Ports was mentioned. So was the seat of Batman, held by Deputy Prime Minister Brian Howe. Jennie was 46 and at a crossroads, she thought. She had to decide how she would spend the remaining fifteen-odd years of her working life. By now she had been mooted publicly as a possible successor to Ferguson. Succeeding Kelty was another possibility, especially when the man Kelty had been grooming, Iain Ross, was indicating privately that he wanted to bow out and pursue a different career.

The problem for Jennie was that she could wait for years. Neither Ferguson nor Kelty showed any sign of wanting to leave. They were re-elected for another six-year term, as she was, at the September 1993 congress. She believed they would serve out their terms. Once again she was restless, thinking that possibly she had reached a dead end at the ACTU. Ferguson's job was the one she really wanted. As she later recalled: 'If he was going to stay I was going to look elsewhere.' A parliamentary career now seemed to her the way to advance her career—in fact complete it—satisfying her need for a new challenge as well as her curiosity about how far she could go in political life.

Talk of Jennie's future went quiet for more than a year after the Melbourne Ports rumours. She, too, put serious thought of Federal politics aside until an historic rule change by delegates at the ALP national conference in Hobart on 27 September 1994. It guaranteed women a 35 per cent share of winnable State and Federal seats by 2002. The man whom Jennie regarded as her key supporter, the Prime Minister himself, hailed the new quota as 'a defining moment' that would shape the character of Australian politics and reshape the Labor Party.[3]

Joan Kirner, the former Victorian Premier, had led the push for female quotas in winnable seats. Aware in advance of the likely breakthrough, Jennie attended the conference to savour the moment with many of her ALP sisters, among them Meredith Burgmann, Pam Allan and recently acquired friends, Carmen Lawrence and Kirner. The conference came to a temporary halt after the rule change was passed when Jennie and other excited women delegates and observers invaded the floor to celebrate the victory. They danced and cheered and even cried, and then partied long into the night at the Wrest Point Casino Hotel where the conference was held.

The ALP had prominent women in its ranks, including two former premiers, Lawrence and Kirner, and had promoted women such as Susan Ryan and Ros Kelly to the Federal ministry during the Hawke–Keating years. But the number of female parliamentarians was still pitifully low. In the House of Representatives for example, women held only nine of Labor's 78 seats. The ALP rule change was important for Jennie because it reignited her thoughts about running for Parliament. The probability of her finding a seat was higher now but at 47 she had to act soon lest the younger generation of women pass her by.

Her only opportunity for advancement at the ACTU depended on one of the ACTU's two top officials, Ferguson or Kelty, standing aside. Still neither showed any inclination to do so. Kelty preferred to operate behind the scenes and was committed to shepherding through to completion the structural reforms to the union movement he had begun in the mid-1980s. He had never been interested in an alternative career, especially not parliamentary politics. He showed no sign of leaving, even when his protégé, Iain Ross, left to take up a vice-presidency of the Industrial Relations Commission in March 1994.

Ferguson, whose job was the more suited to Jennie's talents, had publicly ruled out a parliamentary career and said he wanted to stay in his job. But given the precedents set by former ACTU presidents Bob Hawke and Simon Crean, a switch to Federal politics did not seem out of the question. Ferguson's obstacle was that his ALP connections remained in Sydney and he had developed none within the ALP Socialist Left since arriving in Melbourne. He also appeared to have restored a passable, albeit cool, working relationship with Kelty. This reinforced Jennie's view that he was likely to remain ACTU president for some considerable time. She recalled:

I believe that you stay in a job and give it your best—but I see people staying around too long and they should move on. And it just seemed at the time from all the conversations taking place that Bill's and Martin's intentions were to run another term.

Jennie was new not only to the ALP but also to the complex factional make-up of its Victorian branch. Consequently she had no historical link with its competing factions—or their leaders. The main rival factions were the right-wing 'Labor Unity' and left-wing 'Socialist Left'. Two smaller factions were the 'Pledge', a hard left-wing breakaway from the Socialist Left, and the 'Independents', a small non-aligned group.

The natural faction for Jennie was the Socialist Left and the person whose support was vital to her run was Senator Kim Carr, the faction's leader and chief powerbroker in the Victorian ALP Left. Carr was tall, dark-haired with a beard and glasses, bearing a strong resemblance to the Irish Sinn Fein leader, Gerry Adams. He was known as a tough operator, applauded by his supporters for his effectiveness and for always honouring agreements but attacked by his critics for a dictatorial style in running his faction. He had good contacts in the Victorian union movement, such as Wally Curran from the Meat Workers' Union and John Corsetti from the AMWU. A serious student of left-wing ideology, he originally ran the Socialist Left faction as a teacher at working-class Glenroy Technical School. Teachers in the staff common room had been puzzled sometimes about why Carr spent so much time on the telephone.

As for past runs for positions of power, Jennie relied on someone as a backer and go-between. Her friend Jenny Doran, an ACTU industrial officer, happened to be a key figure in the Socialist Left and had introduced her to Carr. In discussions with Jennie, Carr said he wanted to help her, even though she had been in the Labor Party for only a short time. He suggested a Victorian Senate seat. There was a vacancy open for the third position on Labor's Victorian Senate ticket, to which the Left was entitled under a factional agreement with the Right. Jennie was the favourite but had to compete in a pre-selection ballot with Julia Gillard, a Melbourne lawyer. While Carr supported Jennie, it was also politically convenient for him to do so. He wanted to block Gillard. Although she came from the Socialist Left, Gillard was an opponent of Carr's from a group within the faction called the Socialist Forum. In hindsight, Jennie accepted that some of Carr's enthusiasm for her candidacy was 'less enthusiasm for me as opposition to Gillard'.

With the backing of Carr, Jennie finally ended speculation and broke her public silence about her parliamentary ambition on 20 October 1994 by announcing, via the media, that she intended to run for the Senate. As an internal matter for the Victorian ALP, the Prime Minister normally would not become involved. However, his office gave Jennie's candidacy a boost by happily declaring Keating's 'high regard' for her.

Kelty did not want to lose Jennie from the ACTU. He had asked her to stay but accepted that she had to make her own way for the future. Declaring her run, Jennie said, 'I had hoped that a bit further down the track the opportunity might be there. The opportunity has come along now and maybe I won't get it again.'[4]

Although positive about the decision she had made, a dramatic one after twenty years in union politics, there was a sour note to the occasion for Jennie. Her backer and friend at the ACTU, Jenny Doran, spent a day going around union leaders who belonged to the Socialist Left faction to secure their signatures of endorsement on Jennie's ALP pre-selection nomination form. They all signed. Doran did not seek Kelty's signature because although he supported Jennie, Kelty was not a member of the Left and his endorsement was not relevant to the ballot. Doran did, however, approach Martin Ferguson because he was in the ALP Left and his prestige as ACTU president could help Jennie's cause. But Ferguson refused. Doran recalled his angry response when she asked him in his office:

Martin hit the roof. It was incredible! I just wanted to get out of the room because the temperature went up 500 degrees! He hated her and wouldn't do anything that advanced her interests. She had come along to the ACTU and got along with Bill . . . Martin had come along and tried to set up his own power base.

Ferguson's refusal to sign Jennie's nomination form made no practical difference to Jennie's chances of winning ALP pre-selection but Jennie recalled that she was 'very hurt and upset' when Doran told her about Ferguson's response. It demonstrated clearly the deterioration of their relations.

The pre-selection ballot on 4 December was a breeze for Jennie. She was elected unopposed when the Socialist Left closed ranks behind her. Guillard withdrew to avoid risking a nasty split, but there was lingering bitterness in sections of the ALP Left that she had missed out. Jennie was now assured of the third spot on Labor's ticket, behind Senators Robert Ray and Barney Cooney, for an expected half-Senate election to be held in conjunction with the next election of the House of Representatives due before mid-1996.

The third spot on the Senate ticket that Jennie had scored was described as 'winnable' but in truth it was marginal. In a normal half-Senate election where six out of twelve Victorian seats were to be decided, three were the most that either of the two major political parties could hope to win.[5] The existence of minor parties such as the Democrats and the Greens, which could win Senate seats because of the proportional voting system used for the Upper House, made the third spot for Labor or the Coalition vulnerable.

Once Labor's unlikely re-election was taken into account, then Jennie's number three spot was even more vulnerable and she appeared headed for defeat. Jennie argued to the contrary, estimating she had a 'not unreasonable chance' of winning the seat. At the last half-Senate election in 1993, Zakharov had won her seat from the third position. Jennie claimed that her own personal support in the Victorian community would be sufficient to ensure she won the necessary votes. She claimed to be 'building a profile' not by virtue of her ACTU position alone but also from a Monday morning weekly chat slot she had started on Melbourne's ABC Radio station, 3LO, with host Peter Couchman.

Jennie over-estimated her profile. While she could claim some public recognition in Victoria as the first woman member of the ACTU executive and most senior woman union official in the country, she was still a newcomer to Melbourne and largely unknown there because she had spent most of her union career living in Sydney, working for a NSW union. Her profile carried much greater weight in NSW, residue from the media exposure she received in her battle with Terry Metherell.

If, as Jennie claimed, she had not been worried about the possibility of losing from her third position on the ALP ticket, she may not have taken the action she did following Senator Olive Zakharov's unexpected death on 6 March 1995. Despite being on the ticket for the next half-Senate election, Jennie hoped that she would be nominated by the Victorian ALP to fill the late senator's position as a casual vacancy. After all, like Jennie, Zakharov came from the Socialist Left.

For Jennie, the beauty of filling a casual vacancy was that she could enter the Senate immediately, as Labor's nominee to replace Zakharov, without any of the uncertainty attached to contesting a seat at the next election from the vulnerable third position on the party ticket. She would also gain the chance to see out the final year of Labor's term in Parliament. If her admiring Prime Minister won the next election, he might assist her promotion to a ministry. If he lost, Jennie would remain in the Senate well after the election because Zakharov's seat was not due for election until 1999.

Despite her best hopes, any expectation Jennie had to succeed Zakharov was misplaced. The above scenario came to naught. Although Zakharov was from the Socialist Left like Jennie, her seat was already promised to the Right upon retirement under a deal agreed between Carr and the Right's leader, Senator Robert Ray. This pre-arranged deal was part of a series of trade-offs between the two faction leaders in the complicated but normal negotiations over internal pre-selection of candidates for Federal parliamentary seats that had been conducted during the 1994 Hobart ALP conference and beforehand under a ten-year agreement.

Jennie was the meat in the sandwich of these factional dealings. Neither Ray nor Carr was prepared to unravel the deal for her. Carr said he was obliged to honour his agreement with Ray and Ray insisted on sticking to it. Carr's ability to alter the deal was limited because he and Ray had agreed on a 50–50 split for ALP Senate seats in which Ray had given away two out of three 'winnable' Senate positions to the Left for the next election. Carr recalled:

> We did put the case that we [the Socialist Left] should take [Zakharov's] spot and then in a mischievous way the Right said, 'well of course' and we said, 'well, we will'. Then they hit the roof—and said it was a breach of the agreement. So there was no question, in terms of her, about honouring that agreement 50–50. That's significant because at the time we [the Socialist Left] were under 40 per cent of the vote—so it was a good arrangement for us.

Jennie was unacceptable to Robert Ray not for any personal reasons, but merely because she came from the wrong faction. He was not about to give up his arrangement with Carr and thereby put the Right at a disadvantage. Jennie's public profile was not so high that she could demand that Ray or Carr make way for her. While factional dealings were Ray's priority, he *did* replace Zakharov with a woman. In keeping with the ALP push for female candidates, he agreed that a woman should take the seat and nominated the Right's Jacinta Collins to fill the vacancy.

When Jennie complained to Carr about her situation, he

This photograph of Jennie, who still smokes, was taken at her Haberfield home not long after she was elected general secretary in September 1979. She took periods of time-off before and after Paddy George's death in June 1980.

Jennie with Jack Mundey (right) and her stepfather, Vladimir Feodosiu (left). She was attracted to Mundey's flamboyant nature and his heroic persona.

Wiry, boyish-looking Simon Marginson, the bright union research officer four years Jennie's junior with whom she had a relationship that lasted almost five years. He is pictured in 1982 at the cellar door of a Margaret River vineyard—collecting wine became a hobby for both of them.

Jennie moved to Canberra in late 1982 so she could live with Simon Marginson but regularly returned to Sydney to visit her mother and stepfather, Vladimir. Here she is with Marginson and Vladimir.

'How do we top this?' said Jennie heading to the dais to address a 50 000-strong rally of teachers, parents and students who filled Sydney's Domain to protest against Terry Metherell's education reforms. (Courtesy NSW Teachers Federation)

Jennie addresses the rally before marchers pour into Macquarie Street and demand, unsuccessfully, to speak to Metherell at Parliament House.

When Jennie was elected an ACTU assistant secretary in 1991 she agreed to pose next to a life-size bust of Bob Hawke, the most spectacular ACTU president in the organisation's history. She dismissed speculation that she would run for the presidency, but the incumbent, Martin Ferguson, was entitled to draw some uncomfortable conclusions. (Courtesy of Fairfax Photo Library)

A special moment. Jennie celebrates her appointment as ACTU president-elect at the 1995 ACTU Congress in Melbourne. With her are her mother, Natasha, and ACTU secretary Bill Kelty. (Courtesy of Brett Faulkner, *Australian*)

The admiration's mutual. Jennie George and Prime Minister Paul Keating enjoy a moment together at the 1995 ACTU Congress hours after she officially became president-elect. Jennie had helped Keating to his election victory in 1993 by campaigning in marginal seats and repeated the effort in the ill-fated 1996 campaign. (Courtesy of Fairfax Photo Library)

Jennie George and Cathy Bloch remain close after many years of friendship. They first met while members of the Eureka Youth League in the 1960s.

The ACTU's big day in court at the height of the Weipa dispute, 20 November 1995. The room is packed with media and union faithful. At the bar table Jennie chats with Bob Hawke, rehabilitated as the ACTU's chief advocate for the Industrial Relations Commission proceedings in Sydney. Bill Kelty, not unusually, keeps his head down and shies away from the cameras. (Courtesy of Fairfax Photo Library—Andrew Meares)

Jennie takes the lead outside the courtroom to announce a great victory for the ACTU in the Weipa dispute after an emotional Hawke claims to have destroyed CRA's case. (Courtesy of Fairfax Photo Library—Dean Sewell)

Mixing with workers, Jennie sips a beer in the steamy heat of Weipa on 28 November 1995. She had a job to do though—to convince workers to give up their strike after the ACTU reached a setttlement with CRA in Sydney. (Courtesy of Fairfax Photo Library)

reminded her that she had already won pre-selection for the third position and should be content with that. He stressed that while he was now number one on his half of the Senate ticket due for election in 1999, he had begun his Senate career in 1990 from the third Senate spot—even though he was leader of the faction. He argued it was legitimate for Jennie also to stand for the marginal position first.

Jennie was far from content. She became angry and frustrated about the way the Victorian ALP's factions worked. It also occurred to her that Carr might have a personal interest in holding her back from Zakharov's seat. If she took Zakharov's seat, then in pre-selections for that half of the Senate due for election in 1999, she might displace Carr from his number-one position and relegate him to the marginal position that had been Zakharov's seat.

In continuing discussions with Jennie about her future, Carr said that if she was unhappy with her spot on Labor's Senate ticket, then she could stand for a Lower House seat. He suggested two safe Victorian Federal seats—Maribyrnong and Batman—but could assure neither of them to Jennie. Maribyrnong was available because the sitting member, Alan Griffiths, had decided to quit at the next election after resigning from the Keating ministry over a dispute about a Moonee Ponds sandwich shop he owned. The problem for Jennie was that the Right, not Carr's Socialist Left, controlled Maribyrnong. The only hope she had of winning Maribyrnong rested on the fact that the leading Right candidate, Bob Sercombe, had antagonised some in his own faction. If enough ALP members from the electorate's Right faction could be convinced to switch their pre-selection votes from Sercombe to her, she had a slim chance of winning.

The other seat, Batman, first mentioned as a possible for Jennie in 1993, was equally uncertain but for different reasons. Held by the Deputy Prime Minister, Brian Howe, Batman *was* a Socialist Left seat. It was not available yet but Carr's faction knew it would be available 'sooner or later' when Howe announced his anticipated retirement. Carr put the proposition to Jennie. He recalled, 'It was a case of "should there be a vacancy in Batman"—that kind of approach'.

Jennie rejected standing for either seat. According to Carr, she told him that she did not believe they were secure enough. Jennie's critics claimed she wanted a Senate seat with its non-specific statewide electorate because she did not want to do the hard work of a local member in a Lower House seat, dealing with voter grievances and ingratiating herself with a local community. Carr attributed her reluctance to different reason. He recalled, 'It struck me that there might be other issues—what I assumed to be Ferguson, involving changes within the ACTU and that she might stay at the ACTU [to become president]'.

Indeed there were rumours during the early months of 1995 that Ferguson wanted to quit the ACTU for a seat in Federal Parliament. The strongest, which Ferguson vehemently denied, was that he would return to NSW and take the ALP seat of Banks, held by his factional ally Daryl Melham.

According to Jennie, her name was mentioned in connection with a number of Lower House seats when factions were looking around to defeat a particular candidate, such as Sercombe. She recalled: 'I have always made it very clear that the only position for me would be an Upper House seat because I don't have an established record of community activity.'

As weeks passed, Jennie's anger intensified over her rejection for Zakharov's seat. It seemed obvious to her that she was the best candidate. She was also just the sort of high-profile woman the ALP had declared it needed when the 35 per cent quota was set in Hobart. She even had the personal endorsement of the Prime Minister. Were these factors not enough for the male powerbrokers to accept her?

Jennie was entitled to feel disgusted because her ability and experience counted for nothing in the dealings of the men who ran the factions and filled Zakharov's seat. A woman had filled the position, but only because it suited the Right to do so. Where Jennie's anger was unjustified was her naivety about how the ALP worked—the political realities of its factions and the consequences of having been a party member for a short time. She was also egotistical in believing that she was entitled to a seat and that the admiration of the Prime Minister should give her carte blanche. She even convinced herself that jealousy had played a part in holding her back because of fears that Keating would favour her above others if she entered the Senate.

Jennie vented her fury and frustrations at a restaurant dinner on 15 May with union friends and journalists, the start of a three-day meeting of the ACTU's revamped 100-member council held in the Victorian beach-resort town of Lorne. All night she harped about not gaining a seat in Parliament, saying she was the best candidate and yet the ALP still would not hand her Olive Zakharov's Senate seat, or Maribyrnong for that matter. As the night wore on, she commiserated with the author and her old Kent Street Mafia friend George Campbell, who sympathised as he was also engaged in a battle to win the numbers for a NSW Senate seat.

As Rex Hewett among others had observed, Jennie often processed her thoughts in moments of crisis by returning to them again and again in social situations, primed by alcohol. So it was at Lorne. By the time she returned to Melbourne she had made up her mind to withdraw from the Senate race altogether and stay at the ACTU. It was a risky call—Jennie could have looked weak given that it was known she wanted to leave and had gone out on a limb to win pre-selection for the Senate. However, she handled her withdrawal with aplomb, issuing a carefully worded statement on 18 May that was gracious in its loyalty to the ALP and betrayed none of her bitterness. It said:

> This morning I notified the State secretary of the ALP of my decision to withdraw from the Victorian ALP Senate team.
>
> Since my pre-selection to the Victorian Senate team in December

last year, a number of significant changes and developments in the trade union movement have caused me to reconsider my nomination.

Since my pre-selection a number of senior and experienced male and female leaders in the movement have either departed, or signified their intention to leave.

This comes at a time when the union movement is facing a significant challenge to turn around the decline in union membership, and where collective experience is needed more than ever.

In addition, the ACTU is working on a number of key issues aimed at encouraging women to join—such as pursuit of equal pay, family and maternity leave, and access to superannuation.

I have been asked by many people in the movement and particularly by the ACTU secretary, to reconsider my decision in light of the challenges facing us and the changed circumstances.

I feel confident that there are many capable women who can replace me on the Senate team, and that in light of the circumstances outlined, the most effective contribution I can make on behalf of working people is not to leave the ACTU at this stage.

Following the recent Budget, I believe the ALP is in a strong position to go on to win the next Federal election. I intend to be as actively involved as I was in the last Federal election campaign to secure the re-election of the Keating Government.

The unspoken subtext to Jennie's statement was that she was fed up with the ALP's deal makers and gender politics. But the key to her decision to stay was her reference to Kelty and the role he played in persuading her. Kelty never wanted Jennie to leave the ACTU and doubted she could win from the third Senate spot. Speaking to her privately during the Lorne conference, Kelty's first concern was that she remain because of the exodus of senior-level union officials. Among the men who had departed 'or signified their intention to leave' were Iain Ross, Peter Robson and George Campbell. Women in the same category were Anna Booth, Pat Staunton and Marilyn Beaumont. The departure of these senior women in particular was disturbing for Kelty because it upset the ACTU's attempt to boost female representation.

But there was an underlying though related reason for Kelty's concern. If Ferguson were to quit, Kelty had no replacement waiting in the wings of sufficient status or ability—or of the right gender—to become ACTU president. For some years, Kelty had been close to Anna Booth, secretary of the Clothing Trades Union. The general view was that Ferguson's eventual successor should be the first woman president and Booth was touted as Kelty's preference. Although she toyed with the idea, Booth lived in Sydney, had two young children and did not want to shift to Melbourne because she was married to a barrister establishing a Sydney practice. She had recently chosen to bow out of the union movement for a job in private enterprise. Keeping Jennie was important for Kelty—her level of experience would always make her attractive but especially in the event that the ACTU presidency became vacant.

Jennie had no prior warning that Ferguson was contemplating his departure, despite rumours that he was interested in the Sydney seat of Banks. She no longer had any communication with him at a personal level. She also claimed to have no early signal from Kelty that he would support her for the ACTU presidency.

Kelty had some knowledge of Ferguson's thoughts of leaving, though he did not hear it from Ferguson himself. Instead Ferguson confided to several of his union friends outside the ACTU that he and his wife, Trisha, were agonising about whether to stay in Melbourne or pack up and return to Sydney, partly because they wanted no interruptions to their children's high school education. Kelty learnt of Ferguson's deliberations second-hand. It did not mean that Ferguson was definitely leaving but Kelty needed to be prepared.

The announcement on 20 June 1995 of Brian Howe's immediate resignation as Deputy Prime Minister and his intention to retire from the Victorian seat of Batman at the next election surprised everyone. It was believed that Howe would go in the not-too-distant future but even in recent months he had told people in his faction, the Socialist Left, that he did not intend leaving yet. Keating was among the few to know in advance, having held private discussions with Howe over a three-week period. They finally reached an agreement on the Saturday evening of 17 June (after inquiries by the *Sunday Age* newspaper to Howe's office indicated information was leaking) that Howe would stand down on 20 June and be replaced with a minimum of fuss in preparation for the next election.[6]

The timing of Howe's announced resignation was politically exquisite. It came on the first day of hearings by a West Australian Royal Commission into the role of the State's former premier, Carmen Lawrence, in a 1992 divorce petition that defamed a Perth woman, Penny Easton, and preceded Easton's suicide. Since moving to Federal politics and becoming Health Minister in March 1994, the 'younger, brighter' Lawrence had been compared favourably with the 'tired, earnest' Howe and was regarded by ALP powerbrokers as his successor as Deputy Prime Minister. But allegations about Lawrence's role in the petition had changed all that, taking the gloss off her image. Howe had feared Lawrence ever since she entered Federal Parliament and did not want her to succeed him.[7] Lawrence's presence also threatened the chances of her fellow West Australian minister, Kim Beazley, succeeding Howe. Beazley was Howe's preference for Deputy Prime Minister. By resigning when he did, Howe effectively blocked Lawrence and assured Beazley the job. Lawrence accepted she was out of the running and agreed not to stand. In a neat transition, Howe resigned and the ALP caucus elected Beazley unopposed on the same day.

The other feature in the timing of Howe's resignation, however coincidental, was the way it proved crucial for the future of Martin Ferguson—and ultimately Jennie George. If Howe had stayed on, the entire course of ACTU history may have differed. By announcing he would not stand again, Howe's Victorian seat of Batman was suddenly vacant for the next election, just when Martin Ferguson was contemplating whether to stay or quit as ACTU president. Ferguson had been close politically to Howe but had no advance warning of Howe's departure. Now he was presented with a big opportunity and had some serious thinking to do: would he run for Batman? Doing so was fraught with difficulty even though Ferguson had the prestige of the ACTU presidency behind him. He still had no base in the Victorian ALP Left and was regarded as an outsider. To win pre-selection, Ferguson would have to strong-arm his way past the ALP's two leading candidates, Theo Theophanous from the Socialist Left and Jenny Mikakos from the Pledge, both of whom had strong local branch support and no intention of stepping aside for anyone.

Jennie had just started a two-week holiday at a resort in Vanuatu when Howe announced his decision to retire. It took nine days for her name to emerge as an important piece of the jigsaw. She was lying by the pool on June 29 when a fax arrived, sent by her office secretary in Melbourne. It was a copy of a Canberra report from the *Age* newspaper that day, titled 'Ferguson pushed for Howe's seat', which confirmed that Ferguson was being promoted to run for Batman. What excited Jennie was that the article prominently declared that Ferguson's departure would clear the way for her to take the ACTU presidency.[8]

It seemed remarkable. Here she was, in absentia, sunbaking on a South Pacific island. The media back home was saying that, as if by magic, she was assured of winning the most senior public position in Australia's union movement.

It was not that simple, of course. After having missed out on Zakharov's seat, Jennie was the 'obvious candidate' because Kelty had helped her back on the path to the ACTU presidency, positioning her in the event of Ferguson's departure. Within the ACTU, the sentiment from Kelty down was that electing the first woman president—Jennie in particular—could help solve the union movement's recent problems in attracting women recruits.

She also was thought to be the best person to appeal to the general community for support and to carry the union side of public debate if Labor lost the next election and unions faced a hostile Coalition government.

On holiday in Vanuatu with Jennie were her mother, Natasha, and Natasha's friend, Vera Shihoff. Jennie had shouted the trip for each of them. When she told them the news, Natasha expressed caution. 'I said to Jennie, "in such chauvinistic unions, you will be the only woman!" I said "No, better not". She said, "I will see, Mum".'

When Jennie returned from Vanuatu a few days later, she plunged back into her work. From Sydney, she talked by telephone to Kelty in Melbourne about the transition of the ACTU leadership, then boarded a flight bound for Perth. Her job in Perth was to play a leading role in the public campaign of unions against legislation proposed by Richard Court's West Australian Government imposing severe curbs on union activity.

Before Jennie left for Perth, however, there was a major financial transaction of a personal nature that needed completion. She had to speak to her bank manager about finalising a new property purchase. Back in April, when Jennie was in turmoil about her future—to leave the ACTU or stay—she had made a decision to move back to Sydney. She wanted to be close to her mother again and eventually retire in her home city. In the short time she was involved with the Victorian ALP, she had also become so jaded about the horse-trading of its male powerbrokers that she wanted to leave the State behind. After several rounds of house-hunting, Jennie had bought a brand-new unit in Manly, the northern beach suburb of Sydney, and planned to make it her home. Did this signal that she did not intend to take up the opportunity that Ferguson's likely departure offered her? After all, the ACTU presidency was traditionally based in Melbourne. Just as she was being touted as the next ACTU president, she appeared to be making Sydney her home again.

PRESIDENT

All the signs favoured Martin Ferguson making the leap into Federal politics and clearing the way for Jennie to become the first woman ACTU president. Ferguson's decision had nothing to do with her, of course. He and Jennie disliked each other intensely now. For Ferguson, however, there were powerful reasons to make the transition. It was a neat resolution of his frictions with Kelty but more compelling was that politics ran in his blood. He was the son of Jack Ferguson, a former NSW Deputy Premier. His brother Laurie already had a safe seat in Federal Parliament and if he wanted a seat in Parliament too, he would be a fool if he did not make his run now, while ACTU president, by exploiting the precedent set by Bob Hawke and followed by Simon Crean.

Ferguson ended speculation about whether he would stand for Brian Howe's seat on 12 July 1995 when he submitted his name for ALP pre-selection for Batman just hours before nominations were due to close. Despite her mother's misgivings, Jennie had already made up her mind to stand for the ACTU presidency if Ferguson decided to leave. Considering Ferguson's continuing status as president, Jennie stated her ambition diplomatically but left no doubt:

> If and when there is a vacancy, I will throw my hat in the ring.
> Martin still has a big challenge ahead of him and he's still president
> of the ACTU until such time as he is successful in his pre-selection
> for Batman. I will stand on my experience and record.[1]

Although still plagued by insecurities from time to time and a little nervous about the responsibility she stood to assume, Jennie did not have the hesitation she had in the past in declaring her run. She was more confident about her abilities and accepted that fortune had put this prize her way after the blight of the Zakharov affair:

> It's always my judgment that if Martin had stayed another term,
> which was what I was expecting, that Anna [Booth] would be the
> first female president. That was just a chance freak of history that
> he left when he did and I was there to take on the job.

There was no need to count votes. Jennie was the only serious candidate and it quickly became clear that she would be elected unopposed. She received a groundswell of support from union leaders across the factions—a mark not only of her quality as a candidate but also testimony to the way Kelty had succeeded in easing deep-rooted factional tensions of the past.

Only one person, Stan Sharkey, the successor to Tom McDonald as national secretary of the renamed Construction Forestry Mining and Energy Union (CFMEU), expressed the opinion in public that he wished Ferguson were staying. Sharkey's view was not driven by personal animosity towards Jennie. He liked her. But he also liked Ferguson and reflected the desire of a number of union officials who wanted Ferguson to stay as a counterbalance to the power of Bill Kelty. This group also appreciated that Ferguson's rough edges appealed to blue-collar workers and that he had created a useful role for himself helping to solve difficult industrial disputes such as the strike at Tasmania's APPM paper mill in Burnie.

Despite Sharkey's initial comments, within days he and his union quickly swung behind Ferguson for Parliament and Jennie for the presidency. Along with other unions, the CFMEU abandoned support for the Socialist Left candidate for Batman, Theo Theophanous, and pledged the pre-selection votes it controlled to Ferguson.

Kelty's main concern in all of these dealings was to see that Ferguson succeeded once he had declared he wanted Batman—because Kelty wanted Jennie in the ACTU presidency. The ALP hierarchy too had to ensure Ferguson succeeded. It could not risk the severe embarrassment of having an ACTU president fail. A reluctant Kim Carr, as head of Victoria's ALP Socialist Left, came under strong pressure to accommodate Ferguson—to the point of threats of intervention by the ALP's Federal executive if he did not. After much acrimony, Ferguson's rival candidates, Theophanous and Mikakos, withdrew from the pre-selection race on 12 August so he could win without a fight.[2]

Most of Jennie's anger about her own failed run for Parliament had faded—but the irony was not lost on her: Ferguson, a male outsider from Sydney, could strong-arm his way into a safe Victorian seat but she, a woman who had ALP pre-selection, could not.

As soon as Ferguson secured his pre-selection, Jennie was thrust into the ACTU's frontline, even though she was not due to be officially anointed president-elect until the following month at the ACTU's congress. It was agreed with Kelty that from now until Ferguson officially resigned as president at the Federal election, Jennie was to take over most of Ferguson's public duties. She would serve out the rest of his term as president—due to expire in September 1997—when Ferguson officially resigned at the election. In the meantime, Ferguson was to be a figurehead, but remaining in the background as he acquainted himself with his new electorate.

Jennie's first opportunity to step into her new role came just days after Ferguson secured Batman pre-selection. On 15 August she took the role of ACTU spokesperson to the assembled media, normally reserved for the president, for the first time after the day's proceedings of the ACTU executive in Melbourne. For Jennie, it was also the first time she spelt out what her goals would be as head of the trade union movement. Her three main priorities, she said, would be to get back in touch with rank-and-file unionists, to boost union membership and, in the lead-up to the next election, expose to workers what she regarded as the harmful effects of the Coalition's industrial relations policy. The challenge for unions, she said, was to speak a language that workers understood and to be seen as staunch defenders of their aspirations:

> The first thing I want to do is actually to get out of 397 Swanston Street and spend time at the coalface and get a feeling for the concerns of working people. I had a salutary experience last week going to a clothing factory and seeing how much things that had meant so much to me, like equal employment opportunity, had hardly touched the lives of migrant women workers.[3]

Jennie also stressed that while she was 'well known for coming from the Left' she would not act in a factional manner as ACTU president by favouring one side or the other. She did not intend to follow the example of her predecessors by representing the ACTU at the International Labour Organisation—she would leave this task to other officials while she concentrated on local issues. She also could not resist at least one last swipe at the male-dominated factional system of the ALP. There was an obvious personal tinge to her complaint about the failure of the party to promote women of merit or to place them in winnable seats as promised:

> The irony is that we will probably see fewer women in Parliament representing Labor after the election than we have at the moment—but I think this can only be [rectified] when the Federal executive

bites the bullet. I mean, if you leave women to the mercy of factional power plays, then we are not going to achieve the target that the Labor Party has set.[4]

The main opportunity for Jennie to set down her priorities for the presidency was a set-piece speech at the ACTU congress in Melbourne on 27 September. It followed a celebratory ritual that day in which she was officially anointed 'ACTU president-elect'. For this stage-managed occasion, Jennie invited her mother and a large collection of guests, mainly women colleagues and personal friends, to join her on the congress podium at Melbourne University's Wilson Hall. She wanted them to share the proud moment when she was officially declared the next ACTU president and significantly the first woman to hold the position leading Australia's 2.3 million-strong union movement.

Amid balloons, streamers and bouquets of flowers, Jennie stood between Natasha and Bill Kelty. Those behind her included Senator Cheryl Kernot, Joan Kirner, Anne Summers, Cathy Bloch, Mavis Robertson, Helen Hewett, Rex Hewett, Sharan Burrow, Wendy Caird, Margaret Reynolds and Father Frank Cappo. As Jennie was endorsed president-elect by acclamation, Helen Reddy's feminist anthem, 'I Am Woman', was played over the public address system. Jennie led everyone in singing along.

Once the festive part of the occasion was over, Kelty paid tribute to Jennie, describing her as 'simply the best' and saying she had always carried a torch for battlers, working people and women. He continued:

> Jennie George, we are proud to have you as our president in the future. The battles will be tough. The battles are there to be fought and are there to be won. Women have not had it easy in politics and they have not had it easy in the union movement. When Jennie became the first woman on the ACTU executive, it was a pretty old-fashioned male chauvinist show. Jennie changed it. It is not easy being 'one out', but at the end of the day, Jennie won her battle and won it convincingly.[5]

Jennie then launched into her inaugural speech as president-elect, building upon the themes she had enunciated the month before. The speech was important because what she said this day would become the standard against which her presidency would be measured. After declaring that her endorsement was a victory for all women, Jennie admitted to having no blueprint for the job and said she had a steep learning curve ahead, considering her experience was mainly with white-collar, public sector workers in education. There was an agenda beneath the public modesty, however. Her main pledge to congress delegates was to address the needs of working people and to ensure she knew what these were by spending time meeting them in their places of work. These visits would also contribute heavily to her role in an ACTU recruitment campaign:

> I think to be a good, effective spokesperson for the union movement, I have to understand how people are feeling, what they've lived through, what their aspirations are, what their expectation of the union movement is. So a lot of my time over the next two years will be spent on what might appear to some to be very mundane issues, but to me [they are] the fundamental issues that will decide our strength into the future. I'll be very involved in workplace organisation issues and, as I say, I'll be very involved with affiliates, spending time with you and your members and seeing at first hand the diversity of jobs that are undertaken by our people.

Also rating highly for Jennie was defeating what she defined as a 'tremendously important ideological agenda' of the Coalition parties. The anti-union agenda had taken root first in Victoria under Jeff Kennett, then spread to Western Australia under Richard Court, whose recent legislation she labelled the most anti-democratic the country had seen in attacking the collective representation of workers' interests. At the next Federal election, there was a strong possibility that a Coalition Government led by John Howard would come to power and implement its own tough agenda to curb union rights and privileges. Jennie stressed the importance of historic ties between the union movement and the ALP. She reminded the audience of her 'huge admiration for Paul Keating' and recounted achievements of Labor's reign such as a national superannuation scheme, Medicare, family allowances, a child-care relief system and paid maternity benefits, that she said would not have been possible if the party was not in government. But the prospect of a Coalition election victory prompted her pledge to congress delegates to seek formal negotiations with the Australian Democrats, the Greens and minority parties, mindful of their crucial position in holding the balance of power in the Senate and ability to ensure the passage of legislation. Her priority here was to ensure the minority parties understood the need to protect the award system, so it remained a 'safety net' to protect workers' minimum pay rates. She also intended to strengthen links with community groups, especially welfare organisations regarded as the union movement's natural allies, such as the Australian Council of Social Service, the Brotherhood of St Laurence and the Catholic Social Justice Commission. She intended to continue her work on Aboriginal reconciliation, believing that the union movement had an obligation to extend a hand to people 'who are often in worse situations than even the most vulnerable in our ranks'. The finale to Jennie's speech was an assurance that she would be a fair president:

> What I want to say to all the unions is, you know where my commitments lie. They are solidly of the Left and I will never walk away from that. But I can assure you that as president-elect I have no interest in factional games and neither do the members whom we are elected to represent. I don't think, quite frankly, they care where we stand politically, providing we do the job and deliver the benefits that they all expect from being a member of the union. So I'd like to say to all unions, I thank you most sincerely for the trust and confidence you've placed in me and, as I say, I hope I will live up at least to half the expectations.
>
> In conclusion can I thank all my friends who've come along

to share this special moment, both inside and outside the union movement—I thank them for their personal support. And last, but most importantly, I thank Mum for making it all possible, for making the sacrifices to give me a good quality public education. I thank her for her love and support and I think she's very proud that the opportunities this country gave me, and her, will be put to good effect.

This was a day of wonderful celebration for Jennie, charged with goodwill and hope. It would remain one of the fondest memories of her life. Among congratulatory letters and cards Jennie received was one from Simon Marginson's parents. It niggled her that she heard no word from Marginson himself and that he did not drop by the Wilson Hall to congratulate her personally—considering he worked just nearby on the university campus.

One of the letters Jennie cherished most came from Bob Hawke:

Dear Jenny [*sic*]

First of all, my sincere congratulations on your uncontested ascendency to the Presidency of the ACTU. I believe it is a fitting recognition of your integrity, talents and total commitment to the cause of the working men and women of Australia. It is pleasing to me that this important position is held by a principled person from the Left and, for the first time, by a woman.

May I say on a personal note as one who knows how much I owe to my own mother that I appreciate your constant reference to the indebtedness you feel to yours.

Every period in our history has carried its particular problems and challenges for the trade union movement and its leadership. Certainly, the present and the years ahead of you are no exception. It seems to me that the secret of success in meeting the challenge is always the same—to understand the fundamental forces of change that are occurring in our own society and the international community in which we are inevitably enmeshed and, while remaining true to the basic principles of our movement, adapt and create policies and programs that will best harness the power of those forces in protecting and advancing the interests of working people.

I regret that because of a temporary bad back I was not able, on medical advice, to be with you for the ACTU dinner on Thursday night. If sometime when you are in Sydney it would be possible to have a yarn, I would love to do so.

Again, My congratulations and with every best wish,

Yours sincerely,
BOB HAWKE

For all the shared celebration and outpouring of congratulation that echoed through the hall and in the well-wishing correspondence, the future for the union movement and Jennie's own role as its leader looked anything but positive. She was endorsed as the next ACTU president at a crisis point in union history. The obstacles confronting unions were so immense and outside her control that Jennie's chances of being regarded as a success in the job were seriously undermined.

Despite strength of numbers in some traditional blue-collar areas, union memberships were in serious decline as a proportion of the total workforce. Recent figures also showed that for the first time, union numbers were down in absolute terms. Over the past five years the total membership had fallen from 2.7 million to 2.3 million despite growth in the employment market.

Unions were not popular because of a poor public image dating back to their industrial militancy of the 1970s and because some of them had failed to adapt their approach to modern circumstances. Media coverage often still focused on strikes, reinforcing the negative side of union behaviour in the public mind.

Unpopularity aside, the reason for belonging to a union was no longer readily apparent to the majority of the community, especially the affluent middle class that formed its bulk. For them good pay and working conditions appeared guaranteed and not under any obvious threat that required union protection. The hard battles fought earlier in the century to win community standards of working life that most enjoyed—such as minimum pay, hours of work, sick leave and annual leave—were taken for granted. The materialistic society that Australia had become had little concern for the historical role of unions in having built and maintained those standards, even though one in ten people was unemployed.

From their humble beginnings in Australia in the 1850s, unions had undergone a turbulent history in the early twentieth century, eventually becoming part of the institutional make-up of the country as registered organisations and respondents to awards overseen by the Conciliation and Arbitration Commission.[6] According to 'census' figures of union returns provided to the Australian Bureau of Statistics, union members as a proportion of all employees peaked in 1953 at 63 per cent. These census figures showed that a majority of the workforce continued to belong to unions throughout the 1960s and 1970s but the trend was distinctly downwards. The proportion of union members had slumped to 40 per cent by 1995. Most disturbing for unions, however, was a separate survey-based measure of total membership adopted by the Australian Bureau of Statistics that was generally regarded as more accurate. These figures showed that union membership when Bob Hawke became Prime Minister stood at 42 per cent of the total workforce and by 1995 had fallen to just 33 per cent. The most significant part of these results—and the cause of union alarm—was the private sector in which the bulk of people were employed, where membership had slumped to just 27 per cent. Unions stood to become politically and socially irrelevant if this rate of decline continued unabated.[7]

Kelty had recognised the problem in the mid-1980s. Under his leadership, the ACTU had devised a number of counter-measures to try to reverse the decline. A paper he released in 1986 called *Future Strategies* outlined a program of union amalgamations to turn Australia's traditional craft-based unions into about 20 broad industry-based unions, in the hope that large, well-resourced organisations could stem the tide. With the advent of a decentralised wage system, these large industry unions were meant to become more self-reliant, less dependant on the ACTU for direction and able to use enterprise bargaining as a recruitment tool.

Kelty himself kick-started the process of reducing 150 federally registered unions and a myriad of state-registered unions by devising rules, approved by the ACTU congress, under which unions were defined as principle, significant or other. A 'principle' union would continue to exist as a dominant entity among the lucky 20 and swallow up others. A 'significant' union had secondary status in any amalgamation and could exist as a division of a larger union. A union referred to as 'other' was headed for oblivion.

By 1995 Kelty had come close to his model of 20 industry unions, a remarkable feat of his leadership considering the factional divisions he encountered and the reluctance of many officials in the old craft-based unions to lose their little empires.[8] The way Kelty had succeeded was by a combination of persuasion and sometimes outright bullying. He also received specific help from Labor: the Federal Government forced many small unions into mergers by passing legislation that none was permitted to have less than 10 000 members.

However well intended, Kelty's plan did not halt the union membership decline. Altering the structure of unions by itself was not enough to make a difference. Many became too distracted by internal fights over the spoils of power—and the difficulties created by too many officials for too few positions at the top of merged unions—to bother focusing on recruitment as Kelty wanted them to.

In search of other methods to retain or sign-up union members, Kelty encouraged a range of incentive schemes, including discount home loans, travel, insurance, credit cards and other financial services. While these incentives were up and running, still they appeared to have no impact on the central problem they were meant to address. At the 1995 congress, Kelty announced his latest plan to revive unions by transferring ACTU funds back to unions specifically for recruitment. He set a target of 200 000 new members over the next two years and the training of 300 new organisers to help in the task.

In his farewell address to the congress after Jennie was anointed president, Martin Ferguson conceded that despite its best efforts, the union movement had failed to capture 'the hearts and minds of a new generation' of young people entering the job market. Yet it was crucial to the survival of unions that they capture this young generation. Women, who may have welcomed Jennie's appointment as a sign of changing attitudes, also had turned their backs on unions. They were entering the workforce at a faster rate than men but most were not interested in signing up with a union. Organised labour was regarded as out of touch.

Another major difficulty for unions was the changing composition of the job market. Part-time and casual jobs, always a troublesome area for recruitment, were increasing at the expense of full-time employment. New industries, often geographically disparate and therefore difficult for unions to target, were springing up in the financial services, hospitality, retail and tourism sectors at the same time jobs in formerly labour intensive and highly unionised industries such as manufacturing and mining were on the wane.

Having inherited public responsibility for this complex issue of union decline, the factor that stood to work still further against Jennie's ability to lead any rearguard campaign against it was that the fall was occurring in an increasingly hostile political environment. Companies such as the mining giant CRA had launched major offensives on union strength, competing for the loyalty of union members by offering workers non-union individual employment contracts, often at higher rates of pay, which destroyed the collectivist principle that lay at the heart of unionism.

The most galling aspect of these contracts for many unions was that their new style of 'direct relationship' between employer and worker—designed to shut out unions—was happening when the movement's supposed soul mate, the Labor Party, was still in office nationally. Keating's Government had made some token protest about the behaviour of CRA and other anti-union companies. But it had also recognised reality after twelve years in office by giving legal recognition, for the first time, to a form of non-union bargaining in Federal laws introduced in 1994 by the Industrial Relations Minister, Laurie Brereton. To union leaders who had played their part in maintaining wage restraint for the sake of employment and economic growth in the 1980s, and thought they were partners with Labor in an Accord that had endured for all of the Government's term, it was a difficult reform to stomach.

Tensions in the Labor–ACTU relationship, especially from among the left-wing unions to whom Jennie owed her allegiance, were surfacing openly now and Jennie would have to deal with them. It appeared to many officials that, first under Hawke and now Keating, Labor was as good as aiding and abetting an anti-union culture by pursuing policies that made sacrifices to the god of economic rationalism and failed to take into account the party's historic relationship with the union movement.

If there was lingering resentment among unions about Labor, however, it paled by comparison with the fearful apprehension about what lay ahead if a Coalition Government led by John Howard won the next election. Keating was expected to call the election sometime in the first three months of 1996. If the Coalition won, as anticipated, Jennie was destined to spend her entire ACTU presidency cast in a reactive role, continually opposing the government over policy changes and receiving no thanks for a potentially pressure-packed, soul-destroying task. The last ACTU president cast in that role was Cliff Dolan during the dying days of the Fraser Government. By comparison, Jennie's immediate predecessors Crean and Ferguson had enjoyed a smooth ride, basking in the glow of the Accord with Labor, enjoying the privileges of political influence and access to power it bestowed for their entire terms in the presidency.

Howard and his industrial relations spokesman, Peter Reith, had not unveiled their revised industrial relations policy since the Coalition's defeat at the 1993 election. But there was enough detail available—combined with some tough anti-union rhetoric coming from them both—to know that winding back union power was on the agenda. Already Howard and Reith had indicated strong support to companies wanting CRA-style non-union contracts. An obvious target for Coalition attack was the Industrial Relations Commission, which Howard and Reith regarded as a hindrance to labour market reform because of its clubbish atmosphere and monopoly over registered enterprise agreements. If the commission came under attack, so too could awards—the detailed system of minimum pay rates and conditions it supervised which unions held sacrosanct and Jennie had pledged to protect.

Against such adversity, what could Jennie do? The challenges she faced were arguably much more difficult than those of her predecessors. If the union movement was unable to project to the general population what it stood for and had achieved under a friendly Labor Government, its capacity to do so during her term as ACTU president when—as expected—an openly hostile Howard Government achieved office was doubtful. Her chief role, as the ACTU's public spokesperson, stood to be seriously undermined if the slide in union membership reached the critical point where unions were judged irrelevant. Some commentators believed unions had reached that point already. The mainstream media would simply lose interest in what Jennie said or did if she was perceived to be speaking on behalf of a non-representative union rump.

At a personal level Jennie faced some stiff challenges too. Support for her ascension to the ACTU presidency indicated that the union hierarchy was ready to reach out to women and take their needs into account. But Jennie was to lead an organisation whose constituent unions were still a predominantly male bastion. In tough, traditional blue-collar areas such as construction, manufacturing, mining and transport, old chauvinistic attitudes were difficult to shift. Women were often not treated seriously.

Not being taken seriously was never likely to be a problem for Jennie. She was accustomed to dealing with men in power and had been on the ACTU executive for more than a decade playing an active part in debates and decisions on major issues. She had a strong personality and a capacity to be tough when necessary. She also was at the forefront of debate on issues such as equal pay, child care, paid maternity leave and family carers' leave. In the male den of some unions, she might face a hard time occasionally but could hit back as hard as she received.

Would Jennie have the discipline and stamina to be ACTU president? Earlier in her career she had liked to burn the candle at both ends and she still liked to party. She had also opted out of high-profile jobs for an easier existence several times during her 25-year union career and cited pressure among the reasons. She was about to step into the most high-pressure role she had ever encountered—on the national stage, under constant scrutiny and dealing with the toughest union officials and politicians in the country.

She was, by her own admission, highly sensitive to criticism. As a single woman she also lacked the level of support of many men or women in comparable leadership positions. Emotionally Jennie was as passionate and tormented in her personal life as she had ever been. She had entered into several relationships with men after Joses Tuhanuku, mostly short and ill-fated, and no-one had filled the void in her life. The only real constant remained her mother about whose health Jennie worried and whom she saw as much as possible. She telephoned every evening, after 'The 7.30 Report', shortly before her mother retired and they spoke in Russian, 'It's my only regular date. Eight o'clock every night with me mum. I think that's wonderful. It's a shame it's up to Kerry O'Brien [the program's host] to keep my mum alert.'

Jennie's vulnerable side was difficult to detect in her public presentation. She had acquired a professionalism and sense of duty in her public life that overrode any demons in the background. As a union politician, she had good instincts but relied on advice before making major decisions. Partly from both experience and maturity, Jennie had developed the capacity to master any given situation, whether it was addressing a public meeting, giving a media interview, or chairing a meeting. She was skilled at learning a brief quickly, was very articulate and could pitch her words to suit the audience. She was inventive, never repeating a speech as many politicians do, always changing the tone and content. She was thoughtful and careful in her public utterances, almost never making gaffes but prepared to be controversial or outspoken if her cause required it. Party officials, community groups or factory workers would hear very different speeches from her on the same topic, each targeted at their level and range of interests. The audience she wanted to target most—workers—listened attentively and she was greeted warmly whenever she visited factories or offices.

Jennie did not need a written text for her speeches. She wrote her own when a formal set of words or a serious oration was called for. The only occasions her speeches relied heavily on ACTU staff for assistance were for making intelligible technical economic or legal issues that she conceded were beyond her expertise.

The ACTU president with whom Jennie and all others would be compared, Bob Hawke, was often described as having 'charisma'. Jennie had a different style altogether from Hawke's but certainly had some of his attributes. She was an excellent communicator and had a 'presence' when she entered a room. She was gregarious and had a liking for alcohol—for which Hawke had been renowned. Like Hawke,[9] she used to get drunk, though she never imbibed during working hours and had toned down her party lifestyle from her wilder early years. One of the amazing things about Jennie was a capacity to go out late, be among the last to leave a party, and yet arrive appearing alert and chirpy the next morning to chair a meeting or give a speech. Hawke had a similar reputation. He did not have normal hangovers and 'got up after maybe an hour's sleep, bright-eyed and bushy-tailed'.[10] Jennie was not spared hangovers. She was proud, nevertheless, that she had never missed an appointment after a late-night cocktail of alcohol, cigarettes and lack of sleep. Jennie's friends joked about her morning-after reserves, citing her 'peasant' Russian constitution. She put it down to responsibility instilled in her by her mother, 'Never once in my life—ever—have I had a good time but not fronted up the next day. I might front up with baggy eyes, I might not be totally in control, but I have never walked away from a public commitment.'

Unlike Hawke, known as a gaudy dresser in his days as ACTU president, Jennie dressed conservatively. She always looked immaculate in women's business suits or a coat and slacks. She always wore make-up and dyeing her brown hair blonde in the 1990s had made a difference to her appearance, softening the impact of her trademark spectacles. Despite Jennie's communication skills, the most obvious drawback of her public presentation was that she came across as too harsh and fierce. Away from the media spotlight, Jennie was generally friendly and easily engaged people in conversation—but this lighter side of her personality was submerged under the stern image she presented in speeches and interviews.

While Jennie had a good, clear speaking voice, it had become deeper as she got older, exaggerated by years of smoking. Her rasping tones did not assist positive perceptions of her among the non-union majority who did not know her. Jennie *was* an intense person but she did like to laugh and had a good sense of humour. While disliking small talk, she loved to know the latest gossip, especially if it related to herself. Unfortunately she was not adept at mixing this lighter, jovial side of her personality with her professional role to present a softer, more rounded image.

Critics attacked her for carping and for resorting to the language of outdated class warfare. While her admirers focused on her content and commitment, many ordinary listeners found the tough exterior a turn-off, lacking in warmth.

The radio host Alan Jones described Jennie as the only woman in Australia who could turn a glass of milk into yogurt by just staring at it, while a most unkind sexist riddle doing the rounds was, 'what do you call a rottweiler in lipstick?' Answer: 'Jennie George'. Still other critics, almost always men, insisted on calling her 'Jennie George-o-sorous' or reversing her name to 'George Jennie'.

One occasion that provided an opportunity for Jennie to display spontaneity and wit in public was as a panellist on the ABC Television comedy program 'Good News Week'. It was handy for her image because it showed off to those who did not know her that Jennie George was not some one-dimensional woman who only talked the jargon of politics and industrial relations or was trapped in an ideological time warp.

At times Jennie could have helped herself by adopting a less defensive approach and by attempting to show more of her charm and openness, which she was capable of using to good effect in personal contact. Jennie's reasoning was that levity did not fit her job ('I'm not there to be nice') and indeed few of the issues she talked about were laughing matters. She was there to represent workers' interests. Her carefulness with words in public also required a high level of concentration when she answered questions from journalists, giving comments that would be beamed across the country and could easily be misconstrued if she put the wrong emphasis on something.

Jennie was, however, more at ease in public than her predecessor, Martin Ferguson. Her better command of the language meant she was always going to be the more polished media performer. She did not use clichés or mangle her words like

Ferguson. Her meaning was straightforward, unlike another predecessor, Simon Crean, who was polished but whose use of the language was so contorted and riddled with jargon that precious few people could understand what he was saying. For clarity and directness, Jennie was a public advocate for the ACTU on a par with Hawke. It remained to be seen if she could achieve anything like his impact.

WORKING WITH KELTY

Jennie's ability to work effectively within the ACTU was always going to depend on her relationship with Bill Kelty. That relationship had improved dramatically since early clashes over the Accord and Kelty's reluctance to take women's issues seriously. After Jennie was elected as ACTU assistant secretary, they became very close. From Kelty's side, affection for Jennie grew out of an appreciation of her 'substance' and her record as a fighter for her cause. Their bond, professional and personal, rested on a firm foundation of mutual trust. But so it had appeared between Kelty and Ferguson. It could prove a major problem for Jennie, as it had for Ferguson, if there were a serious difference of opinion with Kelty once she was president. Indications were that a similar rift was unlikely, however.

Jennie appeared indelibly dedicated to Kelty and uninterested in building her own power base within the ACTU. Unlike Ferguson she accepted her role and was unlikely to challenge Kelty's dominance of the ACTU. They might have minor differences of opinion but Jennie went out of her way to work with Kelty rather than pull against his leadership. She trusted him to support her as she carried the burden of public responsibility for the country's union movement. He trusted her not to undermine his authority. Jennie reflected on her view of the ACTU presidency and how she regarded her responsibilities as clearly defined:

> Martin had a different view of the presidency than I do—and that was to be a very interventionist president. My view about the rules of the game is that the secretary runs the administration and makes the decisions about the allocation of industrial responsibilities. The constitution of the ACTU says quite clearly that the president's function is to be the main public spokesperson and to represent the ACTU in a variety of public forums. I think some of the tension between Martin and Bill was the overlap of responsibilities, which thankfully Bill and I do not have. We do what we think should be done within the confines the organisation gives us.

The reference to the constitution was Jennie's acknowledgment of the practical limits of her power. Historically, the ACTU president was both the power and the public face of the organisation. Throughout the 1970s, for example, Bob Hawke was the dominant figure. The secretary, Harold Souter, had responsibility for administration but lacked ultimate control. The shift in power from president to secretary began after Hawke left the ACTU. His successor, Cliff Dolan, did not exert the power and authority at his disposal and was removed from much of the ACTU's daily running. In the 1980s, first as assistant secretary to Peter Nolan and then as secretary in his own right, Kelty gradually overshadowed Dolan as the pivotal figure in the ACTU. In the mould of Souter, Kelty disliked the limelight and preferred to work out of public view. But he did not shy away from power and gradually came out of his shell to accumulate enormous authority and influence across the union movement.

When Simon Crean, national secretary of the Storemen and Packers' Union, was shaping up as Dolan's successor in 1985, Kelty cut a deal with him. Crean was friends with Kelty and they hailed from the same union. He agreed to support a constitutional rule change mooted by Kelty at that year's congress that recognised officially how the ACTU had operated of late by handing most of the executive powers to Kelty. Under the revised constitution, Kelty acquired a long list of responsibilities that included administration, finances, staff and implementation of policy and decisions of the congress and executive. He was also to 'generally supervise and direct work of the ACTU staff'. Crean and all his successors as president were left with the function of principle spokesperson and chair of meetings. There was no executive role for the president beyond 'carrying out the policy and work of the ACTU'.[1]

The president could try to influence ACTU decisions and intervene in industrial disputes but had to face the fact that Kelty was kingpin. Jennie did not dispute the reality of Kelty's power. In fact, it suited her. What needled her, however, were recurring suggestions that she was beholden to Kelty and owed her position to him:

> Martin got the presidency because of Bill, absolutely. I didn't get the presidency because of Bill. I got the presidency because I had the runs on the board and I got it in my own right. I'm not Bill's handmaiden, or his little patsy. I'm me, I'm myself, I'm capable. Of course there are times when we have differences—though very rarely. I can't think of a time when we've ever had an ideological difference.

Jennie's claim that she was supported for the presidency because of her experience was essentially right. But she could not have won it without Kelty's endorsement and his role in positioning her for the job cannot be overstated. Kelty also had in mind a different presidential role for Jennie compared with Crean and Ferguson.

Presentation in the mass media was not an important consideration when Albert Monk was president before Hawke. Since Hawke, who had achieved hero status thanks to his media exposure, it had become everything. Dolan, the stop-gap president after Hawke from 1979 to 1985, was a pleasant man but poor media performer. Crean, president from 1985 to 1990, presented well in the media even if his convoluted language—'Creanspeak' as it was known—became bogged down in jargon and lost the listener. The chief purpose of Crean's presidency was to help win support from the corporate sector in the early days of Hawke's Government when the ACTU and Labor wanted to dispel fears that the economically reckless behaviour of unions during the Whitlam years would be repeated.

Crean succeeded, his calm reassuring tones and suave business-suit image putting doubters at ease and ably selling the virtues of the Accord. It appeared, however, that Crean was too successful. A survey commissioned by the ACTU when it hired public relations firm Burson-Marsteller showed that a side effect of the ACTU's new style was that blue-collar workers, the union movement's traditional base, had become disillusioned with its leadership. Enter Martin Ferguson. Kelty handpicked Ferguson to succeed Crean. They had first discussed the subject in January 1988 when they ran into each other during family holidays on the NSW South Coast and Kelty confirmed to him that Crean intended to enter Federal Parliament at the next election. As months passed, Kelty talked Ferguson into accepting the presidency when Crean made his expected move.[2]

Ferguson's chief role as president was to win back the support of alienated blue-collar workers. His broad Australian accent and rough edges appealed to the target group, even though or perhaps because he was a poor media performer.

Jennie's role was different again. She was far superior to Ferguson as a media performer, even if she came across harshly at times. In anticipation of a hostile political environment in the event of a Howard victory at the next election, Kelty's task for her was to reach out to the non-union community for support, especially unconverted women and young workers entering the job market. She was also to use her persuasive powers to put the case against proposed changes to industrial laws by Howard that unions did not want.

To the general community it seemed as though Jennie George was the main power inside the ACTU because of her title and because she was the focus of public attention. It suited Kelty for this misconception to be perpetuated because he regarded dealing with the media as a chore and did not like being subject to its scrutiny. He also did not come across well on television. His mass of white curls, apparent frown and dour temperament contrasted oddly with the clean-cut coiffure looks and manner of those who interviewed him occasionally for news and current affairs programs.

For the media cognoscenti, aware of Kelty's real status inside the ACTU, however, his rare public appearances attracted heightened interest. Great significance was put on his utterances, often justified when he gave an outline of the ACTU's future directions or, as he discovered his powers as an orator in union forums, took a firm stand on issues and sent loud warnings to his political enemies. Though he pleaded lack of interest, Kelty appeared to know how to exploit the media. He did not court journalists but sometimes chose certain moments or media outlets to plant information about policies or planned job appointments. Like Jennie, Kelty was also highly sensitive to criticism although he did not bite back at individual journalists as quickly as she did. He read almost everything that was written about him and had a long memory for particular details of newspaper reports he disliked.

While Jennie and Kelty were close professionally and communication between them was friendly and open, they were never in each other's pockets. They hardly ever socialised, though Jennie had been invited to Kelty's house in Eltham and had attended a football match with him to watch his favourite team, Essendon.

Jennie believed that one of the main reasons she and Kelty

got on well together was their similarities. She could hardly have meant their personalities—socially she was gregarious and chatty; he was shy, spoke quietly in personal conversation and often shrugged as a way of expression.[3] One of Kelty's favourite topics of conversation was his passion, Australian Rules football; Jennie was ambivalent about sport. Their ethnic origins were also vastly different—hers was Russian; his was Anglo–Celtic. She was a migrant from a non-English-speaking background; he was not. Rather Jennie was referring to the fact that they had succeeded in life after sharing in common an impoverished background, raised by single parents.

Kelty grew up in the Melbourne working-class suburb of Brunswick. His mother was a single parent. Like Natasha, Kelty's mother had a hard life, struggling to make ends meet for the family by working as a cook after Kelty's father deserted them. Kelty was raised by one of his sisters for much of the time because his mother worked:

> The fact that I was brought up by my sister, I suppose, leads you to understand how really hard it is for women. I didn't have to be told the way it was like. My mum never got straight shifts, so I didn't have to get told how hard it was for people to bring up their kids working broken shifts, working ten 'til twelve o'clock. I knew about being down the back of the class, missing school. So I know how hard it is. I think Jennie has a similar background to that, and because you do understand it, I think you are sympathetic.

A bright student, Kelty was fortunate to gain a scholarship for tertiary education and graduated with a good economics degree from La Trobe University. He began his union career as a research officer for the Storemen and Packers' Union. Then Harold Souter recruited him in 1974 to work in the backrooms of the ACTU. Early on, Kelty had modelled himself on Souter and looked upon him as a father figure. But after 1977, when he became an ACTU assistant secretary, Kelty became much closer to Hawke. When Hawke left the ACTU for Canberra, he wanted Kelty to accompany him as his researcher and administrator—but Kelty felt his future lay with the union movement. Hawke's biographer, Blanche d'Alpuget, gave an indication of their closeness when she recorded how Kelty was in tears as he made the farewell speech to Hawke at an office party in 1979.[4]

Like Hawke, Kelty was also a fervent admirer of Charlie Fitzgibbon, the leader of the Waterside Workers' Federation. Fitzgibbon was the man Hawke had wanted to succeed him as ACTU president, only to accept Cliff Dolan as a compromise candidate when it was clear Fitzgibbon lacked the numbers. Kelty gave his impression of Fitzgibbon to author Shaun Carney. It left no doubt about Fitzgibbon's significance in his life but could have applied as a self-description. It also provided an insight into Kelty's later unflinching loyalty to waterside workers:

> If ever I wanted to aspire to be a union official, if there's an ideal that you would want to aspire to, then that ideal is Charlie Fitzgibbon. He is the person I've had the greatest respect for, he is a person I think who has all the qualities of a union official. He is tough, he works hard, he has a very flexible mind. He can talk to people in straight terms, there's nothing convoluted about what he has to say, people understand him precisely. He's not theoretical, a very practical person, but he's always thinking about the future, never the past. He is a man truly of vision. He is singularly the most impressive union official that I have ever dealt with.[5]

Kelty had learnt to be a tough union negotiator from his early days at the ACTU, cutting deals during bargaining disputes in the strike-prone oil industry. His infamous line to employers was 'pay up or we'll fuck you'. In the years since, he had become a reformed man. He was still given to rough language, privately or publicly when he felt the need, but had become a disciple of the Accord, which was founded on restraint. Kelty was behind all the Accord agreements with Labor, their primary architect along with Keating and aided invariably with input from Laurie

Carmichael. Beginning as a highly centralised model of wage fixing in the 1980s, the Accord ended up becoming the mechanism to deliver a form of managed enterprise bargaining in the 1990s. Under the new model, the Industrial Relations Commission took a backseat role—so employers and workers could conduct their own negotiations—except to formally approve registered enterprise agreements and set minimum award standards for pay and conditions.[6]

Enterprise bargaining was not new. Kelty had been an expert exponent in the rough-and-tumble 1970s when the unsophisticated objective was to use union muscle to extract as high a pay rise as possible in negotiations with employers. An important difference about the 1990s model Kelty and Keating proposed was that unions undertook not to go for broke. Instead unions agreed to continue observing their commitment of the Accord years to an annual average wage target, linked now to maintaining a low inflation rate of 2–3 per cent.

The wage target, as an average, did not preclude some wage deals being too high. It was a means nonetheless for Kelty and Keating to manage the system nationally in that it imposed overall restraint. Low-income workers who lacked bargaining power relied on small 'safety net' rises in minimum award pay rates and conditions granted by the Industrial Relations Commission to offer some compensation for rises in the cost of living. Unions with bargaining muscle carried the responsibility that if they negotiated too many deals with pay rises that far exceeded the national wage target, they would deny the prospect of a 'safety net' rise being granted to low-income workers.

Kelty had driven the move to an enterprise bargaining system in response to pressure to do so from John Howard and the Business Council of Australia. He re-fashioned it to suit the objectives of the union movement and the Labor Party. From Kelty's point of view—despite the opposition of some unions and women's groups to bargaining—it was better to introduce a bargaining model that fitted the Accord's historical concern to look after low-income earners. The alternative was to risk a bargaining model foisted on the union movement by a future Coalition government that could see a return to the wages free-for-all of the 1970s with its accompanying high inflation and high unemployment.

The chief complaint from unions about the ACTU model of enterprise bargaining—especially from vociferous critics of Kelty such as the secretary of the NSW Labor Council, Peter Sams—was that it mistakenly downgraded awards and the Industrial Relations Commission. Sams argued that Kelty was doing the Coalition's work for it. The complaint of employers—apart from some enterprise pay deals being too large—was that the ACTU model was really 'industry', not 'enterprise' bargaining, because unions tended to make large uniform pay claims and launch campaigns across whole sectors instead of linking negotiations to the needs of particular workplaces.

Jennie was wedded to the ACTU's official policy of enterprise bargaining but had some sympathy for the view of Sams (though not the way Sams directed his anger personally at Kelty) about the need to maintain strong awards enforced by the commission. She was aware that the award system might be the union movement's strongest line of defence against pressure for cuts to pay and conditions if Howard won the next election. Stressing the sustained importance of awards was also her strongest argument against critics of enterprise bargaining from within the women's movement who continued to protest that female employees were worse off under the new system.

In late 1995 Jennie decided to tackle head-on the criticisms of employers about the union preference for industry bargaining—also known as pattern bargaining—in a speech launching a report prepared by the University of Newcastle. She claimed that common, industry wage claims were often the 'best outcome' because they could guarantee stability across an entire sector when a settlement was reached. Citing the CFMEU's 15 per cent pay demand for the building sector—to be spread over a two-year period—she said that once the results of negotiations were tallied, the annual average from big and small building sites would be 5 per cent. Such an outcome, she argued, was economically sustainable and would not upset the ACTU's agreed wage target.[7] Jennie had no personal knowledge of what the building claim or any other would do for the country's aggregate wage figures. Economics, as she admitted, was never her forte. Her defence of pattern bargaining did reveal once more, however, her ability to master a brief. She was relying on information provided by ACTU staff, which she had distilled into an argument that could be readily understood by the public.

When Jennie discussed taking over the ACTU presidency with Kelty, her condition of accepting the job was that she wanted to spend more time in Sydney. What she meant was that she intended to run the presidency in a way it had never been done before by basing herself in Sydney, not Melbourne where the ACTU traditionally had its headquarters. In July 1995, the same month she had declared her candidacy for the presidency, she had completed the property settlement on a comfortable new unit in Sydney's Manly. She moved in soon after. When in Melbourne, Jennie continued to live temporarily at the unit she owned in Elwood—but a two-city, two-house arrangement was not affordable indefinitely. An ACTU president was paid $72 000 a year. Jennie had no family but her income did not make her rich—she had to make a choice.

One of the bonuses of Jennie's good relationship with Kelty was his ready acceptance of her settling back in Sydney. As she intended to make her presidency very much a travelling show—visiting workers in offices and factories and mines to ascertain their 'feelings'—her logic was that it did not matter whether she was located in Melbourne or Sydney. The question would inevitably arise though: could her presidency work if she was not in touch with the day-to-day administration of the ACTU as other presidents had been?

The past experience of Cliff Dolan—who lived in Sydney but spent four days a week in the Melbourne office—was evidence of how an out-of-town ACTU president was not necessarily in touch with the organisation. Dolan was often not present to see what deals Kelty brokered in his absence. Jennie accepted that her presidential role was primarily as ACTU spokesperson. She also had regular communication with Kelty. Nevertheless, her physical absence from the ACTU most of the time was a potential problem.

When working in Sydney, Jennie first used an office on the floor of an ACTU financial services company in Market Street, then switched to an office nearby in the building of the ACTU's State branch, the NSW Labor Council, in Sussex Street. The council's secretary, Peter Sams, relished the idea of Jennie using his premises. He liked her but her presence also served his political purposes. He could work with Jennie as ACTU president while at the same time conducting his long-time feud with Kelty over Kelty's attacks on the Industrial Relations Commission. To Sams, Jennie's presence also meant that the ACTU was recognising the reality that Sydney had overtaken Melbourne as Australia's business capital and was the home of most union head offices. Jennie explained her move in less symbolic terms, though she conceded that unions in Sydney were 'happy to have an ACTU president more readily available':

> I am in Melbourne every second week and often when I am in Sydney I go to Bundaberg or somewhere else. It is the nature of the job that I travel probably more than any other officer and get more speaking engagements than a lot of them do. And yes, Bill always understood that my staying depended on my capacity to be in Sydney to have some responsibility to my Mum. So it seemed to work without anxiety and the Sydney people liked it.

Soon after stepping into the ACTU presidential role, Jennie left no doubt that Sydney had become her 'home' again by making several important gestures. She quit the Victorian ALP and became a member of the local Manly branch. She also attended the NSW ALP's annual conference in Sydney as a delegate, not a Victorian visitor. As months passed, she tried to spend as many weekends in Sydney as possible, relaxing with friends and family before another five-day onslaught of worksite visits and speeches. The final confirmation of Jennie's move was the sale of her Melbourne unit. From then on, Melbourne was very much second-string living. When working at the ACTU's headquarters, she had use of a room at a friend's home.

Jennie's move to Sydney and promise to 'get out of 397 Swanston Street and spend more time at the coalface' meant that she ran the ACTU presidency in an unprecedented way. It was a bold experiment for the ACTU. She was like a roaming satellite on a continuous speaking circuit, not using the role like her predecessors who, besides fulfilling their public duties, spent part of most days in the Melbourne office, sleeves rolled up, liaising with staff, hunched over the telephone or immersed in paperwork. Jennie did catch up with office business during her semi-regular stints in the ACTU's Melbourne headquarters. But she mainly arranged her work itinerary from Sydney or wherever she happened to be—courtesy of daily telephone chats to her assistant, Denise Power, in the Melbourne office.

As the months passed, Jennie complained about the exhaustion of constant travelling, of a never-ending list of speaking engagements and of the disconcerting side of frequently ending a day's work in a motel room in a strange town far from home, sleeping between someone else's sheets. She had to admit, though, she had chosen to do her job this way.

THE BATTLE FOR WEIPA

Weipa was a most unlikely place to start a union war. It was also a most unlikely destination for Jennie George to test her ACTU presidency. The red earth mining town near the far north tip of Queensland usually attracted people who were prepared to tolerate its oppressive damp heat and extreme isolation to make a buck—not union officials taking a symbolic national stand with implications for all workers.

For almost two years, unions at Weipa's bauxite mine and kaolin plant operated by CRA, one of Australia's largest mining companies, had resisted company efforts to switch workers from collective union agreements to individual employment contracts that did not permit union representation. By October 1995 more than 400 had signed contracts, which offered up to $20 000-a-year more than the unionised rate. That left a hardcore of 75 workers, faithful to the union cause, who went on strike when negotiations with CRA for a new collective wage agreement showed no sign of progress.

The Weipa strike would have amounted to little if it were an ordinary bargaining dispute. But within a month Weipa grabbed national headlines when CRA initiated legal action to sue strikers for interfering with company business. The strike had made little difference to the mine's production because the overwhelming majority worked on. So the strikers had engaged in a novel but highly dangerous tactic to try to block bauxite exports leaving Weipa's harbour by darting between the giant transport ships in dinghies powered by outboard motors.

CRA's threat to sue workers was the trigger Bill Kelty had been waiting for to justify an all-out assault on the company. The moral imagery was powerful: a mining Goliath sues a small band of workers and denies them the significant salary increases granted to others who perform the same work. On 13 November 1995 Kelty chaired a strategy meeting of unions in Sydney which foreshadowed the most disruptive campaign of national strikes seen in decades to support the Weipa miners. First on the list of sympathy strikes were the nation's ports, then its coalmines, oil refineries, factories, and on it went.

The union trouble could not have come at a worse time for the Keating Government, deeply disturbed about the impact on Labor's prospects at an election just months away. But Kelty had more at stake than Keating's survival and was prepared to put the ACTU's partnership with Labor at risk. The strike at Weipa was part of a much bigger picture involving CRA after the union movement already had fought and lost similar battles at the company's vast iron ore, diamond, gold and aluminium smelting operations around the country. Individual contracts were repugnant to union principles because they denied collective representation. Kelty had tolerated them over the years providing they were not widespread. However, the problem that the CRA model presented him with was that contracts had become a successful *foundation* of employment, not just a minor phenomenon. The potential for employers to repeat this model across the workforce posed a serious threat to the union movement.

Kelty and other union officials had let CRA pursue its contracts strategy for too long before mounting a serious challenge. Belatedly, they tried using legal avenues in the commission to stop contracts at CRA's smelting operations at Bell Bay and Gladstone. But they failed. Now Kelty was taking a stand at Weipa, warning CRA and any other company of the industrial consequences of pursuing an anti-union agenda. The timing of his message was pertinent given that John Howard, who wanted to encourage individual contracts, might become prime minister in a matter of months. Kelty made it clear how seriously he took the Weipa conflict when he addressed the Maritime Union of Australia's national conference in Sydney before chairing a union strategy meeting on 13 November. He said that the fight against CRA would be 'tough, hard and brutal' and he was drawing a 'line in the sand' at Weipa, 'We won't be beaten. We can't be beaten. For us to be beaten is for the union movement to lose its heart, its soul and its purpose.'

Rhetorical flourish or not, once Kelty had uttered these words, it was clear that the Weipa dispute had entered a new realm. One of his deputies, Tim Pallas, confirmed as much, saying the union campaign would be on a magnitude never seen before. In Canberra Keating became increasingly worried. He was due to leave for an APEC meeting in Osaka in three days time but could not do so if a national industrial conflict of such a dimension was spiralling rapidly out of control. Keating telephoned Kelty to ask him what it would take to lift the strike pressure on CRA. Then he telephoned Leon Davis, CRA's chief executive, to stress the need for opening communications between the two sides. Prompted by the Prime Minister, the warring sides began talking by telephone.

Kelty delegated union negotiations to Tim Pallas, an ACTU assistant secretary, who had gone to Canberra for talks over the Weipa conflict and was temporarily using Laurie Brereton's Parliament House office. Davis delegated company negotiations to Terry Palmer, chief executive of CRA's Weipa subsidiary Comalco, who worked out of head office in Melbourne. Faxes were sent back and forth between Pallas and Palmer in an attempt to thrash out a written agreement. Kelty insisted that any agreement Pallas made ensured no discrimination against the Weipa workers. He wanted rights to collective bargaining and union representation and a cessation of legal action against them. After hours of haggling on 15 November, Pallas was so confident he had secured a settlement that he sent a late-night fax to Keating at the Lodge, which said:

> This is a copy of an in-principle agreement between ACTU/CRA. The company have agreed to the wording over the phone, however unable to contact them to sign the document. ACTU are confident this constitutes an agreement.

The next morning, departing for Osaka from Canberra's RAAF Fairbairn airport, Keating relied on Pallas's advice when he told reporters, 'I think we may have a resolution of it. I am optimistic that we might be able to tidy it up by midday or thereabouts.' But Keating was seriously embarrassed when he arrived in Osaka. By then, negotiations between the ACTU and CRA had collapsed and unions began escalating their strike campaign across the country. CRA insisted that the document Palmer had faxed from Melbourne the night before to Pallas did not constitute an agreement because Palmer had not signed it. Palmer had attached a handwritten note to the document, which said:

> Tim, there is a lot here I can agree with but a couple of points give me concern and I need to talk to a few people about them tomorrow morning. I note that it's all one way. Why don't we let the PM go to bed and assure him we will sort out the details tomorrow.

As strikes threatened to shutdown major businesses across the country, Jennie now took her first serious role in the dispute. She publicly blamed CRA for breaching undertakings, declaring that ACTU officials were stunned at the breakdown of negotiations.

She said that any prospect of reducing union disruption had been lost by CRA's stance:

> By walking away from the undertakings given to the Prime Minister and the intransigence displayed today, it is clear in my mind that CRA is not interested in finding a resolution to this dispute.

Palmer denied that CRA had breached any undertakings to Keating and blamed the breakdown in negotiations on obstacles put in the way by the ACTU. In particular he objected to the ACTU's insistence that award workers were entitled to 'equal pay' with those who had signed non-union contracts.

Kelty, meanwhile, had an alternative strategy. Earlier in the week he had sounded out Bob Hawke about whether he would be the ACTU's chief advocate if the Weipa dispute was sent to the Industrial Relations Commission for resolution. Hawke agreed. When the news reached Keating in Osaka on 19 November—the day before Hawke was to leap into action—he was ropeable. He regarded Kelty as a friend yet Kelty had not even forewarned him about Hawke. Hawke's involvement only highlighted Keating's failure to gain a settlement after having predicted, on flawed advice, that peace was near. From Osaka, Keating, unable to contact Kelty, ridiculed Hawke's new role:

> Given the commission's record on the point of discrimination or non-discrimination, I don't think if you were a betting person you would particularly need to concern yourself too much about who the advocate is. I think Marcel Marceau could almost get this one through.[1]

Hawke, accompanied by his former biographer and now his wife, Blanche d'Alpuget, led a large ACTU entourage in Sydney on 20 November for a full-bench hearing that had been called by Justice Deirdre O'Connor, president of the Industrial Relations Commission. O'Connor was disturbed by the level of disruption and was anxious to find a settlement. Jennie acted as Hawke's deputy, sitting at the head bar table with him and Kelty. Behind them the courtroom was packed with lawyers, union officials and media. Famous for his fiery advocacy in early days, Hawke gave a spirited performance and raised Jennie's hopes for a win. She had missed seeing Hawke in his courtroom heyday but was familiar with his exploits. Now she watched admiringly as he harangued O'Connor's bench about how CRA had used 'deceitful and dishonest' methods to de-unionise its workforce and resorted to 'psycho-babble' for its philosophy of direct relationships with employees based on trust, love, dignity, fairness, courage and honesty.

Afterwards, Hawke claimed his arguments had destroyed CRA's case. However, his role had less to do with brilliant advocacy than the attempt by Kelty—using publicity surrounding Hawke's resurrection from the ashes of his 1991 ALP leadership loss to Keating—to pressure CRA into a backdown and to distract community attention from growing union disruption across the country. The added bonus for Kelty was that Hawke's presence was a strong personal gesture. His loyalty to Hawke had been unquestionable when both were at the ACTU and he regretted the gulf that developed between them during Labor's leadership battle in 1991 when Kelty sided with Keating. Now he had made up for the past, rehabilitating Hawke despite the cost of hurting his relationship with Keating.

On 21 November, at the end of two hearing days, CRA made a pragmatic decision to accept a settlement proposed by Deirdre O'Connor. The company agreed to drop all legal action against the Weipa strikers, grant them an immediate 8 per cent pay rise and submit to further hearings based on an ACTU claim for equal pay.

Outside the courtroom, standing next to Hawke as he struggled to hold back his emotions, Jennie took the lead in declaring a 'great victory for fairness and justice' to the assembled media throng. She praised the solidarity of unions and the hardcore members at Weipa. Her broader political message was that the existing system was too good to be put at risk under the control of 'conservative ideologues' wanting to dismantle established institutions such as the Industrial Relations Commission. She said, 'I think the decision of the commission makes it very clear that the pursuit of individual contracts as a calculated strategy to de-unionise and get rid of unions is unacceptable by the law of the land.'[2]

The Weipa settlement was an impressive tactical victory for the ACTU although the company's basic aim—the right to encourage individual contracts—remained in place. There was also a major hitch. One of the conditions of the 21 November settlement was that 'all industrial action ceases immediately'. But the Weipa strikers had so much ill feeling towards the company and resentment towards ACTU officials in Sydney for failing to consult them that at a meeting held that evening they resolved to continue their strike until equal pay with non-union workers was guaranteed in writing.

Kelty was furious with a *Sydney Morning Herald* front-page report the next morning, which revealed the decision in Weipa. The settlement was at risk of coming undone. Brandishing the newspaper article in the commission, Kelty assured O'Connor that it was 'just simply wrong' and that Jennie would go to Weipa early the following week.[3]

The *Herald* report was correct. The problem lay in the ACTU's lack of communication with unionists in Weipa, including one of its own industrial officers temporarily stationed in the town, Bob Richardson. After the *Herald* report, Richardson told ABC Radio that the Weipa workers were determined to carry on their strike because their claim was for equal pay with contract workers, 'It is not more than that and it is not less than that. The people here are going to stay out and continue the activity until that is what we get.'

Jennie arrived in Weipa, a town bitterly divided between union and non-union supporters, on 28 November with a potentially difficult job ahead. Accompanying her were senior union officials from the ACTU's disputes committee—Doug Cameron, national secretary of the AMWU, John Maitland, president of the mining division of the CFMEU, Peter Tighe, national secretary of the CEPU and Steve Harrison, national secretary of the AWU. So far in the Weipa dispute, Jennie had been part of a large jigsaw, adopting a team role much as she had throughout her career. Now success or failure depended crucially on her ability to allay miners' anger and persuade them to return to work. The union hardcore felt immensely frustrated after five weeks on strike and were suspicious of the ACTU's involvement in faraway Sydney—yet they were also honoured, indeed flattered, that the ACTU president-elect had come all the way to Weipa to talk to them. Jennie received a hero's welcome at the airport. Striking miners and their families cheered and held aloft friendly banners as she stepped off the plane.

In Weipa, Jennie's presence was akin to that of a pop celebrity's. Fêted wherever she went about the town, her impact was evidence of the inspiring effect she could have on workers. Nevertheless, her success was not assured. Among the 75 was still a good number who doubted the merit of ending the strike until the battle was won. There was also a psychological barrier to overcome: after such a long strike many felt uncomfortable about returning to work with so much lingering mistrust and loathing directed at CRA management. Much of Jennie's task was to fulfil a symbolic role, helping miners to accept what resuming work meant as well as providing sound reasons why they should return to normal conditions. She had to dispel an unreal sense among them that their five-week organisation of round-the-clock pickets and harbour blockades had *become* their work.

The night of Jennie's arrival was a celebration in Weipa, not the occasion for the arm-twisting purpose of her visit. Under the shelter of tarpaulins at 'Picket Point' by the harbour shore, she and other out-of-town union officials joined the strikers and their families for a celebratory meal of spit-roasted pig and lamb, mud crabs and prawns. The event was important for Jennie to win the confidence of these people who had their own local concerns and were disgruntled about being used as pawns in a much bigger conflict raging between the ACTU and CRA. As the hours wore on, she excelled at establishing a rapport with the strikers, sipping beer to cool down in the ever-present humidity as she chatted and traded anecdotes. She spoke to them of their concerns and listened to their problems with genuine interest. Only later in the night did some tensions surface when the most hardened raised reservations about returning to work without a clear victory. Jennie kept the peace, prepared to discuss the issues and use gentle persuasion but waiting sensibly until a scheduled meeting at the picket the next morning to focus on the official business of her trip.

The strikers did not drive to the picket the following morning. This had nothing to do with the amount of alcohol drunk the night before—rather they indulged in a ritual. Before the meeting they invited Jennie to join them at a nearby wharf to climb aboard the boats used to blockade ships and stage a final triumphant 'sail-past'. It was a curious sight as Jennie's boat, leading a union flotilla, whizzed around the harbour in a show of proud defiance against CRA. Arriving at the meeting by water, she stepped onto the shore as if to claim 'Picket Point' like some explorer.

The ritual over, the hard talking began. Jennie's main message was to praise the strikers for their stand and to stress that it was time to give it up. Several of them challenged her, arguing that it was pointless to stop until all their demands had been met. Jennie responded with a personal guarantee. She asked all to place their trust in her that she would fight for them. She also assured them that unions were prepared to back them again if they were not vindicated in 'equal pay' hearings continuing in Sydney. After lengthy debate, the strikers voted overwhelmingly to support a motion drafted by Doug Cameron which agreed to end hostilities and return to work from the first shift the next day.[4]

Having won her own battle of Weipa, Jennie returned to Sydney on the afternoon flight where Hawke and a team of lawyers continued to fight the war against CRA in the commission. All went quiet around Christmas when hearings concluded—except for a threatened strike in Weipa as miners grew impatient over delays by O'Connor's bench. When O'Connor finally handed down a decision on 23 January 1996, Jennie hailed the result a great victory. O'Connor's bench ruled that CRA must offer the same salaries and working conditions as the other staff enjoyed to the 75 employees on awards who had refused to sign non-union contracts. The result was enough to satisfy union workers at Weipa and, at face value, the ACTU had won what it wanted. CRA had only signed-up workers to contracts with higher pay providing they accepted one-on-one negotiations with no union representation. O'Connor found against CRA for having discriminated against award workers when they achieved at least the same level of performance as non-union contract workers on higher pay.

At a deeper level, however, the Weipa ruling did not change much. O'Connor ruled that in return for the higher pay of contract workers, the award employees had to be prepared to work under the same terms as the contracts, which required longer and more flexible working hours. So the Weipa workers won the right to 'equal pay'—but it was not automatic. And while the CRA campaign to exclude unions appeared to be stymied because the company was no longer permitted to decline to issue contract offers to workers at Weipa who wanted to remain in a union, in practice, CRA had successfully de-unionised almost all of its workplaces anyway (with the notable exception of its coalmines). So a setback at Weipa did not make much difference to CRA's overall policy of treating unions as unwanted 'third parties'. The ACTU's main hope of turning the tide against CRA rested on its ability to use the discrimination findings of the Weipa ruling to woo back members from the company's ranks of contract workers. Jennie acknowledged as much, saying that a Weipa victory was not the end of the war against CRA. She announced a union plan, approved by the ACTU executive, to target systematically every CRA workplace to reverse the spread of contracts, 'The war won't be over until we can win back the hearts and minds of people who have accepted staff contracts in a situation where they had no obvious, alternate, practical choices'.

Where the ACTU achieved its greatest success was in its broader objective, to frighten other companies waiting in the wings to follow the CRA lead. Standing outside the courtroom with a jubilant Hawke after the decision, Jennie said:

> Let me say categorically to any company that has been sitting there waiting for the results of this decision, that if you believe that your strategy was to do the same as CRA, this decision today by the industrial umpire makes that totally unacceptable in the future.

In fact, it was not so much the commission's Weipa ruling that had frightened companies. The commission was chiefly a device for the ACTU to gain a neat resolution of a potentially uncontrollable conflict. The importance of what occurred over Weipa was that it worked as a trial run for the ACTU before the election. The day after Kelty drew his line in the sand, unions had begun a wave of national strikes. The warning of Weipa that Jennie and Kelty successfully sent to the business community was that in the event of a change of government, any company contemplating a similar head-on confrontation with the union movement stood to suffer dreadful consequences.

L A B O R ' S   D E F E A T

Just ten days before the Federal election Paul Keating had called for 2 March 1996, Jennie received a telephone message while campaigning for Labor in the western NSW seat of Calare. The host of ABC Television's 'The 7.30 Report', Kerry O'Brien, wanted to interview her in the Sydney studio that evening about some apparently explosive remarks made earlier in the afternoon by Bill Kelty. Jennie was keen to participate but had several problems. She was caught between Orange and Bathurst, involved in speaking engagements for Labor candidate Rob Allen. Even if flight schedules ran smoothly, her ability to arrive on time at the studio was doubtful. She also was not clear about what Kelty had said. In distant Melbourne, Kelty was reputed to have declared an 'all-out industrial war' if the Coalition was elected. Not unusually, he declined afterwards to be interviewed. O'Brien had turned to Jennie. If Jennie was required to defend Kelty, she wanted to know precisely what he had said first. O'Brien's solution was for Jennie to travel swiftly to Sydney in the ABC's helicopter. He also gave her a full transcript of Kelty's words.

What Kelty said that day became known as 'the symphony

speech'. In one of his rare public appearances—and first official foray into the election campaign—he addressed a packed meeting of union delegates at Melbourne Town Hall. Keating was on the same dais, on hand to speak to the gathering as part of his campaign tour of the country. The effusiveness between Kelty and Keating this day was a public sign that they had patched up their differences after falling out over the Weipa dispute. Kelty never used a prepared text but always thought ahead and chose his words. He acknowledged Keating's presence by drawing on Keating's love of classical music in the metaphors he used to make his point. If the Coalition tried to dismantle award protections, said Kelty, the 'skirmish' against CRA at Weipa would be just 'the first sonata'. He said:

> If they want a fight, if they want a war, they'll have the full symphony—with all the pieces, all the clashes and all the music. I am not sure it will be the 1812 Overture but I will tell you what Paul, it will not be Mahler either.[1]

Kelty also lampooned John Howard's remarks on ABC Television's 'Four Corners' two days earlier that his vision was for Australia's citizens to feel 'comfortable and relaxed'. If Howard wanted to attack unions in the absence of Labor's Accord with the ACTU, said Kelty, unions would set their own targets for pay rises:

> A 10 per cent claim? That would make us feel a bit 'comfortable and relaxed'. But why not 'very comfortable' and 'very relaxed'? Why not 20 or 30, hey? Don't come back whingeing and complaining when we go to the marketplace.[2]

Keating endorsed the thrust of what Kelty said. He agreed that 'if Howard wants an all-out assault on unions, and that is his stated policy . . . then unions owe him nothing in terms of their policy, in terms of wage fixation'. Such talk of all-out industrial warfare with the 'full symphony' and pay claims as large as 30 per cent was highly inflammatory so close to an election. Kelty's colourful quotes figured prominently on television news bulletins that evening, providing great fodder for the Coalition's campaign.

It would not be the first time Jennie was thrust in the role of picking up the pieces after remarks by Kelty. Jennie confided to some that she was annoyed Kelty had gone too far in his rhetoric but would not do so publicly. She told O'Brien on 'The 7.30 Report' that Kelty's speech had suffered from distorted editing on television and radio news to make it appear as though he was declaring all-out war. She said it was time to make clear where the union movement stood. With transcript in hand, she quoted his words to try to show they were not unreasonable. Jennie recalled:

> I said to Kerry O'Brien that if I was going to go on, I wanted the whole transcript of what was said—because what was said was deliberately simplified and distorted. So I had to qualify 'if' all along the way. 'If the Government declares war on the unions, then we will do this or that.

Her defence of Kelty did nothing to halt the next day's headlines or a barrage of criticism from editorial writers and commentators who attacked Kelty's leadership and the destructive capability of the union movement to undermine a democratically elected government. The *Australian* splashed the story across its front page with the headline 'Kelty warns it's war over wages'.

Kelty made no friends among Labor's strategists with his comments either. A number of them regarded his blast as a voter turn-off and blamed him for tipping the scales against the party in some marginal seats. Kelty was a handy scapegoat but his rhetoric was undeniably overblown and negative for Labor. He was making a threat, qualified or not. Kelty insisted long after that he was badly misrepresented and rejected that the sensitive overall context of the election campaign meant his comments were ill-judged. The most he conceded was: 'If there were choices, I wouldn't necessarily use the same set of words.' Jennie continued to stand by him long after the incident, admitting only this much:

> If Bill had realised how it was going to be used, in a way that was detrimental to the ALP, he wouldn't have used those words. We can all be wise in hindsight. No-one is beyond making a statement which gets blown out of proportion and out of context.

Jennie spent the entire five weeks of the election campaign repeating the role she had successfully performed in 1993. She toured almost every state in an exhausting round of speaking engagements, concentrating on trying to swing women voters back to Labor. Under a campaign banner titled 'Women don't risk it', she warned that the election of a Coalition Government would endanger benefits specifically aimed at women such as the maternity allowance and child-care cash rebates. Howard's spokeswoman on women's affairs, Judi Moylan, branded Jennie's campaign a 'scurrilous' attempt to intimidate women. 'It is a blatant lie to suggest that women will lose benefits under a Coalition Government,' said Moylan. Jennie was undeterred. The other major area of concern for her was the award system, of particular relevance to protecting minimum conditions for many women left vulnerable in face-to-face bargaining with employers. Jennie acknowledged that Howard had made a commitment not to dismantle awards but voiced scepticism given the Opposition Leader's admiration for governments in Victoria and New Zealand, which had abolished them. She said:

> What has been seen in both Victoria and New Zealand is that what their bosses most wanted in an unregulated, independent contract environment was to abolish penalty rates, change the hours they worked and restrict leave entitlements. These are issues of considerable concern to women who are combining work and family needs. Many women work on weekends or at other unsociable hours, especially in the health, retail and hospitality industries. Their penalty rates are a huge component of their take-home pay.[3]

As election day neared, Jennie prepared for the worst. ALP polling indicated Labor was headed for a massive defeat. After thirteen years in office, winning a sixth term was always going to be difficult. Keating's unpopularity vastly increased the odds. Howard ran an astute campaign, not letting out too much policy detail to allow Labor room for attack—there was no gift like the GST to save Keating this time. Howard had even neutralised Jennie's scare campaign about the future of awards, saying: 'I give you this rock-solid guarantee—our policy will not cause a cut in the take-home pay of Australian workers.'

Jennie's task, she recalled later, was to give her best in the event of defeat 'to minimise the loss as much as possible'. The magnitude of the defeat surprised her—a 49-seat majority to Howard in the House of Representatives. Nevertheless, she appeared unperturbed at a press conference at the ACTU's Melbourne headquarters the day after the election in which she stood by the Kelty line. With the end of Labor's rule, the Accord was dead. In the absence of the Accord, she said, wage claims would be 'determined by unions in the market place' and they would be higher. Jennie's frosty response to Howard's victory was followed a day later by a rare press conference called by Kelty at which he announced his resignation from the board of the Reserve Bank. In a letter to Howard, Kelty said that his continued membership of the board 'may be inconsistent with my union responsibilities'.

Kelty also dismissed the suggestion of critics such as the assistant secretary of the NSW Labor Council, Michael Costa, that he should consider quitting the ACTU as well because his strategies linking the union movement to a sympathetic Federal government were flawed. Kelty said, 'There is no way given this challenge I will ever walk away from the union movement. This is about as exciting as it's going to get—and I'm going to be here.'

A sympathetic government was indeed no more. But Kelty had been preparing the union movement's defence lines for this moment for years. He was ready in 1993 but Labor's win had given the ACTU a reprieve. Despite the backdrop of union decline, strategies for collective bargaining, a wage 'safety net' for the low paid, retirement income, union structures and membership recruitment were all in place ready to confront the Coalition. One advantage of a Coalition Government was, as Kelty put it, 'you know exactly where you stand, that's my political position'. The ACTU leadership was no longer torn in policy terms between representing its union constituency and accepting compromises for the sake of keeping Labor in office.

To be free from ambiguity was not to be free from pain, however. The transition period of learning to exist under a Coalition Government was very difficult for the ACTU leadership after having enjoyed a comfortable ride for thirteen years. Jennie had to bear much of that burden. The day John Howard became Prime Minister the welcome mat in Canberra suddenly disappeared. The ACTU no longer had guaranteed access to ministers and certainly no role in decision-making. Lucrative government grants for areas such as union amalgamations and policy research were stopped. The TUTA, started by Whitlam with government funding, was abolished. Union appointees to government boards could not expect re-appointment when their terms expired. Job cuts on a large scale were planned for the Commonwealth public sector, a valuable stronghold of union membership.

Jennie was now officially ACTU president, her five-month stint as president-elect having expired once Martin Ferguson was elected to Parliament. Her role in the immediate post-Labor era was twofold. First, she was to promote a new union wages policy in the absence of the Accord. Second, she was to shoulder responsibility for a campaign of opposition to the industrial relations legislation that the new Government was expected to introduce to Parliament without delay.

Jennie announced the new Accord-free approach to wages at an ACTU executive meeting held a fortnight after Howard's victory. The AMWU had already set the pace for enterprise bargaining claims by announcing it would seek a 15 per cent rise over two years. In the absence of the Accord, Jennie declared that the ACTU would pursue a new 'living wage' for workers who lacked bargaining power. She said:

> It will be particularly aimed at raising minimum award rates and looking after the needs of those who have been described variously as the working poor—you know, people who are still trying to survive on about $400 [minimum] award rates of pay.[4]

The 'living wage' was a Kelty idea and it was Jennie's job to sell it. Instead of asking the commission to approve a 'safety net' rise of between $11 and $14 a week—negotiated with Labor under the defunct Accord VIII agreement—the ACTU sought a much higher rise. The 'living wage' sounded new but it was really an old idea updated with added sophistication. The point of the exercise was to convince the national wage bench of the Industrial Relations Commission to consider family 'needs' and what it cost to live in the 1990s. This concept was borrowed straight from the 1907 Harvester Judgment by the second chief judge of the Arbitration Court, Henry Bournes Higgins, who set a 'fair and reasonable' wage based on family costs.

The ACTU's new claim was not spelt out in detail until July—a $20-a-week rise in the award 'safety net' plus a new adult minimum hourly pay rate, rising in stages over three years to $12 an hour or $456 a week. When hearings commenced in November, it was the first time in thirteen years that the union movement had tried to convince a national wage bench to grant its claim without a friendly federal government on side.

The Howard Government rejected the 'living wage' but did support an increase in the award 'safety net' of $8 a week for workers on less than the average wage of $677 a week.[5] The main employer group, the Australian Chamber of Commerce and Industry, advocated no rise at all but was prepared to back a $5 allowance for low-income earners.

Jennie was ideal for the task of selling the 'living wage'

particularly because she could reduce quite complex issues to their essence. She also wholeheartedly supported the concept—the claim was targeted (supposedly) at low-paid workers on basic award pay rates. She had always been a staunch defender of the award system and the low paid. Repeatedly, Jennie pointed to a growing disparity in the bargaining system—those with muscle did well while those without fell behind. But her ability to promote the 'living wage' was hampered by the ACTU's isolation now the props of Labor support were gone.

Jennie was also let down by the complicated nature of the claim—and the fact that it became clear not just the so-called working poor stood to benefit. The claim for a $20 rise in the award 'safety net' was unambiguous and simple, if obviously an ambit claim. The complicated part was how three annual rises of $20 were to be absorbed against three separate annual increases in minimum pay rates intended to lift minimum rates overall by an enormous 30 per cent. With the annual inflation rate hovering at 2 per cent, it was difficult suddenly to justify such a large increase when it had not been contemplated just months earlier while Labor was in office. Furthermore, the ACTU sought a 30 per cent increase in *all* minimum pay rates for the sake of maintaining award relativities—even for senior trades workers whose minimum was $960 a week. So the ACTU's argument that the 'living wage' claim was aimed at the low paid was distinctly flawed.

For Jennie, who was not technically inclined, the fine detail of the 'living wage' was a matter for the ACTU's research team whose job it was to frame the figures and economic justification and argue the case in the commission. She had more urgent business at hand in leading the union fight against legislation being drafted by Peter Reith, now Minister for Industrial Relations in Howard's Government. Reith, a gung-ho politician, had wasted no time turning the Coalition's industrial relations policy into legislation. Three weeks after Howard's victory he had a taskforce of three handpicked experts—all known for their anti-union sympathies—working full-time so that legislation could be introduced into Parliament by May.

The industrial relations policy Howard had taken to the election was a watered-down version of *Jobsback!*, the package Howard released in 1993 as the portfolio's shadow minister when John Hewson was Opposition Leader. As Opposition Leader himself, Howard had waited until January 1996 to launch the revised policy to limit the opportunity for a government counter-attack. When he did launch it at the Young Liberals annual conference in Canberra, the publicity was just as he had hoped. Front-page headlines such as 'Howard's pledge: no pay cuts' in the *Sydney Morning Herald* were a clear signal that a planned scare campaign by the ALP–ACTU alliance about wage cuts was doomed to failure. Howard stymied the campaign with his guarantee that workers would not suffer a cut in take-home pay—they would continue to receive the same income including overtime, penalty rates and leave loading.

Nevertheless, his policy had a sting for unions. Although the award system was to remain in place, he intended to sever any union connection with the bargaining stream established by Keating for the majority non-union sector. For non-unionists, he proposed a new form of secret individual contracts called Australian Workplace Agreements for which the only requirement was that they meet a range of community standards, including take-home pay no less than a worker's relevant award rate. The Industrial Relations Commission would lose its control over non-union agreements. Instead, the replacement Australian Work-place Agreements would be registered confidentially with a new bureaucracy called the Employment Advocate. Unions would lose all right to become involved.[6]

Unions stood to lose other rights and benefits as well. While awards were to be maintained as such, they were to be vastly simplified from dozens of detailed conditions to just 20 'allowable matters'. A legal right to strike, introduced by Labor in 1993, was to remain during the bargaining period for an enterprise agreement but sections of the Trade Practices Act outlawing sympathy strikes, watered down by Labor to the point of ineffectiveness, were to be restored. Labor's unfair dismissal laws were to be replaced with a streamlined, less legalistic system.

Following formal approval by union officials, Jennie announced the ACTU's first step of opposition to legislation enacting the Coalition's policy in Melbourne on 19 April. Her immediate concern was to retain workers' existing award conditions—and to this end she issued an ultimatum devised by Kelty. Employers, she said, would be required to guarantee in writing all existing wages and conditions not included in the Coalition's 20 'allowable matters'. If employers refused, they faced industrial action. Award conditions outside the 20 included maximum hours of work, length of shifts, meal breaks, rest periods, rostered days off, redundancy and termination provisions and superannuation. The ACTU ultimatum was a tactic to attempt to make any legal simplification of awards irrelevant—but its chances of success were limited to areas of greatest union muscle. Peter Reith laughed it off as a melodramatic gesture.

Jennie had already met Reith once since the election at his Melbourne office in the city's Treasury Place and they continued to face each other in debates on ABC current affairs programs. She found him a formidable opponent: wily and unflappable. Reith had nothing like the effect on her of her other great ministerial foe, Terry Metherell, who got under her skin by refusing to engage her position. By contrast, Reith had no qualms about talking to Jennie in any forum about anything. In private discussion he was polite but direct. In public debate he thrived on a good verbal joust and was adept at wrong-footing opponents by easily manipulating facts to suit his argument. While Reith was seriously committed to his policy, he did not take himself too seriously like some politicians. Jennie believed she could match Reith but knew she could never take him for granted. She even acquired a begrudging respect for him.

Reith reciprocated—to a degree. While admitting his contact

with Jennie was limited, he said he always found her 'very straight to deal with'.

> I don't mind the Lefties because they might be wrong and misguided but most of them have a thought-out position. Jennie's in the classic mould—someone from a white-collar teachers' union in the public sector, and female.
>
> I don't think her presidency has been a great success for the ACTU. She's not as persuasive for her cause as she could be—but that reflects the union movement struggling to re-fashion itself and Jennie is no more able to do that than Bill Kelty and others at the ACTU.

As the months passed, Jennie led the assault against Reith's Workplace and Other Legislation Bill on a series of fronts. She delegated the technical legal work of going through the legislation line by line after Reith had introduced it into Parliament to ACTU officials Tim Pallas and John Cairns. They spent more than 30 hours in negotiations with Reith attempting to secure concessions but got nowhere. They also spent many hours in Canberra discussing with Labor's new shadow minister for industrial relations, Bob McMullan, possible amendments to the legislation when it reached the Senate.

For herself, Jennie assumed the responsibility of negotiating with the minor parties in the Senate—in particular the Australian Democrats whose support the Government needed if its legislation was to pass the Upper House. Jennie was best placed to deal with the Democrats compared with any other union official because of the rapport she enjoyed with the party's leader, Senator Cheryl Kernot. Jennie had met Kernot and come to regard her as a friend after Keating appointed them both to the Aboriginal Reconciliation Council on six-year terms in late 1991. The council, which met four times a year at different locations around the country and often required an overnight hotel stay, provided an opportunity for the two women to get to know each other. They discovered they shared similar views on life and unwound together after meetings. The aftermath of one meeting in 1994 was a memorable occasion in which Jennie and Kernot ended up in a Cairns karaoke bar with fellow council members Ray Martin, Galarrwuy Yunupingu and Robert Champion de Crespigny singing the Stevie Wonder/Paul McCartney song *Ebony and Ivory*. Now Jennie hoped her camaraderie with Kernot and what she knew of Kernot's personal opinions would prove invaluable to the union cause.

The Democrats had already stated the party's intention to pass Reith's legislation in some form rather than block it outright. Kernot identified six key areas of the legislation that she said broke election promises by the Prime Minister, indicating that these provided the basis for major amendments. Jennie needed to ensure that the Democrats Leader would not back away from her reservations under pressure from Reith and that she would accept as many as possible of the ACTU's own amendments.

An early platform for Jennie to put her case with Democrat assistance came when the party's senators combined with the ALP to force Senate committee hearings which sought public submissions on Reith's legislation in July. Jennie personally appeared before the committee in Melbourne at the start of its nationwide tour. In detail she ran through the ACTU's objections to the bill. She also ensured that unions in every state bombarded the committee with submissions to emphasise the degree of opposition. Except for delaying passage of the legislation in the Senate, the committee made no difference in the end because it split along party lines. The key was whether Reith could secure a compromise in private negotiations with Kernot to gain the Democrats' support.

Besides attempting to persuade Kernot, Jennie's last hope to try to impress upon the Government that its legislation was misguided and out of step with the working people it claimed to represent was another idea of her own making that she called a 'Cavalcade to Canberra'. The cavalcade had a familiar ring to it. It was really a rally by another name that drew once more on Jennie's personal history of involvement in such events. She regarded the anti-Metherell rally as her triumph but also remembered with great fondness the success of anti-Vietnam demonstrations in which she had played a significant part. A large rally in Canberra while Parliament was in session, she believed, was the best way to make the union movement's point.

Jennie had first raised the proposal for a 'Cavalcade to Canberra' in April when she issued the ACTU ultimatum on guaranteeing award conditions. It was settled soon after that the rally would be held on 19 August, the day before the Government delivered its first Budget and the day when the object of the protest—the industrial relations legislation—was to be introduced to the Senate. Timing the rally to coincide with the Budget was important for Jennie because she wanted to join forces with community and indigenous groups. These groups had grave concerns about proposed Budget spending cuts and were likely to participate in greater numbers in an ACTU-sponsored event if it could be identified as a protest against wider measures of the Government rather than the industrial relations legislation alone. Jennie was also concerned about likely Budget cuts but the legislation remained her primary issue. She wanted the rally to have maximum impact—union activism reborn.

R I O T

It was a brilliant start to the day. The sun beamed down, blue sky the perfect complement to the crisp winter air of August as protesters descended on the nation's capital throughout the morning. They came in thousands, by car and bus and interstate flights. An entire train was hired to bring a large contingent from Sydney. Jennie was on hand to greet the train, as it pulled into the station. She was in a positive mood and looking forward to a success, having arrived in Canberra the afternoon before to hold a pre-protest media conference and check last-minute preparations. Jennie predicted that the turnout would be the largest seen in Canberra—a minimum of 15 000 people and possibly as many as 30 000. Her hope was that the sight of such a huge crowd might rattle the confidence of John Howard and his ministers, forcing them to appreciate the depth of feeling against proposed industrial relations legislation and Budget cuts.

The venue for the rally was a lawn area about 200 metres away from the front doors of Parliament House. At this point a stage was erected, facing the opposite direction towards the old Parliament building and Lake Burley Griffin, for speakers to address the crowd. Protesters began gathering on the lawn at about 11.30 on the morning of the rally. All was calm as a band entertained them while they waited for the official proceedings to begin. At the same time a separate crowd—a mixture of unionists, students and Aborigines—also began swelling on the large forecourt directly in front of Parliament House.

Problems began an hour later when supervising police, facing a bottleneck of people at the roadway that divided the lawn and the forecourt, tried to stop a large group of Aboriginal protesters from marching onto the forecourt to join others already there. Union protesters who had arrived by train from Sydney and marched from the station in Kingston up Wentworth Avenue to join the rally also got caught in the bottleneck. Seeing the confrontation between the police and Aborigines, they began chanting 'let them through'. While most joined the main rally on the lawn, a considerable number pushed their way past police with the Aborigines towards the forecourt crowd. Those who made it to the front then surged forward. They broke through a police line established just ten metres away from the entrance to Parliament House and entered the first of two sets of glass doors.[1]

Police formed a human shield to protect a second set of locked doors that led straight into the building's marble foyer and warned what was now an angry mob at the front to retreat. But the mob ignored the warning, instead struggling past police to storm the building. Some used a delivery trolley and a flagpole to prise open the doors and gain access into the foyer. Others used a stanchion ripped from one of the doors as a battering ram to smash their way through a thick side window into the adjoining Parliament House bookshop, which they ransacked and used as another access into the building. Altogether about 100 people broke through, running amok in the foyer until they were either arrested or forced outside by police reinforcements with helmets and shields. Police and protesters were injured in the riot. Among them was a policewoman who was taken to hospital badly bruised after she was punched and kicked to the ground. At least 40 people were taken into police custody. When cleared, the entrance to Australia's place of representative democracy was a mess of blood and broken glass.[2]

At first it appeared to those back on the lawn that nothing was wrong. The crowd listened to speeches from Jennie and other speakers including the Opposition Leader, Kim Beazley, Aboriginal leader Lois O'Donoghue and the Green senators, Bob Brown and Dee Margetts. Jennie was made aware of some early commotion on the forecourt when fellow union rally organisers made a special announcement on the public address system, asking protesters to remain on the lawn. But she had no inkling of more trouble than that until receiving information from Cheryl Kernot's office. Kernot was on the bill of speakers at the rally. One of her staff rang the mobile telephone of the ACTU's media officer, Clare Curran, standing next to Jennie, to advise that Kernot was delayed because she was unable to leave Parliament House to join the rally from the front doors and would have to use a side exit.

The most disturbing evidence of things gone awry was the appearance at the stage soon after of a man with a bloodied face and carrying a police shield. He demanded to address the crowd, threatening Jennie that he and his mates would take over the stage unless allowed to speak. Reluctantly, she let him on. At the microphone the man brandished the shield and boasted: 'Look what we took from the coppers.' When reports of the riot finally reached Jennie from union scouts, she realised immediately that she had a public relations disaster on her hands. Standing by the stage after the speeches had concluded, she became visibly upset. News of the riot was crushing—all her effort squandered by violence 200 metres away. The rally in which Jennie had invested so much of her personal energy was ruined and her opportunity to send a powerful political message to the Government was lost. It was the worst violence seen at the new Parliament House since it opened in 1988.

Jennie had to regain her composure quickly. She and Kelty had previously arranged a meeting with Howard after 3 p.m. in his Parliament House office. It had been intended as a last-ditch attempt to persuade the Prime Minister to water down his industrial relations legislation, ideally reinforced by a triumphant rally. While success was always unlikely it was a hopeless quest now. Shortly before seeing them, Howard visited the foyer to inspect the damage and congratulate police for the way they handled a difficult demonstration. Back in his office to meet Jennie and Kelty, Howard was abrupt. He said he would not negotiate under duress but agreed to meet them again in a fortnight. After just seven minutes, he said: 'This meeting is terminated.' Jennie and Kelty were shown the door. Howard then called a media conference in one of the Parliament courtyards at which he branded the violence 'un-Australian and ugly'. He said:

> I want to make it clear to those involved in that violence, and to the Australian people, that never under any circumstances will my Government buckle to threats of physical violence or behaviour of that kind.
>
> It is a very sad and unhappy day in the life of the Australian Parliament, and those responsible for today's demonstration should feel utterly ashamed of themselves. I don't believe for a moment that those people who smashed their way into Parliament House in any way represent the feelings of mainstream Australia. I think what they did this afternoon will be greeted with revulsion by mainstream Australia.

Jennie was still obviously shaken by news of the riot but mixed with her grief was anger at Howard's attitude towards her and Kelty. Speaking to journalists outside Parliament she said, 'I made it very clear to John Howard that I resented any inference that any incidents that may have occurred during the day had anything to do with the ACTU'.

Kelty had been standing on the lawn with his son listening to the speeches unaware of any trouble until he joined Jennie for their scheduled meeting with Howard. He was reluctant to speak to journalists but one dogged radio reporter pursued him for comment on the riot. He said, 'This is the most successful rally in the history of this country in Canberra. I know nothing of the details of it.'

These remarks attracted widespread criticism when broadcast because—even allowing for his opinion of the main rally and ignorance of other events—they appeared so obviously out of place. The images Australians saw on the evening television news bulletins were those of police bravely battling rioters and the expensive property damage left behind, not sunny-faced rally-goers in a peaceful expression of their democratic rights. Jennie had realised from the moment she was told of the riot that it inevitably would overshadow any positive side of the rally—but Kelty refused to accept this.

Kelty rarely made public appearances but was becoming known for gaffes when he did. First came his 'symphony' speech. Shortly after that he suffered enormous criticism with the disclosure that he had sent a letter to Japanese electric power companies urging them to look elsewhere for coal during a strike at CRA's Vickery mine in the Hunter Valley. Now he was calling a public relations disaster a great success. In coming weeks Jennie would have to defend Kelty—in public and privately to union officials who complained about him—in addition to fending off constant calls for the ACTU to accept responsibility for the riot.

Jennie dined with friends including Cheryl Kernot and Sharan Burrow on the evening of the melee, emotional about the day's events, then retired early to her Canberra hotel room for a tearful night alone. She gained comfort on the telephone from Natasha, who despaired at her daughter's disappointment and the immense pressure she was under. Nevertheless, she found it impossible to sleep.

Unfortunately, the next day Jennie had to return to Parliament House. Being Budget day, her job was to give the official ACTU response after Treasurer Peter Costello delivered his 7.30 p.m. speech. It was also her 49th birthday and she had arranged to have a celebratory dinner with friends after concluding her post-Budget duties. Jennie had to focus her mind on the Budget swiftly and temporarily forget the riot. She watched the Budget speech on television in one of the ALP's parliamentary offices, received a briefing from an ACTU official allowed out of an early-access Budget 'lock-up', then began a hectic round of media interviews in which she criticised cuts to welfare, child care and employment programs.

It seemed she could not escape the previous day's events, however. She took personal offence when Kerry O'Brien described her as 'fresh from the riot' in the introduction to his '7.30 Report' Budget interview. O'Brien meant nothing sinister—it was purely a contextual intro—but Jennie was hypersensitive about the merest suggestion linking her to the violence.

Later in the evening, after her birthday dinner at a Chinese restaurant in nearby Manuka, Jennie's party joined journalists downstairs enjoying post-Budget festivities at The Grange nightspot. Clare Curran, the ACTU media officer, told O'Brien that Jennie was upset with him and that he should have a talk with her before she left. He walked over to her, only to be berated for his 'fresh from the riot' remark. When O'Brien defended himself, Jennie broke down and he comforted her.

From the start, the ACTU leadership adopted a position that it had nothing to do with the riot and refused to accept any responsibility. Indeed Jennie and Kelty could not be blamed for a riot that occurred away from the main rally area. But the ACTU's failure at an organisational level, for which it had to accept responsibility, was plain. The crowd, which police estimated at 25 000, had not come to attend a sporting event but had come to a protest rally about issues that angered them deeply. The possibility of trouble should have been anticipated. A form of self-imposed discipline, such as union marshals, was necessary in addition to the security provided by police but was missing on the day.

By refusing to either accept responsibility or adopt a firm, united position among unions early on, Jennie allowed public criticism of her and the ACTU to run for weeks. In hindsight she believed that her greatest mistake was not convening a special meeting of the ACTU executive the day after the riot to determine a fixed response to the controversy. Instead she bore the brunt on her own, ducking and weaving in her public remarks trying to defend the ACTU's position. Jennie coped with interviewers grilling her about whether the ACTU should accept responsibility by paying for up to $100 000 damage to Parliament House (she refused) but became fed up with attempts to associate her personally with the melee. Howard had a field day in Parliament and outside attacking the ACTU's handling of the rally and singling out Jennie and Kelty for special mention. He told an ACT general meeting of the Liberal Party, 'How dare Jennie George and Bill Kelty pretend that they can wipe their hands of any responsibility for what happened here'. Reflecting on Jennie's plight much later, Peter Reith expressed some sympathy for her: 'Jennie took very personally the accusations about the riot—she took that to heart which she needn't have. I think the ACTU should have got the riot off its chest straight away.'

For Jennie, negative publicity about the riot became so bad as the controversy dragged on that some passers-by in the street abused her. The constant burden of the riot left her feeling exhausted—and alone. Kelty recalled that he supported Jennie, deflecting a fair amount of the criticism. But his support was mainly behind closed doors. He remained cloistered in his Melbourne office and did not stand alongside Jennie to face the public onslaught. As one astute observer and friend of Jennie's put it, Kelty appeared to have 'switched off'.

A week after the riot Jennie became very anxious about rumours she believed were being spread by Labor Party staff in Canberra that she was thinking of resigning as ACTU president for a safe seat in Parliament. Her anxiety was heightened by the knowledge that journalists from two Melbourne newspapers, the *Age* and the *Herald-Sun*, were preparing stories with potentially damaging content about her weeping in public and unnamed sources revealing her alleged desire to quit the ACTU.

In her most distressed moments about the riot, Jennie had expressed doubts to colleagues and friends about continuing, saying, 'Oh God! Is it all worth it?' and 'Public life is just shocking. My name has been vilified and dragged through all the mud.' But her talk was more a way of defusing the pressure she felt. She had no serious intention of resigning. As Jennie's friend Peter Robson said, she could summon great strength despite signs of vulnerability. He recalled, 'She has got a great capacity to draw from her strength even though on the top you see emotion and sometimes tears. Underneath there is some very great depth there, a great capacity to draw on, to dig down deep.'

Feeling her position was being undermined, Jennie decided that the only way to dispel rumours was to confront them head-on. She telephoned several media organisations, including the *Sydney Morning Herald*, to dismiss speculation about her future and blamed a strategy to destabilise her on 'Labor Party sources in Canberra'.[3] Those who knew her thought she meant Martin Ferguson's office—but Jennie would not confirm so publicly. Ferguson's staffers denied any connection with any rumours at the time.

Apart from any scuttlebutt in Canberra, officials from the CFMEU and other unions that had become belated critics of ACTU policy during Labor's rule did canvas privately the possibility that Jennie or Kelty, or both, might step aside. They suggested a new team of, perhaps, John Maitland from the CFMEU and Greg Sword from the NUW, but such talk led nowhere.[4]

As the public controversy raged, ructions among unions also ran unchecked as an internal witch-hunt was conducted to identify those linked to the violence. The CFMEU came under the heaviest attack and was accused privately of having wrecked the rally. It was an easy target because people wearing caps and sweatshirts with the union's insignia were clearly identifiable in the thick of the ruckus from television footage and newspaper photographs. The attitude of the CFMEU's leaders was to dissociate the union completely and to plead that it was not possible to control some of its more excitable members. It also declared that members were 'on their own' if police laid charges.

The CFMEU's defence of dissociation fell apart when the *Sydney Morning Herald* published a front-page story on 31 August revealing that paid officials from the union had played an active part in the riot. At least five officials from the NSW branch were identified in riot pictures and the man with the bloodied face and shield was an official from the CFMEU's South Australian branch. The CFMEU's NSW branch secretary, Andrew Ferguson, was aware that some of his officials were 'involved in the incidents' but had kept quiet about it. The *Herald's* revelation put Jennie in an even more difficult position. All along she had claimed the ACTU was unconnected to the riot and yet now officials from one of the unions that shared responsibility for organising the rally were exposed as having been involved. Despite being ACTU president, Jennie was hamstrung: she was powerless to interfere with the internal affairs of the union and most reluctant to criticise one of the ACTU's largest affiliates. The day after the *Herald* story, Canberra journalist Laurie Oakes quizzed Jennie about the CFMEU's involvement on the Nine Network's 'Sunday' program:

> Oakes: It's now been revealed that a number of the people in the front line of that Budget eve riot at Parliament House were paid officials of a union affiliated with the ACTU. What's your response to that?
>
> Jennie: Well, I read that report in the *Sydney Morning Herald* yesterday. We have a council meeting this week. I've asked for a

number of reports: one from the Federal Police, one from the ACT Trades and Labour Council, and from unions whose members were involved in behaviour that we do not condone. So I'm expecting to make a fuller statement, but certainly it causes me great distress to think that there would be paid union officials that could be involved in behaviour which has done serious damage to the union movement.

Oakes: Now you don't dispute the identification of those people, do you? They've been seen in photographs in the *Sydney Morning Herald*, on television last night.

Jennie: Well, I don't know the people. Let me say this, that as far as I'm aware, there are no charges that have as yet been laid by the police, and I think anyone, including union officials, do have the right to due process of law. No-one in this country is guilty until they're proven to be guilty. So I think we need to keep that in perspective as well, Laurie.

Oakes: It's not just a matter of law, is it? I mean, these people are your people, affiliated with the ACTU, paid by the union movement. Now what are you going to do about it? Are you going to try and get something done to take away their jobs?

Jennie: Well, the secretary of the union has already made it clear in a number of public statements he's made that anyone in his union that is charged with serious offences is on their own. I'd be expecting the union to outline exactly what that means in their report to our council meeting on Tuesday. Look, let me say quite clearly: I will not walk away, I'm not the sort of person who would walk away from responsibility which is properly attributed to the ACTU. But from day one, I was not going to accept responsibility for actions and behaviour that have nothing to do with the mainstream of the union movement. I made that very clear. And I think that when I get the police report, all the people who put the pressure on Bill and myself to accept responsibility will find that even the police come out in their report stating quite categorically that I, on behalf of the ACTU, did everything on that day to put in place what should have been a great day for the union movement.

So, to that extent, that we're able to foresee events that occurred, I'll accept the responsibility that in future we have to learn from that experience. But I did everything requested of me by the Federal Police for that occasion, which was to be, as I said, a peaceful protest rally by the union movement.

Oakes: You seem to be saying there'll only be action against these people, these paid officials of a union that's affiliated with you, you're saying there'll only be action if they're charged.

Jennie: Well, I'm asking the union to advise me what their intent is when they say that anyone charged in their union is on their own.

Oakes: But why are you *asking* the union? You're the president of the ACTU—you're the leader of the entire union movement. Why can't you be proactive and do something about these people?

Jennie: Well, I have been very proactive. I'm the one that's called for the inquiry. I'm the one that's doing the discussions with the police. I've asked the unions to report to me and, after they report on Tuesday, then I will make a statement on behalf of the whole union movement. But I'm not going to assume that people are guilty just because a picture appears on the front page of the *Herald*. I don't know whether or not they are, in fact paid officials of the union. If they are, I view that very seriously, as does the whole union movement, and we would expect the union...

Oakes: If they are, should they lose their union positions?

Jennie: Well, under the Act, anyone charged with criminal offences is not allowed to continue to hold a union job.

The day Jennie tried to put the riot issue to rest happened to coincide with Federal Police making the first of an anticipated spree of arrests following their investigation of the riot. Jennie, however, was far from Canberra in Lorne, the Victorian beachside town chosen once again as the location for a meeting of the ACTU's 100-member council. During council debate, the national secretary of the CFMEU, Stan Sharkey, resisted great pressure from some delegates to take disciplinary action against some of his officials in the absence of any charges laid by police. He declared he would not indulge in any 'McCarthyist witch-hunt'. In light of speculation about their leadership, the council also took the highly unusual step of passing a 'unanimous' vote of confidence in Jennie and Kelty.

The main point of debate was to reach agreement on a resolution about the riot, which Jennie made public after its approval at a joint media conference with Sharkey. The resolution was a piece of ACTU face-saving justification that fell well short of an apology or accepting responsibility as Howard had demanded but did make some admissions and relieved Jennie of her personal burden. It said:

> The ACTU council congratulates all those trade unionists and community supporters, well over 50 000, who rallied and protested in Canberra and many other cities on 19 August 1996 against the Howard Government's proposed industrial relations changes.
>
> The ACTU thanks the broad range of community groups (including ACOSS, FECCA, women's organisations, youth groups and churches) for standing with the ACTU in opposition to the proposed legislation.
>
> The success of the mobilisation of tens of thousands of people on that day was overshadowed by the actions of a small minority of protesters at the Canberrra rally, who engaged in behaviour not condoned by the union movement.
>
> The ACTU council condemns, in the strongest terms, the violent actions of a small minority of protesters at the rally. These acts of violence and destruction of property are totally abhorrent to the union movement and any person found to be involved should receive no support or comfort from our movement.
>
> The actions of these people undermined the collective objectives of the union movement's campaign against the legislation and caused harm to the reputation and standing of the union movement.
>
> The council acknowledges that the organisational arrangements on the day were in conformity with Federal Police requirements, but clearly inadequate to handle these unforeseen events. Accordingly, a

protocol will be developed for future rallies and protests as requested by the Australian Federal Police Association.

The ACTU council regrets what occurred, including injury to police and staff, but is not responsible for the actions of a small minority of the 30 000 participants at the Canberra rally. Individuals who act outside the collective framework and damage the collective standing of the union movement will receive no support or comfort from the movement.

The ACTU council believes that all citizens are entitled to the due processes of law. Should individual union officials or union members be charged and found guilty of serious offences, the council is of the firm view that disciplinary action by the unions is warranted.

While the actions of the tiny minority have undoubtedly done harm to the collective union movement, the extent of the union and community opposition displayed that day highlights our determination to continue to campaign in opposition to the Howard Government's industrial relations legislation.

At the very least, Jennie had wanted the Canberra rally to stiffen the resolve of the Democrats, the Greens and Independent Senator Brian Harradine, who held the fate of government legislation in their hands by virtue of holding the balance of power in the Senate. In this objective, the riot did not sabotage her efforts and she achieved as much as she could have hoped. As expected, Kernot negotiated a compromise with Reith that ensured the passage of the Workplace Relations Bill. The compromise announced on 27 October, which committed the Government and Democrats to supporting 181 amendments to the original bill, gave Reith enough latitude to hail a great victory for reform. The bill officially became law on 1 January 1997. However, some important concessions were made that reflected the political pressure Jennie had maintained despite immense adversity. She had remained in Canberra the entire week that the bill was debated in the Senate, responsible for the outcome of ACTU negotiations. She recalled:

> At that stage I went through it paragraph by paragraph. So I would say of all the people in the ACTU, I take responsibility for all the

shortcomings or otherwise of the final package to the extent that I was able to make it better, I think. I can rightly claim some responsibility for that.

I managed to retain a role for the umpire [in non-union individual contracts] despite the fact that the tests are very hard before the umpire can intervene, and the fact that contracts were to be checked to ensure workers were not disadvantaged. I helped retain the equal pay provisions in line with the ILO convention on equal pay. Having the capacity for arbitration of paid rates awards was only secured very much towards the end.

I think the greatest disappointment where I could have done better was particularly in the area of secondary boycotts because the Democrats themselves had a party policy on that [of not restoring old law]. Cheryl walked away from her own party's policy on that. I guess she termed it a compromise.

The day after Kernot's deal with Reith on the legislation was announced, Jennie declared that she wanted the Democrats to re-open negotiations with the Government, claiming the party had backtracked on certain parts of its policy in making a compromise. Jennie did want changes but her protest was more a token gesture than a serious demand—part of her concern was to deflect internal union criticism about the ACTU's reliance on the Democrats. Jennie had no choice except to use the Democrats to secure changes and she freely admitted as much. She also refused to apologise for thanking the Democrats for improving what was a 'fundamentally flawed' bill.[5]

It took months for Jennie to recover emotionally from the riot. With friends over the Christmas and New Year holidays she still sifted through what went wrong. Personally, she eventually made a full recovery. Her ACTU presidency was not so fortunate. Whenever she attended public gatherings from then on, the cameras would be waiting for another riot.

21

HOLDING THE LINE

When Bill Kelty walked out of the courtroom on the tenth floor of the Industrial Relations Commission in Sydney on 22 April 1997 all television and radio microphones suddenly turned his way. 'Will you comment on the wage decision, Mr Kelty?' a reporter asked. 'No, Jennie's making comment,' he replied, and disappeared down the corridor. Kelty's grand idea to combat a harsh new political environment without the Accord—the 'living wage' claim—had been trounced by the commission only minutes earlier. He left it to Jennie, standing alone, to cope publicly with a significant defeat.

When she emerged, Jennie's response was tough and defiant. She criticised the commission's refusal to meet the needs of those she called the working poor. In particular, she was irritated that the commission had bowed to pressure from the Reserve Bank not to grant the claim because of likely adverse effects on interest rates and inflation. 'There is one law for the rich and one for the poor,' she declared. In a split six-to-one vote, the full bench headed by Justice Deirdre O'Connor had just granted an extra $10 a week to workers without an enterprise bargain and set a new minimum wage of

$359. The bench rejected the ACTU claim for a $20 increase in the award 'safety net' as well as the first stage of a proposed 30 per cent increase in minimum pay rates.

No-one had expected the ACTU to win the whole claim but the enormous gulf between the claim and the small amount allowed was a powerful reminder of the adversity confronting the union movement—and Jennie as its frontline leader. Personally Jennie took the defeat well and was at ease in defending the ACTU's position—the public pressure was also nothing like the intensity she had experienced after the Canberra riot and she was able to deflect criticism of the ACTU claim elsewhere. But the 'living wage' defeat was indicative that no matter how hard she tried, circumstances worked against Jennie putting her stamp on the ACTU presidency. She had assumed the mantle as head of the Australian union movement just as the ACTU's influence was fading. As had happened to former State premiers Carmen Lawrence and Joan Kirner, the men who had traditionally wielded power had been prepared to back a woman when the political cycle looked like turning sour. The key difference was that while political parties always bounced back sometime, the trend of union decline showed no sign of reversing or even slowing, no matter how much energy Jennie exerted.

Jennie had made public declarations, after chairing several quarterly meetings of the ACTU executive, that anecdotal evidence based on 'going round the table' surveying union officials was that the membership decline had 'bottomed out' and that the ACTU's recruitment drive was working. But official Australian Bureau of Statistics results told a different story—that the long-term collapse was continuing. Figures released in February 1997 showed that only 31 per cent of the workforce belonged to a union, down a further 2 per cent from 1995. In the private sector, which accounted for the bulk of employees, union membership was just 24 per cent of the workforce, compared with 55 per cent in the public sector. Worse looked yet to come in the face of major job shedding in the Commonwealth Public

Service and the effect of Reith's legislation outlawing compulsory unionism.[1]

By necessity, Jennie had made boosting union membership one of her chief priorities. Yet it was patently clear that she was bound for failure. It was not through any particular fault of hers, just that the magnitude of the task of reversing the long-term trend was beyond the capability of any single person in the limited time available.

When Martin Ferguson was still in the chair as president, the ACTU had set a target to increase total net membership by 200 000 by mid-1997. It was a target that Jennie had supported wholeheartedly and again endorsed when she took over the presidency. As the deadline neared and it became clear that there was no chance of the target being achieved, she had little choice but to change tack. Instead of talking about target numbers, she shifted emphasis to the role unions could play in the fight for 'job security'. The change of focus was a good way for Jennie to tap into the increasing uncertainty unionists and non-unionists alike felt in their working lives. Job security had always been a union objective. By stressing it now, attention could be deflected from the failure of the ACTU to reach its stated recruitment goal.

The plan to increase membership appeared destined for oblivion just like some other ACTU recruitment schemes, among them a proposal Jennie supported to offer 'cut-price' associate membership to workers faint-hearted about joining a union and another to open 'shopfront' union agencies in suburban shopping malls. Still another, fanciful in hindsight, was the ACTU's proposal to set up a 'people's airline' that was supposed to compete with the major carriers by offering workers cheap travel to holiday destinations.[2]

As the ACTU's official spokesperson, Jennie was constantly trapped in a reactive role, regardless of what initiatives she announced to try to keep the union movement on the front foot. Such a role, where the negatives outweighed the positives, was a recipe for frustration and exhaustion. Her job became, much as she described it, 'just holding the line, trying to defend our position'. One method of coping with the largely negative role in which Jennie was cast was to ration her public appearances. In doing so, she was accepting Kelty's advice to her. Not being on tap for the media to comment on every political development gave her more presidential bearing, her pronouncements carrying greater weight if delivered sparingly. Jennie explained, 'I don't want to be on the media too often because you can suffer from over-exposure. Too much tends to blur the role of ALP politician and union leader.'

Jennie was also expressing her appreciation of the predicament the ACTU had faced since the late 1980s when it came to be regarded widely as just an arm of the Labor Party. She sought to make the ACTU stand as an independent organisation that was recognised for what it was supposed to be, the country's peak union council. A breather from public appearances also helped her to rebuild her energy and fulfil one of her other stated priorities, to 'spend time at the coalface' in the form of worksite visits to hear the concerns of ordinary people. Such visits doubled as Jennie's contribution to the ACTU's recruitment drive, although in truth their value beyond maintaining membership levels was limited because she was mainly preaching to the converted.

Although the 'rationing' theory for her public appearances had merit, absences from the media spotlight did carry a serious risk for Jennie. When the reality of an all-pervasive information age was juxtaposed with a union movement in the doldrums, the days and sometimes weeks that passed without Jennie's name featuring in public debate only reinforced the growing perception that unions were no longer relevant.

Jennie's style of leadership, consistent with her past, was to be inclusive when chairing ACTU meetings and working with the ACTU executive team. While kept advised of events, she saw her job as being the organisation's front person and stayed clear of policy formulation, carriage of test cases, industrial negotiations and the internal management of the ACTU. These areas she left to Kelty and his assistant secretaries Greg Combet and Tim Pallas. Indicative of her inclusive nature—unlike her predecessors—Jennie felt no threat to her position by giving free reign to Combet or Pallas to take over the public running on various issues. In fact she actively encouraged them, especially in the technical legal matters or bargaining negotiations she regarded as beyond her expertise. Typical of such issues was the Court Government's repeat attempt to have its so-called 'second wave' of anti-union legislation passed in the West Australian Parliament. Jennie made several trips to Perth to address union rallies and at one point held more than two hours of (unsuccessful) talks with Premier Richard Court over the issue. But she left most public comment and hands-on negotiations to Pallas.

One area where Jennie hoped her presidency could make significant and lasting inroads was better pay for women. The ACTU had won equal pay, officially, following ACTU test cases in 1969 and 1972 that eradicated blatant discrimination by guaranteeing women the same minimum pay rates as men. Jennie wanted to score a major success in the unregulated area of 'over-award payments' so that women were guaranteed the same *earnings* as men. Total earnings of women were still only 85 per cent of men's earnings, and on average women who received over-award payments received only 55 per cent of the amount earned by men.[3]

Fighting for equal pay was also a way for Jennie to appease those in the women's movement who argued that enterprise bargaining put female workers at a disadvantage. Jennie had defended the ACTU line at the Sydney congress in 1993 when women had demonstrated over equal pay. A year later she had clashed with women friends such as Meredith Burgmann at a Macquarie University seminar, claiming that an ACTU analysis of statistics showed that enterprise bargaining was not the cause of a widening earnings gap between men and women.[4] As one woman observer noted:

> When Jennie gave that speech she presented figures some of the sisters thought were spurious. While everyone was very cross about it, no-one thought it was coming from her. No-one was angry with her personally because she was following the ACTU line.

As ACTU president, Jennie had the opportunity to partly stem criticism of the ACTU's position by actively seeking to end remaining discrimination over women's earnings. During the latter part of 1995, as the Keating Government headed for electoral defeat, the ACTU cast around for companies it could use in a test case in the Industrial Relations Commission to prove the point of a disparity in earnings. Finding a test case was not an easy task because the ACTU had to pick watertight examples of discrimination where the pay records of individual women employees could be held up to scrutiny against those of men performing the same or similar work who were paid more. Typically, whenever a test case was found, the company concerned made a settlement with its women employees that made any union claim invalid.

Jenny Doran, the ACTU industrial officer charged with running the case, finally settled on three companies—HPM Industries and Utilux in Sydney and John Sands in Melbourne. The women in these firms performed semi-skilled process work. They earned about $375 gross a week and could earn $20 a week less than men on a lower grade than themselves once bonuses and other over-award payments were considered. Jennie optimistically launched the test-case claim as a major ACTU initiative in December 1995, at a media conference in Sydney with her friend and colleague Doran. But problems began almost as soon as the case was launched.

The ACTU had picked companies employing semi-skilled process workers under the Metal Industry Award because it believed that manufacturing would prove the best example for its argument. Yet in doing so it came head to head with one of the more astute and pragmatic employer organisations, the Metal Trades Industry Association (MTIA). The MTIA accepted that women had been treated unfairly in the past but argued that competency standards, not gender, should rule rates of pay. It was determined not to have its members used for any test case on discrimination that would put them in the spotlight in setting general standards. During the course of 1996, while the case was listed before the Industrial Relations Commission, the MTIA's industrial relations director, Roger Boland, reached settlements in two of the three companies by direct negotiation. In doing so he robbed Jennie of her treasured test case because more than one company was needed to satisfy the requirements of the commission.

During 1997 Boland negotiated a deal for the third company, HPM Industries, under which the union claim was to be arbitrated by Commissioner Jim Simmonds. Simmonds subsequently dismissed the claim but accepted that a better avenue for the union to pursue it was by a traditional method of testing the work value of men and women at HPM. On these grounds the HPM women had a good argument to put—but the outcome could have no legal significance outside the company. Once again, Jennie's attempts at gaining a positive result in a major issue during her ACTU presidency had been foiled. A disappointed Jennie told her colleagues in the women's movement that she had tried her best—and that the battle was not over. Her fallback position was to campaign generally on behalf of low-paid women, stressing that union membership was the best remedy for those who lacked bargaining power to gain anything from the model of 'one-on-one' negotiations that Reith was encouraging under his Workplace laws.

Jennie's campaign for women on low pay was brought sharply into focus in late May 1997—but not in the way she had intended. In the preceding months the Textiles Clothing and Footwear

Union had run what it called a 'Fair Wear' campaign which urged retailers to sign a code of practice stipulating that they would accept wholesale clothing only from those manufacturers that guaranteed fair wages and conditions to their workers. Jennie was a champion of the cause. It had been a long-running and vexatious issue for the union movement: how to police the exploitation of home workers, mainly migrant women with poor English who earned as little as $2 an hour making garments sold to the public at premium prices. Signatories of the code included Just Jeans, Witchery, Jacqui E., King Gee, Peter Weiss, Najee and Sara Lee. But a number of retail chains, such as Sportsgirl, would not sign up.

Jennie agreed to speak at a protest of unionised clothing workers held outside the Sportsgirl store in Sydney's Pitt Street Mall on 30 May 1997. She told the gathering that it was a disgrace that up to 300 000 outworkers were exploited at home and in sweatshops and called for a consumer boycott of retailers refusing to sign the code. She said:

> What we've got to say to these companies is that we will generate a consumer boycott and refer to these companies and their shops as shops of shame. They've got a choice—they can either be shops of integrity or shops of shame.[5]

After her speech, in a pre-planned move, Jennie then strode into the Sportsgirl store, about 100 protesters and media following behind her. Confronting a young shop assistant at the counter, she demanded to see the store manager. When the manager arrived, Jennie brandished a winter jacket with a $200 price tag. Why, she asked the manager, were outworkers paid less than $9 to make the garment? With television cameras rolling, Jennie continued: 'You should put the pressure on your company because it is a disgrace that women at home are getting only $2 an hour. The manager replied: 'I ask you to leave the store please. You are invading the store.' Jennie then turned to the shop assistant, who had insisted she did not make the clothes, and said: 'How would you feel? You are covered by an award here. These people are working at home with no protection.'[6]

As a media stunt, Jennie's store 'invasion' worked by drawing maximum attention to the issue. But as a public relations exercise to bring the non-unionised majority behind her in support of the Fair Wear campaign it backfired badly and showed poor judgment on her part. In that evening's commercial television news reports the emphasis was placed more on a confrontation than the fight for a just cause. The images beamed across the country were those of an aggressive Jennie, surrounded by angry protesters, clashing with shop employees. Less than a year after the Canberra riot from which she had struggled to dissociate the ACTU, here was apparent evidence of Jennie engaging in overbearing union behaviour. This was sure to alienate the non-union audience to which the ACTU had hoped to appeal. It reinforced negative perceptions of unions generally and of Jennie personally.

The most strident anti-ACTU media coverage came from the next morning's *Daily Telegraph* with a strongly critical editorial headed 'The bully girl of unionism'. While accepting that payment of miserable wages to outworkers was a grubby practice, the editorial pointed out that Jennie's target was misdirected and should have been company executives closer to her 'weight division' rather than ordinary women employees:

> ACTU president Jennie George is supposed to be the human face of the union movement, the one you can trust and need not fear. Tell that to the young women who were going about their perfectly legal duties in a Sydney clothing shop yesterday when Spinning Jennie whirled in. Ms George berated the women for the management decisions of employers. It was part of an unpleasant stunt . . . If Ms George wanted to draw attention to herself she succeeded. If she wanted to recruit members she was a dismal failure. The peak union group should seriously re-examine its general tactics and acknowledge that it has yet to live down the disgraceful assault on Parliament House last August.[7]

Even more damaging to Jennie than this editorial in the major
metropolitan newspaper that reached deep into the worker heartland in Sydney was the accompanying cartoon by Warren Brown.
It portrayed Jennie as an axe-wielding Viking, the words 'ACTU
youth recruitment program' emblazoned on her chest, raiding
the Sportsgirl store with bearded marauders. A shop assistant
looked aghast behind a cash register.

Politically Jennie left herself vulnerable to attack from the
Federal Government. John Howard obliged, accusing her of
bullying tactics, while Peter Reith, never one to miss the chance
for point-scoring, called on her to apologise for 'humiliating'
Sportsgirl staff and said the incident reminded people of the 'ugly
side of unionism' shown by the Parliament House riot. Jennie,
stung by the criticism and refusing point-blank to apologise,
accused the Government of blowing the incident out of proportion. She said:

> I went out of my way to be polite. I did not address my complaint
> personally to the shop assistant. The Government should worry
> about its own lack of progress on behalf of outworkers. Reith is
> just using every opportunity to criticise us.[8]

Within days the controversy had passed. But it served as a
potent reminder of the damage that the Canberra riot had already
done to Jennie's presidency. Her opponents were always ready
to revive it as an issue to hurt her. The lesson for Jennie was
that the ACTU had to be careful how its actions would be
perceived if community support was to remain a chief priority
as she stated it was.

Jennie did not dwell on the incident for long—as she did
after the riot. But she again revealed her thin skin when it came
to media criticism. She was happy for the ACTU's media officer
to telephone the *Telegraph* journalist who wrote a news report
of the incident, Mark Robinson, to attack him for the paper's
coverage. In future she would snub Robinson, just as she had
Paul Molloy from Melbourne's *Herald-Sun* following his post-riot

coverage the year before. Even though she was the union move-ment's voice in the media, Jennie was prepared to shun major newspapers she believed had crossed her on a few key occasions. She did this even at the expense of losing ACTU access to media outlets with mass distribution that spoke directly to the union movement's core constituency.

Jennie's chief focus, the national government in Canberra, remained her real enemy. The legislation that Peter Reith had pushed through Parliament was mild in its restriction of union activity compared with the model some of the most zealous promoters of reform had wanted and that State premiers Kennett and Court had put in place. But Reith was only warming up. The Coalition missed few opportunities to undermine union influence and, contrary to earlier denials, more legislative changes were planned.

The much-anticipated main event, however, was a union war on the waterfront. Since their days in Opposition, Howard and Reith had attacked the poor productivity levels they claimed prevailed on the docks. They wanted to tackle the closed shop of the Maritime Union of Australia (MUA). More than twelve months after the Howard Government's election in March 1996, the tone of the rhetoric indicated it was only a matter of time before fireworks on the waterfront began. In its absence a dispute in the coal industry involving a seasoned ACTU foe, CRA (renamed Rio Tinto), had become the headline dispute and an important test for union strength.

Rio Tinto's mines in the NSW coalfields remained the only under-performing area of its vast resource interests across the country. For many months the company had wanted to force an end to century-old work practices over which the CFMEU retained control, thanks largely to its closed shop. The company had fought a protracted battle at its Vickery mine near Gunnedah during the dying days of the Keating Government, only to settle for a compromise in the Industrial Relations Commission and eventually close the mine. Now able under Reith's Workplace Relations Act to use tougher legal sanctions against unions for illegal strike action while avoiding the intrusion of the commission, the company was determined to press for changes at its Hunter Valley No. 1 colliery, a rich mine near Singleton employing 430 CFMEU members. The issue came to a head during July 1997 when, using management labour, Rio Tinto attempted to restart the mine during a strike. Given that the CFMEU was refusing to compromise on work practices sought by Rio Tinto, the company's strategy was to exhaust the union side. Rio Tinto was prepared to lift the temperature of the conflict to such a high degree that there was the strong possibility of an all-out conflict with the union forced to use illegal sympathy strikes. If unions blocked the transport of coal by train from the mine to the port of Newcastle and then tried to stop export shipments out of the country bound for Asia they could be liable for enormous financial damages for interference with trade.

Jennie entered the fray as ACTU spokesperson with the task of garnering wider community support for the miners' cause. It was not an easy task. She faced the company's slick propaganda machine pumping out information daily about miners on salaries of $85 000 or more who indulged in 'rorts'. Jennie's counter was to simplify the issue to what she considered its essence—much disputed by Rio Tinto and, to some extent, by the facts. Repeatedly, she attacked what she said was a company agenda to put all miners on non-union individual contracts as it had done, according to a corporate philosophy of the early 1990s, at its non-coal enterprises across the country. The Hunter Valley strike, Jennie argued, had major implications for the general community. It was important to take a stand here so that workers in low-paying jobs without bargaining power could not have contracts forced upon them. The political message laced through Jennie's rhetoric was that the dispute had been 'well engineered'[9] by Rio Tinto with collusion from Peter Reith.

Indeed Rio Tinto *was* offering non-union contracts at Hunter

Valley No. 1 to those who wanted them. About five workers had signed up. The company also was receiving active encouragement from Reith's office in its endeavours. Yet Rio Tinto executives also knew that any hope of breaking the CFMEU's stranglehold in the coal industry, given the union's history of solidarity in the Hunter Valley, was fanciful. Its chief goal was to break union control in determining, by seniority, everything a miner did from allocation of jobs, shifts, promotions and who was laid off in an economic downturn. If successful, the effect would be to reduce the influence of the CFMEU—though falling far short of de-unionising the workforce.

Among the claims and counter-claims, there was some sense to Jennie's argument as she sought to protect the old-style union line. Suggesting that coalmining conditions in the Hunter Valley had implications for the community generally was doubtful (the CFMEU's influence in coal far outstripped that of unions in most workplaces), but there were wider implications for the coal industry. A victory for Rio Tinto at Hunter Valley No. 1 would create momentum for similar changes the company wanted at other mines such as its nearby Mount Thorley colliery. Once changes spread throughout the entire Rio Tinto coal group in NSW and Queensland, other companies would have to follow suit to remain competitive. Already the Atlantic Richfield Company (ARCO) was taking an aggressive approach in pursuing contract employment at its Curragh and Gordonstone mines in far north Queensland, prompting union walkouts.

As conflict across the coal industry deepened, Jennie became the living symbol of the union cause. Visits she made to the mining communities of NSW and Queensland had a dual purpose: mustering community support for the union cause and lifting the spirits of the individual workers in the middle of strikes who were under heavy political pressure to give up. In the mould she had set while campaigning for Paul Keating during the 1993 election campaign, she made touring the lifeblood of her ACTU presidency. Wherever she went—speaking to miners' strike meetings at Singleton Civic Centre or attending miners' family days in the far north Queensland town of Emerald, she received a hero's welcome.

With no end in sight to the Hunter Valley dispute, Jennie's main hope was that the Industrial Relations Commission would intervene to force a settlement on both sides that would stop conflict escalating out of control. An old-style forced settlement was the last thing Rio Tinto wanted, believing it could not win all it wanted this way. The commission's powers to intervene were limited under Reith's Act. Under the new rules, the commission was meant to stay out of industrial disputes and let the two sides thrash out their differences. But it could legally terminate the bargaining period and impose arbitration on two warring parties if satisfied that the dispute threatened significant damage to the economy, or part of it. This limited precondition suggested that unions would have to manufacture a strike catastrophe—or threaten to do so—to justify commission intervention.

Jennie, who had been a firm believer in maintaining a role for the commission as umpire since her presidency of the Teachers' Federation (and believing that its rulings would not swing too far against the union line), emphasised the possibility that the Hunter Valley strike would erupt into a national confrontation. But she was playing a delicate rhetorical game. She could not appear to be encouraging confrontation. To do so would make Jennie politically vulnerable to Reith, ready to accuse her of inciting trouble. She also risked a heavy financial liability for herself and for unions in the event that companies later took court action for secondary boycotts.

Demonstrating how seriously the ACTU was taking the Hunter Valley conflict, Jennie chaired a special meeting of national union leaders on 11 July in Sydney. Her main objective was to underline the need to stop industrial action spreading. But two days later, in a television interview on Channel Ten's 'Meet the Press', she publicly raised the possibility that it would spread, 'I think the ground has been well paved for this to potentially loom as a very big major national dispute. That's what Howard wants—it's not what we want.'[10]

Peter Reith immediately jumped on Jennie's comments:

> Jennie George likes to see national disputes. The fact of the matter is she can't spread this dispute; she can't spread it because the Workplace Relations Act is a major disincentive to the conduct of secondary boycott action by other unions.[11]

Throughout the Hunter Valley dispute Justice Alan Boulton of the Industrial Relations Commission had convened several hearings as both Rio Tinto and the CFMEU tested the limits of Reith's Workplace Relations Act. By the end of July he called them together. While not imposing a result, he did persuade both sides to accept a temporary truce, ending a six-week strike, so they could attempt to resolve differences by negotiation.

It was a convenient pause in hostilities for Jennie. Personally it freed her of engagements so she could celebrate her fiftieth birthday on 20 August 1997. She did so with a week of parties in Sydney, including one at the State Parliament in the ministerial office of her friend Pam Allan, and another at a Leichhardt restaurant that was strictly for her network of women friends including Cathy Bloch, Meredith Burgmann and Sharan Burrow. Two more birthday celebrations were hosted at the homes of friends—one by Paula Rix from old Eureka Youth League/Communist Party connections and another by Rex and Helen Hewett (in Melbourne). The parties were joyous affairs for Jennie, full of chatter and memories, and opportunites for friends to pay tribute to her achievements. The Rio Tinto truce also enabled Jennie to prepare for the union movement's major policy forum, the ACTU congress in September, at which she would officiate for a full five days.

The future of the ACTU's leadership had become a serious question in the lead-up to the congress. Kelty had been secretary since 1983, through Labor's entire thirteen-year term in national office and since. Consideration had to be given to who would eventually replace him. Jennie was still relatively new to the ACTU presidency—barely two years in the job. Hawke had spent a decade as president but his three successors Ferguson, Crean and Dolan had since set a standard of five years in office. Jennie was not expected to exceed that time. Nor had she been inclined to remain for long periods in high-profile jobs that she found wore her down.

Inside the ACTU organisation Jennie continued to receive support from Kelty and they enjoyed close professional ties. They were at one on most issues. But in the public mind Kelty had become a liability: the perception of him was that of a union leader who was either invisible or ridiculous. He either said nothing or, on rare appearances, was given to aggressive outbursts with exaggerated rhetoric. By comparison, Jennie was firm but measured in her utterances, always careful not to stray to extremes. Time and again she answered for Kelty when he did not elaborate on a public position he had adopted or tried to salvage something defendable when he had gone out on a limb. It made her task of selling the virtues of the union movement to the community and attracting new recruits all the more difficult.

The pattern had started with Kelty's pre-election 'symphony' speech and was followed by him calling the Canberra rally a great success. Kelty had been the architect of the 'living wage' claim that was comprehensively rejected yet he would say nothing about it on the day—he did not even stand by Jennie's side as she fielded questions. It was hugely embarrassing for Jennie that the day after she had branded the 'living wage' decision 'one law for the rich and one for the poor' Kelty appeared in a Melbourne court to give character evidence for former Coles Myer chief Brian Quinn.

Kelty had declined to speak for the low paid when it mattered but spoke for a man facing jail after conviction on a multi-million dollar fraud over lavish home renovations. Even Kelty's closest allies found this latest incident a serious lapse of judgment that showed him to be out of touch with his constituency. Kelty later offered several oblique explanations about why he spoke up for Quinn but already his links with business identities such as Lindsay Fox and Solomon Lew had drawn criticism from within union ranks. When combined with overall disenchantment about his leadership style and his closeness to Keating during Labor's reign, serious questions were asked about whether Kelty should remain in office.

Jennie's position was under no threat. But the Quinn episode in April 1997 crystallised the thinking of several left-wing union officials—not Kelty's usual opponents from the NSW Right—who spoke privately about the need to persuade Kelty not to seek re-election at the ACTU congress in Brisbane in September. Only one official, CFMEU leader Stan Sharkey, was prepared to canvas publicly that Kelty's leadership was in question, saying it was 'on the agenda'.[12] Talk of a serious move against Kelty was soon abandoned, however. The main reason was the lack of a feasible replacement—the man Kelty was grooming, Greg Combet, was thought not yet ready.

At a Left caucus during the ACTU executive meeting held in Newcastle in May 1997, Kelty and Jennie were assured of the faction's support in the upcoming congress vote. The tacit condition of support, however, was that Kelty would not serve out his full six-year term. There was no such pressure, tacit or otherwise, for Jennie to go before the end of her next term in 2003. However, few expected that she would see out the full six years.

The September congress, held in Brisbane's Town Hall, was significant in policy-making terms for the ACTU. It was the first held since 1981 in which Labor was not in power federally and the first since the death of the Accord. For Jennie it was significant as the first in which she would preside from the chair as ACTU president in her own right. The congress was also important symbolically for Jennie: she was to be elected as president by the congress, rather than serving out the rest of Ferguson's term as she had since he resigned.

Jennie's election was a formality: no candidate stood against her and none had a chance of winning anyway, such was the mass support for her leadership. Yet Jennie could not resist. She quizzed several people shortly before the congress, including journalists, asking if they had heard whether she was likely to be challenged. Her questioning exposed once more her innate insecurity but was also a method to doubly assure herself that no wildcard nomination was likely to spoil her smooth re-election.

The congress week was a marked contrast in styles between the two main ACTU leaders, Jennie and Kelty. From the chair Jennie ran proceedings in a most disciplined, efficient fashion. For the entire week she curbed her usual away-from-home predilection for partying late, instead retiring early so she could be as sharp as possible to face any unpredictable moves from the floor.[13] She let Greg Combet take the lead in major debates on wages and the waterfront, the clearest signal yet that he was being groomed to eventually succeed to Kelty. Jennie's main address to congress was measured and unemotional, striking a balance that recognised the adversity the union movement faced while attempting to boost morale. Threats of strikebreaking troops or trainloads of strikebreakers would not deter the union move-ment, she declared. She read a scorecard of recent enterprise bargaining campaigns in which unions had won wage rises, a long list crossing many occupations. 'They thought and hoped we would collapse but we haven't—and what's more we won't,' she said.[14]

By comparison, Kelty appeared to be functioning on raw emotion all week. He was close to tears on at least four occasions during addresses he made to the congress. During one, a reply to a moving speech by Aboriginal leader Lois O'Donoghue, he was lost for words. It was Kelty, however, who effectively set the agenda of the congress during a passionate speech in support of the Maritime Union of Australia (MUA). His purpose was to win a vote of united support for the union if a much-anticipated assault on its coverage of waterfront workers began. But his speech, bellicose and full of highly emotive language, also served notice on the Federal Government and stevedoring companies about the dire consequences of such an assault. All unions, declared Kelty, would stand behind the MUA no matter what force was used to destroy the union. 'To weaken the Maritime Union of Australia is to weaken the union movement as a whole. The day we give away that support is the day we rip out our own heart and leave it pumping in irrelevancy.'

As tensions heightened that a major battle was imminent after media reports of a secret Federal Government plan devised to break the MUA, Kelty warned:

> The only promise to John Howard is this. If you seek to destroy the Maritime Union of Australia, we will be there and you won't have a picket of 30 people, or a picket of 40 people. You won't have a picket of 500 people. You will have the biggest picket that has ever been assembled in the history of this country.

While Kelty thundered his warning of the retaliation that awaited a major assault on the MUA's power, the union movement's immediate challenge remained the fight against Rio Tinto in the coal industry. Three days after the ACTU congress ended, following almost seven weeks of truce, negotiations over work practices at the Hunter Valley mine broke down and the CFMEU's strike resumed. Jennie stuck to her position throughout that a settlement imposed by the commission was the only way to solve an intractable conflict. But she had to face up to tensions within the CFMEU leadership, particularly at a local level, which was reluctant to risk a commission-imposed settlement that might go against the union by ending precious working conditions, seniority in particular.

While the CFMEU wrestled with what to do and 8000 coalminers held a short-lived sympathy strike across the Hunter Valley, unionists staged a protest outside the Prime Minister's

ACTU presidents—past and present—pictured at a union fund-raiser just days before the Federal election Labor lost in March 1996. From left, Cliff Dolan, Martin Ferguson, Bob Hawke, Simon Crean and Jennie. (Courtesy of Fairfax Photo Library—Warren Clarke)

In Peter Reith's Melbourne office at Treasury Place just weeks after the Coalition's 1996 election victory. Jennie, seated left, leads a delegation with Bill Kelty and ACTU assistant secretary Tim Pallas. Reith is seated in the right corner. (Courtesy of Fairfax Photo Library—Tina Haynes)

Jennie in a buoyant mood greets a train packed with union protesters at Canberra's railway station on the morning of 19 August 1996. She hoped the day would be a triumphant protest against the Howard Government's Workplace Relations Bill but it all went horribly wrong. (Courtesy of Fairfax Photo Library—Mike Bowers)

In the most violent scenes ever witnessed at Parliament House in Canberra, rioters break through the front doors, overshadowing the union rally a mere 200 metres away. (Courtesy of *Canberra Times*—Gary Schafer)

A case of double standards. Bob Hawke could get away with crying in public, but Jennie was pilloried for it. (Courtesy of Ron Tandberg)

Jennie, always a champion for low-paid workers, addresses a small rally outside the Sportsgirl store in Sydney's Pitt Street Mall in May 1997 in support of exploited clothing workers, some earning as little as $2 an hour. (Courtesy of NSW Teachers Federation)

In an orchestrated move following the rally, Jennie walked into the Sportsgirl store with media and protesters in tow. She was asked to leave, but only after confronting a shop assistant and then the manager. The *Daily Telegraph* called her 'the bully girl of unionism' and she was lampooned by the newspaper's cartoonist, Warren Brown. (Courtesy of Warren Brown, *Daily Telegraph*)

Jennie has had a lot to ponder as her ACTU presidency has been pitched against constant adversity with union membership in decline and a hostile political environment. (Courtesy of Alan Moir, *Sydney Morning Herald*)

Jennie addresses a group of workers outside Courtroom 1 of the Industrial Relations Commission, Melbourne, in October 1996, at the start of hearings to decide the ACTU's 'living wage' claim. (Courtesy of Fairfax Photo Library—Joe Armao)

Despite new recruitment strategies and gimmicks such as cheap credit cards and travel, the ACTU appears not to have been able to arrest the decline in union memberships. (Courtesy of David Rowe, *Australian Financial Review*)

Jennie with Kim Beazley and the Labor Party's star recruit, former Australian Democrats leader Cheryl Kernot, at the ACTU-sponsored Whitlam Lecture at Sydney Town Hall in November 1997. The subject was the Republic, a cause close to Jennie's heart. (Courtesy of Fairfax Photo Library—Nick Mar)

(Left) A big kiss for Jennie from a wharfie on 21 April 1998, the day the MUA won round one of its Federal Court battle with Patrick Stevedores to save the jobs of sacked workers. She was in Adelaide visiting picketers. (Courtesy Chris Mangan, *The Advertiser*, Adelaide) (Right) Back in Melbourne, Jennie gives the thumbs-up sign as she is driven from the Federal Court to Webb Dock to celebrate the MUA's second round victory on 23 April 1998. (Courtesy of Craig Hughes, Herald and Weekly Times)

A euphoric Jennie on 4 May 1998 in a tent outside Patrick's Darling Harbour terminal in Sydney celebrates the announcement of the MUA's High Court victory upholding reinstatement of the sacked wharfies. In a study in styles, the MUA's John Coombs, seated opposite Jennie, remained measured—he knew there was much haggling to go. (Courtesy of Fairfax Photo Library—Adam Pretty)

Jennie George was passionate about fighting to save the jobs of sacked wharfies in the waterfront dispute—but there was much more at stake for her. A defeat for the MUA would have amounted to a major crack in the union movement's armour and a major boost for Peter Reith's anti-ACTU crusade. (Cartoon courtesy of Alan Moir, *Sydney Morning Herald*)

Jennie George has made touring workplaces the lifeblood of her ACTU presidency. Wearing a customary hard hat, she talks to workers on a visit to the BHP steelworks, in the company of Bill Kelty, following an ACTU executive meeting in Newcastle. (Courtesy of Fairfax Photo Library—Louise Kennerley)

Sydney office on 1 October. The CFMEU, much to Jennie's relief, had learned a lesson from the Canberra riot as officials wearing 'marshal' insignia were on hand to keep the peace. Jennie addressed the crowd, the Hunter Valley dispute dominating her speech as she attacked the Government's support for what she called Rio Tinto's 'cold-hearted pursuit of profits' at the expense of mining communities.[15]

Jennie's role in the dispute, especially after the protest outside his office, appeared to get under Howard's skin. A week later he launched a blistering personal attack on her during a Liberal Party function in Launceston, rejecting her credentials as a spokesperson for 'the legitimate interests' of employees:

> See her for what she is, somebody who is trying to defend the indefensible, somebody who is trying to preserve a set of arrangements which are holding back productivity, denying higher wages to her own members and as someone who is selfishly pursuing the interests of the trade union movement to the detriment of the people that the movement is meant to represent.[16]

Jennie hit back at Howard, saying his decision to focus on her personally showed she was doing her job:

> What Mr Howard fails to state is that the union has agreements with every other mining company in the Hunter Valley bar Rio Tinto. We cannot allow an unfettered management prerogative without the rights of workers being taken into account.

When CFMEU leaders finally agreed among themselves that a commission settlement was the only way out of their dilemma, Jennie played an important part in commission proceedings in Sydney that ran through the first week of November 1997. Prominent industrial barrister Wayne Haylen carried the union legal argument in front of Justice Boulton. Jennie presented a submission that by comparison was very short—yet its importance cannot be understated. Political rather than legal in content, she set out to leave no doubt in the judge's mind about the practical consequences of failing to intervene. Jennie was not one of the union strategists running the union campaign—she left that to key CFMEU officials John Maitland, Tony Maher, Mick Watson and Mick Kelly. But what she had to contribute now was the prestige of her office, leading the country's unions as president of the ACTU. In a special statement, using her status to the utmost, she told Justice Boulton that she had an obligation to advise him that escalation of strikes beyond the mine to a national basis was 'inevitable' if he did not intervene. 'This is no idle threat,' she said.[17]

Three days later Boulton responded as Jennie had wanted, forcing an end to the official bargaining period that permitted legal strike action and forcing a return to pre-strike work practices while both sides started the process that could lead to an old-style arbitration settlement.

Jennie's contribution to the CFMEU's cause encapsulated the heart of her ACTU presidency—that of a campaigner. She was able to communicate well with the workers she represented, to gain their confidence whether delivering a morale-boosting speech or mixing with them socially. Her broader communication role was to distil complex issues to their essence to try to win the public debate. Her success with workers was undisputed. Her success in other forums was mixed. Indeed the victory for Jennie and the CFMEU over Rio Tinto was short-lived. The company immediately lodged an appeal to a commission Full Bench, which it later won in January 1998, forcing the CFMEU back to direct negotiations with Rio Tinto without any enforced result from above. The 'inevitable' conflict that Jennie had warned of if the commission failed to intervene never occurred. But by then, the union movement was distracted by a much larger confrontation. The war on the wharves had begun and Jennie was in the middle of it.

WATERFRONT WAR

Long before he became Prime Minister, John Howard had made known his contempt for the MUA and its predecessor, the Waterside Workers' Federation. Unimpressed with a halving of the stevedoring workforce and improvements in container lift rates that occurred under Labors reform agenda, Howard was determined to end the closed shop on the waterfront, one of few remaining. He attributed lagging productivity on the docks, compared with international standards, almost entirely to what he called a 'union monopoly', and when he finally led the Coalition parties into government after thirteen years in Opposition, the MUA was destined to be his primary target for an assault on union power.

Howard's impatience with the progress of reform was understandable. Even during Labor's term a number of government ministers became frustrated to the point of exasperation in their dealings with the MUA, such was its resistance to change. The MUA's power far outstripped that of other unions (with the exception of the CFMEU in the Hunter Valley coal industry). It controlled workers' rosters, shifts, promotions and even the number of people operating equipment. The key difference between Howard and his predecessors when it came to waterfront reform was that he appeared to support a form of shock treatment as the remedy rather than bumble along in the vain hope that the MUA would co-operate freely.

Jennie knew that the waterfront confronted her with potentially the biggest battle of her presidency and that, given the resources available to a government, even the collective might of the union movement would not necessarily be strong enough to stave off defeat. Yet, she recognised that a loss for the MUA in the present climate was intolerable because it carried widespread ramifications for the union cause generally. The MUA was one of the smallest unions in the country, covering just 4000 stevedores and roughly the same number of seafarers. Its culture was old-fashioned and did not reflect the predominantly white-collar union movement of the 1990s. Yet the MUA was also a union that was rich in history, one of the ACTU's most loyal affiliates, reputedly the toughest union in the country, and the most obvious symbol of the union movement's remaining strength. For a movement in decline confronting a hostile government, destruction of the MUA's power would amount to a major crack in its armour from which it might never recover.

While Jennie was ready to play a prominent role in any waterfront onslaught, she knew that she would not be alone, but would be part of a team effort. Primary leadership rested with John Coombs, the MUA's gritty white-haired national secretary, as it was his union in the Government's sights. The ACTU had adopted a policy of unions taking responsibility for their own destiny and its job now was to offer support. Kelty delegated Greg Combet to assist Coombs in negotiations and with strategic advice. Jennie's role was to take an important public profile, providing comment to the media and boosting the morale of workers who would be caught in the conflict. She was most conscious of trying to co-ordinate her actions with Coombs in such a way that she did not overshadow him and hijack what was essentially his war to win.

The Government's main problem in pursuing the MUA was that it was not the employer of waterfront labour and therefore not in a position to directly lead any assault. An early proposal, promoted by Howard's Minister for Transport, John Sharp, to shut out the MUA—and encourage a new company on the docks prepared to hire only non-union labour—had failed. The alternative was to convince one or both of the two existing national stevedoring companies that did employ the labour, Patrick and P&O Ports, to fight the Government's war. In the first year of Howard's Government both companies had been shy of such a proposal, not merely because they were without legal weaponry while they awaited passage of Peter Reith's industrial laws. Even after the laws were introduced in January 1997, Patrick and P&O's primary concern was that they would fail to gain sufficient financial and political support from the Government. During a lengthy strike in which cargo could be stranded on the docks for weeks, business realities could force the companies to back down unless adequate support were offered—especially as Kelty had promised the 'biggest picket' in the country's history.

Determined to press ahead, at vast cost the Howard Government commissioned several consultants' reports on the best way to reform the waterfront—code for neutering the MUA. The contents of these reports remained confidential but sacking the MUA workforce during a waterfront strike and replacing it with new non-union labour was believed to be the favoured option.

The fight began in late September 1997 in the far north Queensland port of Cairns, an unlikely place to begin an assault on the MUA's power, considering only a handful of workers was involved. The shipping company International Purveyors dropped a local stevedoring firm that used MUA labour and in its place planned to use some of its own in-house non-union employees to load cargo bound for the giant Freeport mine in Indonesia. Peter Reith, whom Howard had put in charge of waterfront reform following John Sharp's resignation as minister over a 'travel rorts' scandal, fully backed the company's move. In response, John Coombs chose not to use traditional means of union retaliation such as Weipa-style sympathy strikes that risked financial penalties for secondary boycotts under the Government's new laws. Instead, he outmanoeuvred the company and the Government by drawing support from the International Transport Workers Federation (ITF) to successfully pressure the owner of the first ship to be loaded by non-union labour, the *Java Sea*, not to berth in Cairns. After hasty negotiations, International Purveyors backed down, not wanting to risk further bans on its international operations just for the sake of a small-time shipping outfit in Cairns. The union movement had won the first round.

Though unknown publicly, planning for another operation to thwart the MUA was already well advanced. A group of 35 men, including retired army personnel and other soldiers on leave, was being recruited by private interests for a secret mission to the Middle East port of Dubai. They were to be trained there as a non-union workforce to later replace the MUA in Australian ports. In early December, just days before the trainees were about to leave for Dubai, Coombs learned of the operation courtesy of a source he came to call his 'Number One Friend'. After making checks to rule out a hoax, he gave the information to the Federal Opposition, which enjoyed a bonanza in the last days of the parliamentary session before Christmas exposing the Dubai 'industrial mercenaries' and trying to link the Government to the venture. Reith denied any prior knowledge but lent his support to the plan. The training exercise failed because Coombs, wasting no time, boarded a flight to London and persuaded the ITF to issue warnings to the government of Dubai that it faced an international blockade unless the training agreement was abandoned. Dubai authorities, fearing loss of trade, complied with the demand by revoking the visas of the stevedoring trainees. They returned home, their mission unfulfilled.

The next development came in late January 1998 with the

news, again leaked in advance to Coombs, that Patrick's chief executive, Chris Corrigan, planned to sub-lease part of his company's Webb Dock stevedoring facilities in Melbourne to P&C Stevedores, a company wanting to train a non-union workforce. Just who was financing the training exercise remained mysterious but an old union foe, the National Farmers' Federation, admitted to owning the company. The union response this time was for the workers from Patrick's terminals at Webb Dock to strike in protest and picket the terminal gates, protesting against 'scabs' training to take their jobs. It became a festering dispute with claim and counter-claim. Coombs charged that Corrigan—with government backing—was the mastermind behind the Dubai exercise, as well as the Webb Dock leasing arrangement, both being precursors to replacing his entire workforce with trained non-union labour.

Jennie visited the MUA picket at Webb Dock many times, welcomed with cheers. Intent on keeping spirits high for what could be a lengthy battle, she gave speeches, mixed freely among the picketers and even donned an 'MUA here to stay' T-shirt over her business clothes in a show of camaraderie. Such was her popularity, picketers and their families queued for her to sign their T-shirts. She was the workers' hero, a symbol of the fight they vowed to wage to the end.

In mid-March Coombs revealed more leaked information about a plan by Corrigan to sack his entire Patrick workforce of 1400 at Easter. Corrigan denied such a plan. He had also denied involvement in the Dubai exercise or that the Webb Dock leasing arrangement formed part of any grander company scheme against the MUA.

On 7 April, three days before the Easter long weekend, tensions came to a dramatic head. Using the cover of darkness, at 11 p.m. large teams of security guards, some wearing balaclavas, entered Patrick terminals around the country with dogs and forced MUA workers on late shifts off the premises.[1] No access was to be given to MUA members from that time forth. In their place 350 non-union contract workers recently trained at Webb Dock were bussed inside the gates as a replacement workforce. This was the culmination of a well-planned and intricate corporate manoeuvre.

Six months earlier, Corrigan had secretly transferred his employees to four Patrick companies now described as 'labour hire' firms. These companies were effectively empty shells because ownership of equipment and other assets was transferred to upstream parent companies in the Patrick group, owned by the publicly listed Lang Corporation. Just hours before security guards entered the Patrick gates, a meeting of the board chaired by Corrigan had made a formal decision to stop funding the 'labour hire' companies for wages. The companies were then declared insolvent and placed voluntarily in the hands of administrators for likely liquidation. As a result, all 1400 full-time workers and a further 600 casuals were left without jobs. There was no role for the Industrial Relations Commission as the umpire because the workers were left without entitlements and no apparent legal right to claim unfair dismissal.

Jennie was woken shortly after 5 a.m. the next morning at her Manly flat by a telephone call from her mother. 'Jennie, Jennie, you must get up . . . ' cried Natasha, alarmed after having heard the early news bulletin on ABC Radio. Natasha knew her daughter would have an ordeal ahead of her and needed to be prepared. Jennie was not surprised at the sackings, given rumours of their likelihood, but she was taken aback by the audacious method of their execution. Her first move was to contact Greg Combet in Melbourne for an early-morning briefing. Combet had been alerted immediately the security guards entered the Patrick gates and had already branded the sackings 'disgraceful and un-Australian' in overnight media comments. Now Jennie hit the airwaves, putting the union position on ABC Radio's 'AM'. Her chief objective at this early stage was to win the public relations battle in the community by explaining how the Patrick sackings were relevant to everyone. She declared that the company's actions posed a threat to the job security of all workers if the tactics were allowed to succeed and were used elsewhere. She also tried to link the Federal Government directly to the Patrick strategy, alleging it had colluded in hurting ordinary workers. 'We are up against the worst political conspiracy this nation has seen in 100 years,' she said.

By mid-morning Jennie was at MUA headquarters in Sydney's Sussex Street talking through the crisis with Coombs and nervously pacing the floor as he fielded calls to discuss tactics. Together they drove to Port Botany, the largest of Patrick's two Sydney terminals, to address picketers about the fight ahead. It was afternoon by now. The crowd was a mix of sacked workers and a large media contingent that had assembled to record the event. The host of Channel Nine's 'A Current Affair', Ray Martin, arrived by chauffer-driven limousine to host his show from the picket line. He greeted Jennie with an embrace. 'This is terrible, Ray, just terrible,' she told him.

To loud cheers, Jennie promised the sacked workers that the ACTU would support them 'until the end' and the conflict would only end when they won back their jobs in a unionised workplace with the MUA representing them. She also pitched her message for the wider media coverage of the event:

> I want every worker in Australia to understand that it is the wharfies today but who is next? Is it coal workers tomorrow, is it nurses the day after, teachers the day after that? What it means is that any worker in any union in this country is not safe from the threat of being dismissed.

As in the past, Jennie left the actual running of the dispute to others while she devoted her energies to her real strength: campaigning. Again, some officials privately criticised Jennie for not involving herself in the nuts and bolts of the dispute as her immediate predecessors, Ferguson, Crean and Hawke would have done. But she perceived her role differently: she believed that she was best suited to talking about the broader implications of issues thrown up by the sackings, while leaving Coombs to do most of the running—including media commentary. One of her strongest arguments on the issue of fairness, she believed, was to repeatedly remind the general public of an admission during the dispute by the Prime Minister on 'A Current Affair'. When Ray Martin had asked Howard why Patrick wharfies in Hobart who had been commended for their productivity were also sacked, Howard replied without hesitation that it was *because* they were members of the MUA.

Jennie never faced Howard one-to-one during the waterfront conflict. She did, however, engage Reith in a number of debates on radio and television that relieved Coombs of some of the burden while broadening the scope of the union case. She followed Reith on the Nine Network's 'Sunday' program to rebut his remarks early in the dispute. She also faced Reith on the ABC's '7.30 Report' and sat beside Coombs on Nine's '60 Minutes' for a prearranged contest between Reith and Corrigan, which, predictably, became a slanging match that did not shed much light on the subject.

A central part of Jennie's contribution was visits to sacked workers and their families on MUA picket lines at Patrick terminals. Her most frequent visits were to the main pickets at the largest ports close to home—East Swanson and Webb Dock in Melbourne and Port Botany and Darling Harbour in Sydney. But she also travelled to pickets in Brisbane and Adelaide, intent on boosting the morale of the MUA troops who faced a long wait outdoors as the weather grew cold with the approaching winter.

At an organisational level, Jennie's role was to help maintain unity in the union movement. This she did by chairing a hastily convened ACTU executive meeting in Sydney the day after the sackings. She chaired another meeting a fortnight later. The point of these, besides giving Coombs an opportunity to brief the country's top union officials about the conflict, was to reconcile several opposing views in the union hierarchy. Jennie had to hose down militants—among them Coombs's deputy, Tony Papaconstuntinos—who wanted to escalate the conflict into widespread sympathy strikes across the country. She understood that such a response, conceived in anger, made no sense tactically because it would engulf the entire union movement, destroying any hope of controlling the outcome. The ensuing chaos would hand a clear advantage to Patrick and the Federal Government by blurring the issues in dispute. Unions not immediately connected with the dispute could also be up for huge damages claims and any hope of community support would be sabotaged. The other compelling reason to focus on unity was to quell grumbling in the union hierarchy. While militant elements were eager for stronger action, others felt the MUA had brought trouble upon itself by failing to accept compromise earlier. The doubters harboured resentment about being dragged into a potentially damaging conflict not of their making. Jennie had to calm such feelings because the ACTU could not afford any damaging public splits at this delicate stage.

The counter-strategy agreed by the ACTU was based on containing the industrial response to Patrick itself by imposing pickets that would stop cargo entering or leaving company terminals. The longer pickets remained in place, the more commercial pressure would be imposed on an isolated Patrick to concede that it could not restart business with its replacement workforce. Meanwhile, P&O Ports, which showed no interest in following rival Patrick's lead, was to be kept running at all costs with MUA labour.

The pickets at Patrick's terminals appeared a crude means of union defence but proved to be a highly effective weapon. No longer was Kelty's prediction of the 'biggest picket in history' so far-fetched. It was an apt description of what he had had in mind all along. If the company sought injunctions to remove individual picketers—as it did—the MUA–ACTU plan was to replace them with others, over and over, from a multitude of unions, in such a way that no legal action could ever be effective.

The Government and Patrick had expected a campaign of national strikes. The ACTU did not dissuade such speculation in the media—indeed privately it lent encouragement as a tactical ploy to wrongfoot its opponents.

The second part of the union strategy, ultimately the most crucial of all, was based on a case run by the MUA's lawyers in the Federal Court alleging an 'illegal conspiracy' involving Patrick and the Government. It specifically named Corrigan and Reith. Outwardly the MUA's objective was to use the judicial system to have the sackings overturned and to secure massive damages. But the legal and industrial objectives were intertwined. Gaining an interim injunction in the Federal Court that restored the status quo by compelling Patrick to reinstate the sacked workers before the conspiracy case was heard in full would hand the MUA a tactical advantage (and a moral victory of sorts). With workers back at the gates rather than protesting outside, there would be added weight in the MUA's favour to force a negotiated settlement. If none were forthcoming, the MUA intended to proceed with the conspiracy case, which its legal team were confident of winning.

Jennie experienced what she described as a series of 'emotional highs and lows' during the court battle. She joined in the spontaneous union rejoicing when the MUA won interim reinstatements in the Federal Court on 21 April, Justice Tony North having found 'there is an arguable case that Patrick have engaged in an unlawful conspiracy'.[2] In Adelaide that day, Jennie shared the moment with wharfies on the picket line. Several rushed to embrace her. The excitement was short-lived—she was soon let down when Patrick would not accept the result and challenged the ruling in two appeals.

Jennie was cautious as she sat in the Melbourne courtroom for the appeal ruling by three judges of the Federal Court on the evening of 23 April. She forewarned her supporters that 'tonight is not the end' and that ahead lay a full trial to press the union case that the sackings were illegal. When the ruling again went the MUA's way, however, Jennie made no attempt to contain her exuberance. Hugged by MUA officials such as national organiser Mick O'Leary, her face beamed. She gave the 'thumbs-up' sign for the cameras as she was driven away to East Swanson dock to celebrate with the picketers, hopeful of a quick return to work. Another letdown was quick in coming as Patrick rushed to the High Court, where it secured a freeze on the Federal Court ruling and was granted leave to appeal once more.

As Jennie waited nervously in the days leading up to the final verdict in the High Court, she gave full vent to her public campaign at an indoor rally of 2000 unionists in the lower Sydney Town Hall on 28 April. The crowd gave her a hugely warm reception. In an impassioned speech, she likened the union movement to a family. She said:

> The truth about this dispute is not about productivity, it is about the politics of union bashing. And I tell you Mr Howard—when you mount an attack on one of our family, you face the rest of our family . . .

But there was a hint of caution in Jennie's words that betrayed the uncertainty she was feeling about how the waterfront conflict would end:

> I don't think we're going to win it in the courts of law. Whatever happens in the High Court, it by itself does not get the jobs back of those workers who have been unfairly and illegally sacked. So please don't raise your hopes too high. Don't go home thinking it's all over, because it's not.

Jennie coped with the pressure of the waterfront conflict remarkably well. Finally, it appeared, she had left behind the trauma of the Canberra riot. The fact that she worked in a team, did not have to shoulder the entire responsibility alone, and was not subjected to vicious criticism helped keep her at ease.

The harshest public assessment of the ACTU leadership's role during the conflict came from the *Sydney Morning Herald*'s acerbic political columnist Alan Ramsey. Kelty, wrote Ramsey, had appeared as 'Moses in miniature' to deliver his warning about the consequences of an assault on the MUA at the September 1997 ACTU Congress but was now revealed as a 'neutered' blusterer. Nowhere to be seen, Kelty left 'all the hack work defending the ACTU's corporate interests' to Jennie. While directing the brunt of his criticism at Kelty, Ramsey also dismissed Jennie's ACTU presidency as ineffective. She was just another woman exploited by the men when it suited their interests to do so, in this case by Kelty:

> Bill Kelty, still the real power at the ACTU, however moribund, remains in his headquarters bunker in Melbourne as union dominance of the waterfront is systematically shredded by the Government and its well-heeled allies, while George, as his protege, protector and mouthpiece, fights the war Kelty so graphically committed the ACTU to last September, but in which, now that battle is joined, he takes no visible part.
>
> . . . As when the men in Labor turned to Joan Kirner in Victoria and Carmen Lawrence in Western Australia and, now, Cheryl Kernot in Canberra, to try to stop the rot with some all too obvious manipulation of political imagery, so Jennie George is simply inconsequential window-dressing in what is happening in the gradual erosion of unionism at large, a process hastened, ironically, by Labor itself.[3]

Ramsey's remarks were as pertinent as they were cutting. Kelty had become an issue of the waterfront dispute by virtue of his invisibility, and Jennie appeared to be covering for him. A day later the *Daily Telegraph* columnist Piers Akerman also reminded readers of Kelty's absence after all the breast-beating the previous year:

> Who would have suspected that Bill Kelty, the pint-sized prima donna of the trade union movement, would have gone missing in action? What's that? Where's Wally? Where's Wally indeed. Where is the tow-headed little fellow who promised the mother-of-all

picket lines, the full symphony? If he is half as smart as his self-publicity would indicate, he is hunkered down in a Melbourne pub hoping he won't be noticed because his industrial muscle has gone the way of all flesh.[4]

After having handed ACTU responsibility for the waterfront to Combet, Kelty was nowhere to be seen. Many believed he was uninvolved—though they were misguided to think so. Kelty's rationale for keeping a low profile was that this was Combet's opportunity to demonstrate his preparation for eventually succeeding Kelty as secretary (to which Kelty's staunchest opponents had the ready riposte: why wait?). Jennie appreciated that having Kelty away from the continual pressure of the frontline meant that he could keep a watchful eye on the strategic direction of the union campaign. Though out of sight, he provided Coombs and Combet with a constant stream of advice on tactics, and conducted significant behind-the-scenes negotiations to keep the peace with a number of large non-stevedoring companies caught up in the conflict.

Apart from his dislike of the media, Kelty's poor public image was reason enough to stay silent. He was so demonised after adverse commentary about some of his rhetorical flourishes that he knew he was no asset to the public campaign. Nevertheless, the Ramsey criticism in particular stung him, enough to prompt his appearance on the East Swanson picket in Melbourne just days later, arm-in-arm with Joan Kirner and other political figures, prepared to be arrested if it came to that. Even then, it seemed Kelty could not help himself. In a burst of extreme hyperbole, he compared the tactics used against the MUA with the political environment that led to the creation of Nazi death camps.

Jennie, hypersensitive about criticism such as Ramsey's in the past, was not hurt by it now. She regarded Kelty as having been subjected to an unfair attack. That the brunt of it was directed at him, not her, helped her overlook it. Even the assertion that she was 'inconsequential window-dressing' seemed to sweep over her without much effect. 'I knew it wasn't true,' Jennie recalled. 'I'd got to the stage where I didn't take that sort of criticism seriously anymore.' Her response was the same when Piers Akerman branded her a 'dated figure' in one of his regular columns and a *Daily Telegraph* editorial called her a 'dinosaur'.[5]

That Jennie was not constantly at centre-stage, as Hawke had been when ACTU president, *was* a mark of the ACTU's fading influence in union politics of the 1990s. Yet to dismiss Jennie as mere window-dressing was unfair, denying her the legitimate symbolic role she had developed as the country's most prominent union figure. The presidency still carried prestige even if it was not what it once was. While Jennie had failed to achieve her stated goal of reversing union decline, and those who expected her election as president to quickly re-invigorate the union movement were destined to be disappointed, she had certainly triumphed in uniting a movement much bruised after Labor's defeat.

One of the most enduring images of Jennie from the entire waterfront conflict was her spontaneous response to the final appeal ruling by the High Court on 4 May, which essentially upheld reinstatement of the workers six-to-one. She waited for the result with Coombs and other senior MUA officials on a wet Sydney day inside a cramped tent erected near the gates of the MUA's picket at Patrick's Darling Harbour terminal in Sydney. As the news was broadcast from a television set perched in the corner, Jennie stood, shouted in elation and shook her arms above her head. She had warned unionists not to pin their hopes on the court but could not help an impulsive, excited response at the moment of truth. It was a study in styles. Coombs, restraining his emotions, remained seated opposite her with a sober look, wary of overreacting to what could prove to be a Pyrrhic victory. The picture of a jubilant Jennie and subdued Coombs was splashed on front pages of newspapers across the country the next day.

Coombs was right to be cautious. Non-union workers from

P&C Stevedores, the company contracted by Patrick to take over stevedoring work, were ousted immediately but it took a further three days before the MUA workforce was permitted through the gates at Patrick terminals. Delays were caused by intense wrangling between the MUA and Patrick over the procedure for an orderly return and Patrick's demand that some wharfies involved in disturbances on the pickets be denied re-entry. Also of concern to Coombs was that liquidation of the Patrick labour hire companies employing the reinstated MUA workers remained a possibility because the High Court handed more control over their fate to Grant Thornton, the accounting firm appointed by Patrick to administrate them.

Jennie was at the East Swanson dock in Melbourne shortly after 6 p.m. on 7 May when the first workers marched triumphantly through the gates. Arm-in-arm with the MUA's national organiser, Mick O'Leary, and others, she led a 'guard of honour' to the gates, shedding joyful tears as she experienced all the euphoria of the symbolic win against Patrick. All about her there was cheering and chants of 'THE WORKERS, UNITED, WILL NEVER BE DEFEATED' and the now familiar 'MUA, HERE TO STAY'. The return-to-work came exactly one month after the sackings, ending protest pickets around the country. 'They said we wouldn't do it—but we did!' Jennie exclaimed.

Her role in the waterfront dispute now complete, Jennie withdrew from the excitement of the frontline, weary but positive that the MUA would survive the war largely intact. Her life could resume its normal pace, freed from the intensity of campaigning that can only be physically and emotionally sustained for so long. The weeks ahead became a tough slog of negotiations as Coombs and Corrigan aimed for a settlement. The threat of damaging litigation after the conspiracy case was given the go-ahead in the Federal Court prompted Corrigan to seek compromise rather than risk all. His negotiations with Coombs focused on ensuring a permanent return-to-work by the MUA, subject to a significant reduction in jobs and reform of work practices to make Patrick more profitable. In return all court action was to be dropped. About 600 out of the 1400 full-time MUA workers were to take redundancy packages funded by the Federal Government (repaid over time by Patrick by means of a levy). Approximately 100 of those made redundant were expected to return immediately as unionised contract workers in maintenance, security and cleaning. Employees were to be transferred out of the insolvent Patrick 'labour hire' firms and into solvent Patrick companies further up the corporate stream. Big changes to work practices—among them the reduction of some work crews from three to one and the end of the infamous 'double header' shifts that maximised wharfies' earnings—meant that Corrigan would secure significant improvements to productivity.

It took until early September for the settlement to be formally concluded as the MUA and Patrick haggled over details. The main hurdle, however, was how to resolve legal action initiated late in the conflict by the Australian Competition and Consumer Commission (ACCC) against the MUA, seeking to recover damages on behalf of small businesses hurt by union pickets that blockaded the movement of cargo on the docks. The ACCC chairman, Professor Allan Fels, while insisting he was not taking sides, said he believed the MUA had committed an unlawful boycott under the Trade Practices Act. As a condition of withdrawing the ACCC's action, Fels wanted the MUA to pay millions of dollars in compensation and give undertakings not to breach the boycott again.

In an extraordinary twist, Patrick agreed to foot the bill by paying $7.5 million into an ACCC special fund for small business. Fels explained away the curious industrial precedent of Patrick assuming financial liability by saying, 'We never said to the MUA "You have to pay".'[6]

For its part, the MUA gave undertakings to the Federal Court, as demanded by Fels, not to breach secondary boycott provisions for two years. The union was also bound under the terms of its agreement with Patrick to refrain from industrial action for three years. Neither was a particularly onerous condition considering no-strike clauses were a standard feature during the life of enterprise bargains.

Patrick also paid all the MUA's legal bills and paid wharfies arrears for lost wages during the dispute. By its own estimates, the company lost $50 million and faced having to repay the Federal Government a large part of publicly funded redundancy packages estimated at $90 million.

While the MUA won the reinstatement of all wharfies in the short term, it ultimately lost more than double the number on redundancy packages it had been prepared to concede before the sackings occurred. It also lost a swathe of union-controlled work practices that had given the MUA a strong say in how Patrick's terminals were run.

There was no outright victor because compromise was made on all sides. But a clue as to 'who won', as business commentator Alan Kohler noted, was Corrigan's agreement to pay the $7.5 million, in order to seal the truce, to victims of the alleged illegal boycotts orchestrated by the MUA. 'There was no suggestion the damage was caused by Patrick, but it paid anyway and helped preserve the union's bank account.'[7]

Corrigan judged that he would eventually recoup his losses now that 'entrenched rorts and inefficiencies on the waterfront' were gone. A former merchant banker who regarded the struggle with the MUA in cost efficiency terms, he was probably right. But the MUA also maintained its threshold position—the union closed shop survived the onslaught while Corrigan's ruthless plan to replace his workplace fell apart. The astronomical cost of the dispute to Corrigan carried a powerful message of deterrent to employers generally (just as Jennie and Kelty had hoped). Any that followed Corrigan's example did so at their peril.

Polling at the start of the waterfront conflict had convinced the Government that it had strong community support for its full backing of Patrick's actions. Wharfies were unpopular and it was agreed widely that something had to be done to improve flagging productivity on the docks. Howard and Reith had reinforced the negative view of wharfies early on, incessantly referring to the high salaries they earned and their 'rorts'. However, as the full import of how the sackings had been conducted sank into the public consciousness, sentiment changed. According to a number of opinion polls, while a clear majority continued to support waterfront reform, a majority also opposed the Government's handling of the issue, particularly by Reith.

So many of the allegations surrounding the waterfront conflict proved to be correct. Corrigan *was* behind the Dubai and Webb Dock training exercises. And the fact that his corporate strategy depended so heavily on an understanding reached months earlier that the Government would legislate to guarantee redundancy payments for workers sacked was powerful evidence to argue advance government participation in the plan, despite ministerial denials inside and outside Parliament. Reith continued to deny foreknowledge, even when confronted with evidence that he intended to provoke a dispute with the MUA, that his own advisers were in regular contact with Corrigan from early on, and, according to journalist Pamela Williams in the *Australian Financial Review*, that he too was deeply involved.[8] The day after the first MUA wharfies walked back through the gates to resume work, Reith had still continued to fudge the issue:

> What I can say is that both companies—not just Mr Corrigan but both companies—had given consideration to various strategies but, as to which strategies they might adopt in the future, that was a matter for them, always a matter for them. There's no denying we had a lot of discussions with companies in lots of sectors about what the strategies might be for them in managing their circumstances . . .
>
> As to what decisions they've taken, the fact of the matter is we were not aware of any decision taken by Mr Corrigan to replace

his workforce, and in respect of overseas training in Dubai, the fact of that was simply news to us until it was publicly exposed.[9]

Though not leading the strategy against Patrick or the Government, Jennie's contribution was significant in conveying messages that eventually changed public opinion: that wharfies were sacked *because* they were unionists and, that if wharfies could be sacked this way, so could other workers. Reith had entered the waterfront conflict predicting confidently that 'those former employees of Patrick's are not going back' and that 'the monopoly is definitely over'.[10] He left it politically wounded, linked too closely to a failed, much-maligned company strategy, in large part thanks to Jennie's efforts in public debate. She raised questions that lingered in people's minds about whether the strong-arm tactics of undemocratic countries had been transplanted to Australia. She recalled:

> I don't think the union could have taken on Patrick and the Government by itself. In me, it was useful to have a female voice to counter the public view that this was a male union with male issues. I was able to show that it was not just confined to them but was relevant to everybody.

23

HORIZONS

Jennie knew that the Federal Government had plans for other battles just as fierce as the war on the waterfront. Peter Reith admitted when the conflict was at its height that he had an industry hit list. Next in line for special treatment were unions in construction, meat processing, coalmining and—predictably— the rest of the MUA's closed shop in stevedoring and shipping. But, the MUA's successful retaliation stalled Reith's plans. He could not continue so brazenly on his crusade now that the union movement had demonstrated how strongly it was able to defend its territory; neither could he do so in the face of public unease about the way in which the wharfies were sacked. The approaching Federal election—which Howard was expected to call early—was also an important reason for Reith to retreat. The Government needed to present an image of calm and stability during the campaign, not acrimonious division.

The respite freed Jennie from combat mode. She would again play a role in the election campaign—but in the meantime she was able to savour some of the more positive aspects of her life, professionally and personally.

Lost in the all-consuming waterfront dispute had been Jennie's contribution to a number of causes close to her heart, including the push to make Australia a republic. On 2 February, at about the time the MUA's protest at Webb Dock began, she went to Canberra as an elected delegate to the two-week Constitutional Convention called to determine the republican model that might be put to voters in a referendum. Jennie's background was especially relevant to her republicanism—as a Russian migrant born in Italy it made little sense to her that a modern Australia coming to terms with its identity should retain a constitutional monarchy in which the Queen, as head of State, resided in Britain. She believed that an Australian head of State could 'reflect the nation's sense of self-worth' while continuing to recognise the importance of the historical, cultural and institutional links that exist between Britain and Australia.

Elected on the Australian Republican Movement (ARM) ticket led by Malcolm Turnbull, Jennie supported the 'minimalist' model in which the political system would remain essentially the same but a president, who would be appointed by a majority of Federal parliamentarians, would take the place of the Queen's representative, the Governor-General. Jennie's place on the ARM ticket was proof of how republicanism crossed party political lines. While she spoke on behalf of ACTU affiliated unions (all had expressed support for an Australian republic), the ARM representatives included Liberal and Labor supporters.

Just days after the two-week convention began there was serious doubt about whether Jennie would be able to participate in it, when events at Webb Dock in the brewing waterfront dispute forced her back to Melbourne. Her friend and ACTU colleague Jenny Doran—an unsuccessful teammate on the ARM ticket—sat in Jennie's place as a proxy for much of the convention. But Jennie was able to return the following week to present her main address.

Her speech to convention delegates in the old Parliament House building on 11 February was an important boost to the ARM's campaign because she argued against the popular view in the community that a president should be directly elected by the people. While understanding the 'democratic sentiment' that lay behind support for a directly elected president, she believed such a system held grave dangers:

> It would, of necessity, result in the politicisation of the selection process. All political parties would be involved and it is likely that, ultimately, a major party candidate would be selected. We would end up with a politicised office of head of State. We certainly could end up with a politician, even if we did not start with one. Some colleagues here are so passionate about not giving more power to politicians but, in my judgment, direct election would in no way prevent this from occurring.[1]

Jennie also acknowledged the deep cynicism in the community about the representative nature of the political process but argued that if Australians elected politicians to govern on their behalf, 'we should be prepared to trust them with the selection of our head of State'. As a compromise, she suggested a variation of the original ARM model, that the people have a role in nominating candidates. The parliament would then choose the head of State from the publicly nominated list.

Although a staunch opponent of the direct-election model, Turnbull was prepared to consider Jennie's proposal and the idea for indirect community involvement was included in the communiqué released at the convention's conclusion. 'Jennie and I are too disciplined to be saying things in public that we hadn't worked out in private first', he recalled.

Another positive development for Jennie overshadowed by the waterfront dispute was the full-bench ruling of the Industrial Relations Commission on the second stage of the ACTU's 'living wage' claim on 29 April. While the decision again fell short of the ACTU claim, it was not the obvious defeat that the first ruling, a year earlier, had been. After arguing for a $20-a-week rise in the minimum award pay rates (and ridding the original claim of some of its complexity), the bench, headed by the new commission president Justice Geoffrey Giudice, awarded $14 to workers earning less than $550 a week. Workers on $550 to $700 received $12 and those on more than $700 received $10. The minimum weekly wage set twelve months earlier was increased from $359 to $373.

The result was much closer to the ACTU claim than the previous decision and vindicated Kelty's view that the ACTU should keep 'bowling up' the 'living wage' again and again. The $14 rise was a blow to Reith. He had argued once again for an $8 across the board rise and claimed anything above that figure was economically unsustainable. The nation's main employer group, the Australian Chamber of Commerce and Industry, had wanted no increase. Giudice's bench was prepared to recognise the 'needs' of the low-paid as the ACTU asked. It set what Giudice, a former industrial barrister with a history of representing employers, called 'fair minimum standards' for workers in the context of Australian living standards.[2]

Jennie had accepted that the ACTU was unlikely to receive what it sought but took heart from the decision's recognition of the needs of the 'working poor'. Campaigning that day in the thick of the waterfront dispute, she hailed the result as a victory for up to 1.5 million low-paid workers struggling to survive:

> More than half are women, often employed as part-time or casuals, working longer and irregular hours. They have little industrial strength and are easily exploited by unscrupulous employers. Most left school early, and many have only basic language skills.[3]

One of the most noticeable aspects of Jennie's demeanour during this demanding period of her career was that she seemed more contented than in the past. Though still in need of reassurance, a significant reason for this change was a development in her personal life. She had been linked with several men in recent years, in particular a senior politician from the NSW Left. At last, however, she had found happiness with someone with whom she was considering a long-term future. Jennie had become close to Denis Lennen, the Victorian secretary of the National Union of Workers. Their relationship drew much approval from Jennie's closest friends, long anxious for her to find a companion to share her life and ease some of the pressure she had shouldered alone. Helen Hewett said:

> Jennie doesn't just want someone to go out to dinner with and have a good time. She wants to have a relationship—she wants to have a mate. In Denis she's found someone who is very easy to be with. He's not demanding and understands what the pressures are like for her. He gives her space when she needs it—they're not 21 anymore so they don't have to be together all the time.

Yet the relationship also raised a few eyebrows—Lennen was not from the Left as most observers would have expected but from the ALP's right-wing Labor Unity faction in Victoria. A decade earlier it would have been inconceivable for Jennie to be associated romantically with someone from the Right, such was the factional divide. But now she was the hero of both Right and Left, able to mix easily with both, having evolved into a pragmatic union politician. She had acted as a bridge between the warring factions when the reasons for their differences appeared more personality-based than ideological. Now she was reflecting that political maturity in her own life. Jennie said:

> Instead of coming home to emptiness, I have someone to talk to. Denis and I are in the same realm of work so we share a lot of the same interests. It's made me much happier and more grounded.

Long separated from his wife, Lennen was several years Jennie's senior and generally well regarded. His sense of humour was important to her. He could lighten Jennie's mood when her work highlighted the intense side of her personality, as it did much of the time. He also showed some amusement at Jennie's unorthodox interest in astrology—she still read her stars regularly and occasionally had her 'chart' prepared by friend Annie Robertson. Jennie said: 'Denis laughs about it. He's like Paddy—a Pisces—so we're fire and water.'

Jennie could not leave behind completely the complications of the past, however. The most obvious being that she had begun a relationship once again with someone who lived interstate. This was not a major problem though as she was now able to travel more as part of her work, and it meant that Jennie began spending more time in Melbourne, and therefore more time in the ACTU office, to the delight of ACTU officials.

It was important to Jennie that she now had someone with whom she could share special times in her life, such as being named as one of Australia's 100 'living national treasures'. She had been chosen in a public poll conducted by the National Trust in December 1997 to determine those who had contributed most to the national heritage. It was an honour for Jennie to be among those selected. She excitedly rang her mother when told her name was on the list.

Lennen accompanied Jennie to a gala dinner held at the Sydney Town Hall on 18 February 1998, at which she was among those presented with a certificate, medal and silver plate. The red carpet treatment was a pleasant change from defending union battlelines. Jennie's only reservation about the evening was hearing John Howard, himself named as one of the treasures, remark that he did not think some of the 'treasures' could be described as such. 'I thought he meant me and maybe [Aboriginal leader] Mick Dodson,' Jennie said. 'I thought it was uncharitable.'

W hen Labor was swept out of office in the Federal election landslide of 1996, the party's strategists believed it would take at least two terms to win again—and probably more if the economic cycle favoured the Coalition. The benign Kim Beazley, Keating's replacement as Labor Party leader, was handed the seemingly insurmountable task of trying to claw back 27 seats amid lingering community resentment about the party's thirteen-year rule.

Jennie thought a win at the next election was virtually impossible. Nevertheless, she had to approach the coming campaign seriously. It was not just a matter of restoring the electoral base for a future Labor win—the chance of a Labor victory (as slim as it seemed) was the fillip the union movement needed in a hostile climate with its membership still on the wane.

On July 1 1998—the same day that all awards officially were to be reduced to just twenty 'allowable matters'—Beazley and his industrial relations spokesman, Bob McMullan, announced what they called a '10-point rescue plan' aimed at rolling back all of Reith's Workplace Relations Act. In part they were responding to signs that the public was tired of change and deeply worried about job security. But their revamped policy was clearly a result of the union fight Jennie had led to keep the old system. Jennie had declared that the ACTU did not want a formal Accord in future—but the 'rescue plan' was an Accord in all but name.

For Jennie the policy's centrepiece was important because it advocated the restoration of all the powers of the Industrial Relations Commission removed by Reith's Act, chief among them the commission's ability to intervene and arbitrate disputes. In her official response she issued a statement from ACTU headquarters welcoming the policy. She stressed the historic institutional role of the commission as an umpire and pointed to the fact that the waterfront dispute might have been avoided altogether if the commission had not been denied by law its dispute-settling role.

The rescue plan also addressed Jennie's other great source of annoyance—the erosion under the Coalition of awards as a protection of minimum entitlements. She was enthused by Beazley and McMullan's pledge to stop the stripping of awards and to empower the commission to restore award conditions already lost. She also endorsed their proposals to give priority to collective agreements over individual contracts; to abolish the Employment Advocate that ran the Coalition's system of non-union contracts; to strengthen union rights to enter workplaces; and to replace secondary boycott provisions of the Trade Practices Act (that were a deterrent against sympathy industrial action) with a watered down version.

Beazley had declared his desire to 'produce a new act and a new system for Australia into the twenty-first century'. The model he proposed, however, was distinctly a step back in time. It matched Jennie's preference for a strong arbitrator in the middle when the two sides could not sort out their differences, but also restored regulation and union privilege against a worldwide trend of labour market flexibility.[4]

What worried Jennie most about the prospect of a second Coalition election victory was Reith's confirmation that he intended to implement another round of industrial relations changes. Reith wanted secret ballots before any industrial action, the right for employers to have legally protected strikes suspended and further unspecified cuts to awards. The thrust of these proposals was clear—Reith was bloodied by his fight with the MUA but remained determined to destroy the ability of unions to operate through awards and the commission.

While she continued to doubt Labor's ability to regain office, Jennie harboured some hope because of community disquiet about Howard's unsure leadership, a parade of ministerial resignations and funding cuts to nursing homes, job programs, health and education. She knew, however, that Labor's main chance rested on none of these things. Rather, it came down to Howard's uncharacteristically risky decision to fight an election over a tax 'reform' package, at the centre of which lay a GST voters had rejected in 1993.

Howard announced his package with much fanfare on 13 August, based on a 10 per cent GST and compensatory sweeteners including tax cuts paid for out of the Budget surplus. High-income earners fared best from the tax cuts. Once adjustments for the elimination of wholesale sales tax were made, Howard claimed that prices would increase by an average of just

1.9 per cent. Pensioners and other social welfare recipients were to receive top-ups to their benefits to cope with the effects of a GST.

The GST was anathema to Jennie—a regressive tax that ran counter to all she stood for. In Canberra on the day of the tax policy launch to respond to Howard's announcement, she told journalists that the GST was a 'massive new tax' hidden behind the glitter and sparkle of tax cuts, in which low-income earners would be hit hardest. She said that ACTU estimates put the inflationary impact of the GST at 3 per cent in its first year and workers on $30 000 would be worse off—even with an offered $16.15-a-week tax break.[5]

Beazley announced Labor's tax package in response on 27 August based on no GST and retaining the existing tax structure, but with a tax credit for 'battlers' earning between $30 000 and $50 000 a year. The alternative from Beazley targeted precisely the group Jennie wanted to see helped and—not surprisingly—she supported it wholeheartedly.

All along Howard was operating according to a tight timetable—intending to rush to the polls so he could minimise any potentially damaging scrutiny of his package and avoid the recall of Parliament, where he would face an onslaught from the Opposition. Three days after Beazley's response on tax, which was received coolly in the media, Howard called an election for 3 October.

Jennie's role in the five-week campaign was to repeat her efforts of the 1993 and 1996 elections. Under a schedule set down for her by the ALP's national secretariat in Canberra, she toured mainly the eastern states. It was Beazley's job, as Opposition Leader, to run the headline campaign across the nation announcing policy initiatives and rebutting the Coalition's record. Jennie's was a secondary role, much more grassroots, to try to swing voters from the marginal seats that were once Labor's heartland back to the party. She spoke to workers in factories, country townspeople in the street and old folk in community centres. While Jennie was accustomed to life on the road, it was a test of stamina nonetheless. In the first week she concentrated on marginal seats in Queensland, sweeping through Hinkler in the far north and Oxley and Petrie just outside Brisbane. Then she crisscrossed NSW, starting in the western Sydney seat of Lindsay, flying west to Orange in the seat of Calare and on to Coffs Harbour, the stepping-off point for tours of the north coast seats of Page and Richmond. At the start of the third week, she flew to Launceston to travel around Bass and Braddon—then back to Sydney so she could honour several prearranged ACTU-sponsored commitments, including the launch of a book of cartoons on the waterfront dispute, *War on the Wharves*. At the beginning of week-four she was in Melbourne for the ACTU-sponsored Whitlam Lecture, given by Bob Hawke on 21 September. The next day she flew back to Brisbane in readiness for Labor's official campaign launch on 23 September, but returned to Melbourne when it was over so she could tour the Victorian regional seat of Bendigo. In the final days of the campaign, Jennie went to South Australia to accompany Labor candidates in Makin, Adelaide and Kingston, finally returning to Melbourne to be with Denis Lennen and close friends on election night.

Each electorate tour worked according to a rough plan, Jennie often started with a breakfast 'launch'. She tried, on average, to visit three workplaces a day and usually conducted a campaign 'walk' through town shopping malls, speaking to locals. Her aim was to gain as much local media exposure as possible. To do this, Jennie had to be fully acquainted with issues of concern in each electorate. This required briefings from candidates in advance and a daily stream of telephone calls to her assistant at the ACTU in Melbourne, Denise Power, who faxed summaries and news-paper clippings to wherever Jennie happened to be.

'It was non-stop,' recalled Power of Jennie's movements. 'There was one day when the itinerary was three pages long—it was incredible.'

In Launceston, for example, Jennie started her tour with an early breakfast speech on behalf of Labor's candidate for Bass, Michelle O'Byrne. Her next day and a half in Bass and Braddon included visits to Launceston's general hospital, museum, brewery, a yacht club, a sheet metal plant, the weaving mill at Davenport and the soon-to-be closed pulp mill at Burnie.

While tailoring her message to suit the audience, Jennie concentrated on industrial relations and job security. In factories she told workers that Labor's proposed overhaul of Reith's laws was the only way to guarantee minimum standards and a decent work environment. She argued that the only way to reduce an unemployment rate still hovering above 8 per cent was a return to government-funded job creation programs, not the Coalition's system of farming out employment services to private agencies that was on the brink of collapse.

Jennie's general message on the GST concentrated on food and how low-income earners would be worse off because they spent a greater proportion of their income on essentials. She challenged the assumption that prices would rise by only 1.9 per cent. It was also misleading, she believed, for the Coalition to say people spent an average 18 per cent of income on food when pensioners, for example, spent well over a quarter of their income on food. To an audience in Adelaide in the last days of the campaign, Jennie said:

> Put simply, the government package is unworkable and regressive. It shifts the tax burden from income to consumption, from business to consumers, from direct to indirect tax, and most seriously, from high income to low-income earners.[6]

Beside her concern about Labor's chances of winning, the most disturbing element of the campaign for Jennie was the electoral threat posed by Pauline Hanson. Since losing her endorsement as the Liberal Party's candidate in the Queensland seat of Oxley for making 'inflammatory and insensitive' remarks about Aborigines during the 1996 election campaign, Hanson had become a political phenomenon.[7] Elected as an Independent and then forming her own party, One Nation, she fed on ignorance, prejudice and fear in the electorate, drawing support from people disaffected with the major parties and ready to blame others—from Aborigines and Asian migrants to single mothers—for their woes. The problem for Jennie was that many of the disaffected came from her own constituency—unionised battlers willing to listen to someone like Hanson who was prepared to challenge the political order even if she was ignorant of the facts and had none of the answers.

As a migrant herself, embodying the success story of hundreds of thousands of people who made Australia their home in the wave of post-war migration and who contributed to the richness of the country, Jennie found the xenophobic and otherwise narrow-minded message of Hanson particularly repugnant. Under Hanson's rationale, families such as Jennie's with no English and few possessions might never have been allowed to enter the country. Yet a potent reminder of Hanson's impact was that Jennie's own mother was a Hanson admirer and, while she wanted Beazley to win the election, was considering voting for One Nation. Jennie and Natasha argued again and again—in Russian—about Hanson's merits. In spite of her own experience, or perhaps because of it, Natasha warmed to Hanson's view that life was too easy for migrants now and that too many Asians were entering the country. She compared the indentured labour system that her generation knew with the government assistance available to migrants in the 1990s. 'Mum admires Hanson's courage and that she is shaking up the political system,' explained Jennie.[8]

In her campaign travels, Jennie tried to convince unionists who might be persuaded to support One Nation to stick with Labor by arguing it was wrong for individuals to be made 'scapegoats' for the failures of society and governments. She also drew upon Hanson's voting record in Parliament, saying Hanson might claim to represent working battlers but had acted against their interests by supporting

Reith's original Workplace Relations Bill 'in its entirety' when it was introduced in the House of Representatives in 1996.

Jennie demonstrated her repudiation of the values and policies of Hanson in practice by joining a coalition of community leaders who co-signed a statement condemning the policies of Hanson's party and pleading for racial tolerance. The grouping—organised behind the scenes by Bob Hawke to bring together leaders of unions, business, welfare and churches—was a coup for Hawke and a rare chance for Jennie (and fellow signatory Bill Kelty) to show unity with an ACTU opponent in normal circumstances, Stan Wallis, president of the Business Council of Australia.[9]

As election-day neared it became clear that Howard's Government was likely to be re-elected, despite some opinion polls favouring Labor. Howard's victory, with a much-trimmed House of Representatives majority, was disappointing for Jennie—but not unexpected. She was gratified that Labor scored a slight majority of the overall vote on a two-party preferred basis, providing her reason to argue that Howard lacked a 'mandate' for specific policies. She was also gratified that Hanson's One Nation Party fared poorly. Hanson lost her own seat while her party secured just one—a Senate position in Hanson's home state of Queensland.[10]

The return of the Howard Government meant that the pattern of Jennie's ACTU presidency—in opposition—was now set for the rest of her term in office. It was her hope that the Government's inability to gain control of the Senate would prevent the passage of further legislation antagonistic to unions and that the the level of resistance by organised labour during the waterfront dispute would deter a further industrial assault on union power on such a grand scale.

Jennie George will be remembered as the most left-wing ACTU president in many years, a former communist who remained true to many of her 'Left' ideals despite becoming pragmatic in the business of union politics. She has vehemently opposed the privatisation of public assets such as Telstra and rejected the NSW Labor Right's attempts to sell that State's electricity grid. She has retained her faith in strong public schooling and health systems, even arguing for constitutional protection of the right to a quality education.

While Hawke, the ACTU's most high profile president, carved out a role for himself as a dealmaker, Jennie will be remembered for her strength as a campaigner. To her, leadership is about defining issues and then seeking practical, intelligent means to attain her goals. When she has not been able to achieve them—she has reverted to the role of careful politician, able to redefine and compromise. 'Job security' is now her catchcry.

Jennie remains severe and impenetrable to many in the community who know only her media persona and she has often been stereotyped as a 'masculined woman'.[11] However, she radiates warmth and shows a contradictory mix of firmness and vulnerability, self-absorption and generosity of spirit to those who know her personally.

She has done the hard work by breaking through the union glass ceiling to the benefit of other women. She has competed under male rules while, as she puts it, adding the breadth of female conditioning with characteristics such as listening, supporting and consulting. After Jennie's lead, women officials in the union movement no longer have to operate according to traditional male values. Kelty acknowledges:

> She changed the organisation without trying to destroy it, and that in some ways is so much harder. She tried to build it internally by a demonstration of character. That alone gives her a place in history—it's not just being the first. Being first is all right but a lot of people are first and disappear. She was first and persisted. She argued and cajoled and changed the organisation.

As she plans her departure from the ACTU presidency, and contemplates what ambitions she has left to fulfil, Jennie has put a greater emphasis on finding more balance in her life. No longer does she want to say she is making sacrifices for her career. She wants to devote time to her partner but also to her mother, never far from her thoughts and still the closest person in her life.

Speculation persists that Jennie will cap her career by moving to politics as three of her recent predecessors have done. When the pressure of the ACTU presidency was at its greatest in the early days of the Howard Government she had considered bowing out shortly after the election, which Howard called ahead of time in 1998. However, as time passed Jennie has grown more comfortable in the presidency and aims to stay on, ideally until the ACTU congress scheduled for Wollongong in July 2000. She has cooled on the idea of federal politics but a future in NSW politics is a possibility. She has toyed with seeking a seat in State Parliament if one becomes available at the right time.

From the humble beginnings of a refugee camp in war-torn Europe to pursuing a public life that has taken her to the pinnacle of Australian trade union politics, Jennie George has persisted against the odds in a brave journey that has shown the way forward for those who follow.

N S W T e a c h e r s '
F e d e r a t i o n p r e s i d e n t s a n d
s e c r e t a r i e s 1 9 4 0 s t o 1 9 8 0 s

President

Sam Lewis 1945–51

Harry Heath 1952–54

Don Taylor 1955–63

Sam Lewis 1964–67

Jack Whalan 1968–1971

Len Childs 1972–73

Eric Pearson 1974–5

Barry Manefield 1976–81

Max Taylor 1982–83

Ivan Pagett 1984–85

Jennie George 1986–89

Secretary

Harry Norington 1944–62

Matt Kennett 1962–63

Ivor Lancaster 1963–75

Max Taylor 1975–79

Jennie George 1980–82

Vic Baueris 1983–88

ACTU presidents and secretaries

President

Bill Duggan 1927–1932

Albert Monk 1932–1943

Percy Clarey 1943–49

Albert Monk 1949–69

Bob Hawke 1969–79

Cliff Dolan 1979–85

Simon Crean 1985–90

Martin Ferguson 1990–96

Jennie George 1996-

Secretary

Charles Crofts 1927–43

Albert Monk 1943–49

Reg Broadby 1949–56

Harold Souter 1956–77

Peter Nolan 1977–83

Bill Kelty 1983-

APPENDIX 3

The Accord

The original Prices and Incomes Accord, agreed between the ACTU and Labor in 1983, provided for increases in award pay rates every six months, indexed according to rises in the CPI. The rises were granted by the Conciliation and Arbitration Commission (later renamed the Industrial Relations Commission) in return for union commitments to make no extra claims.

Accord Mark II, negotiated in 1985, saw Kelty agree to Keating's request for a 2 per cent discount of the ACTU's wage claim to take account of the price effects of the devaluation of the Australian dollar, in exchange for a promised tax cut. The discount was the first of a series of real wage cuts, killing off the Accord's original assumption that wage indexation would fully compensate workers for rises in the cost of living. The most radical aspect of Accord II, however, was Labor's support for a 3 per cent ACTU wage claim based on productivity, to be paid by employers as contributions to a new universal superannuation scheme.

Accord III, negotiated amid a crisis over Australia's current account deficit in 1986, resulted in a further real wage cut, leaving no doubt that wage rises indexed to inflation were finished. It also started a move from a centralised wage model controlled entirely by the commission to a decentralised model that linked pay rises to productivity. Under what was called a 'two-tier' system, all workers received a flat $10-a-week rise in 1987. To receive a further 4 per cent, they had to trade off work practices in negotiations with employers. The commission created what it called a 'structural efficiency principle' to guide productivity negotiations.

Accord IV resulted in two pay rises in 1988, one of 3 per cent and another of 2.5 per cent, six months apart. Unions had to undergo restructuring of their awards—according to the commission's structural efficiency principle—to achieve the rises.

Accord V linked pay rises to skill so that workers at the bottom of the income scale received $20-a-week and those at the top $30-a-week, paid in two halves, six months apart, and in exchange for further restructuring of awards.

The turning point for the Accord was Mark VI in 1990 when Kelty responded to pressure from within unions for an end to wage restraint and to pressure from the business community for wage deregulation by embracing a form of enterprise bargaining. Workers who failed to achieve enterprise bargains with their employer would receive $12-a-week and a top-up of superannuation. Kelty encountered a major hitch when the Industrial Relations Commission rejected the Accord for the first time in its entirety, judging that the parties lacked the 'maturity' for enterprise bargaining and deferring the superannuation claim. Instead, the commission granted an across-the-board 2.5 per cent rise in 1991 providing unions renewed their commitment to the structural efficiency principle. Late in the year, the commission agreed after intense pressure from Kelty to condone enterprise bargaining while the Government, again under pressure from Kelty, legislated to enforce higher contributions to superannuation funds from employers.

Accord VII, negotiated three weeks before the 1993 election, reaffirmed enterprise bargaining as the primary means of delivering pay rises but set a target that the national average for wage rises should not exceed a band of between 4 and 5 per cent. Workers unable to strike bargains would receive a 'safety net' pay rise of $8-a-week. The commission accepted an ACTU claim under Accord VII for two further annual safety net rises over the next two years that was linked to an Accord target of increasing employment by 500 000 jobs.

Accord VIII, negotiated before the 1996 election, followed the pattern of the previous agreement while providing for slightly higher 'safety net' pay rises in a range of $11–14 a week. Its implementation, as for 1993, was dependent on Labor winning the election. The agreement was abandoned, as was the Accord concept, when Labor lost. However, the principle of enterprise bargaining and small 'safety net' pay rises for workers without bargains continued to apply once the Coalition took office.

NOTES

INTRODUCTION

1   Albert Monk is counted twice because he was ACTU president two times, 1932–43 and 1949–69. In the intervening years he was ACTU secretary.

CHAPTER 1   REFUGEES

1   Catherine Panich, *Sanctuary?*, Allen & Unwin, Sydney, 1988, p. xiv.
2   Egon F. Kunz, *Displaced Persons: Calwell's New Australians*, Australian National University Press, Sydney, 1988, p. 94.
3   ibid. p. 95.
4   ibid. pp. 95–6.
5   ibid. p. 18.
6   ibid. p. xvii. Estimates of the total number of Russian immigrants under the IRO's auspices are difficult because of the lengths to which Russians went to disguise their Soviet nationality. Some estimates suggest 10 000 or higher.

CHAPTER 2   CHILDHOOD YEARS

1   Bevin Alexander, *Korea: The lost war*, Arrow Books, Great Britain, pp. 1–3.
2   'Implementing Red Bill not easy task' and 'Union moves to whip up fight on red bill', *Sydney Morning Herald*, 19 October 1950.
3   Kunz, *Displaced Persons*, pp. 139–40.

CHAPTER 3   TEEN REBEL

1 Ray Davies, *X-Ray: The unauthorised autobiography*, Viking, London, 1994, pp. 186, 188, 209, 235.

CHAPTER 4   PADDY

1 W. J. Brown, *The Communist Movement and Australia: An historical outline—1880s to 1980s*, Australian Labour Movement Publications, Sydney, 1986, p. 259.

2 Stuart Macintyre, *The Reds: The Communist Party of Australia from origins to illegality*, Allen & Unwin, Sydney, 1998, p. 328.

3 Audrey Blake, *A Proletarian Life*, Kibble Books, Sydney, 1984, p. 89.

4 Gregory Pemberton ed., *Vietnam Remembered*, Weldon Publishing, Sydney, 1990, p. 138.

5 Greg Langley, *A Decade of Dissent: Vietnam and the conflict on the Australian home front*, Allen & Unwin, Sydney, 1992, p. 62.

6 Donald Horne, *Time of Hope: Australia 1966–72*, Angus & Robertson, Sydney, 1980, p. 53.

CHAPTER 5   MARRIED TO THE PARTY

1 Langley, *A Decade of Dissent*, p. 91; Denis Freney, *A Map of Days: Life on the Left*, William Heinemann Australia, Melbourne, 1991, p. 224; Pemberton ed., *Vietnam Remembered*, p. 149.

2 Freney, *A Map of Days*, pp. 226–7.

3 Bernie Taft, *Crossing the Party Line: Memoirs of Bernie Taft*, Scribe Publications, Newham, 1994, p. 152.

4 Gerard Henderson, *Menzies' Child: The Liberal Party of Australia 1944–1994*, Allen & Unwin, Sydney, 1994,   p. 109.

5 Eric Aarons, *What's Left? Memoirs of an Australian Communist*, Penguin, Melbourne, 1993, p. 118.

6 Freney, *A Map of Days*, p. 236.

7 ibid. p. 236.

8 'Teachers labelled', *Bankstown–Canterbury Torch*, 27 October 1971.

9 'Communist program for education', *Bankstown–Canterbury Torch*, 1 September 1971.

CHAPTER 6   RUNNING FOR OFFICE

1 John O'Brien, *A Divided Unity! Politics of NSW militancy since 1945*, Allen & Unwin, Sydney, 1987, p. 1.

2 ibid. p. 1.

3 ibid. p. 38.

4 ibid. p. 93. Norington quit the Communist Party after 1950. He was active in the ALP thereafter.

5 ibid. pp. 110, 202.

6 ibid. p. 13.

7 About 84 per cent of all NSW teachers were members of the federation by the mid-1970s.

8 Jim Hagan, *The History of the ACTU*, Longman Cheshire, Melbourne, 1981, p. 224.

9 ibid. O'Brien, *A Divided Unity!*, p. 75. O'Brien's reference to 'cheap labour' comes from a federation leaflet in Equal Pay and Equal Opportunity files of the NSW Teachers' Federation archives called *Concerning women teachers: facts you should know*.

10 Ann Harding, 'Union's first lady seeks public support in teachers' crisis', *National Times*, 11–17 May 1980.

CHAPTER 7 DEATH OF A MARRIAGE

1 Taft, *Crossing the Party Line*, p. 186.

CHAPTER 8 AFTER PADDY

1 Philip Chubb, 'Teachers plan big campaign', *National Times*, 11–17 May 1980.

2 Andrew Casey, 'Teachers strike again tomorrow', *Sydney Morning Herald*, 3 February 1981.

3 Jennie George, *Sydney Morning Herald*, 25 July 1981.

4 Andrew Casey, 'Teachers' Federation leader to stand down', *Sydney Morning Herald*, 4 August 1982.

CHAPTER 9 THE ACCORD

1 *Statement of Accord by the Australian Labor Party and the Australian Council of Trade Unions regarding economic policy*, Melbourne, February 1983.

2 Shaun Carney, *Australia in Accord: Politics and industrial relations under the Hawke Government*, Macmillan, Melbourne, 1988, p. 18.

3 ibid. p. 21.

4 Keith Martin, 'PM got it wrong, ACTU says as unions back deal', *The Sydney Morning Herald*, 22 February 1983.

CHAPTER 10 EXECUTIVE STATUS

1 Andrew Casey, 'Teachers' Federation leader to stand down', *Sydney Morning Herald*, 4 August 1982.

2   Rowena Stretton, 'Jennie makes her own history', *Herald* (Melbourne), 20 September 1983.
3   Sarah Chester, 'A top unionist who won't be Queen Bee', the *Age*, 21 September 1983.
4   Marie Reiss, 'Jennie aims for top job', *Daily Telegraph*, 12 April 1985.
5   Luis M. Garcia, 'Teachers' Federation will again lean Left', *Sydney Morning Herald*, 22 November 1985.

CHAPTER 11   CAVALIER POLITICS

1   Luis M. Garcia, 'Teachers' leader top of Cavalier class', *Sydney Morning Herald*, 23 January 1986.
2   Marie Reiss, 'Cavalier attitude comes under fire', *Daily Telegraph*, 28 January 1986.
3   Anne Susskind, 'The teachers' great stateswoman', *Sydney Morning Herald*, 19 May 1986.
4   Jennie George, 'The President Writes', *Education*, 7 December 1987.
5   ibid.
6   'Pioneering unionist', *National Times*, 18 January 1987.

CHAPTER 12   THE METHERELL CAMPAIGN

1   Malcolm Farr, 'The Maverick in Metherell', *Daily Mirror*, 26 July 1988; Tony Stephens, 'The education of young Terry', *Sydney Morning Herald*, 3 September 1988.
2   Matthew Moore, 'First blood: Greiner strikes, going gets tough—everyday charges rise, bureaucracy squeezed', *Sydney Morning Herald*, 3 June 1988.
3   Anne Susskind, 'Suddenly, Metherell seeks public's views', *Sydney Morning Herald*, 29 June 1988.
4   Matthew Moore and Anne Susskind, 'Greiner puts muzzle on Metherell', *Sydney Morning Herald*, 6 July 1988.
5   ibid.
6   Anne Susskind and Matthew Moore, 'Govt to schools: We won't budge—50 000 rally in protest, schools shut across State, *Sydney Morning Herald*, 18 August 1988.
7   Anne Susskind, 'Teachers' leader calls end of term', *Sydney Morning Herald*, 23 February 1989.
8   Jennie George, 'Where to on the wages front?', *Education*, 20 October 1986; Jennie George, 'Time for action on the 4 per cent', *Education*, 12 October 1987; Jennie George, 'The 4 per cent', *Education*, 23 November 1987. Jennie maintained the federation's opposition to the two-tier system but ultimately acquiesced, citing an ACTU congress

decision in 1987 that it was 'transitional in nature' and negotiations would resume soon to replace it.

9   see Brad Norington, *Sky Pirates: the strike that grounded Australia*, ABC Enterprises, Sydney, 1990.

CHAPTER 13   MELBOURNE CALLING

1   The Australian Conciliation and Arbitration commission was renamed the Australian Industrial Relations Commission in 1988.

2   Steve Lewis and Mark Davis, 'Carmichael ends the long march', *Australian Financial Review*, 13 September 1991.

3   Anne Susskind, 'Ms GEORGE the FIRST', *Sydney Morning Herald*, 21 September 1991.

4   Karen Harbutt, 'Exit Laurie, enter the workers' heroine', the *Australian*, 10 September 1991.

CHAPTER 14   TAKING SIDES

1   Paul Kelly, *The End of Certainty*, Allen & Unwin, 1992, p. 68.

2   Mark Davis, 'Kelty and Ferguson—tension in the union', *Australian Financial Review*, 22 July 1991.

3   Brad Norington, 'ACTU split on return of Keating', *Sydney Morning Herald*, 10 December 1991.

4   Bob Hawke, *The Hawke Memoirs*, William Heinemann Australia, Melbourne, 1994, p. 557.

5   Kelly, *The End of Certainty*, p. 640.

6   Brad Norington, 'Double-or-nothing threat by unions', *Sydney Morning Herald*, 2 July 1991; Brad Norington, 'Accord's future lies with push for super', *Sydney Morning Herald*, 4 July 1991; Brad Norington, 'Keating push behind Kelty attack on Budget', *Sydney Morning Herald* 27 August 1991; Kelly, *The End of Certainty*, p. 641.

7   Anne Susskind, 'Ms GEORGE the FIRST', *Sydney Morning Herald*, 21 September 1991.

8   Shane Green, 'Search is on for female successor', the *Age*, 24 July 1993.

9   Brad Norington, 'Done deals or done over?', *Sydney Morning Herald*, 17 May 1993.

10   Mark Davis, 'ACTU's top woman challenges wages gap', *Australian Financial Review*, 7 July 1994.

11   Sheryle Bagwell, 'Libs, ACTU act affirmatively', *Australian Financial Review*, 1 September 1993.

CHAPTER 15   THE CANDIDATE

1   Shane Green, 'Two ACTU officials tipped for Canberra', the *Age*, 3 June 1993; Peter Wilson, 'George denies ambition as MP', the *Australian*, 30 June 1993; Shane Green, 'Search is on for female successor, by George', the *Age*, 24 July 1993.

2   Shane Green, 'Search is on for female successor, by George', the *Age*, 24 July 1993.

3   Margo Kingston, 'Keating hails victory for women: conference vote for 35% quota a defining moment', *Sydney Morning Herald*, 28 September 1994.

4   Nicholas Johnston, 'George says its time to make her run', the *Age*, 22 October 1994; Ewin Hannan, 'Senate bid support for George', the *Australian*, 22 October 1994; Brad Norington, 'George push for Senate', *Sydney Morning Herald*, 21 October 1994.

5   Under the split system for election of senators on six-year terms, half the Senate faced election every three years except in the event of a double dissolution of Parliament when both Houses of Parliament faced the electorate.

6   Tony Wright, 'Labor clears the decks: key pieces of poll jigsaw now in place', *Sydney Morning Herald*, 21 June 1995; Geoff Kitney and Tony Wright, 'Decision forced by tired image: How the deputy's baton was finally passed on with a minimum of fuss', *Sydney Morning Herald*, 21 June 1995.

7   Margo Kingston, 'Wrong time to clear the numbers, says Lawrence', *Sydney Morning Herald*, 21 June 1995.

8   Innes Willox, 'Ferguson pushed for Howe's seat', the *Age*, 29 June 1995.

CHAPTER 16   PRESIDENT

1   Ewin Hannan and Sid Marris, 'George would be elected unopposed to leadership of ACTU', the *Australian*, 13 July 1995.

2   If they had not withdrawn, Theophanous and Mikakos would have made Ferguson's task of winning harder and bloodier, politically. But they faced an uphill battle anyway by this stage because a majority of the half of pre-selection votes that were determined by a central ALP panel, not by the local branches, had swung behind Ferguson.

3   Mark Davis, 'George reveals battle plan', *Australian Financial Review*, 16 August 1995.

4   Brad Norington, 'ALP all talk on women, says George', *Sydney Morning Herald*, 16 August 1995. Jennie George had a point. After setting a target for women to contest 35 per cent of winnable seats by 2002,

the ALP looked like going backwards because several retiring women MPs were to be replaced by men, and others in marginal seats were at serious risk of losing at the election. Jeanette McHugh, retiring from Grayndler, was to be replaced by Anthony Albanese. Wendy Fatin was to retire from Brand in favour of Kim Beazley, who was switching from his very marginal seat of Swan, to be contested by a woman, Jane Saunders. Other marginal seats with women in danger of losing were Macquarie, held by Maggie Deahm, and Lowe, held by Mary Easson. The only likely gain for women was Jagajaga, where Jenny Macklin was replacing Peter Staples.

5 Ewin Hannan, 'It's my party and I'll sing if I want to', the *Australian*, 28 September 1995.

6 Renamed the Industrial Relations Commission in 1988.

7 The 'census' figures are contained in ABS 6323.0. The 'survey' figures are from ABS 6325.0.

8 By 1995 there were still 40 federally registered unions in existence. All the same, Kelty had established his model of about 20 industry unions. Most of the remainder was in the process of amalgamations with larger unions.

9 Blanche d'Alpuget, *Robert J. Hawke: A biography*, Schwartz Publishing Group. 1982, pp. 95–6.

10 ibid. p. 96.

CHAPTER 17 WORKING WITH KELTY

1 *Australian Council of Trade Unions: Constitution, rules and standing orders*, January 1992, pp. 7–8.

2 Brad Norington, 'Bland ambition', *Good Weekend*, (*Sydney Morning Herald* and *Age* magazine), 29 February 1992.

3 Carney, *Australia in Accord*, p. 24.

4 d'Alpuget, *Robert J. Hawke*, p. 393.

5 Carney, *Australia in Accord*, p. 24.

6 See Appendix 3 (p. 361) for outline of Accords I–VIII.

7 Brad Norington, 'ACTU lends weight to 15% pay push', *Sydney Morning Herald*, 9 November 1995.

CHAPTER 18 THE BATTLE FOR WEIPA

1 Brad Norington and Geoff Kitney, 'Keating mocks Hawke's new role for ACTU', *Sydney Morning Herald*, 20 November 1995.

2 Mark Davis, 'CRA forced to submit', *Australian Financial Review*, 22 November 1995.

3 Brad Norington, 'Strikers reject ACTU peace', *Sydney Morning Herald*,

22 November 1995; Brad Norington, 'ACTU tries to calm strikers', *Sydney Morning Herald*, 23 November 1995.

4   Brad Norington, 'Prawns, pork, beer and tough talking', *Sydney Morning Herald*, 29 November 1995; Brad Norington, 'Strikers put faith in George to win the war', *Sydney Morning Herald*, 30 November 1995.

CHAPTER 19   LABOR'S DEFEAT

1   Shaun Carney, 'Keating, Kelty seek one more electoral record', the *Age*, 22 February 1996.

2   Sid Marris, 'Kelty warns it's war over wages', the *Australian*, 22 February 1996. Kelty repeated his warning the next day. He said: 'Without an Accord there will be no controlling wage inflation. A breakout will be purely and simply the result of not having an incomes policy. Without a social partnership, and the Coalition's aggressive and provocative stance, hostility and disputation are inevitable.' Tony Wright and Brad Norington, 'Howard vows consensus', *Sydney Morning Herald*, 23 February 1996.

3   Brad Norington, 'ACTU lures female support with dire warnings', *Sydney Morning Herald*, 13 February 1996.

4   Brad Norington, 'ACTU bid to lift pay of "poor" workers', *Sydney Morning Herald*, 14 March 1996.

5   The figure supported by the Government happened to be the amount sought by the ACTU in Accord VII: three pay rises of $8 over three years, the last of which was only recently granted. Nevertheless, the ACTU had no compunction in criticising the Howard Government for a Scrooge mentality.

6   Tony Wright, 'Howard's pledge: no pay cuts', *Sydney Morning Herald*, 9 January 1996.

CHAPTER 20   RIOT

1   Georgina Windsor, 'Protest turns ugly in rush of emotion', the *Australian*, 20 August 1996.

2   Brad Norington, 'Batons used as rioters storm Parliament', *Sydney Morning Herald*, 20 August 1996.

3   Brad Norington, 'ACTU is being targeted: George', *Sydney Morning Herald*, 30 August 1996.

4   ibid.

5   Michael Millett and Brad Norington, 'Call for Kernot to renege on workplace deal', *Sydney Morning Herald*, 29 October 1996.

CHAPTER 21 HOLDING THE LINE

1   Michael Millett, 'Unions suffer huge drop in membership', *Sydney Morning Herald*, 4 February 1997; Mark Davis, 'ABS statistics show union membership is still dwindling', *Australian Financial Review*, 4 February 1997; Mark Davis, 'Unionisation rate may be "bottoming out" ', *Australian Financial Review*, 6 January 1997. In January 1997 the ABS annual trade union census based on questionnaires completed by unions themselves reported that membership levels had remained steady at 35 per cent, hence Jennie's optimism about the decline having 'bottomed out'. But survey data released in February 1997—generally regarded as the more reliable of the ABS's two series on union membership—showed that membership levels had continued to fall. They were down 2 per cent over the past two years to 31 per cent.

2   Mark Davis, 'Unions: Kelty's last stand', *Australian Financial Review*, 1 March 1995; Mark Davis, 'ACTU Air: coming to a shop near you', *Australian Financial Review*, 28 February 1995; Brad Norington, 'Union scheme to attract the faint-hearted', *Sydney Morning Herald*, 18 May 1995; Brad Norington, 'ACTU to enter the discount shopping business', *Sydney Morning Herald*, 12 December 1996. Of all its proposed schemes, ACTU shopping and home loan services did hold some promise. But they were attractive chiefly to existing members, and not useful as recruiting tools.

3   Brad Norington, 'Back into battle', *Sydney Morning Herald*, 14 December 1995.

4   Mark Davis, 'Australia's top woman challenges wages gap', *Australian Financial Review*, 7 July 1994. According to the ABS, the average total earnings of women fell from 85.8 per cent of male earnings in 1992 to 84.4 per cent in 1993. Jennie argued against the orthodoxy of the women's movement that a wage system based on enterprise bargaining was the cause. She said that the decline in women's earnings was affected by more overtime worked by men and larger over-award payments going to men. She also claimed the election of the Kennett Government in Victoria contributed to a discrepancy in that State affecting the national average.

5   Mark Robinson, 'The union boss and the shop girl', *Daily Telegraph*, 31 May 1997; Brad Norington, ' "Shops of shame" targeted by unions', *Sydney Morning Herald*, 31 May 1997.

6   ibid.

7   'The bully girl of unionism', *Daily Telegraph*, 31 May 1997.

8   Brad Norington, 'ACTU head stands firm over protest', *Sydney Morning Herald*, 3 June 1997.

9   Jennie George, 'Meet the Press', Network TEN, 13 July 1997.

10 ibid.

11 Brad Norington, 'ACTU warns of national mine dispute', *Sydney Morning Herald*, 14 July 1997.

12 Paul Molloy, 'Kelty's future "on the agenda"', *Daily Telegraph*, 28 April 1997.

13 Jennie was wise to be on guard. On the second-last day of the congress, left-wing union officials staged a walkout during an address by Graham Roberts, the new president of the financially troubled right-wing Australian Workers' Union. While the only hiccup for Jennie as chair of the congress, it was also politically embarrassing for her. The walkout came just 24 hours after unions had given a unanimous pledge to remain united to protect the Maritime Union. It seemed unity did not extend to all. Furthermore, the walkout overshadowed the positive news coverage Jennie had hoped to gain from the former chair of the Aboriginal and Torres Strait Islander Council, Lois O'Donoghue.

14 Brad Norington, 'Unions ready to fight for waterfront, even if military is called in', *Sydney Morning Herald*, 2 September 1997.

15 Brad Norington, 'Mining dispute: 8,000 out', *Sydney Morning Herald*, 2 October 1997.

16 Brad Norington, 'PM slams Jennie George', *Sydney Morning Herald*, 9 October 1997.

17 Brad Norington, 'Intervene or mine strike will spread nationwide, IRC warned', *Sydney Morning Herald*, 5 November 1997.

CHAPTER 22   WATERFRONT WAR

1   The MUA had waged or threatened to wage industrial action in all Patrick terminals, using their legal right to strike allowed under registered bargaining periods for enterprise agreements. But at the time security guards entered the company gates around the country, MUA workers in Melbourne were the only Patrick employees on strike.

2   Brad Norington and Helen Trinca, 'Wharfies' win in danger', *Sydney Morning Herald*, 22 April 1998.

3   Alan Ramsey, ' "Blood and thunder" Bill noticeable by his absence', *Sydney Morning Herald*, 15 April 1998.

4   Piers Akerman, 'Where's Wally, the faceless leader', *Daily Telegraph*, 16 April 1998.

5   Piers Akerman, 'PM exposes camouflage of wharfare', *Daily Telegraph*, 9 April 1998; Editorial, 'Taking an interest in the firm', *Daily Telegraph*, 23 April 1998.

6   Brad Norington 'Patrick to pay $7.5 million picketing bill—company

that took on wharfies coughs up again in final twist to dispute', *Sydney Morning Herald*, 4 September 1998.

7　Alan Kohler 'Docks war not over yet,' *Australian Financial Review*, 8 September 1998.

8　See Pamela Williams, 'Corrigan's cabal: the inside story of how the Government joined the plot to crush a union', *Australian Financial Review*, Weekend Edition, 29–30 August 1998; Pamela Williams, 'Postcards from Dubai: the disarray in Corrigan's cabal', *Australian Financial Review*, 31 August 1998; Pamela Williams, 'The minister, the mercenaries and the madness at Webb Dock', *Australian Financial Review*, 2 August 1998.

9　Peter Reith, media doorstop, Treasury Place, Melbourne, 8 May 1998.

10　Peter Reith interview with Laurie Oakes, 'Sunday', Nine Network, 12 April 1998.

CHAPTER 23　HORIZONS

1　Jennie George, Address to constitutional convention, Canberra, 11 February 1998.

2　Brad Norington, 'Low-paid workers granted $14 increase', *Sydney Morning Herald*, 30 April 1998.

3　Jennie George, ACTU statement on 'living wage' decision, 29 April 1998.

4　At the very least, the policy proposed returning to Laurie Brereton's 1993 legislation and appeared to be a further regression so far as the increased concentration of power in the commission's hands went. Despite instances in which workers were worse off, the evidence so far was that award-stripping under Reith's model had forced unions in coal and manufacturing, for example, to embrace more flexible arrangements while not diminishing wages and conditions regarded as community standards.

5　Helen Trinca, 'Inflationary hoax, says ACTU', *Sydney Morning Herald*, 14 August 1998.

6　Jennie George, election campaign speech notes, September 1998.

7　The furore over Hanson began when she wrote to an Ipswich newspaper, the *Queensland Times*, saying: 'How can we expect this race to help themselves when governments shower them with money, facilities and opportunities that only these people can obtain no matter how minute the indigenous blood is that flows through their veins, and this is what is causing racism.' Hanson later told the *Courier-Mail* that Aborigines were the main instigators of crime and violence, and could walk into any job. Paul Chamberlin, 'Dumped Liberal candidate defiant', *Age*, 16 February 1996; Greg Roberts and Jodie Brough, 'I'm a scapegoat, says sacked Lib', *Sydney Morning Herald*, 16 February 1996.

8 Howard extended the qualifying period for new migrants to receive unemployment benefits from six months to two years. He also reduced the country's overall immigration intake and immigration for the purpose of family reunions. The effect was to reduce Asian immigration, considering most family reunions were Asian. These changes reflected not only Howard's own inclinations but also pressure from Hanson.

9 Tony Parkinson, 'Matchmaker Hawke forms united front against One Nation', *Age*, 27 August 1998. The joint statement was co-signed by Jennie George, Bill Kelty, Stan Wallis (Business Council of Australia president), Dr George Pell (Catholic Archbishop of Melbourne), Dr Keith Rayner (Anglican Archbishop of Sydney), Cardinal Edward Clancy (Catholic Archbishop of Sydney), Michael Raper (ACOSS president) and Diane Shteinman (Executive Council of Australian Jewry). The statement was read by eminent medical scientist Sir Gustav Nossal. Hawke had already tried to organise a similar grouping of prime ministers, former and serving. Howard declined to be part of it.

10 Hanson had moved from Oxley to the adjacent seat of Blair following an Electoral Commission redistribution that was thought likely to result in Oxley returning to Labor at the next election.

11 Jennie George, 'Women and leadership', address to the University of South Australia, Adelaide, 4 April 1997.

BIBLIOGRAPHY

Books

Aarons, Eric 1993 *What's Left? Memoirs of an Australian Communist*, Penguin, Melbourne

Alexander, Bevin 1989 *Korea: The Lost War*, Arrow Books, London

Baker, Glenn A. 1982 *The Beatles Down Under*, Wild and Woolley, Sydney

Blake, Audrey 1984 *A Proletarian Life*, Kibble Books, Malmsbury

Brown, W. J. 1986 *The Communist Movement and Australia: An Historical Outline—1880s to 1980s*, Australian Labor Movement History Publications, Sydney

Bucciotti, Achille (chief ed.) 1987 *Italy*, Instituto Geografico de Agostini, Novara

Callus, R., Moorehead, A., Cully, M. and Buchanan, J. 1991 *Industrial Relations at Work: The Australian Workplace Industrial Relations Survey*, AGPS, Canberra

Carew, Edna 1988 *Keating: A Biography*, Allen & Unwin, Sydney

Carney, Shaun 1988 *Australia in Accord: Politics and Industrial Relations Under the Hawke Government*, Macmillan, Melbourne

Crosby, Michael and Easson, Michael 1992 *What Should Unions Do?* Pluto Press, Sydney

Crowley, Frank (ed.) 1974 *A New History of Australia*, Heinemann, Melbourne

Cumming, Fia 1991 *Mates: Five Champions of the Labor Right*, Allen & Unwin, Sydney

Dabscheck, Braham 1995 *The Struggle for Australian Industrial Relations*, Oxford University Press, Melbourne

Dabscheck, Braham and Niland, John 1981 *Industrial Relations in Australia*, Allen & Unwin, Sydney

d'Alpuget, Blanche 1977 *Mediator: A Biography of Sir Richard Kirby*, Melbourne University Press, Melbourne

d'Alpuget, Blanche 1992 *Robert J. Hawke: A Biography*, Schwartz Publishing Group, Melbourne

Costa, Michael and Duffy, Mark 1991 *Labor, Prosperity and the Nineties: Beyond the Bonsai Republic*, Federation Press, Sydney

Davies, Ray 1994 *X-RAY*, Viking, London

Easson, Michael (ed.) 1990 *Australia and Immigration: Able to Grow?* Pluto Press, Sydney

Ewer, P., Hampson, I., Lloyd C., Rainford, J., Rix, S. and Smith, M. 1991 *Politics and the Accord*, Pluto Press, Sydney

Freidan, Betty 1965 *The Feminine Mystique*, Harmondsworth, Middlesex

French, Marilyn 1978 *The Women's Room*, André Deutsch, Great Britain

Freney, Denis 1991 *Map of Days: Life on the Left*, William Heinemann Australia, Melbourne

Greer, Germaine 1970 *The Female Eunuch*, MacGivor & Kee, London

Hagan, Jim 1981 *The History of the ACTU*, Longman Cheshire, Melbourne

Hawke, Bob 1994 *The Hawke Memoirs*, William Heinemann Australia, Melbourne

Henderson, Gerard 1994 *Menzies' Child: The Liberal Party of Australia 1944–1994*, Allen & Unwin, Sydney

Horne, Donald 1980 *Time of Hope: Australia 1966–72*, Angus & Robertson, Sydney

Hurst, John 1979 *Hawke: The Definitive Biography*, Angus & Robertson, Sydney

Kelly, Paul 1984 *The Hawke Ascendancy*, Angus & Robertson, Sydney

Kelly, Paul 1992 *The End of Certainty: The Story of the 1980s*, Allen & Unwin, Sydney

Kennett, Matt 1969 *The Teachers' Challenge: Professional Standards and Public Service*, Alpha Books, Sydney

Kunz, Egon F. 1988 *Displaced Persons: Calwell's New Australians*, Australian National University Press, Sydney

Langley, Greg 1992 *A Decade of Dissent: Vietnam and the Conflict on the Australian Home Front*, Allen & Unwin, Sydney

McHugh, Siobhan 1993 *Minefields and Miniskirts: Australian Women and the Vietnam War*, Doubleday, Sydney

Macintyre, Stuart 1998 *The Reds: The Communist Party of Australia from Origins to Illegality*, Allen & Unwin, Sydney

Mundey, Jack 1981 *Jack Mundey: Green Bans and Beyond*, Angus & Robertson, Sydney

Nicholson, Nigel 1973 *Alex: The Life of Field Marshal Earl Alexander of Tunis*, Weidenfeld and Nicolson, London

Norington, Brad 1990 *Sky Pirates: The Pilots' Strike that Grounded Australia*, ABC Books, Sydney

O'Brien, John 1987 *A Divided Unity! Politics of NSW Teacher Militancy Since 1945*, Allen & Unwin, Sydney

Panich, Catherine 1988 *Sanctuary?* Allen & Unwin, Sydney

Pemberton, Gregory 1990 *Vietnam Remembered*, Weldon Publishing, Sydney

Pullan, Robert 1980 *Bob Hawke: A Portrait*, Methuen, Sydney

Rowbotham, Sheila 1979 *Beyond the Fragments: Feminism and the Making of Socialism*, Merlin Press, London

Scammell, Michael 1985 *Solzhenitsyn: A Biography*, Hutchison & Co, London

Taft, Bernie 1991 *Crossing the Party Line: Memoirs of Bernie Taft*, Scribe Publications, Newham

Thomas, D. M. 1997 *Alexander Solzhenitsyn: A Century in His Life*, St Martin's Press, New York

Uren, Tom 1994 *Straight Left*, Random House, Sydney

Williams, Pamela 1997 *The Victory: The Inside Story of the Takeover of Australia*, Allen & Unwin, Sydney

Other references

Maps: Europe, National Geographic Society, *National Geographic Magazine*, Washington, December 1993; Italy, Instituto Geografico de Agostini, Novara, 1975

Newspapers: Sydney Morning Herald, Age, Australian, Australian Financial Review, Daily Telegraph, Herald-Sun, Courier-Mail, Advertiser, Sun-Herald, Sunday Telegraph, Canberra Times, Canterbury-Bankstown Torch, Sun, Mirror, National Times, Tribune

Radio: 2BL, 2UE, 3AW, 3LO

Television: '7.30 Report', 'Four Corners', 'Lateline' (ABC), 'Face to Face' (Channel Seven), 'A Current Affair', 'Sixty Minutes', 'Sunday' (Channel Nine), 'Meet the Press' (Channel Ten), 'Dateline' (SBS)

Australian Bureau of Statistics: 6325.0 Trade Union Members, Australia; 6323.0 Trade Union Statistics, Australia (discontinued 1996)

ACTU Congress papers 1985–97

ACTU, 'The need for fairness in the workplace', ACTU response to the Federal Government's 'The reform of workplace relations—implementation discussion paper March 1996', April 1996, Melbourne

ACTU Constitution, rules and standing orders, 1992 Melbourne

ACTU, Future strategies for the trade union movement, 1986 Melbourne

Australian Industrial Relations Commission, National wage cases and safety net reviews 1983–1997

Australian Security Intelligence Organisation (ASIO), personal file of Jennie George 1966–67; National Archives of Australia.

Education, Journal of the NSW Teachers' Federation, 1986–89

Jennie George, speeches, papers and files

Jobsback! The Federal Coalition's industrial relations policy 1992

Life membership: NSW Teachers' Federation, Sydney, 1989

Norington, Brad 14 December 1996 'Soft heart, hard line', Good Weekend Magazine, *Sydney Morning Herald*

Party records, Communist Party of Australia.

Sams, Peter 5 July 1991 ACTU wages strategy: a discussion paper, Sydney

Statement of Accord by the Australian Labor Party and the Australian Council of Trade Unions, February 1993, Melbourne

INDEX

Herald-Sun, 313
Hewett, Helen, 97, 98, 103, 106, 108, 117, 154, 184–5, 318, 239
Hewett, Peta, 117–18, 184–5
Hewett, Rex, 50, 63, 97–8, 103, 106, 108, 117–18, 184–5, 204–5, 229, 239, 318
Hewish, Pam, 83
Hewson, John, 207, 285
Higgins, (Justice) Henry Bournes, 283
High Court, 335, 338
Hills, Pat, 113
Hitler, Adolf, 73
Holding, Clyde, 219
Hornibrook, Tim, 84, 102, 111
Howard, John,
  attacks Jennie George, 296, 313, 323
  first Budget as Prime Minister, 289, 294
  Opposition industrial relations spokesman, 207, 209, 261
  Opposition Leader, 240, 247–8, 261, 278, 280–1
  Prime Minister, 282–3, 285, 289, 293–4, 296, 314, 322–3, 325–7, 332, 249, 352, 258
  rock-solid guarantee on awards, 281, 285
  waterfront reform, 325–7, 332
Howe, Brian, 220, 227–8, 231–3, 235
Hughes, John, 93
Hungary, uprising of 1956, 66
Hunter Valley mine dispute, 315–18, 322–4

individual employment contracts, 246–7, 266–9, 275–6, 315–16, 350
Industrial Relations Commission

(formerly Australian Conciliation and Arbitration Commission), 188, 200, 211, 261–2, 271–2, 275, 283, 285, 304–5, 309, 314, 317, 330, 346–7, 350–1
inflation rate target under Accord, 261
International Labour Organisation (ILO), 238
International Purveyors, 328
International Refugee Organisation (IRO), 7, 14, 18
International Transport Workers Federation (ITF), 328
International Year of Women 1975, 91
Irene, *see* Ostrovsky, Irene

Jamieson, Suzanne, 74–5
Jobling, Doris, 49, 56, 82, 84, 91
Jobsback!, 209, 285
Johnson, Heather, 135
Johnson, Lyndon, B., 55–6, 64
Junior Eureka League, 45, 140

Keane, Mike, 106, 108
Keating, Paul, 52, 126, 130, 176, 201, 210–11, 232, 277–8, 285
  Accord, 130, 176, 191, 232, 309, 314, 316, 320, 349
  award 'substitutes' comment, 270
  becomes Prime Minister, 202
  election victory 1993, 210–11
  election defeat 1996, 281
  George, Jennie, admiration for, 219, 223, 225
  Hawke, leadership battle with, 197–202
  Kelty, close to, 176, 191, 197
  'Marcel Marceau' comment, 270